Popular Housing and
Urban Land Tenure
in the Middle East

Popular Housing and Urban Land Tenure in the Middle East

Case Studies from Egypt, Syria, Jordan, Lebanon, and Turkey

Edited by
Myriam Ababsa
Baudouin Dupret
Eric Denis

The American University in Cairo Press
Cairo New York

Chapters 1, 3, 4, 8, 9, 10, 11 and 12 were translated from the French by Samira Druilhe.

An earlier version of Chapter 6 appeared as "The Genesis of a Mosque: Negotiating Sacred Space in
Downtown Beirut," EUI Working Paper RSCAS 2008/17. European University Institute, Florence,
2008. Reproduced by permission.

Some material in Chapter 8 is drawn from "Contrer la précarité par la sécurisation foncière et la
légalisation: enjeux et opportunités dans le Monde arabe et en Égypte," Revue Tiers Monde, no. 206
(2011/2012), 75–93. Reproduced by permission.

Dar el Kutub No. 11767/11
ISBN 978 977 416 540 5

Dar el Kutub Cataloging-in-Publication Data

Ababsa, Myriam
        Popular Housing and Urban Land Tenure in the Middle East: Case Studies from Egypt,
    Syria, Jordan, Lebanon, and Turkey / Myriam Ababsa, Baudouin Dupret, and Eric Denis.—
    Cairo: The American University in Cairo Press, 2012
        p.   cm.
        ISBN 978 977 416 540 5
        1. Middle East   I. Title
        956.015

1 2 3 4 5   16 15 14 13 12

Designed by Sally Boylan
Printed in Egypt

To André Raymond

Contents

Tables

Illustrations

Figures

Contributors

Myriam Ababsa is a research fellow in social geography at the Institut Français du Proche-Orient (IFPO), Amman. Her work focuses on the impact of public policies on regional and urban development in Jordan and Syria. She currently runs the Atlas of Jordan research program (funded by the French Embassy and the European Commission). She has written *Amman de pierre et de paix* (2007), *Raqqa, territoires et pratiques sociales d'une ville syrienne* (2009), and co-edited with Rami Daher *Cities, Urban Practices and Nation Building in Jordan/Villes, pratiques urbaines and Nation Building in Jordan* (2011). She holds a PhD in geography from the University of Tours, France.

Valérie Clerc is an architect who has a PhD in urban planning from the Institut français d'urbanisme (Université Paris 8, France). She is a researcher at the Institut Français du Proche-Orient (IFPO) in Damascus, where she runs the Urban Observatory of the Middle East. Her research concentrates on informal settlements, land and housing issues, urban policies, and urban planning practices and principles in the cities of the Global South. Among her many publications are: *Les quartiers irréguliers de Beyrouth: Une histoire des enjeux fonciers et urbanistiques en banlieue sud* (2008) and *Les marchés fonciers et immobiliers des quartiers informels à Phnom Penh* (2009). Her work focuses on Lebanon, Cambodia, and Syria. She also supervises a program on housing and poverty in the Middle East at the IFPO.

Agnès Deboulet is professor of sociology at the Ecole Nationale Supérieure d'Architecture de Paris La Villette. She holds a PhD in urban studies from the Institut d'Urbanisme de Paris, Université Paris XII. She is a member of CNRS, AUS research unit. She is co-editor, with R. Hoddé and A. Sauvage, of *La critique architecturale. Questions, frontières, desseins* (2008). She is also co-editor, with I. Berry-Chikhaoui and L. Roulleau-Berger, of *Villes internationales. Tensions et réactions des habitants* (2007); with B. Destremau and F. Ireton, of *Dynamiques de la pauvreté en Afrique du nord et au moyen orient* (2004); and, with I. Berry-Chikhaoui, of *Les compétences des citadins dans le monde arabe. Penser, faire et transformer la ville*(2000).

Eric Denis has a PhD in urban and economic geography and town planning from the University of Caen, France. He is a senior research fellow affiliated with the Centre national de la recherche scientifique (CNRS). He was based for ten years in Cairo, Egypt, and Khartoum, Sudan. He is currently affiliated to the French Institute in Pondicherry, India. He is the editor of several volumes on Middle Eastern geography and urban studies, including *Villes et urbanisation des provinces égyptiennes* (2007), *Atlas of Cairo* (2000), and *Géographies de l'Egypte* (1994). He is the author of some fifty scientific papers and books, notably *Access to Fresh Water, Clean Environment and Right to Urbanism Affiliation* (Working Paper, Middle Eastern and Central Asian Studies Group). He is co-administrator of the Foncier et Développement website and a member of the editorial committee of *Etudes Foncières*. He has been involved in applied research on land access and security of tenure and is currently co-leading a program on world urbanization (e-Geopolis) supported by the Agence Française de Développement and the World Bank.

Baudouin Dupret holds degrees in law, Islamic and Middle East studies, and political science. He is a senior research fellow at the Centre national de la recherche scientifique (CNRS), in Paris. He is also guest lecturer in Islamic law and socio-legal sciences at the universities of Louvain and Strasbourg and at L'Ecole des Hautes Etudes en Sciences Sociales (EHESS), Paris. He currently runs the Centre Jacques-Berque in Rabat. He has published extensively in the fields of the sociology and anthropology of law, legislation, and media, especially pertaining to the Middle East. His current work involves a praxiological approach to the production of truth in Arab contexts, including courts and parliaments, scientific expertise, the media, and religious education. He has co-edited several special issues of scientific journals and numerous books, including *La Charia* *aujourd'hui: Usages de la référence au droit islamique* (2012) and *Ethnographies of Islam: Ritual Performances and Everyday Practices* (co-edited with Th. Pierret, P. G. Pinto and K. Spellman-Poots). He has also authored several books on law and norms in Egypt and other Arab contexts, including *Adjudication in Action: An Ethnomethodology of Law, Morality and Justice* (2011) and *Practices of Truth: An Ethnomethodological Inquiry into Arab Contexts* (2011).

Myriam Ferrier is currently a PhD candidate in political science at the Institut d'Etudes Politique in Grenoble. Her research focuses on the way both the Syrian parliament and the government administration address the issue of urban organization. She spent several years in Syria at the Institut Français du Proche-Orient (IFPO) in Damascus. She is the holder of master's degrees on the Middle East from the School of Oriental and African Studies (SOAS) in London and the Institut d'Etudes Politiques de Paris.

Zouhair Ghazzal is professor of historical and social sciences at Loyola University, Chicago, and a member of the Institute for Advanced Study, School of Social Science, Princeton. He is the author of *L'économie politique de Damas au XIXe siècle* (1993) and *The Grammars of Adjudication* (2007). He is currently completing a book on Syria's contemporary criminal system, *The Textuality of Crime*, and working on the ways of life in marginal urban settings in Lebanon and Syria.

Falk Jähnigen studied architecture at the Technische Universität Berlin, specializing in urban development in fast-growing metropolises. During his studies he conducted research on the subject of informal development in Tashkent, Beirut, and Damascus. He completed his research with a proposal for a project to upgrade informal settlements in southern Beirut. He currently works as an architect and city planner in Berlin.

Franziska Laue studied architecture at the Technische Universität Berlin, specializing in urban development in a global context, and resulting in graduation on a comparative study focusing on informal settlement issues in Dhaka, Ouagadougou and Damascus. She is currently involved in the publication of a long-term case study of the Jeramana neighborhood, near Damascus, and works as a DED-advisor within the Syrian German Urban Development Program, managed by the Deutsche Gesellschaft für Technische Zusammenarbeit GmbH (GTZ).

Etienne Léna studied architecture and urbanism at the School of Architecture of Versailles. He worked as an architect at the Institut Français du Proche-Orient (IFPO) in Damascus. He is currently an associate professor at the École Normale Supérieure d'Architecture in Grenoble, and a research fellow at the École Normale Supérieure d'Architecture in Toulouse. He is also a practicing architect. He is the author of several research papers, including "Les maisons de parpaings," in Baudouin Dupret, Zouhair Ghazzal, Youssef Courbage, and Mohammed al-Dbyat, eds., *La syrie au Présent* (2007), and "Le Dar Majarish à Muhajat. Dispositifs spatiaux, systèmes constructifs: une étude de cas," in Pascale Clauss-Balty, ed., *Hauran III, l'habitat dans les campagnes de Syrie du Sud aux époques classiques et médiévales* (2008).

Jean-François Pérouse graduated from the Institut National des Langues et Civilisations Orientales (INALCO) in Paris. He has a PhD in geography and urban planning from the University of Reims-Champagne-Ardenne. He was formerly associate professor in political and urban geography at the University of Toulouse-II, France, and worked as a researcher at the Institut Français d'Etudes Anatoliennes (IFEA-Istanbul). Since 2007, he has been an assistant professor at Galatasaray University, Istanbul. He is a member of the editorial board of the online *European Journal of Turkish Studies* (www.ejts.org) and has published numerous papers on urban issues in contemporary Turkey.

Marion Séjourné received a PhD in geography from the University of Tours, France. For ten years she worked as a researcher at the Centre d'Etudes et de Documentation Économiques, Juridiques et Sociales (CEDEJ) in Cairo, where she studied policies and projects relating to the regularization of informal settlements in Egypt. Her research interests include land, urban illegal issues, policies of housing, urbanization, Geographic Information Systems (GIS), and planning in developing countries. She has also been a consultant to various international organizations and development aid agencies, including the United States Agency for International Development (USAID), the World Bank, the Institute for Liberty and Democracy (ILD), and the Deutsche Gesellschaft für Technische Zusammernarbeit GmbH (GTZ), and has provided training for development policies, planning, and governance. She is now a research assistant at the Université Paris 7-Diderot. She is the author of "Historical Background of Informal Settlements," in *Cairo's Informal Areas Between Urban*

Challenges and Hidden Potentials, Facts, Voices, Visions (2009); and, with David Sims, of *The Dynamics of Peri-urban Areas around Greater Cairo, Concept Note, Egypt Urban Sector Update* (2008).

Ward Vloeberghs is currently assistant professor at the École de Gouvernance et d'Économie de Rabat, Morocco, where he is also deputy director of the Centre for Research on Africa and the Mediterranean (CERAM). He is also associate researcher at the Centre Jacques Berque (CJB, Rabat). Vloeberghs has a PhD in political science from the University of Louvain on the political dimensions of religious architecture in contemporary Beirut. His research interests lie in the politics of architecture and in dynastic power as well as in foreign policy issues, especially in societies of the Arab world. He has lived for several years in Egypt, Lebanon, and Morocco.

Introduction

Forms and Norms: Questioning Illegal Urban Housing in the Middle East

Myriam Ababsa, Baudouin Dupret, and Eric Denis

This book aims at describing and taking seriously two major transformations that have been observed in the Middle East during the last thirty years: first, the accelerated changes in public policies toward neighborhoods characterized as irregular or illegal, and second, the claim that this form of housing in urban areas constitutes the ordinary and majority condition.[1]

There is nothing specific or original about these observations; and indeed the aim of this volume is to emphasize their banality in favor of empirical work aimed at *describing* interactions specifically located within the urban sphere. This is as part of a wider trend within the social sciences that seeks to think afresh the ways in which to observe societies of the Middle East.

Here, and for longer perhaps than anywhere else in the world, the mode of analysis remained constrained by a dualistic way of thinking, one which pitted state apparatuses against populations utterly deprived of any ability to influence their governments' policies. The few works that dealt with illegal urban housing in the Middle East underscored the lack of institutionalized forms of governance, especially when contrasted with India and Latin America, where neighborhood associations and nongovernmental organizations are active in the protection of squatters' rights.[2] However, several new studies dealing with strenuous avenues of political participation in

Cairo (Singerman 1996), political participation on the street as the locus of popular micro-interventions and the quiet encroachment of the poor on the city of Tehran during the 1980s (Bayat 1997), and ordinary citizens' participation in the Arab world (Berry-Chikhaoui and Deboulet 2000), made it possible to break with this burdensome tradition. They all proposed relevant tracks for researching urban space through examination of the most ordinary interactions around which agreements take place.

Without falling into the trap of radical readings of Middle Eastern politics, which had a tendency to overshadow analyses of the simplest daily interactions (cf. Hoodfar 1997), and which contributed in turn to denying any efficacy to "limited democracy" regimes, these approaches share a real heuristic force. They establish a *continuum* between different modes of action and bind ordinary citizens, public agents, and entrepreneurs to one another through their daily interactions. Recent work in legal anthropology (cf. Dupret 2006) testifies to such an approach: through the observation of daily practices within local tribunals, it shows how legal norms are produced and how the relationship with positive law is constructed. The precise description of interactions, routines, and ordinary practices sheds light on the way in which 'bits and pieces' of cities, neighborhoods, or broader urban formations appear, are reproduced, balance each other, evolve, and transform. It seems therefore unproductive to continue thinking about changing urban environments exclusively in terms of social contradictions and profound inequalities. Exploring the ways in which agreements are reached and compromises emerge proves much more heuristic, even in a context of highly asymmetrical relationships. It does not equate to an irenic vision of empirical realities; rather, it aims to eschew criticism in favor of close attention to the day-to-day mechanisms that make up urban phenomena.

In the context of the daily practices and legal documents negotiated by inhabitants, we observe a crossing of institutionalized borders, which are in turn blurred and re-made with the cooperation of state agents. As the anthropologist Fredrik Barth puts it, border drawing is a collaborative or conflictual, and thus social accomplishment, the sides of the divide concurring in the definition of the "wherefrom I speak" that is necessary in interaction. This means that instead of dichotomies pitting permanence against change, public against private, and state against society, it seems more fruitful to adopt an endogenous perspective. This approach reflects real experiences and processes that therefore appear far less contradictory and chaotic than when observed through broad and fixed categories.

Illegal housing constitutes the most obvious example of the rejection of such a dichotomy. Although illegal housing, by definition, infringes upon formal legal rules, it has become the norm for the majority of the inhabitants in all the metropolises under study in this volume—Beirut, Cairo, Damascus, Istanbul, and Amman. It is less heuristic than ever, as we closely scrutinize this so-called illegality, to describe and analyze this quiet and steady production of housing—with all its buildings and life investments—as partaking in a scheme that pits formal against informal or legal against illegal, therefore shaping two separate markets, informal and formal real-estate networks, and legal systems (cf. El Kadi 1990). Similarly, the analysis from above, which considers the authoritarian state as dominating its 'non-citizens,' whom it controls in a patron–client relationship while maintaining them within a no-law margin via illegal housing, falls short, regardless of the importance of relations of dominance and the unfair use of force to back arbitrary decisions. Here again, denouncing inequality cannot account for its operational modes; moreover, such an approach radically erases what social practices are in terms of complexity, fluidity, order, and (conflicting) negotiation and collaboration.

Let us go further with the example of the law, around which many contributions to this volume revolve. The study of legal practices can follow different tracks. The theory of legal pluralism, which posits the co-existence of multiple laws alongside state law, was once fashionable. Instead of the state as sole producer of the law, this theory held that law-making was the production of a multiplicity of semi-autonomous and self-regulated social fields. According to this perspective, the state itself is little more than the aggregate of multiple social fields. Whereas it is perfectly legitimate to posit the law and the state as objects of sociological analysis, the unlimited extension of the notion of law-making to any form of normativity seems excessive. Instead of the legal dichotomy between the monism of state law and the pluralism of non-state instances, we suggest a double shift in our viewpoint: On the one hand, it is necessary to analyze normative systems close to state law, in the sense that they are grounded in written or oral rules which a group of specific persons is deemed to know and interpret, that they are endowed with persons in charge of their enforcement, and they are referred to by people as a legal system alternative to state law; on the other hand, it is also necessary to examine the ways in which people grasp their legal environment, understand it, and act in the relevant contexts, constantly reconciling a plurality of social norms to the unified character of the law in force. This is the challenge of the praxeological approach to law, which seeks to study, while faced with multiple customary systems, fluctuating legal practices, and the impact of hegemonic state laws, the organizations and hierarchies designed in an endogenous manner by the people involved in a specific course of action. These organizations are necessarily neither institutionalized nor stable. Contexts of interaction lead people to establish circumstantial hierarchies, to select priorities, and to proceed to what is conventionally called 'forum shopping.' However, the same contexts can also compel them to act within one system rather than another and to have no choice in competent legal forums, which nevertheless does not mean that they have no specific practice of these instances.

This praxeological approach to law asks how inhabitants produce their legality in practice: through the payment of taxes or fines which are used as means to warrant a right; through the use of seals, a finance ministry's official forms; engineer's documents; notary documents; evidence required by the Cadastre Department; or the use of 'customary' contracts (very widespread in Jordan and Syria).

The chapters in this volume defy theoretical dichotomies, for which they substitute a close observation of ordinary situations. Nothing contributes more to the understanding of how urban societies are produced than the detailed, not-too-interpretive description of the ways in which housing deemed a priori illegal is secured, a transaction concluded, a conflict resolved, the breadth or the use of a street in construction is determined and enforced, and so on. Add to that the description of how a land-titling policy is conceived of, formerly recognized equipments are claimed, a neighborhood is equipped with electric wires, sewerage systems, school facilities, and asphalted roads. The ambition of the volume is to restore the obvious continuum in the consolidation, building after building, of the popular neighborhoods of the cities under study, while showing the proximity of social relationships and the forms of solidarity that are mobilized.

Instead of looking for the Middle East's specificities in politics, we suggest adopting a research policy that scrutinizes the 'proximate': denying the holistic and culturalist exception for the sake of the study of daily *routines* and practices. The first ambition is therefore to upgrade the knowledge of urban land tenure dynamics, eventually underscoring the banality of current trends (something that can hardly be reconciled with the quest for something specifically characterizing the Middle East taken as a whole).

We assumed that there is a tendency for these neighborhoods to be considered afresh by the actors of urban politics—government employees, counsellors, international experts, and development agencies. This approach induces new relationships, and new contexts of interaction between inhabitants and the agents of urban development, urbanism, and taxation agencies. All these situations make more palatable (because they are more diverse and numerous) the possibilities for negotiation and adaptation involved in complex and pluralistic forms of governance. This holds true for social science analysis, the methodological and epistemological renewing of which is closely connected to the dynamics of 'real life,' and has a direct impact on it (in a looping, or feedback, effect which is essential with regard to what was stated above).

As urban planning disappears in favor of juxtaposed projects and delegated urban development, there is a momentum for the tacit acknowledgment of the positions/possessions that were previously acquired and of their regularization. Access to networks of urban services depends on criteria of profitability and on the inhabitants' financial capacity; networks no longer belong to the sovereign power of ministries and urban public agencies. In the same way, forced and massive dispossessions orchestrated by ruling governments disappear, giving way to "market evictions" (Lasserve 2007), which introduce new forms of land and tenure insecurity in the very place where land titling procedures appeared to guarantee stability (see Chapter 11 in this volume by Jean-François Pérouse).

The current convergence of urban land markets and the blurring of the line dividing legal and illegal lead us to regard urban dynamics as being less regulated than previously assumed and therefore inherently uncertain and unstable. They also lead us to consider the period that was dominated by public intervention, which gave way in the early 1990s to economic liberalization without political democracy, as a long 'bracketing' of urban construction. Today, the production of urban forms on the scale of plots, buildings, transactions, or even the more ambitious projects of developers, appears in a clearer and more assertive manner. Obviously, the evident liberalization of the city's 'production forces' encouraged us to observe the inhabitants' strategies to secure and transfer those properties.

Nevertheless, it is impossible to ignore the fact that the 2010–2011 revolutionary movements in the Middle East represent popular protests against the trend of economic liberalization led by authoritarian governments. In Egypt in particular, economic reforms of the 1990s have had a considerable effect on popular housing, inducing greater pressures on land access, land grabbing by businessmen, and greater insecurity of tenure.

The issue of historical development is a background one, since the dynamics we observe are not new in any sense, be they in architecture, popular urbanism, or in the realm of legal regulations. The dynamics of urban relationships described here can be traced back to modes of urban growth that have existed in the Middle East since at least the Ottoman unification. These represent ordinary ways of producing urban units, according to forms that are suitable, inherited, and still active, and hence according to what Bernard Lepetit (1993) called the "traces" of history.

The Many Forms of Ordinary Housing, Law Production, and Public Action

This perspective is essential. The urban environment is not a neutral theatrical stage, but, through its geometric shapes and inhabited and invested forms, it represents the existing sum of all the interactions that make up the city. The form, whether spatial, architectural, administrative, or legal, is a constraint with which all the city's agents must come to terms. Therefore, the form is normative, not in the sense that it directly causes an action, but in the sense that it sets the conditions within which action takes place (cf. Wittgenstein 1921; Petitot 1985).

That is why the first part of this volume deals with the study of ordinary forms and methods that are used to build, juxtapose, and compose buildings in the shape of streets and neighborhoods. Panerai and Noweir's pioneering work on the spatial and architectural shaping of popular neighborhoods in Cairo is very important in that respect (Panerai and Nowier 1990). In the same way, we also seek to describe grammars of normativity, whether legal, when practices articulate formal rules and their local enforcement, or conventional, when negotiation and compromise allow neighbors to adjust and adapt to one another.

In Chapter 1, Etienne Léna details the stages of construction of an informal settlement in the countryside near Damascus. He analyzes the unified look created by the use of concrete blocks, then examines the negotiations related to passageways between houses, and describes the physical connections created between houses by the water pipes attached to artesian wells. He examines the complexity of informal urban landscapes in the countryside around Damascus, made up of groups of buildings and visible networks based on social networks of kinship and the neighborhood.

In Chapter 2, Baudouin Dupret and Myriam Ferrier analyze the various documents held by the owner of an apartment in a building built without a permit in the heart of the Yarmouk Palestinian camp in Damascus.

They show that this case comprises a series of acts of sale of the stories of the building on land which was probably unsuitable for development. They reveal the wordplay used to give the informal property a coherent legal form, as well as the many practices used to prove ownership when a defect precludes the use of ordinary legal techniques.

Taking a similar approach in Chapter 3, Myriam Ferrier follows, step by step, the strategies for the registration of informal property in Syria, including the use of proofs of payment of property taxes. The most common procedure is to present the informal property as forming part of an undefined block *(mush'a)*. This complex reclassification is always aided by collusion between owners and government officials. Through these processes, the property becomes liable to taxation, and the Land Registry Department's terminology is used to award the property legal status.

In Chapter 4, Marion Séjourné gives a thorough account of the different procedures for registering property built in violation of town planning and land laws in Cairo, depending on the various types of land and transactions involved. She uses the concept of "quiet encroachment" to describe the various methods used by Cairo's residents to try to regularize their property without following all the numerous steps normally required of them by law, or by spending a fortune in bribes. She demonstrates that the Egyptian authorities themselves tolerate informal settlements for lack of any institutional solution to the chronic shortage of affordable housing.

Chapter 5, by Franziska Laue, is based on fieldwork carried out in Jeramana, a village that was once in the Ghouta and now forms part of Greater Damascus. She studies the architectural development of two streets located on agricultural land. She concludes that middle-class households have no choice but to build their own homes, and underlines the flexibility of concrete blocks, cement, and reinforced concrete pillars for adapting housing to income and family size. She thus shows that construction techniques allow for the use of better materials as incomes rise.

In Chapter 6, Ward Vloeberghs studies the stages of the design, construction, and symbolism of the Muhammad al-Amin Mosque in Beirut, and analyzes the formal and informal mechanisms involved in the creation of an exceptional urban edifice. He examines the land registry plans, the positions, and statements of all the stakeholders, and the legal practices and architectural projects involved, in order to describe and consequently interpret the methods of appropriation and dispute of a public space whose sacredness is reinforced or challenged by its political use.

Zouhair Ghazzal, in Chapter 7, studies various aspects of urban informality and methods of property registration in informal settlements in Aleppo, as well as the tribal codes that govern social relations in these neighborhoods. He describes how, by making a false declaration of breach of contract in court, the parties officially set out the details of a plot and the names of its owners. Ghazzal carries out a micro-sociological study of working-class neighborhoods in Aleppo in order to show that their residents handle crimes and homicides themselves, following customary tribal law, before referring cases to the police. This "cognitive style" used by social stakeholders (Garfinkel 2005) allows Ghazzal to recreate simple property negotiations. He shows how people manage legal issues themselves, with a range of consequences for methods of real-estate trading.

The second part of this volume looks at the normative conditions of daily practices related to land and tenure mobilization and thus of housing, neighborhood shaping, transactions, and conflict resolution in the urban context, thereby offering a new reading of government action in and on cities through case studies. These workings are understood as participating in the ongoing and negotiated reformulation of urban territories, emerging in precise contexts that deserve to be specified, and not as actions determining the unfolding of all the practices that take place on the ground or in the process of implementation.

In Chapter 8, Agnès Deboulet analyzes Egypt's local adaptation of policies to eradicate slums. She seeks to demonstrate how political objectives to regularize and renovate informal housing settlements, especially those on public land, are limited by the added difficulty of a newly required procedure of legalization or land titling that is extremely complex and time-consuming, if not impossible to implement. It also tends to produce new forms of exclusion by pitting legalized property owners against those who do not hold title deeds, thereby marginalizing tenants. These programs are also unsuccessful because of new safety and environmental regulations that justify the eviction of squatter settlements, sometimes because conditions are regarded as dangerous for the residents themselves. The flexibility of procedures that are negotiated on a daily basis and which produce popular housing on a massive scale is therefore still disputed, while no integrating alternative has ever gone beyond the stage of an experimental 'best practice.' However, repeated government interventions remain limited in scope. Given the scale of self-built dwellings which house the majority of city residents, tacit acceptance is still the norm, while the issues of a chronic lack of housing safety and reliance on the goodwill of government staff remain to be addressed.

In Chapter 9, Eric Denis reviews Hernando de Soto's work in Cairo on the legalization of illegal housing. He underlines how his lobbying of the highest authorities in the country helped develop the concept of the individualization of working-class property in favor of owners, rather than of occupiers/possessors. Far from regarding this program as having stopped short of its goals, he lists and makes connections between a series of reforms, ranging from mortgages to the registration of property, that have fundamentally changed land issues in informal neighborhoods. Land markets have thus been able to converge, benefiting the financial sector, which now has access to these legalized properties. The commodifcation of the registrated properties has meant neither empowerment nor a reduction in residents' poverty.

He thus demonstrates how economic reform programs are negotiated on a daily basis in unequal relationships, initiating and legitimizing many decisions, and accruing new procedures and opportunities that tend to complicate courses of action to secure tenure. In 2007, this set of reforms gave rise to one of the first public-sector strikes tolerated in public for decades, with the occupation and setting up of a camp for several weeks by the employees of the land-tax department of transfers, which led to the proliferation of social and political movements that helped spark the revolution of 25 January 2011.

In Chapter 10, Myriam Ababsa studies the evolution of policies for the rehabilitation of informal settlements in Jordan, showing that they are contingent on the residents' degree of citizenship and the fact that policies changed after the peace accord with Israel in 1994. While illegal settlements built by Palestinian refugees were rehabilitated by the Housing and Urban Development Corporation, those built following Transjordanian rural depopulation were rehabilitated locally by municipalities. From 1980 to 1997, Jordan was the first Arab country to implement the developmentalist ideology recently fostered by the World Bank, which involved the residents of informal areas in all the stages of renovation of their homes and enabled them to become homeowners. This titling policy was subsequently abandoned in favor of a single policy of provision of services.

In Chapter 11, Jean-François Pérouse studies informality in the city of Istanbul, and underlines the overuse of the term *gecekondu*. He shows that the public authorities themselves breach property laws and distort the notion of public property. He argues the existence of a real-estate mafia, and describes the processes used by various formal and informal authorities to facilitate property embezzlement. Due to land shortages, title deeds are often canceled, in the name of the fight against crime and terrorism, thus opening the way to lucrative deals. The study of the discourse and standards used by stakeholders to justify their actions shows how a façade of legality (formal law) is nonetheless maintained.

In Chapter 12, Valérie Clerc studies the Elyssar project, developed in 1995, which aimed to destroy large areas of informal settlements located in the southern suburbs of Beirut, whose residents had been displaced from southern Lebanon. The project was abandoned due to resistance from Hezbollah and Amal. The study of the cases put forward by the various stakeholders shows that notions of justice and law are based on the political agendas of each party. At the same time, 'rights to the city' are refused to stigmatized Shi'is and rural populations.

In the final chapter, Falk Jähnigen describes the many stakeholders involved in urban planning for two informal settlements in the same southern suburbs of Beirut. He studies resident committees that support Hezbollah and organize basic public services in return for municipal financial support, and Jihad al-Binaa, the branch of Hezbollah in charge of building basic infrastructure. Hezbollah's refusal to invest in the urban renewal of informal settlements, because it considers that to be a duty of the state, is detrimental to economic development in this coastal area, which has great economic potential.

The day-to-day transactions and relationships thus described in this volume eschew generalizations and allow the authors to assert a continuum between past and present practices, something that is lacking in most studies of urban housing. These studies remain frozen in time, because of their focus on reform, in the antithesis between ordinary housing and state intervention. Customary law acquires a kind of mythical status, becoming the reform's panacea to the predicament generated by positive law, which includes generalized illegal housing (Durand-Lasserve 2004), whereas in fact such dichotomies exist more often in scholarly representations than they do in ordinary practices. If this collective work contributes to something, it is to a renewal in ways of thinking about Middle Eastern urbanity (Dakhlia 1998), by taking into consideration the forms of urban production, the practices which underlie them, and the norms which constrain them, in ordinary, universal terms that can be understood well beyond the borders of the Middle East.

Notes

1 This book was written as part of a research program on public policy and legal practice on the management of informal settlements supervised by Baudouin Dupret within the ANR (l'Agence Nationale de la Recherche) "Citadain" program: "City and Law in the Arab World and India" (2006–2009), directed by Philippe Cadène (Paris VII).

2 According to Nezzar AlSayyad, urban informality in Latin America involves political belonging and sets a relationship of reciprocity between groups of squatters and the state, whereas in the Middle East, to the contrary, the depoliticizing of informality sanctions the squatters' projects; in Latin America, squatting develops or is boosted in contexts of political change— polls for instance. These same changes tend to take place in the Middle East during phases of economic change (AlSayyad 1993, 14).

References

AlSayyad, Nezar. 1993. "Informal Housing in a Comparative Perspective: On Squatting, Culture, and Development in a Latin American and a Middle Eastern Context." *Review of Urban and Regional Development Studies* 5 (1): 3–18.

Bayat, Asef. 1997. *Street Politics: Poor People's Movements in Iran.* New York: Columbia University Press.

Berry-Chikhaoui, Isabelle, and Agnès Deboulet, eds. 2000. *Les compétences des citadins dans le Monde arabe: Penser, faire et transformer la ville.* Tunis: Irmc, Paris: Karthala, Tours: CNRS Urbanisation du Monde arabe (Urbama).

Dakhlia, Jocelyne, ed. 1998. *Urbanité arabe. Hommage à Bernard Lepetit.* Paris: Sindbad-Actes Sud.

Dupret, Baudouin. 2006. *Le jugement en action. Ethnométhodologie du droit, de la morale et de la justice en Égypte.* Geneva: Droz.

Durand-Lasserve, Alain. 2007. "Market-Driven Eviction Processes in Developing Country Cities: The Cases of Kigali in Rwanda and Phnong Penh in Cambodia." *Global Urban* Development 3 (1). http://www.globalurban.org/GUDMag07Vol3Iss1/Durand-Lasserve percent20PDF.pdf.

———. 2006. "Market-driven Evictions and Displacements: Implications for the Perpetuation of Informal Settlements in Developing Cities." In M. Huchzermeyer and A. Karam, eds., *Informal Settlements: A Perpetual Challenge?*, 202–27. Cape Town: University of Cape Town Press.

———. 2004. "La gestion foncière néo-coutumière dans les pays d'Afrique sub-saharienne." In Charles Goldblum, Annik Osmont, Isabell Diaz, eds., *Gouverner les villes du Sud. Défis pour la recherche et pour l'action.* Paris: UNESCO.

El Kadi, Galila. 1990. "L'articulation des deux circuits de la gestion foncière en Egypte : le cas du Caire." In Philip Amis and Peter Lloyd, eds., *Housing Africa's Urban Poor*, 103–22. Manchester: Manchester University Press.

Garfinkel, Harold. 2005. *Seeing Sociologically: The Routine Grounds of Social Action*. Boulder, CO: Paradigm Publishers.

Hoodfar, Homa. 1997. *Between Marriage and the Market. Intimate Politics and Survival in Cairo*. Berkeley: University of California Press.

Lepetit, Bernard. 1993. "Une herméneutique urbaine est-elle possible?" In Bernard Lepetit and Denise Pumain, eds., *Temporalités urbaines*, 287–99. Paris: Anthropos.

Panerai, Philippe, and Sawsan Noweir. 1990. "Du rural à l'urbain." *Égypte/Monde arabe*, Première série, 1, Modes d'urbanisation en Égypte. http://ema.revues.org/index182.html.

Petitot, Jean. 1985. *Morphogenèse du Sens*. Paris: Presses Universitaires de France.

Singerman, Diane. 1996. *Avenues of Participation: Family, Politics, and Networks in Urban Quarters of Cairo*. Princeton, NJ: Princeton University Press.

Wittgenstein, Ludwig. 2001 (1921). *Tractatus logico-philosophicus*. Paris: Gallimard.

1

Mukhalafat in Damascus:
The Form of an Informal Settlement

Etienne Léna

Ancient Informal Settlements

In 1936, in his preliminary report, René Danger, a land surveyor and town planner working on the Plan for Development, Extension, and Embellishment of the city of Damascus (Danger 1937),[1] was already concerned by a phenomenon of illegal construction in the market gardens that surround the city and the risks this posed for city resources (Danger 1937). Danger, who had a legalistic vision of his role, proposed, on the basis of urban rules developed in the metropolis, the creation of a *non-aedificandi* zone for gardens. Several years later, in their report on a new town plan of Damascus, Ecochard and Banshoya only mentioned the informal housing environment in the zone plan key: a 500-meter-wide belt of gardens around the city had to be preserved in order to "stop illegal constructions" (Friès 2000).

These attempts to restrict construction in the 'Ghouta'—as the oasis surrounding Damascus is called—had little effect. From 1984 to 1994, the population of Damascus grew by 67 percent, with 40 percent living in the informal settlements around the city, causing certain large areas of the Ghouta to disappear over a very short period of time (Balanche 2006).

Around the time Danger began to notice cheap constructions in the city gardens, Damascus had just expanded at its northern and southern districts, in places such as Amara, or the north of Midan.[2] These lots were also built on market garden land on the edges of already urbanized districts, and were observed and described as "urban facts," even if there is no trace of the transactions that led to them that could shed light on their legality or otherwise (Arnaud 2006).

Today, many buildings in the suburbs of Damascus are illegal and built quickly using poor-quality concrete blocks. Although these constructions recall those described by Danger, the scale and organization of the illegal districts *(mukhalafat)* bear a strong resemblance to the descriptions of lots found in the suburbs of Damascus that were urbanized in the mid-nineteenth century, suggesting that illegality notwithstanding, we are also facing a clear "urban fact" (Rossi 1990).

In planned urbanization, rules are pronounced in order to set guidelines for what should be regarded as conforming to the norm. Those rules give shape to the city through definitions of density, limits, surface areas, aspects of construction, functional allocation, and so on (Laisney 1988). The parameters to be taken into account in an 'informal' housing process do not follow promulgated rules but result from factors that are not legally formulated: the nature of the urbanized land, its structure before the construction of buildings (division of land, nature of subsoil, land pressure felt on the sector, nature of existing infrastructures), and the terms and methods of 'acquiring' the land. There are also rules and constraints that those who build the lots effectively impose on themselves: whether these are due to their financial means, or their respect for certain rules of behavior (Akbar 1988).

Mukhalafat of Daraya

After a brief survey of different areas around Damascus, for this study we chose a specific district north of the town of Daraya, which is about eight kilometers southwest of Damascus, along the road to Jerusalem (Fig. 1.1 and 1.2). The main reason for its transformation was not rural depopulation but rather the massive process of urban renewal a few kilometers north that led an already urbanized population to build in this area. The survey was carried out by a team of four Syrian architects and architectural students, together with a research fellow in sociology. As there was no prior authorization from the authorities for this research to be carried out, houses were only documented with the owners' consent.

The result of this campaign was the registration of sixty-seven houses[3] and five lots, surveyed in an area measuring 1,000 by 400 meters. Ten title deeds

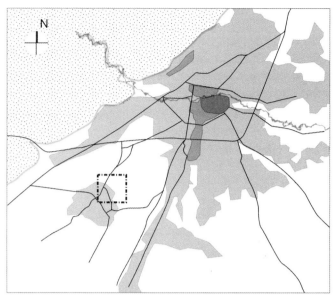

Fig. 1.1: Location of Daraya, southwest of Damascus. Illustration by Etienne Léna, from Google Earth 2007.

Fig. 1.2: Location plan for surveyed plots in Daraya. Dark gray indicates plots surveyed. Illustration by Etienne Léna.

were photographed.[4] Aerial photographs from 2006 and 2007 made available by GoogleEarth® and a page of the Daraya land registry of 1930 drawn by Camille Duraffour, allowed us to situate the houses in their surroundings.

Although the results cannot lead to representative statistics, they give a very good picture of the diversity of building processes. A wide range of different kinds of buildings was visited, and the area studied showed different stages of development: from agricultural land still being cultivated, to single houses becoming complex buildings; from single units to the creation of a lot; from plans to houses under construction. Within that area we could observe all the stages of development of this area of the city.

Manufacturing Units: Concrete Blocks, Frames, and Houses

The characteristic feature of the informal districts of Damascus suburbs is the gray uniformity of the concrete block constructions. The blocks are produced in small factories like the one established in the sector we studied. Two workers run the factory with a small concrete press. The blocks are stored on the edge of a 620-m² plot. One laborer mixes the concrete with a shovel and pours a mixture of sand, gravel, cement, and water into the press. It is then vibrated with an engine, and produces concrete blocks 40 cm long x 15 cm wide x 20 cm high. Average daily production is approximately three hundred concrete blocks. The second laborer organizes the blocks once they have been pressed: he lays them out on the ground so that the concrete sets uniformly, arranges them in a low wall ten courses high and 40 cm thick, maintaining spaces between the blocks to finish the setting, and finally stacks them packed together for sale. Each concrete block is sold for 15 Syrian Pounds (SYP).[5]

The main construction system used to build houses or buildings is based on a post-and-beam frame, filled with concrete blocks (Fig. 1.3). For it to be economical, this system must adapt to the surface area to be covered and the quantities of materials (steel frame and concrete) required. According to the laborers questioned on a house building-site, the most economical length is approximately 4.5 m for beams with a cross-section of 20 cm width x 25 cm height. The foundations form a network of beams 50 cm in height, cast directly on the ground, which leads to the progressive raising of the public road system. Posts with a cross-section of 20 cm x 40 cm are then erected at a level equivalent to fifteen to seventeen courses of blocks.

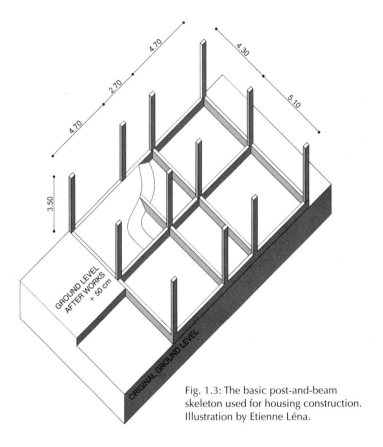

Fig. 1.3: The basic post-and-beam skeleton used for housing construction. Illustration by Etienne Léna.

Almost all houses and buildings are built following this system. For example, house 501, built on a plot measuring 11.20 m x 11.2 m, or 125.4 m², with six rooms (a family living room, bedrooms, and guest sitting rooms), a kitchen, a bathroom, and a staircase to access the roof, required approximately 3,500 concrete blocks for its construction. According to the contractor building the house, the selling price of his labor is SYP4,500/ m², 50 percent of which is allocated for a bribe with which to secure an administrative blind eye to a period of three days during which the house must be built. Because the owner of house 509 refused to pay his share, the construction was partially demolished three times by the municipal authorities.

The construction process is therefore very rapid and requires many laborers. After drawing out the limits of the plot, four or five carpenters build the formwork out of wooden board for foundations (Fig. 1.4). The iron framework is erected immediately afterward, on the same day. Then

Fig. 1.4: Carpenters building formwork out of wooden board for foundations.
Photograph by Etienne Léna.

about twenty workers mix and pour the concrete into the foundations. It takes two days and about ten workers to cast the posts that support the first floor, to cast the floor itself, and fill the framework with concrete blocks.[6] All openings are walled up immediately, and the front door is fitted to ensure the safety of the equipment that will be stored inside for the duration of the building work. The whole operation takes between three and five days. Props to support the upper floor are kept in place for a week for the concrete to set. The rest of the building is then completed, either by specialized professionals (carpenters, electricians, and plumbers), or by the future occupant. This second stage can take much longer, depending on the financial means of the future occupant.

Two Dominant Models: Courtyard Houses and Villas

Although the structural system described above leads to homogeneous standards regarding the dimensions of each room, the survey revealed different types of buildings. Among the sixty-seven houses documented, there are three main types, two of which are dominant and can be linked to·known models. Since the third type is mainly characterized by its compactness and a lack of outdoor space, designed to take full advantage of the lot's assigned area, we will call it 'speculative.' Other buildings stem from the two main categories: farm houses, which are related to the courtyard type, and multistory buildings, which derive from the villa type. The documented houses can be classified as follows:

- Four farm houses
- Twenty courtyard houses, three with a veranda along one front wall; built on plots of between 78 m² and 650 m² in size, the surface area of the houses is between 49 m² and 274 m². Apart from the two largest houses, the rest occupy an average surface area of about 70 m² on plots that are an average 150 m² in size. (Houses: *104, 201, 203, 305, 309, 401*, 402, *403*, 405, 409, 410, *411, 414, 416*, 419, *504, 505*, 507, *508*, and *513*.)[7]
- Twenty-nine 'speculative' houses: their surface area varies from 41 m² to 135 m² on plots of approximately the same surface area. The average size is around 80 m² of living space. Four of them have been transformed into three-story buildings. (Houses: 101, 105, 106, 107, *202, 301, 302*, 303, 304, 308, *311*, 312, *314, 315, 316*, 406, 412, *413, 415*, 418, 421, *501*, 509, 512, 514, 520, 521, 522, and 523.)
- Fourteen villas: built on plots ranging in size from 122 m² to 1,025 m², the houses cover areas of between 92 m² and 167 m². The average-sized houses use up 127 m² on land measuring about 295 m². (Houses: *102*, 103, *307, 310, 313, 317, 404, 408*, 417, 420, 506, *510, 515*, and *518*.)
- Two family units: built on plots that are quite large, they combine different kinds of construction for different members of a same family. (Houses: *306, 511*.)

A comparison between the built surface areas of courtyard houses and of speculative houses shows that they take up similar-sized areas; courtyard houses are built on larger plots of land because of the additional area allocated to the courtyard. More surprisingly, the built surface area of a villa occupies an area equivalent to that of the plot of land of a courtyard house. The plot area for the villa is consequently twice that of the surface area of the building (Fig. 1.5).

Courtyard houses (Fig. 1.6)
Courtyard houses are the oldest model of house, usually referred to as "Arab houses." However, *al-beit al-rifi* corresponds best to this type, as the term *beit 'arabi* generally refers to historical courtyard houses of the Damascene type, where a courtyard organized around an *iwan* is often surrounded by a two-floor construction. The houses documented here rarely have a second floor and never have an *iwan*. This type of house is also found in the countryside, where houses are extended as required, around the edge of the plot, progressively creating the courtyard (Léna 2007).

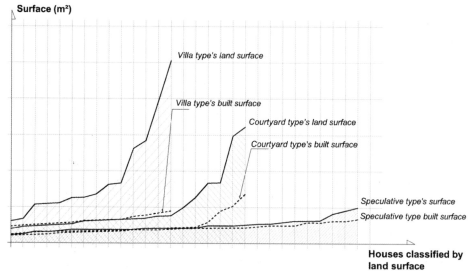

Fig. 1.5: Built versus land surface for different kinds of houses.
Illustration by Etienne Léna.

Among the twenty houses of this type, two of them can be considered as paradigmatic models: 203 and 507. Two houses of this type are larger: 104 and 305, with a succession of rooms along a veranda facing onto the courtyard. Twelve other houses are more compact versions on smaller plots of land. Numbers 203 and 507 occupy plots of land measuring 198 m² and 255 m² respectively, with courtyards making up 61 percent and 73 percent of the property. The built surface area is relatively similar for both houses: 77 m² and 70 m². The entrance opens directly onto the courtyard, which leads onto a toilet, a shower room, and a kitchen, followed by a living room and two other rooms (either two bedrooms or a bedroom and a storage room).

The main differences between the houses lie in the position of the veranda (507) and the way in which the stairway connects the different rooms (203). This is due in part to the different positioning with respect to the road and the direction of sunlight. This type of house is characterized by the fact that the whole house is organized around the courtyard. Differences in size between these houses arise mainly from the number of rooms set around the courtyard. Only in the smallest houses are the rooms smaller in size. The plan is usually organized with the entrance next to the toilet (except for three houses), the bathroom, and the kitchen. In seven

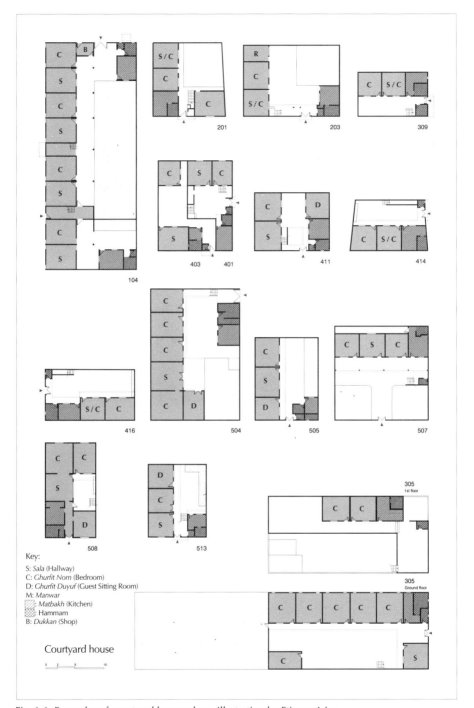

Key:
S: *Sala* (Hallway)
C: *Ghurfit Nom* (Bedroom)
D: *Ghurfit Duyuf* (Guest Sitting Room)
M: *Manwar*
: *Matbakh* (Kitchen)
: Hammam
B: *Dukkan* (Shop)

Courtyard house

Fig. 1.6: Examples of courtyard house plans. Illustration by Etienne Léna.

houses the toilet is separated from the other rooms that require plumbing by a corridor, and placed under the stairs. All but three of the houses have stairs to the roof, which serves as a terrace. The staircase is usually connected directly to the entrance (in ten houses) and the landing overhangs the front door.

Villa houses (Fig. 1.7)

The term 'villa house' is used to refer to a building that is erected in the center of its plot of land. The villa house has a more recent history, dating back to the late-nineteenth to early-twentieth century in Damascus. It is based on a layout that radiates out from a central room. This layout was used widely in René Danger's plan for Damascus, as the regulation that was applied to all the city's extensions required that constructions should be set back by three meters from the plot boundary (Arnaud 2006). The bourgeois aspect of such a model is perhaps one important reason for its use nowadays.[8] In fact, in the area studied, villas are always built with a single floor level, with a roof kept as 'land reserve' for the construction of an additional dwelling and in the meantime serving as a terrace. The staircase is systematically placed in a privileged position relative to the entrances to both plot and dwelling; a villa always has the potential to become a multistory building for a number of nuclear families, whereas a courtyard house never has an extra story added.

Villas are characterized by a central sofa, which is a central room that works more or less like a courtyard and leads to various other rooms. It is interesting to note that none of the villa-type houses has the kitchen positioned in direct relation to the entrance: it is always linked through the sofa. Compared to the courtyard house, where the kitchen is related directly to the entrance, one can regard this fact as revealing of changes in certain social practices.

Speculative houses (Figs. 1.8 and 1.9)

The speculative house is characterized by its small size and compactness. Twenty-two dwellings out of twenty-nine have similar designs. Fifty percent of these are apartments on different stories (apartments 106; 202 and 202b; 301 and 302; 314, 315, and 316; 413; and 523). The entrance is systematically associated with the stairway, which leads to a central room called either a salon or *ma'isha*, referred to here as a sofa, which leads to the other rooms. Lavatories are located beneath the stairway (in eleven cases), and sometimes there is a second lavatory (in five cases), when the surface area so allows (above 85 m²). The entrance gives direct access to a

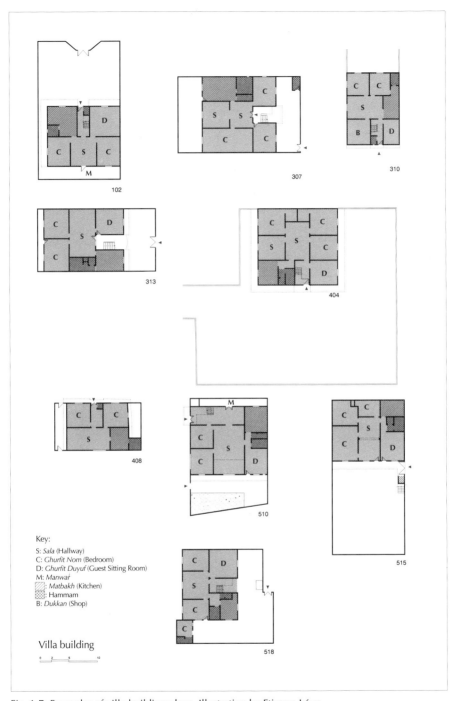

Key:
S: *Sala* (Hallway)
C: *Ghurfit Nom* (Bedroom)
D: *Ghurfit Duyuf* (Guest Sitting Room)
M: *Manwaṙ*
░: *Matbakh* (Kitchen)
▨: Hammam
B: *Dukkan* (Shop)

Villa building

Fig. 1.7: Examples of villa building plans. Illustration by Etienne Léna.

Fig. 1.8: Examples of plans of speculative-type multistory buildings and plans of plots on which several houses for different members of the same family are built. Illustration by Etienne Léna.

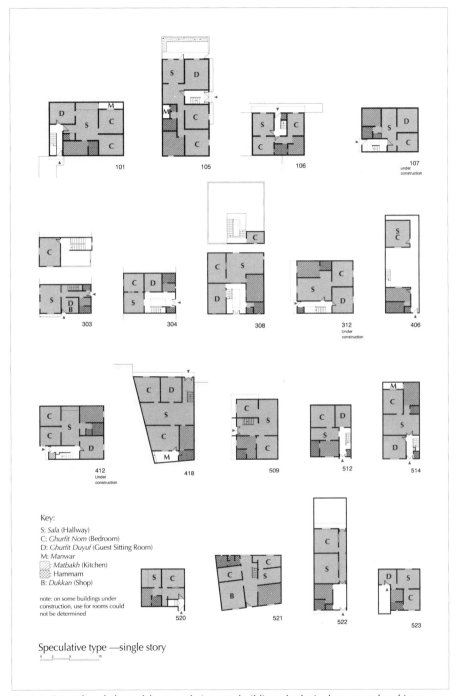

Key:
S: *Sala* (Hallway)
C: *Ghurfit Nom* (Bedroom)
D: *Ghurfit Duyuf* (Guest Sitting Room)
M: *Manwar*
▨ : *Matbakh* (Kitchen)
▧ : Hammam
B: *Dukkan* (Shop)

note: on some buildings under
construction, use for rooms could
not be determined

Speculative type —single story

Fig. 1.9: Examples of plans of the speculative type buildings, both single story and multistory.

guest sitting room *ghurfit duyuf* (in fourteen cases), in order to compensate for the lack of privacy. Because of the design, the presence and role of the central sofa, and its distance from the kitchen and bathroom entrances, this type of house can be compared to a villa house.

There is no direct correlation between the number of rooms and the surface area of the house: up to a certain point, a larger plot of land results in larger rooms. A three-room house measures between 50 m² and 110 m² (in sixteen cases), a four-room house measures between 100 m² and 185 m² (in five cases), and a five-room house measures between 125 m² and 165 m² (in three cases). Only three houses have two rooms each.

We noticed that houses with similar designs were built in very different ways: in a single stage or by progressive development on the plot of land. Three houses (304, 308, and 522) illustrate this point: the courtyard was gradually reduced and transformed into rooms, leaving the staircase in an open-air stairwell. However, as those houses were developed progressively as the need arose, the stairwell remains larger than those left in houses built on the basis of an original design (as is the case of house 301). In any case, the staircase remains open unless the house becomes a multistory building—to be occupied by different families—in which case the staircase is closed.

Somehow the speculative type borrows from both models of villa (the central sofa) and courtyards houses (the open-air stairway).

Architectural Systems for Neighborhood Management

The entrance is obviously the main element determining relations between a house and its exterior, and in certain courtyard houses it is the only such determining factor. In a very narrow space, the entrance reveals and leads on to many small spaces and describes uses and social relationships with the help of architectural features such as the staircase landing, which overhangs the entrance door. In order to enlarge the threshold outside, the posts that support the landing allow space for an electricity meter, a hand basin for guests, or a curtain that separates the threshold from the inside. Inside, the stairs provide extra space before the house's interior (Fig. 1.10). The front garden of villas is an extension of the entrance; vegetable salesmen remain at the gate, far from the front door.

Ways of letting light into the house are also an import consideration: the small size of speculative houses means that light must be brought in from the surroundings walls, which can cause conflict between neighbors. Several solutions were noticed.

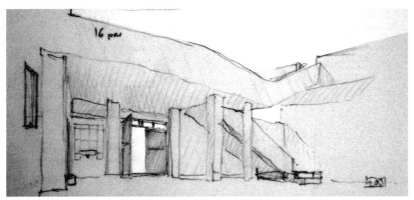

Fig. 1.10: Beyond the door, inside the courtyard. To the left are the sink and hamman for guests, and to the right is the staircase, which houses the temporary storage area and electric meter. Illustration by Etienne Léna.

There are different kinds of windows, and their position in the walls is set according to the function they are meant to serve. There are two models of large window: one is made of steel with a large fixed frame that is 120 cm square with a smaller opening frame of 80 cm square; the second is 160 cm x 110 cm and made of aluminum. They are most often set above 1.8 m high, unless they open onto a private space (the *manwar*, see below). When their purpose is mainly for ventilation, they are smaller and built above 2.5 m. The glass is usually translucent, letting in light but allowing no view. Smaller windows, 50 cm wide and set just below the ceiling, are used mainly for ventilation, but also let light in (Fig. 1.11). Such apertures are found in kitchens and bathrooms, as well as in living rooms, where the window may be set in shelves built into the walls.

Fig. 1.11: Different openings serve different functions (view, light, ventilation). Photograph by Etienne Léna.

Fig. 1.12: The *manwar* is a narrow courtyard that allows light into the house; it can also be used for laundry or general storage. Photograph by Etienne Léna.

Fig. 1.13: When a plot is too small to allow for a complete *manwar* reaching ground level, the *manwar* stops a few meters above ground, creating an alcove beneath. Photograph by Etienne Léna.

The *manwar*, 'place with light' (Figs. 1.12, 1.13) is a small courtyard located to the rear of the lot. It is about one meter wide and of variable length, and used to hang out washing or store furniture. It also brings light into the living room or kitchen. Windows looking onto the *manwar* are placed lower down on the wall, at a height of one meter, and have clear glazing. When light is needed in the center of the house, the *manwar* can stop 2.3 m above ground; this creates a kind of alcove with a lower ceiling in the room, which is most often the sofa.

In courtyard houses, the kitchen and bathroom traditionally have lower ceilings than those of the living rooms, as they do not need similar temperature control. Their rooves serve as outside storage, especially for the water tank. In villas or speculative-type houses, this difference in ceiling height allows room for a space called a *saqafi*, which is used for storage. It can be open to the exterior with windows in order to allow in light, not into the storage room itself, but into the main room behind it.

The roof terrace also creates the need for distance, as each house has a view onto the neighbors. In order to preserve privacy, parapet walls are built two meters high along the street or toward the house beside. Those walls are also a way to allow for the future vertical extension of the house.

These arrangements are easily adaptable to different configurations. They are used all the time in speculative housing due to conditions of extreme density, but are also found in larger houses, always allowing for original uses of rooms and lighting.

Urbanization Processes

As mentioned before, during our fifteen-day study we saw firsthand the different stages of transformation from agricultural land to the building of two houses.

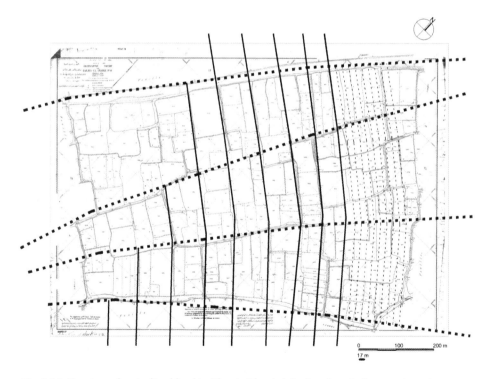

Fig. 1.14: Structure of agricultural land in Ghouta. The dark broken lines indicate main pathways, corresponding to irrigation channels; the solid black lines indicate the land's secondary structure, while the lighter dotted lines show the division of the land into 17-m-wide strips. Illustration by Etienne Léna.

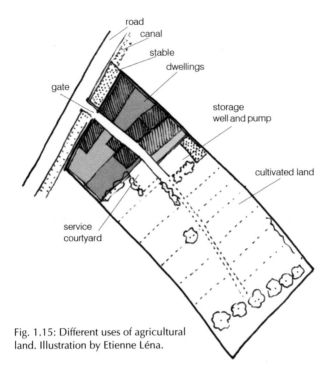

Fig. 1.15: Different uses of agricultural land. Illustration by Etienne Léna.

Agricultural land

Agricultural plots of land were originally irrigated by a canal network from Deranye. The main branches are still in service, mainly following a parallel northeast/southwest axis about 180 m to 230 m apart, with roads running alongside them. Perpendicular canals form a smaller network, which extends to strips of cultivated land. The minimum width of these strips of land is about 17 m, and their width increases in multiples of this value (17 + ½ 17 = 25 m, 3 x 17 = 51 m, and so on) (Fig. 1.14). The strips of land are then divided along their length into agricultural plots of land. Their surface area can therefore vary greatly—from 700 m² to more than 9,000 m².[9] Land that is still cultivated today is mainly used for market gardens, orchards, or olive tree plantations, and sometimes cereal farming. The boundaries of the plots of land are marked out by 30-cm-high banks that contain irrigation channels and serve as pathways. Nowadays, the tertiary canals are in poor condition and only partially serve their function, by transporting polluted water. Instead, water for irrigation is provided by wells equipped with mechanical pumps.

We visited two plots that are still cultivated. The plot described here is located 800 m from mainly urbanized land. The agricultural plot of land measures about 3,000 m²; four courtyard houses are built along a line that is twenty-five meters in from the main road. A 3.5-meter-wide central path gives access to the houses and to farm buildings (a cowshed, pump, and storage), finally leading to the cultivated land. This path is closed with a gate on the main road, and every house has its own door connecting the inner courtyard to the central path (Fig. 1.15).

The farm layout prefigures the way farmland is urbanized: a central path, the distribution of plots of land to members of the same family cut from the originally cultivated area, and the use of a shared well. On this very basic scheme for organizing the land, there will be great variations depending upon the processes for densification.

Parceling of land (Fig. 1.18, Fig. 1.20, a, b, c)

First of all, crops are abandoned and the land soon returns to fallow. The fruit trees which grew on it are left to die, then are cut down and sold.[10] Canals are no longer maintained. The owner—later considered as the 'original' owner—organizes the sale or the transfer by inheritance of his land. He can go through the land registry department, which records the division, which is perfectly legal so far, and demarcate the land based on the land registry established by Camille Durrafour in 1930. Their work may also be carried out outside their official working hours, less formally. In any case, they always use the topographic tools provided by the department and their work is accurate.

Nevertheless, the involvement of the land registry department in the demarcation process is not a sufficient guarantee to protect the construction. For example, house 509 is the first construction on an agricultural plot of land that had been abandoned and returned to the state of bare earth. At the time of our study, lines, breeze blocks, and posts that had been used to mark out the plot of land could still be seen. But the construction itself had been partially demolished by the municipality at least three times. Once lots are defined, they are transferred by inheritance or sold. Even advertising is informal: the 'real-estate' advertisements for the sale of building land may be tagged on walls with the salesman's cell phone number (Fig. 1.16).

Following the principle that a central path should serve houses within the farm, the initial owner insists that there be a right of passage between three and five meters wide. This encumbrance is shared by the buyers of

Fig. 1.16: Advertisement for sale of building on wall reads *ard li-l-bay'* ('land for sale').
Photograph by Etienne Léna.

lots adjoining the passageway, and the road is created by the setting back of any construction by 1.5 m to 2.5 m from the boundary of the plot. When the width of the initial plot does not allow for the creation of two lots on either side of the pathway, the owner can enter into an agreement with the neighboring owner to share the encumbrance, or he can reduce the path to half its width; this is often seen in access to plots created by multiple subdivision. This central path is called a *hara*, 'alley,' which, by extension, gives its name to the passageway and all the houses built along it. None of the alleys were asphalted and all are cul-de-sacs. This system of lots served by a cul-de-sac is not a new one, since it can be seen in Amara, which was built during the nineteenth century (Arnaud 2006). The plots of land served by the passageway can be subdivided until they reach a minimum size. The smallest lot measures approximately 3 *qasaba* and an average lot measures approximately 10 *qasaba*.[11]

The following scenarios of land parceling show the variety of situations and actors and the specificities they engender:

In lot L700 (Fig. 1.17), the original landlord occupied a long plot of land at the back (house 504, measuring 337 m²). Some of the lots which border the four-meter-wide access road were built by members of his family, while the rest were sold to third parties. The plot of land adjacent to house 504, with a surface area of 315 m², was further divided after being resold. The last owner of the lot built the concrete shells of three houses (including 514 and 311), creating a new access alley 1.5 m wide upon his

Fig. 1.17: *Hara* L700: Two initial plots of similar size give rise to different processes of densification: plots 504, 514, 406, and 507 were built by the same family, and plots 514, 311, and the shaded plots to their sides were built by the same contractor. Illustration by Etienne Léna.

L700

own plot. During our stay one of the dwellings was sold again and was under completion.

On lot L703 (Fig. 1.18), two initial neighboring owners agreed to share the right of passage to the alleyway. The owner of the northern plot of land, having divided his land officially, kept two lots along the main road, one to rent to a craftsman and the second for his son who built his villa on it. A third plot of land was kept near his own house to create a private vegetable garden which he fenced in with wire netting. The remaining four were sold. Among them, one was divided again into two units, arriving at what could be said to be the minimum surface areas (520 and 523 have surface areas measuring 49 m² and 52 m² respectively), which were developed by their respective buyers into a house and a two-story building. On the south side, on the land of the second owner, a large villa was built on the road, in order to be rented out. A second plot next to this one was was divided into three parts, and a small alley 1.5 m wide created to serve the rear lot. The house built on the rear lot has just a single window, which opens onto the pathway. For this house, there was also some negotiation with the owner of the bordering southern plot of land: the boundary of the original agricultural

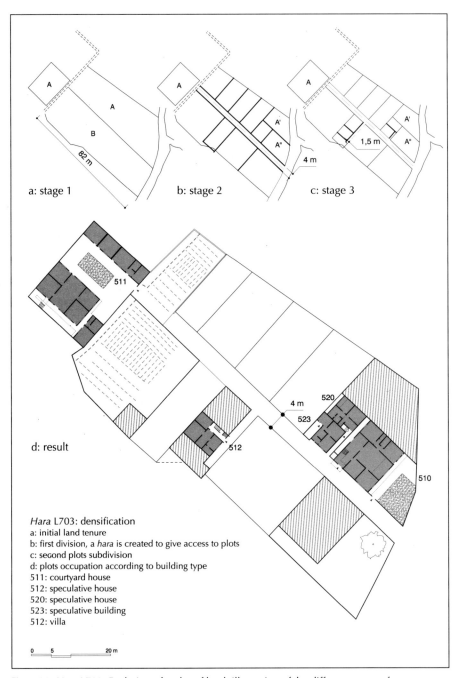

a: stage 1   b: stage 2   c: stage 3

d: result

Hara L703: densification
a: initial land tenure
b: first division, a *hara* is created to give access to plots
c: second plots subdivision
d: plots occupation according to building type
511: courtyard house
512: speculative house
520: speculative house
523: speculative building
512: villa

Fig. 1.18: *Hara* L703: Evolution of a plot of land. Illustration of the different stages of division and a plan of the final result.

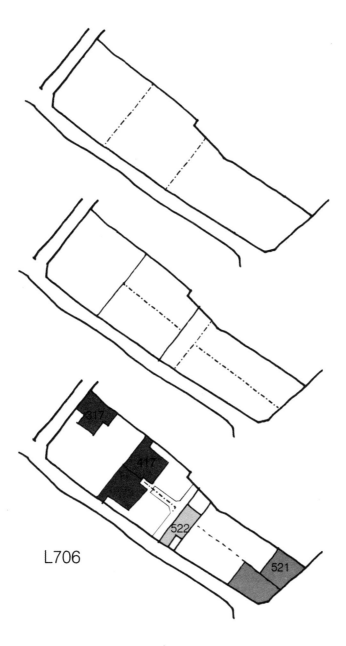

Fig. 1.19: *Hara* L706. From an initial plot divided between three brothers, processes of densification lead to diverse solutions. Illustration by Etienne Léna.

plot cuts diagonally through both plots of land, so the officers at the land registry modified it, by retroceding a triangle of land in order to allow for the construction of a four-sided building. The new boundary line is marked out with a red line painted on the party walls of the house.

Another method has been used by a family on lot L706 (Fig. 1.19), where part of the original farmland was divided between three brothers. One lot is occupied by a single villa, the second by two semi-detached villas (one is 417), the third lot was sold and divided again into two lots: one is occupied by a long house (522, 107 m²), whereas the other, much bigger house (521, 625 m²), has been further divided into two: for the buyer and his son, who share a large garden, which is considered as a land reserve for future extension.

In lot L701, we were only able to visit one house (508). The whole plot of land, measuring 840 m², belongs to one family, and has four houses (speculative or courtyard types) and a workshop on the main street. The *hara* is four meters wide, totally private, and has a gate. The first floor of some of the houses covers the alley in places, like the *sibat*[12] seen in the old districts of Damascus.

Grouped families are not always on a single plot of land. House 313 and those adjoining it, 518, 416, 414, and 415, are occupied by members of the same family. They are in different *hara*s, but all of them lie within a radius of one hundred meters. This community is made visible through the use of the same brown and red paint with similar ornamental motifs on all the houses (Fig. 1.20, d).

Groups of constructions often share features: the same wall coating, flooring, type of décor, and windows. This is particularly noticeable in some sections of lots: L704, L705, L707, and L708. The owner of house 301 explained that in his *hara* (L707), some of the other owners had joined forces in order to reduce construction costs by having one contractor build all their houses, which explains the homogeneous features. These co-partner strategies can have variable compositions, as in one *hara* where the group of owners who joined forces to pay the contractor was different from the group of owners who joined forces to finance the drilling for a common well.

Lot L708 shows all these various situations along a *hara* that is 4 m wide by 115 m long. The first two houses and a carpenter's workshop belong to the same family, while the rest are speculative constructions. And according to their immediate context, the constructions will be completed differently: all those situated on the north side of the passageway have a

Legend (top right):

⌒ Approximative area of houses that share the same well
• Well
▨▦ Houses from the same family group
▬ Houses built by the same company

Legend (bottom right):

▨ Agricultural exploitation
▨ Courtyard house
▨ Villa
▬ Speculative house
▬ Multistory building

Diversity of geography
a: original land (from C. Durrafour's plans—1936)
b: *haras*
c: houses built (in gray—built plots not surveyed)
d: spatial repartition (families, water, company)
e: repartition of the types

Fig. 1.20: Beginning with the original land tenure, the strategy of parceling lots and the formation of associations of families or owners in order to buy the land, build houses, and share water, create a very intricate landscape, wherein different urban geographies can arise. Illustration by Etienne Léna.

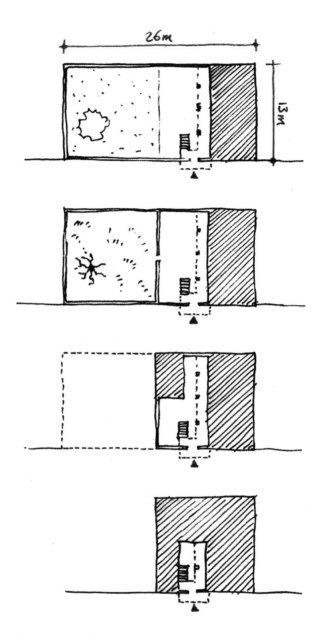

Fig. 1.21: Progressive densification of a single plot, from top to bottom. The dotted lines in the third image down indicate a part of the plot that has been sold. The hatched lines indicate growing construction on the same plot. Illustration by Etienne Léna.

manwar built on the outside edge which looks out onto cultivated farm-land, whereas the constructions south of the path have kept the one-meter strip on which to build the *manwar* at a later date, probably because of the more 'private' nature of the land (narrow and fallow) between this lot and its neighbor. The rest of the *hara* mainly contains purely speculative con-structions, where, in the absence of a house belonging to the initial owner, there is no large lot left.

These *hara*s create a robust structure for the urbanized territory, even if they don't make up a real network of streets, as they are cul-de-sacs for the most part. Nevertheless, the rhythm created by entrances over-whelmed by the staircase landings gives the *hara*s a specific identity.

Densification

This urbanized territory is not fixed once the houses are built. The den-sification process continues on the building itself, whether horizontally, on free space within the plot of land, or vertically by stacking.

South of the studied area, four nearby houses, which occupy plots of land on both sides of the street, give a clue to one of the densification processes.

The two courtyard houses 515 and 309 are juxtaposed on the south side of the street (Fig. 1.21). They have the same layout, with a line of rooms along the courtyard, perpendicular to the street. House 515 is on a plot measuring 12.5 m wide by 26 m long, while 309 is slightly shorter. The plot's length is subdivided between the house, its gravel courtyard, and the garden. But in 309 the garden is derelict, separated from the courtyard by a wall of concrete blocks, and has a passage; the garden is considered as a land reserve for a future sale. On the other side of the street, houses 308 and 411 occupy plots of land 10 m deep, perpendicular to the street, 10 m and 13 m long. They are also courtyard houses, with a wing built per-pendicular to the street. When we visited, building work had just finished in house 411 to cover part of the courtyard, creating a new room and reducing the opening to the sky to a small stairwell. The courtyard could be considered as the second land reserve.

This kind of horizontal densification is sometimes planned from the beginning of the construction process, as in house 406, where initial rein-forcement allowed for the casting of a new slab to cover a forthcoming room.

From a House to a Multistory Building

The concept of the villa allows for new dwellings to be built on top. The speculative type of house can also be transformed. House 301 underwent a similar densification process, which was the result of the financial means of the owner. On a plot of land measuring 82 m², bought for SYP140,000 in 2005, the owner built two rooms, a kitchen, a bathroom, and an access staircase from the ground floor, all located around a courtyard, after which he moved in. One year later, he was able to cover the courtyard, transforming it into a central sofa. Then, when the first level slab was completed, the owner sold its roof for an amount equal to the initial purchase price but with a surface area which was smaller because of the space used for the two *manwar*s: a small 8 m² courtyard on the side of the house, and a second one only allowing light through a fanlight into the sofa. When the roof was sold, a new house was built on top (number 302). The open staircase was then enclosed and modified to make two separate entrances for the dwellings, although the ground-floor owner keeps the right of access to the roof, which houses his water tank.

A similar process led to the creation of a small collective building on lot L707. One stairwell serves the three dwellings 314, 315, and 316. The surface area of each story is reduced by the space taken up by the *manwar*s of the story below. If on the ground floor the *manwar* is the only means of getting light from outside without creating a view into the other apartments, on the other levels, light can be obtained directly from outside. The *manwar* is intended, then, to avoid plunging views from one story to the one beneath, thereby protecting neighbors' privacy.

Services

Because of the illegality of their constructions, owners cannot claim to benefit from public services such as water, sewerage, or electricity. Regarding the water supply, generally a 60-m-deep borehole is drilled, and water is distributed to one or several homes. The owner of the land on which the well is drilled can sell the water, taking payment for maintaining the well, or charge for the electricity used by the pump; thus the price of water varies from zero to SYP3,000 per year.[13] When a connection to a well is unavailable, some occupants have water delivered by truck. Water distribution is independent of the geographical limits of lots; it corresponds more to human geographies (Fig. 1.20, d). According to its owners, house 104 shares its artesian well with fifty homes, but we counted seventeen pipes taking water from the well, which led to houses in different *hara*s (Fig. 1.22). Included among them were houses at the end of lot L708, even though most of the houses built on this lot get water provided by the initial owners of lot L708, who built their houses (419) at the entrance. The

Fig. 1.22: Seventeen pipes taking water from a well to different houses in a *hara*.
Photograph by Etienne Léna.

owner of a well has no obligation to share his water: the owner of farm 523–524 refuses to distribute water from his well to anyone, even to his siblings settled next to his land.

In 2005, in lot L707, the joint owners living in the same *hara* financed a well and the construction of a concrete water tank on the roof of an unoccupied house; the tank was filled using a pump. From that tank, every joint owner obtained their water through their own means, sharing the cost of maintenance and electricity for the pump. Two years later, when the house on which the water tank was built was occupied, the tank was demolished and every joint owner installed their own pump from the well in order to supply water directly to private plastic tanks on the rooves of their houses.

Drinking water is distributed by truck every two or three days and costs SYP10 per twenty liters.

Domestic sewage is evacuated through septic tanks adapted to the size of each house. The sewerage pit is generally dug in the path of the *hara*. House 501 has a septic tank that is 2 m long and 2 m deep and built with concrete blocks spaced at intervals. The pit is emptied three to four times a year by specialized firms, which advertise with paintings on the walls of the district.

In order to provide safe electrical installations, the municipality regularly installs electricity in all houses upon the request of the owner. In the interim, certain owners claim to obtain their electricity from illegal installations.

In the earliest *hara*, closest to the Daraya ring road, owners joined forces in order to get a mains sewerage network from the municipality. The system was built under the main road, on the edge of the illegally urbanized land. We were told two different versions of the story. One was that the owners of the different *hara*s had to pay for the system that connected them to the mains network, and the second version was that this was also paid for by the municipality. However, all agreed that the owners had to pay for the part of the system that was built under each *hara*'s passageway.

Geography (Fig. 1.20, d, e)

On a relatively homogeneous plot of land originally dedicated to agricultural use and organized according to an irrigation system, comes a level of urbanization that creates a very intricate urban fabric, which could be described as chaotic (Fig. 1.23). But closer examination shows that the differents strategies and processes used by different owners to build on the land generate different geographies that do not blend seamlessly into each other.

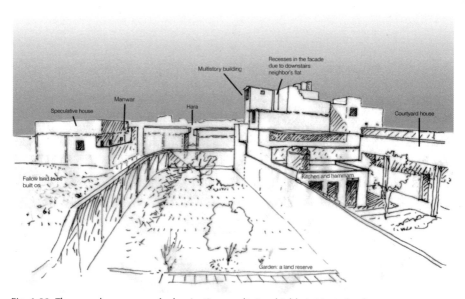

Fig. 1.23: The complex process of urbanization results in a highly intricate landscape. Illustration by Etienne Léna.

One possible geography is determined by the subsoil, by the land itself, which strongly affects the shape of the urban structure. The canal network generates divisions and strips of land that determine the built organization. Therefore the *hara* considered as a whole (the street and the houses that surround it) determines the structure of the parcels of land. And just as canal networks end in lots requiring irrigation, so do street networks end in cul-de-sacs, each cul-de-sac highlighting the individual design of the initial owners, who only regarded their land as a potential source of profit and not as part of a wider urban plan.

The second geographical system reflects families that group together on the same plot of land while preserving some land for the future growth of that group, or which identify themselves by way of common architectural features.

The third one could be the geography of types of architecture, pointing the way to rising land prices and therefore describing the history of urbanization and a familiar evolutionary pattern: agricultural land first, progressively occupied by courtyard houses for the farmers, then villas, when the land was relatively under-constructed, then speculative houses, and finally multistory buildings.

The fourth geography could be that of economic interest, where portions of streets are built on by a single constructor for different individuals, who come together to pool costs at a specific stage of the construction process. The result can be seen in rows of houses that have the same initial design.

Another geography can be determined by water distribution, which is independent of parcel limits and public roads, but the detail of which reveals the balance of power between individuals (who gets water from whom, who shares water with whom, and so on).

The points where these geographies do not overlap are sources of friction and conflict that create the need for negotiation and compromise. These points of friction together with the need to respect certain traditions and conventions are reflected in the urban environment.

Does the complexity engendered by these overlapping geographies and unique negotiations give owners many ways to legitimize their property in order to make illegal constructions permanent in the eyes of the law, or, since each situation calls for a practical solution that an overly exogenous law cannot always allow for, is this complexity the result of a practice of law based on customs?

Notes

1 "Plan d'Aménagement, d'Extension et d'Embellissement." Those plans are issued from Law Cornudet, voted in 1919 in France in order to provide a master plan for cities with populations of over 10,000 inhabitants. Danger is one of the town planners who elaborated this law. Working first with Henri Prost on Cascablanca's plan for extension, he would go on to share his method with France and its colonies, exporting the concept all around the countries of the Mediterranean.

2 Luc Vilan and Yves Roujon, 1997, were the first scholars to provide a description of these lots.

3 Houses received an order number according to the person who carried out the survey: series 100 was conducted by Abd El Ghaman Hamberge, series 200 by Najat Khalil, series 300 by Wouroud Ahdali, series 400 by Kinda El Balkhi, series 500 by the author. Series 600 concerns groups, lots, or particular places that were tracked down by Myriam Ferrier. For this study we numbered interesting groups of lots starting at L700.

4 Title deeds were communicated to Myriam Ferrier, as part of her research.

5 All prices are 2005 prices.

6 The 'post-beam' system in reinforced concrete requires a certain degree of skill from the builder. For example, in a self-built construction such as house 509, the posts are made with blocks set up in posts (40 x 40 cm), and the floors are made partly with a steel beam frame filled with concrete tiles and partly using the usual concrete slabs.

7 Numbers given in italics indicate houses illustrated in this chapter. Others houses were taken into account for the statistics given here, but drawings were not precise enough to be reproduced here.

8 It is possible to argue that the harmony between this existing architectural type and the proposed regulation—which reproduces a morphology that is applied systematically by René Danger to the other cities of the Mediterranean area in which he intervenes—is one of the factors leading to an almost complete fulfillment of the town planning scheme designed for Damascus.

9 The standard unit of measurement for farmland is the *dunum*, which is the equivalent of 1000 m².

10 A small unit for selling olive tree wood was set up about three kilometers north of the site.

11 The unit used to measure surfaces is the *qasaba*, which represents approximately 24.75 m². Ten *qasaba* are the equivalent of a *mod*.

12 Architectural term used to describe a room of a house that covers a street.

13 The statement of certain owners to the effect that they distribute the water free of charge is subject to question, given that there is a minimal cost for maintenance.

References

Abboud, Cha'ban. 2007. "Les quartiers informels de Damas, une ceinture de misère." In Baudouin Dupret, Zuhair Ghazzal, Youssef Courbage, and Mohammed Al-Dbiyat, eds., *La Syrie au présent*. Paris: Sindbad—Acte Sud.

Akbar, Jamal. 1988. *Crisis in the Built Environment: The Case of the Muslim City*. Singapore: Concept Media/Aga Khan ed.

Arnaud, Jean-Luc. 2006. *Damas, urbanisme et architecture, 1860—1925*. Paris: Sindbad—Actes Sud.

Balanche, Fabrice. 2006. "Damas la tentaculaire." In *Villes et Territoires du Moyen-Orient*, no. 2. Institut Français du Proche Orient, online publication of l'Observatoire Urbain.

Bianquis, Anne-Marie, and Guillaume Fantino. 2007. "La Ghouta de Damas, une oasis en mutation." In Baudouin Dupret, Zuhair Ghazzal, Youssef Courbage, and Mohammed Al-Dbiyat, eds., *La Syrie au présent*. Paris: Sindbad—Acte Sud.

Danger, René. 1937. "L'urbanisme en Syrie." *Revue Urbanisme*, no. 55.

———. 1936. *Rapport préliminaire au Projet d'aménagement, d'embellissement et d'extension de Damas*. N.p.: n.p.

Depaule, Jean-Charles, and Jean-Luc Arnaud. 1985. *A travers le mur*. Paris: Centre Georges Pompidou.

Ecochard, Michel, and Gyogi Banshoya. 1968. Plan directeur de Damas, Rapport justificatif. Unpublished report held in Atelier du Vieux Damas, IFPO, Damascus.

"Espaces et formes de l'Orient arabe," *Les cahiers de la recherche architecturale*, nos. 10/11, 1982.

Friès, Franck. 2000. "Damas, 1860—1946, la mise en place de la ville moderne. Des règlements au plan." PhD thesis, Marne-la-Vallée, University of Paris-VIII.

Labeyrie, Irène. 1987. "Damas. Un modèle dominant?" In "Espaces Centrés," *Les cahiers de la recherche architecturale*, nos. 20/21.

Marillot, Olivier. 2006. "La démographie de la province de Damas." Report for IUP, l'Université de Franche-Comté. http://www.mom.fr/IMG/pdf/Damas_Demographie.pdf.

Noweir, Sawsan, and Philippe Panerai. 1989. *L'herbe verte d'Imbaba*. Ladrhaus: Ecole d'Architecture de Versailles.

Rossi, Aldo. 1990. *L'architecture et la ville*. Paris: Livre and Communication.

Roujon, Yves, and Luc Vilan, eds. 1997. *Le Midan. Actualité d'un faubourg ancien de Damas*. Damascus: Institut français d'études arabes de Damas (IFEAD).

2

Selling One's Property in an Informal Settlement: A Praxeological Approach to a Syrian Case Study

Baudouin Dupret and Myriam Ferrier

This chapter addresses the issue of how real-estate transactions are organized in so-called informal neighborhoods in Damascus, that is, city quarters that developed in contravention of laws governing rural lands that are deemed theoretically improper for development. There are many different practices, which may look random, yet they are shaped through a complex relationship to the law, which acknowledges the existence of informal neighborhoods, called *mukhalafat*, in different ways. We shall describe this relationship through a single case study, by analyzing documents kept by the buyer of a property: Mrs. Sabbah.

The apartment Mrs. Sabbah bought is located in the Yarmouk Palestinian refugee camp. The status of its real-estate property is subject to rules that differ from those of other Damascus neighborhoods. For the Land Registry Department, this land is registered as rural and belongs to the northern region of the United Arab Republic.[1] A specific department was created in the 1940s to administer affairs related to Palestinian refugees: the Foundation for Palestinian Refugees (al-Mu'assasa li-l-Laji'in al-Filistiniyyin). Among its responsibilities is the administration of land in the Yarmouk area on which it has a ninety-nine-year leasehold. It is responsible for the parceling out of the land and for its allotment to Palestinian refugees. In parallel, the municipality *(baladiya)*, also called the local council *(al-majlis al-mahalli)*, is responsible for the issuing of building permits and the registration of house tenancy contracts.

Most of the documents consulted concern real-estate transactions for different properties located within the same building, on al-Ja'awna Street, in the camp's historic center, on a parcel of land containing around one hundred buildings. The specific building we are dealing with, which is not registered in the Land Registry, was built in several stages. The initial construction comprised a ground floor and one story. Today, the building has four stories. The documents kept by Mrs. Sabbah and the relating real-estate transactions explain how many stories were added to the building and how they were sold. Mrs. Sabbah's file also includes water and electricity bills plus one house tenancy contract.

These documents can be analyzed in two ways. First, we shall see how they describe the property for specific practical purposes and how, therefore, they do this in different ways. Second, we shall observe how this file, comprising various documents, reflects the complex history of this property, the specific language games that are attached to it, and its internal organization around principles of the contiguity of properties and the succession of legal deeds, in order to secure the buyer's property rights.

Documents Established for All Practical Legal Purposes

Mrs. Sabbah's file comprises six contracts of final sale, two special powers of attorney, one house tenancy contract, and water and electricity bills. These documents do not relate to the same property. The real-estate transactions they account for sometimes relate to unfinished stories, sometimes to built stories, that is, apartments. Nevertheless, the parties who take part in these transactions are related to each other through the close proximity of their properties and the successive character of the contracts (see page 53).

As for the contracts, they (1) put the transaction under God's protection; (2) are titled; (3) declare the sale final; (4) specify the identity of the contract's signatories; (5) define the content of the object of the transaction; (6) stipulate the modalities of the transaction (exchange of a property for money); (7) specify the date of the contract's execution; (8) state everyone's responsibility vis-à-vis the Syrian administration; and (9) specify the conditions under which the sale took place and the contract can be annulled. Moreover, some contracts also (10) mention the payment by one of the parties of a fee to the broker and (11) account for the registration with the Ministry of Finance (Figs. 2.1, 2.2).

The contracts are not all identical. In Mrs. Sabbah's file, the first one was written by an attorney, as indicated by the heading of the document and the comment "written by myself," followed by his signature and stamp. In a preamble the attorney describes the estate concerned by the sale and then states the completion of the sale. In the next five contracts, there is neither a preamble nor any mention of the attorney's role. However, two witnesses have appended their signatures at the end of the deed: "in the full possession of our legal and judicial capacities, we have agreed upon this transaction." These five contracts are written on standard forms, available in ordinary stores. Some parts of the form are left empty, or are more or less completed. The back of the document offers the opportunity to specify the conditions of payment, the inventory of fixtures, and the timetable of installments. These specifications are different in each case, although all the contracts describe the estate sold.

All these sale contracts present themselves as final and binding. In signing this document, the owner gives up all his rights regarding the estate to the buyer. The transfer of the property and the price of the transaction are the subject of two provisions stating the action accomplished by the two parties. The transaction is not registered in the Land Registry insofar as the property itself is not registered. Thus, the buyer's rights are not guaranteed by the Land Registry. However, the transaction is registered, as far as the first three contracts are concerned, with the Ministry of Finance, as indicated by the stamp on the back of the documents. This gives it legal force and serves as testimony to property rights. The fourth, fifth, and sixth contracts are not registered with the Ministry of Finance. The transaction they refer to might be reinforced by the power of attorney given by the seller to the buyer, as is the case with the fifth and sixth contracts. There is, moreover, a handwritten note on these last two contracts, as well as on the third one, which stipulates this procedure indirectly when it characterizes the transfer of the property: "the sale consists of a special power of attorney."

The two powers of attorney completing the file also show common features like (1) a heading; (2) the civil status of the public prosecutor and of the beneficiary of the power of attorney; (3) the public prosecutor's statement and signature; (4) the description of the property concerned by the power of attorney; and (5) the number under which it was registered by the notary. Each power of attorney also defines precisely (6) the competences which have been delegated. Officially written by the public prosecutor, the power of attorney mentions, at the end of the document; (7) the signature,

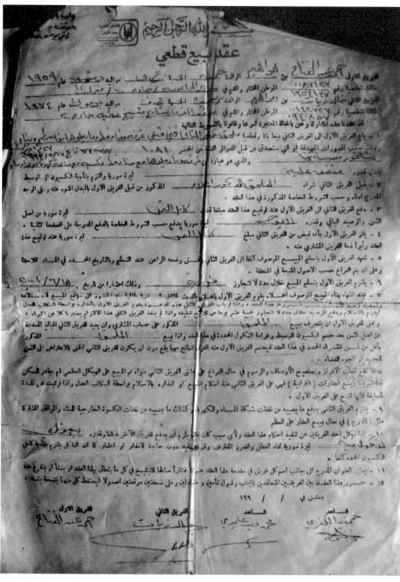

Fig. 2.1: Second contract of final sale (front). (Translation opposite.)

In the name of God the Benevolent the Merciful [1]

Contract of final sale [2] [3]

The first party *Ahmad* ... The second party *Khaled* ... [4]

We have agreed upon the transaction ... according to the following provisions:

1. The first party sold to the second party in a full and final way the *extension situated* ... in return for what was agreed upon.
   /The first party/ committed itself to the payment of the commission to the intermediary person. [5] [6]

2. The second party accepted to buy the *extension* ... in return for *its balance* ... [5] [6]

3. The second party paid to the first party ... the sum of ...
   The remainder ... will be paid according to the special conditions... indicated on page two. [9]

4. The first party declares having received from the second party the sum of ... and has given the final discharge to the buying party.

5. The first party committed itself to leave the estate... in its current condition...

6. The first party committed itself to the payment of the sum ... *immediately*... starting from the date of *18/6/2001*. [6]

7. When the building of the aforementioned estate is completed, the first party announces it ... If the second party does not answer, the sale is considered null and void ... [8]

8. The expenses linked to the [Land Registry procedures] are owed by the second party... [The] taxes ... are owed by the second party ... [7]

9. The second party shall pay the [subsidiary] expenses in case the construction of the sold estate is unfinished. [9]

10. If one of the parties rescinds the contract ... it would be compelled to pay to the other party the sum equivalent to the value of a *final sale* ... [3]

11. The address mentioned beside the name of each party ... is considered as the address ...

12. This contract was made ... in two copies ...

witness / witness of the second party/ first party

Fig. 2.2: Back of second contract of final sale. (Translation below.)

Special provisions for payment [9]

Syrian pounds *an extension made of one room and what overhangs it, above the second floor, has paid the totality of the sum agreed, with the electricity meter and the water meter*

Conditions of subsidiary work
Paint, wood, ceramic tiles *covering as observed* [9]
bathroom and content
kitchen
electricity
[illegible word]
                                        Installments
stamp of the Head Office of Indirect Taxes of the Ministry of Finance, 30 June 2001
[11]
Written 199

Witness / Witness / first party / second party

stamps, and statement of the notary testifying to the respect of procedures and to the authenticity of the deed. Finally, it is dated (8) (Fig. 2.3).

The text of these two powers of attorney forms is identical, and the handwritten parts are the same except for slight details. These powers of attorney concern the last two transactions and correspond to the last two contracts that were also kept by Mrs. Sabbah. There are two types of power of attorney: general, through which somebody confers powers to someone else for any transaction that concerns him/her; and special, through which somebody confers powers to someone else for any transaction concerning a particular property.

The powers of attorney enclosed in Mrs. Sabbah's file are special. The person who sold the property to Mrs. Sabbah conferred to her all the transactional powers concerning this property. In this power of attorney, as in any special power of attorney, the buyer and the seller do not appear as such: the buyer is the prosecutor and the seller is the person to whom the powers are conferred. The power of attorney aims at giving the appointed proxy the capacity to act vis-à-vis the said property as its owner. It gives him or her the right to make transactions, not the right to ownership. So, one can raise the question as to why a power of attorney must be made by the seller to the buyer while normally the sale implies the transfer of all the rights bound to the property. This leads us to question what the power of attorney accomplishes formally and allows indirectly.

The power of attorney is a deed registered by the notary, who is an employee of the Ministry of Justice. It has an official character that affects the whole real-estate transaction. Since the sold property is of a certain type (that is, an apartment in a building constructed on rural land that is not divided into plots and belongs to the state), the transaction cannot be registered at the Real-estate Office. Hence the power of attorney. In other words, the power of attorney serves as a means to testify to a transaction that cannot follow a normal course. The same holds true for the registration with the Ministry of Finance in the first three contracts.

The File Establishing Ownership: Chronology, Language Games, and Instructed Action

Mrs. Sabbah's apartment is located in a building whose construction lasted more than ten years. The first contract dates back to 1996 and indicates that the building is made up of a ground floor and one story. The fifth contract, dating from 18 January 2006, concerns the third-floor apartment and a room built on the fourth floor. Thus, three stories were added

Fig. 2.3: Power of attorney associated with the fifth contract. English translation by Baudouin Dupret. (Translation below.)

The notary
Special number *23* [5]
General number *773* [5]
Register *564* [5]

Special power of attorney [1]
19 January 2006 [8]

I undersigned '*Amir* [2] declare ... having conferred power of attorney [3] to '*Abd al-Fatah* ... [2] to represent me ... in order to buy [description of the flat] [4], to ... sign the contracts ... and to register *the flat* ... with the competent financial and real-estate authorities ... [6] To commit ...; to declare that ...; to receive ...; to execute [real-estate, financial and administrative operations]; to sign ...; [to represent me] for any ... trial against ... [6]

Accordingly, I sign in a written form
name and signature of the public prosecutor [3]
On *Thursday...* Mister '*Abd al-Fatah* ... presented himself before me... And he showed this document established outside the department and asked me to sign it. After having read it to him and having made him understand its consequences and meaning. The signing took place in my presence [7]
Registered after payment of the legal taxes and the required stamps...

between 1996 and 2006. These contracts do not all concern the same property. However, they are linked to each other, not least because they are all included within the same file. Two issues become clear in this respect: on the one hand, the existence of Mrs. Sabbah's property depends on the existence of the stories on which it is built; on the other, it is only possible to testify to the ownership of Mrs. Sabbah's property on condition that one can establish the right of ownership of the person from whom she purchased it. It is for these two related reasons that she keeps the file of the successive contracts that led to her ownership.

Close examination of Mrs. Sabbah's file makes it possible to account for three major features of this process: first, the chronology of the building stages and transactions carried out on the different stories; second, the inventory of the real-estate jargon and language games; third, the description of the principles of the physical proximity of the properties and the successive character of legal instruments leading to the ownership of the apartment, which bring together all the documents.

The chronology
The inclusion of all these documents in one and the same file raises a question which can be answered through the examination of the many links that bind these documents together. Among these links, there is the succession of these documents in a sequence of time that led to the construction of the building in its present form and to the acquisition by Mrs. Sabbah of the ownership of the third-floor apartment. Hereinafter follows the summary chronology that can be established on this basis.

The first contract, dated 8 December 1996, concerns the sale of one half of a story suitable for development, that half having a surface area of 27 m^2, on the second floor of a building comprising a ground floor and a first story with a surface area of 60 m^2. The second contract, dated 18 June 2001, accounts for the selling of an extension of 27 m^2, located on the third floor, and of the story suitable for development above it; that is, a potential extension to the fourth floor. The third contract, dated 27 March 2004, concerns the third-floor extension. The fourth contract, dated 18 January 2006, concerns the third-floor extension plus the non-built story above it. The fifth contract, dated 18 January 2006, concerns the same third-floor extension, plus the story above it, which is now built. Finally, the sixth contract, dated 5 April 2006, concerns the third-floor extension again, without any mention of the room located on the fourth floor. It is only through a discussion with Mrs. Sabbah that we learned this room belonged

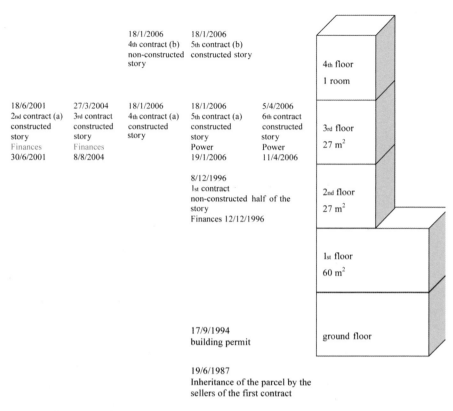

18/1/2006
4th contract (b)
non-constructed
story

18/1/2006
5th contract (b)
constructed story

4th floor

1 room

18/6/2001
2nd contract (a)
constructed
story
Finances
30/6/2001

27/3/2004
3rd contract
constructed
story
Finances
8/8/2004

18/1/2006
4th contract (a)
constructed
story

18/1/2006
5th contract (a)
constructed
story
Power
19/1/2006

5/4/2006
6th contract
constructed
story
Power
11/4/2006

3rd floor
27 m²

8/12/1996
1st contract
non-constructed half of the
story
Finances 12/12/1996

2nd floor
27 m²

1st floor
60 m²

17/9/1994
building permit

ground floor

19/6/1987
Inheritance of the parcel by the
sellers of the first contract

Fig. 2.4: Chronology of contracts and powers of attorney

to her. This room is only partly built and its roof is made of sheet metal. Access to it is through the apartment's kitchen (Fig. 2.4).

Real-estate language games

Real estate and transactions regarding it are formulated with words. We will describe these words and their connections to each another, through what Ludwig Wittgenstein calls "language games." These games accomplish the literary inscription of a material reality (Latour 2002). They produce descriptions that aim at making things, people, and actions enter the realm of categories acknowledged by the law. This is what lawyers know as the characterization process, the main feature of which is to be consequential. We will describe and analyze the main categorization elements of Mrs. Sabbah's file as used in contracts and powers of attorney, that is, the land, the building, the story, and the apartment.

References to the land in the documents of this file mix geographical commonsense and legal administrative terminologies. Some of the contract forms indicate that the real estate is of a *mulk* type, which points to private ownership. The preamble of the first contract specifies that the plot of land is situated "in Damascus, camp of Yarmouk, al-Ja'awna Street, alley *(jadda)* number 10 . . . on plot *('aqar)* number 1081 Shaghur Basatin." The first half of this account is an itinerary that one can follow. It starts from a general location, Damascus, and ends with the precise location of the plot of land, alley number 10, which one reaches as if we were taking a taxi, via al-Ja'awna Street. The second part of this account locates the land with the technical words specific to real-estate administration: the real-estate number (1081) and a name (Shagur Basatin), sometimes preceded by the mention of 'district' *(mantiqa)*, which designates a specific real-estate entity.[2] The next contracts are much briefer regarding the description that locates the land: geographical references are no longer indicated; only the administrative terminology is kept. The real-estate number is mentioned, but there is another term corresponding to it, that of 'report' *(mahdar)*. The association of a number (1081) and a real-estate name (Shaghur Basatin) shows that the word 'report' refers to the real estate and, therefore, this number has a real-estate nature.

The building in which Mrs. Sabbah's property is located is not always mentioned in the documents of the file. When mentioned, two types of terminology are used for the designation of the land. The administrative type copies municipality terminology. It mentions "the building *(bina')* known as the house *(manzil)* number 11 according to building permit number 177." The number (11) associated with the 'house' refers to a document, that is, the building permit, which is not included in the file. It testifies to the registration of the building in municipality records, whereas, as we already know, the real-estate plot on which it is located is itself registered in the Land Registry. The second type of terminology is related to commonsense. The term 'house' *(manzil)* is used more in a domestic than in a legal sense. Moreover, the building is designated in some documents as the Idris Building, which refers to the original owner of the plot of land.

All the properties the successive contracts and powers of attorney refer to are located within the same building, in a vertical axis, according to the constructed or non-constructed nature of the surface area that is sold. If the property is not built, the documents speak of a 'story' *(sath)*, the floor of which is itself specified with regard to the construction on which it is built. Either it is above it (*ma ya'luha*, 'what overhangs it'), or it is situated above (*zahr al-thani fanni* and *sath al-thani fanni*, 'above the story'), or it is associated with it (*ma'a sathiha* or *ma'a al-sath*, 'with its story'). However, in the first contract, the story where the property is located is not only given in relation to the story situated below; it is also complemented by a reference to the surface situated above: 'half the story of the second floor' (*nisf sath al-tabiq al-thani fanni*). When it is constructed, a property is situated vertically in the building by reference to the floor, either implicitly (*thalith fanni*, 'the third') or explicitly (*min al-tabiq al-thalith fanni*, 'of the third floor'). Thus, the term *fanni*, which means literally 'technical,' when associated with a number, refers to a floor, with or without the prior mention of the term 'floor' (*tabiq*) itself. Note that without the term *fanni*, the association of the number with the word 'floor' would have another meaning; that is, it would designate the floor situated below as the ground floor, thereby becoming the first floor.

The property that is sold is sometimes described, when it is developed, using a general term like 'extension' (*mulhaq*) or 'apartment' (*shaqqa*). The content is sometimes specified by the introduction of the formula 'made of' (*mu'allaf min*), through the adjunction of words linked together with the conjunction 'and,' or simply through their juxtaposition without benefit of a conjunction. In other contracts, the terms 'extension' or 'apartment' are just not mentioned. The composition of the property can be given directly—'a room' (*ghurfa*), a living room (*salun*), a bathroom (*munfa'at*), with its story (*ma'a sathiha*)—or indirectly, through the reference to the number of the registered plot on which the building was built, so that the constructed property and the plot on which it was constructed are confused: "real estate *1081* of the district Shaghur Basatin, which consists of a room, a living room, and a bathroom" (*al-mahdar 1081 min mantiqat Shaghur Basatin wa-l-ladhi huwa 'ibaratan 'an ghurfa wa salun wa munfa'at*). Note that the term 'extension' becomes 'apartment' when a room is appended to it. Then, the property is formulated in the following way: "an apartment . . . with its story . . . there is a room on the story (*ghurfa 'ala al-sath*) . . . an extension . . . a room and a bathroom and the building (*bina'*) overhanging them" is mentioned. Sometimes, the surface area (*masaha*) of the property, that is, 27 m², is indicated, as well as its orientation—'south' (*ittijah janubi, janubi*, or *qibli*). The contracts also specify the fact that there are water and electricity meters, which indicate the state of completion of the property. These meters are also used to help ensure legal recognition of the property.

There are language games operating in the description of the property that is sold. The notion of a 'language game' as coined by Wittgenstein (1967) refers to the fact that words take their meaning from their association to one another and through their context of use. A specific language corresponds to any activity with which people are familiar. The meaning of words is not given outright: it comes from words, which, once combined, look similar to those other combinations specific to the many domains of life and language, such as the law. According to Wittgenstein, language games can share a "family resemblance," which shows the type of domain to which they belong. The notion of family resemblance refers to the way in which words associated with an activity share a number of features and therefore often constitute a lexical field. The many language games used are learned through the familiarity people acquire with their environment, its workings, the "forms of life" to which they are associated, "the social practices of a linguistic community which are so deeply rooted that the speakers do not even think about it" (Dupret 2006, 63; Schulte 1992; Wittgenstein 1967).

Bruno Latour explains that in the case of documents, language games achieve the literary inscription of a material property. He stresses the transformation which the writing exercise carries out on the primordial object, that is, the material property, and raises the question of the selective character of writing, which proceeds through shortcuts and hides the mechanisms operating in that very activity (Latour 1996, 43). Literary inscription also has the capacity to establish facts and to make them enter into categories so as to become useful for all further practical purposes. This especially holds true in the domain of law. The writer of a contract, for instance, elaborates it for all practical legal purposes (Dupret 2006, 249). This is often done by obscuring the biographical details of the object of the contract and of the practical conditions of its writing (Dupret 2006, 162). Focusing on its future rather than on its past use, a contract testifies to the transaction that it will perhaps confirm later on.

As for Mrs. Sabbah's file, the language games we described produce legal forms through a process of inscription, that is, through the transformation of a real-estate materiality into a literary reality. The organization of the document into several provisions, the use of archetypal expressions and particular formulations, and the use of template forms, all give it the form of a contract and denote its legal nature. However, it would be simplistic to say that a legal document only reproduces pre-existing forms: although the legal document is the outcome of a process of form *setting (mise en forme)*, it cannot be reduced to the pure product of legal formalism (Latour 2002, 181). Producing forms also means the capacity to produce effects, legal ones, for example.

The literary inscription of a material property is achieved for all legal practical purposes. Regarding real estate, this involves producing a document testifying to the transaction and making it possible for it to be opposed in court. In our case, the language games in the document reveal the informal nature of the property. Indeed, it is through the association of words familiar to people dealing with real estate—words with a family resemblance—that we know it is not only about real-estate law, but also a very specific, though not uncommon, form of this law, that is, real-estate law in informal neighborhoods.

It is clear that the documents in Mrs. Sabbah's file relate to a real estate property. An element of the description of the property is given, while it does not seem necessary, to complete the meaning of another word and to attach it to the family 'real-estate.' The word *mulhaq*, which is a predicate meaning 'added' or 'annexed,' acquires the value of a substantive, and its meaning, 'surface built on the last floor of a building,' comes from its being inserted in a context and associated with other words. Moreover, repeated use of the word gives it a conventional character, so that it can be understood without reference to or association with other elements of the real-estate vocabulary. In the same way, the word *mahdar*, which is a predicate meaning 'that which has been recorded (a statement)' and by extension 'a leaf of the Land Registry,' acquires the meaning of 'land parcel,' and therefore of built property, because of its association with other words. The word has taken on a new meaning through a succession of shortcuts and ellipses.

The fact that the documents of Mrs. Sabbah's file concern a real estate property located in an informal neighborhood is never mentioned directly. Indeed, the absence of any registration in the Land Registry is not explicit. The specific character of this estate is nevertheless expressed through a series of linguistic expressions. This is also the case with the use of terms from everyday language, such as 'Idris Building.' The use of the term 'extension' is another indicator. In Land Registry vocabulary, it refers to a room on the last floor jointly owned by all the owners of the building, which as such cannot be sold. However, in the language game of informal settlements, it refers to the apartment on the last floor, which is privately owned. Lastly, the description of the way the property is vertically located in the building, for example, through the use of adverbial complements indicating place, situates the construction in an informal zone: the property is located through its relationship with another property and not according to its Land Registry number. Physical topology replaces bureaucratic registration.

We see that language games formalized a material reality into a written document, bestowed it with a legal status, and revealed the particular character of the properties relating to the transactions. These properties, which we refer to as 'informal,' are designated in Arabic by the word *mukhalafat*. This encompasses the idea of infringing the legal order of things. It does not amount to illegality as such, but points to the contradiction between the agricultural nature of a plot of land and its development. The expression does not refer to any given category per se, but to an array of practices, habitual and vague, associated by the same language game.

Close proximity of properties and succession of contracts: The retroactive reading of the file

It has been noted that the property that is sold in the last contract is not the same property that was sold in the first: whereas it was initially only half a story, in the end a complete apartment is the subject of the transaction; whereas it was only a story on which the buyer implicitly had the right to build, it ends up as a built apartment. It is the way the file is constituted that allows Mrs. Sabbah (as it allowed all the former owners), to establish the property's history and origin. Because the building is not registered with the Land Registry, there are good reasons to keep all the documents testifying to the transactions related to it. The file in which the documents are gathered together reveals what the documents hide: the property's origin. It is through the detailed and retroactive reading of the file in its entirety that it is possible to describe the many links between the documents and to establish the proximity of the properties and the chronological succession of the contracts. We saw how the documents were written for all practical legal purposes. Now we shall examine the nature of the reading of these documents and of the file they constitute.

The reading of texts, documents, and files consists of what Eric Livingston calls "instructed action," which refers to the fact that reading is an achievement relating two parts (or Lebenswelt pairs): the text and its understanding. The text must be read as a descriptive account, a guide for the action of reading. The reader develops a method of reasoning through his/her leaning on the text's clues, so that he/she can give a coherent meaning to what is read. Understanding a sentence calls for the reader's skill and capacity to mobilize the background knowledge necessary to make sense of the clues. Livingston speaks of a community of readers and of a background knowledge shared by this community. In that sense, reading is a social phenomenon revealed through people's capacity to understand a text.

Recognizing that legal documents constitute a file is a first reading clue. Guided by textual instructions, the reader relates the many different elements constituting the file that together are capable of producing some legal aspect. This is what Latour (2002) calls "bringing a file to maturity." A legal practitioner will read from within the text the information that proves useful for the accomplishment of his work (Dupret 2006). The reader's practical reasoning and capacity to call upon background knowledge make it possible to understand what is said and to pick out relevant information for the purpose of the ongoing activity, that is, for all practical purposes.

The duplication of a mistake in the description of Mrs. Sabbah's property presents a good example of this mechanism of reading for all practical legal purposes. It gives a clue as to the way a document is read. This mistake concerns the parcel's number on which Mrs. Sabbah's property is located. The mistake appears in the fifth and sixth contracts, together with the powers of attorney associated with them. The fifth contract's first page indicates parcel number "1081," whereas the same contract's second page mentions "1881." The power of attorney associated with it as well as the sixth contract (and the second power of attorney) duplicated the mistake. This shows that the person who wrote the power of attorney attached to the sixth contract was concerned mainly with the reading of the fifth contract's second page, the information of which it reproduces. In the same way, the notary who registered the two powers of attorney was exclusively interested in the fifth contract's second page, so that he did not pinpoint the mistake that was accidentally introduced.

In order to understand Mrs. Sabbah's file one must go through the instructed reading of all the documents and the file. Except for the first contract, contracts and powers of attorney are forms, which guide the reader in his/her reading work. The handwritten parts, filled in according to the writer's interpretation of the form's instructions, constitute further clues for the reader, that is, the elements relevant to the establishment of the contracts' succession and the contiguity of the properties of the transaction. They give details regarding the civil status of the signatories of the contract, the description of the property, and the date of the transaction. The succession of sellers, X sold to Y, Y sold to W, W sold to T, and so on, which can be established by the reader of the file through practical reasoning, is a clue to the historical succession of the contracts. The third contract's second page establishes the succession explicitly: "the sale took place according to Mr [T]'s sale contract, which was certified on 30 June 2001 under Number [N1]; he bought it from [X], [Y], and [Z], according to the contract certified by the Damascus Tax Office under Number [N2] dated 12/12/1996."

Close study of the first contract allows us to observe the text/instruction pair for reading. It is organized in three parts. The first part is clearly established: it presents the signatories of the contract. The second part of the contract, that is, its preamble, groups several informational elements presented as the terms of an equation. They are bound together, within the same paragraph, through logical expressions: "considering X, Y, and Z, this agreement was reached." First, there is a description of what is owned by the first signatory to the contract: he is the owner of property X. Second, the second signatory to the contract makes clear his wish to acquire a part of the property (half a story). Third, the first signatory's intention to sell this very story is made explicit. Fourth, it is said that the agreement is reached following the provisions indicated in the third part of the contract, which stipulates the rights and duties of each signatory.

The preamble of this contract indirectly gives the origin of the ownership right of the property. It is grounded in the reader's practical reasoning, which seeks to read the file coherently. The seller owns the property which is the object of the transaction "in conformity with the building permit . . . issued by the local committee of Yarmouk camp," through inheritance. The mention "Yarmouk camp" and the reader's background knowledge make it possible to understand that the ownership is of a particular nature. This interpretation is confirmed by Article 6 of the contract, which reads: "The two contracting parties agree . . . not to breach . . . the rights of Refugees Foundation on the land on which the story is located." Although the origin of the deceased person's property is not specified, it can be deduced from the reader's background knowledge: it is the Foundation for Palestinian Refugees that allocated the parcel to the deceased man, that is, the permit to live in a given place (idhn sakan).

Moreover, the property is not registered as real estate in the Land Registry. It is built on part of a Land Registry parcel which is larger than the property itself. This can be deduced from the use of the preposition "on": the property is not the parcel itself. Another point is added: the property that is sold is not the totality of what the first party declares as

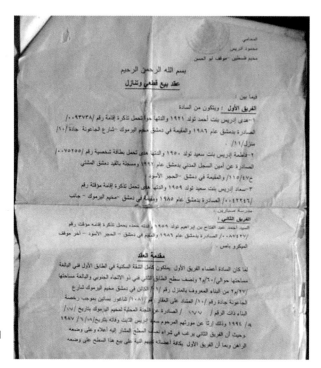

Fig. 2.5: First contract of final sale. (Translation below.)

Attorney Mahmud Idriss, Camp of Palestine, Abou Hassan
In the name of God the Benevolent the Merciful
Contract of final sale and cession

Between:

The first party is the following women …

The second party Mr Ahmed…

[Preamble of the contract]

Considering that the women constituting the first party own the totality of the apartment on the first story, whose surface area is approximately 60 square meters and half the story of the second floor facing the south, whose surface area is 27 square meters, of the building known as building /11/ located in Damascus, Yarmuk Camp, al-Ja'awna street, alley Number /10/, built on real estate Number /1081/, Shaghur Basatin, in conformity with Building permit Number /177/ issued by the Local Committee of Yarmuk Camp, on 17/9/1994, in inheritance of the testament's author, the late Mister Idris al-Thabat, whose death was established on 19/6/1987.

Considering that the second party wishes to purchase half the story of the abovementioned floor in its current state

Considering that all of the members constituting the first party intend to sell this story in its current state, this agreement, which guarantees the rights of both signatories, in full possession of their judicial and legal capacities, was concluded as follows:

his ownership, but only part of it, that is, a story, to which no parcel number is given. The contract makes a distinction between the ownership of a story and the ownership of the land, the latter belonging to the Foundation for Palestinian Refugees. In other words, we can say that the reader's practical reasoning and his affiliation to a community of readers helps him understand the meaning of the text.

The last contract, unlike the first, does not make any logical connection between being the owner and selling one's property. It mainly states the transfer of ownership from the seller, whose title is not questioned, to the buyer. The seller's right is taken for granted, without any need to mention its origin. The first provision indicates that "the first party has sold to the second party . . . a room . . . ," whereas the second provision confirms that "the second party has accepted to purchase the apartment."

Most of the contracts and powers of attorney make no reference to the origin of ownership. It is only through the instructed reading of the file that one can establish the connections between the different documents, give some coherence to the collection of these documents in one and the same file, and trace back the history of ownership. The impossibility of registering in the Land Registry properties located in informal neighborhoods led people to proceed indirectly and to use strategies permitting them to claim their ownership rights.

Conclusion: The Documentary Mechanisms of Real-estate Security

The detailed description of Mrs. Sabbah's file and of all its documents allowed us to identify and understand the various elements of real-estate ownership and the complex relationships they have with one another. We saw how the file's documents were written for all practical legal purposes, and that language games formulate the property and the real-estate transactions concerning a property located in an informal neighborhood. It is the instructed reading of the file, the reader's practical reasoning, and background knowledge that made it possible to make sense of these documents. The file's documents are constituted so as to secure ownership, the origin of which is fragile. The practice of the law and its procedures, of which the file's documents are an expression, are several instructed actions, that is, usages dictated in a more or less constraining way by the norms to which people refer to for the sake of securing their ownership and its authenticity. In other words, the writing of contracts, their registration with the Ministry of Finance, and the use of powers of attorney certified by a notary are used to testify to a transaction that could not follow a normal course of legal procedure.

Notes

1 The United Arab Republic was the sovereign union between Egypt and Syria which lasted from 1958 to 1961.
2 The third contract does not use the word 'district,' but only the predicate 'real estate' (al-'aqariya) to designate the administrative entity. The adjective replaces the substantive it normally predicates.

References

Dupret, Baudouin. 2006. *Le Jugement en action. Ethnométhodologie du droit, de la moralité et de la justice en Egypte*. Geneva: Libraire Droz.
Latour, Bruno. 1996. *Petites leçons de sociologie des sciences*. Paris: Le Seuil.
———. 2002. *La Fabrique du droit. Une ethnographie du Conseil d'Etat*. Paris: La Découverte.
Latour, Bruno, and Steve Woolgar. 1996. *La vie de laboratoire, la production des faits scientifiques*. Paris: La Découverte.
Livingston, Eric. 1995. *An Anthropology of Reading*. Bloomington: Indiana University Press.
Schulte, Joachim. 1992. *Lire Wittgenstein. Dire et montrer*. Translated by M. Charrière and J.P. Cometti. Combas: Editions de l'éclat.
Wittgenstein, Ludwig. 1967. *Philosophical Investigations*. Oxford and Cambridge: Blackwell.

3

Securing Property in Informal Neighborhoods in Damascus through Tax Payments

Myriam Ferrier

The informal neighborhoods of Damascus present the seemingly paradoxical situation in which the inhabitants of a construction that is considered illegal have the right to live in, sell, or even inherit it, and possibly pay taxes on it. Such contradictions may seem surprising. One might expect that any non-compliance with the law would be severely penalized, that infractions would be punished, and that documents issued by the Ministry of Finance stating that the sale of housing built in violation of the law would be used against the inhabitants of such premises. Yet that is not the case: certain forms of registration are accepted in such a way as to enable the inhabitants of these neighborhoods to secure their property. The term 'secure' refers to the fact that the owner of a property can prove his ownership to the government or the court, but also to a possible buyer. Securing one's property may take various forms in Syria depending on the nature of the property. They include registration before the Land Registry, the Notary Public, or the courts after registration with the Ministry of Finance.

This paper aims at describing how people involved in the securing and registration of property manage to qualify the nature of property and the registration procedures it may entail. It will describe how a property which is not listed on the Land Registry because it has been built on illegally subdivided agricultural land, and which violates the urban development plan and the construction code, acquires legal status by being listed on the Ministry of Finance and tax payment registers.[1] I will argue that securing property in an informal neighborhood is the result of (1) a process of qualification, that is, awarding specific qualities to actors or properties, and the interplay of categories and (2) cooperation between civil servants, the majority of whom live in these very same neighborhoods. This hypothesis is based on documents produced by the Finance Directorate of the governorates of Damascus and Rural Damascus and on observations I was able to make in the respective administrative bodies.[2]

The term 'informal housing,' used in World Bank terminology, refers in Syria to very different types of property situations, and procedures for securing property are just as varied. In Arabic, this type of neighborhood is known by the terms *manatiq al-mukhalafat al-jama'iya* or *manatiq al-sakan al-'ashwa'iya*. Some neighborhoods are private properties listed in the Land Registry as agricultural land and may even be included in an urban development plan. In the latter case, construction permits may have been issued, but not respected. Agricultural land may also appear in the development plan while already having been built upon, in which case, the development plan does not correspond to what actually exists, or only corresponds in part. Other neighborhoods belong to the public domain, in which case, parcels are listed on the registers of the Property Office in the name of the Arab Republic of Syria. The owner of private property can sell all or part of his/her property to a buyer by having the transaction certified either by a notary public, a court, or the Ministry of Finance. It is also possible for a transaction not to be registered with an administrative body. In the case of property belonging to the public domain, the land has been taken over by individuals with the tacit agreement or non-interference of the government. This paper deals with neighborhoods of private property.

As far as the legislative framework is concerned, legal texts can seem contradictory. Thus, while successive laws penalize constructions in violation of the law, and order their demolition, a directive of President al-Assad stipulates that any individual whose dwelling has been destroyed for reasons of illegality must be provided with replacement housing (*badal sakan*) or must receive financial compensation (*badal naqdi*).

In addition, because violation is based on the fact of construction rather than possession, the state recognizes ownership of property built in violation of urban planning and the construction code when it is on agricultural land which is unsuitable for development. Thus, gradually, forms of property registration other than those of the Property Office (land registry services) have come into being and become the norm. Theoretically, property registration is undertaken via the Property Office; however, in practice, some steps of the registration procedure with this office have become procedures in themselves; they are recognized as forms of registration and award certain rights.

The owner of a property can thus give a power of attorney[3] *(wakala)* to someone else—the 'buyer'—to sell the property 'to himself' *(li-nafsihi)* and register his name with the Property Office as owner of the property later on. The power of attorney must be certified by a notary public *(katib 'adl)*. Obtaining this certification, which is itself formulated on paper as a step in the registration of a real-estate transaction with the Property Office, has become a procedure in its own right, with its own requirements in terms of documents needed for the registration of a transaction. Certain documents must be obtained from the Ministry of Finance, which plays an essential role in the securing of real estate in informal neighborhoods. It almost plays the role of the Property Office when it records the sale of this type of housing and states on one of the documents it delivers that "although the parcel is unsuitable for development . . . the name of xxx is confirmed as being that of the real owner of the apartment . . ." (see Fig. 3.3: *"tathbit ism"*). The documents issued by the Ministry of Finance prove that no taxes are due on the property.

Registering Informal Property with the Ministry of Finance: A Change of Category and the Sequence of Procedures

When an informal property is registered with the Ministry of Finance, a 'construction in violation of the law' *(mukhalif)* enters into another category; that of a 'construction which has been assessed' *(mukhamman or muqaddar)* and is 'liable to taxation' *(mukallaf)*. This is made possible by the organization of categories as mechanisms of a broader category, that of a 'joint tenancy neighborhood' *(manatiq al-mush'a)*, which replaces the term 'informal neighborhood' in everyday practices of the Ministry of Finance. This category *(mush'a)* refers to the fact that any property registered with the Land Registry equals 2,400 shares *(ashum)* and becomes a joint tenancy property when it is owned by more than one person whose share *(hussa sahmiya)* has no marked boundaries *(ghayr muhaddad)*. While the term *mush'a* rarely appears on administrative documents, it is the underlying conceptual framework and guides the registration process. Indeed, shares may not be registered with the Land Registry, except in the case of inheritance dividing the property, since the Land Registry records geographical limits. The assessment of shares is an activity the Ministry of Finance is entitled to carry out.

Thus, all constructions, whether or not they are in conformity with urban planning and the construction code, can be subject to financial assessment by a ministerial commission if such an assessment has been requested by the owner of the parcel as a whole. This is the first stage of registration. This Commission of First Instance (Lajna Bida'iya) visits the premises, draws up a description, and calculates the tax base. Like an engineer from the Land Registry, the employee from the Direct Taxes Directorate measures and calculates the surface area of the property. The owner is only obliged to produce a statement from the municipality (Fig. 3.1) specifying whether the property is located within or without the urban development plan, as well as another document making it possible to date the construction in order to calculate the tax. In the absence of a building permit, a document from the Electricity Company (*rasm ishtiraq*, or subscription fee) may be provided. The results of this Commission are formulated in an order (*qarar*) (Fig. 3.2). The owner can then sell each unit of property separately by having each transaction certified by a financial officer (*muraqib*) and by paying property taxes and taxes pertaining to the transaction. The buyer is then able to register his name in the financial registers by the procedure known in everyday language as "confirmation of name" (*tathbit ism*) (Fig. 3.3).

This assessment of the first commission uses a first set of categories that is embodied and formulated in a description of the current situation of the property (*wad' rahin*). The document describes the property by combining cadastral, financial, and common languages. Thus, it gives the name of the district on which the property stands ('Shaghur Basatin') as well as the number of the parcel to which it belongs ('344') as they are recorded with the Land Registry. It also gives the reference of the administrative district within the Ministry of Finance ('sixth') and by doing so allows one to cross reference between both administrations.

I will now present the order of the Finance Directorate of the Governorate of Damascus (*qarar mudiriyyat al-maliya*) resulting from the 'confirmation of name' procedure. This order confirms the change in ownership of an informal property, referred to as 'joint tenure property,' on the financial registers, summarizes the procedures leading to the order's issuance, and states that this informal housing unit is a property and is registered as such with the Finance Directorate.

الرقـم :
التاريخ :   / ١٢٢/

الى رئاسـة بلديـــة

تطبيقاً لاحكـام القانون ١٧٨ لعام ١٩٤٥
نرجو موافاتنا بالمعلومات التاليــة :
١ ـ هل العقار رقم محضر   من منطقة
ضمن المخطط التنظيمي ام خارجــه
٢ ـ نسبة المساحة المسموح بـ   ى العقار المذكور عند الموافقة على افرازه
الى مقاسم
٣ ـ عدد الطوابق المسموح ببنائها على العقار المطلوب
٤ ـ هل العقار المطلوب ضمن منطقة سكنية أم تجارية
٥ ـ تاريخ ادخال العقار ضمن المخطط التنظيمي
دمشق في   /   /   ٢٠٠

مدير مالية محافظة
ريف دمشق

Name
Date

To the directors of the municipality

In application of the provisions of Law 145 of the year 1945
We request you to provide us with the following information:

1. Is parcel ('aqar) no. of report (mahdar)...............of district............
   located within or outside the urban development plan?
2. (What is) the proportion of the area of the parcel indicated on the division permit which is suitable for development?
3. (How many) floors is it authorized to build on the requested parcel?
4. Is the requested parcel situated in a residential or a commercial zone?
5. (What is) the date of entry of the parcel in the development plan?

Damascus, .../.../200...
Director of Finance of the Governorate of Rural Damascus

Fig. 3.1: Note adressed to the municipality in order to proceed with the financial assessment of the property. (Translation above.)

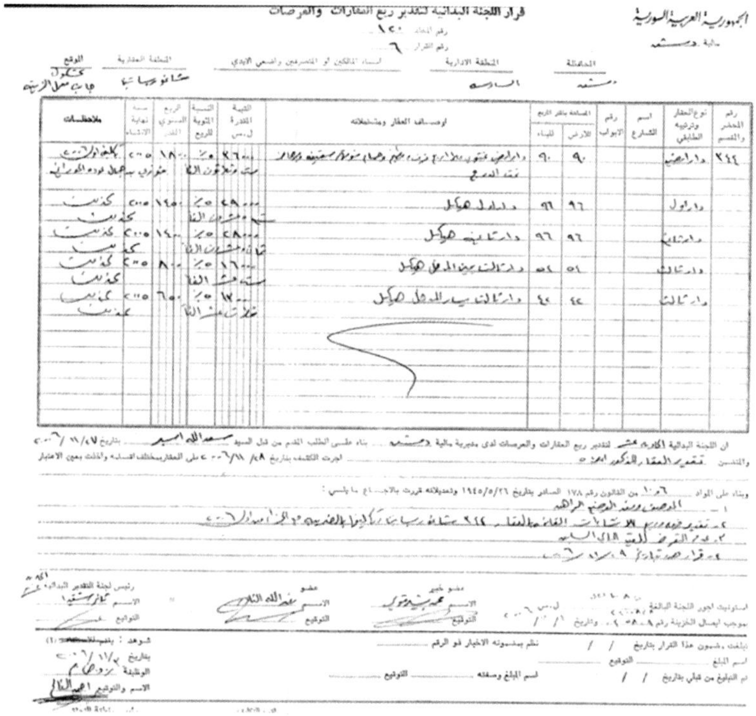
الجمهورية العربية السورية
قرار اللجنة البدائية لتقدير ريع العقارات والعرصات

Arab Republic of Syria/Damascus Finances/
Order of the Property Assessment Commission of First Instance /Volume No. *XXX*/Decision No. *XXX*/

N° of procès-verbal (*mahdar*) or lot (*maqsam*)	Type of parcel (*'aqâr*) and floors	Name of street	N°of door	Area in square meters		Description of parcel (*'aqâr*) and contents	Value estimated in L.S.	Rate of property income	Evaluated annual property income	Year of end of construct-ion	Remarks
				land	built						
344	*house ground floor*			90	90	*Apartment first consisting of four rooms, kitchen, bathroom … storeroom, toilet under stairway*	36 000 *thirty-six thousand*	5%	1800	2005	*Calculation of tax on* ***illegible*** *2006 Faouzi XXX*
	house first			96	96	*Apartment first first works*	29 000 *twenty-nine thousand*	5%	1450	2005	*Idem*
	house second			96	96	*Apartment second first works*	28 000 *twenty-eight thousand*	5%	1400	2005	*Idem*
	house third			54	54	*Apartment third entry right*	1600 *sixteen thousand*	5%	800	2005	*Idem*
	house third					*Apartment third entry left*	1300	5%	650	2005	*Idem*

Fig. 3.2: Order of the First Instance Property Assessment Commission. (Translation above and opposite.)

Governorate : Damascus /Administrative district : *sixth*/ Name of owners, beneficiaries or persons having taken possession of the property : *blank*/ Property district : *Shaghur Basatin*/ Location : *next to XXX*

The eleventh Property Income Assessment Commission of First Instance of the Financial Directorate of Damascus, following the request presented by Mr. *XXX* dated *XXX* 2006, consisting in the assessment of the above parcel, examined the parcel *(kashaf 'aqar) and* its different lots *(aqsam)* on *XXX* 2006, taking into consideration *blank*, and taking into account Articles 1 and 2 of Law No. 178 dated 26/5/1945 and its modifications, collectively decided the following:

1. description according to the present state *(al-wad' al-rahin)*
2. estimation of the value and property income of the installations *(insha'at)* situated on parcel 344 *Shaghur Basatin* and its tax [illegible] 2006
3. no contradiction with the preceding financial statement
4. order published on *XXX* 2006 The Commission received in salary *XXX*, in conformity with the receipt *XXX* dated *XXX* expert member / name *XXX* / signature *XXX* member / name *XXX* / signature *XXX*

Head of the Assessment Commission of First Instance / name *XXX* / signature *XXX*

An interplay of categories: from 'construction in violation of the law' to construction 'liable to tax'

The change in category from 'construction in violation of the law' to 'construction liable to tax' is clearly visible on the following document; an order *(qarar)* signed by the director of the Finance Directorate of the Governorate of Damascus (Da'irat al-Maliya, Muhafazat Dimashq). This document confirms the change in ownership of a property and orders the name of the new owner to be registered on the lists of the Finance Directorate. This 'confirmation of name' document constitutes the link between the two successive owners (seller and buyer) of a single property. In internal administrative language, this official document is also called 'financial taxation' *(taklif mali)*, referring to the fact that a financial assessment of the property has been made and that it is subject to tax. Located on a parcel *('aqar)* that equals 2,400 shares *(ashum)*, the property only constitutes a part of it. It is this part that will be assessed to constitute an

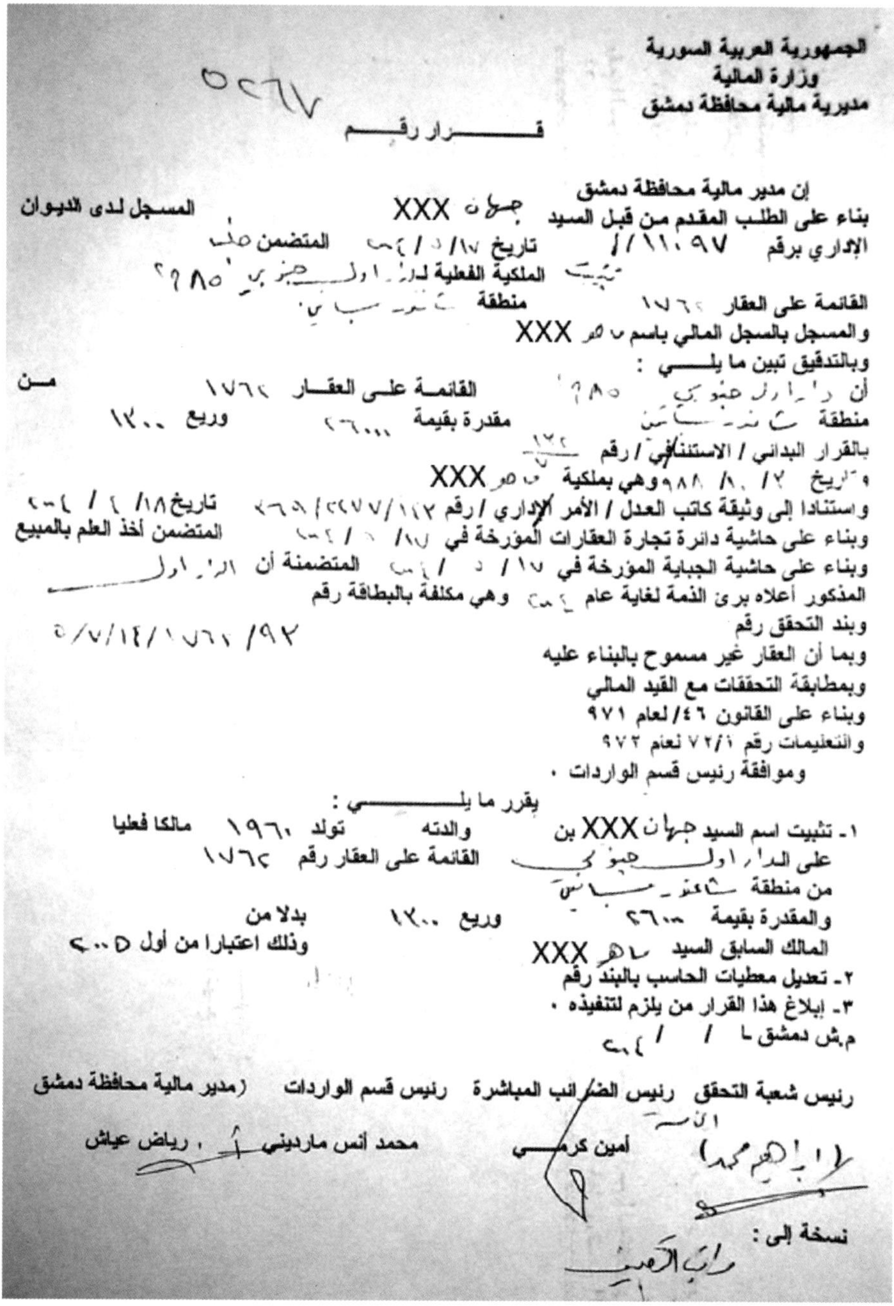

الجمهورية العربية السورية
وزارة المالية
مديرية مالية محافظة دمشق

ق‍‍‍‍‍‍‍‍‍‍‍‍‍‍‍‍‍ـــــــــرار رقــــــم

إن مدير مالية محافظة دمشق

بناء على الطلب المقدم من قبل السيد XXX جــ‍‍‍ان المسجل لدى الديوان

الإداري برقم ٩٧/١١/١ تاريخ ١٧/ ١ / ٩٦ المتضمن عن

الملكية الفعلية لدار اول ... جنز ب... ٥٨٥ ؟

القائمة على العقار ١٧٦٤ منطقة ... سبا ب...

والمسجل بالسجل المالي باسم ٧ صر XXX

وبالتدقيق تبين ما يلـــــــي :

أن د ا ر اول عنو ب‍‍‍‍‍‍ ... ؟ ٨٥ القائمـــة على العقـــار ١٧٦١ مــــن

منطقة ... ... مقدرة بقيمة ٢٦٠٠٠ وريع ١٢٠٠

بالقرار البداني / الاستئنافي / رقم ١٧٢

وتاريخ ١٢، ٨، ٨٩٨ وهي بملكية ... صر XXX

واستنادا إلى وثيقة كاتب العدل / الأمر الإداري / رقم ٢٧٧/١١٢/ ٢٦٩ تاريخ ١١٨ / ١ / ٢٠٠ المتضمن أخذ العلم بالمبيع

وبناء على حاشية دائرة تجارة العقارات المؤرخة في ١٧/ ١ / ٢٠٠

وبناء على حاشية الجباية المؤرخة في ١٧/ د / ٢ ... المتضمنة أن الد‍ا ر اول

المذكور أعلاه برئ الذمة لغاية عام ٥٠٠٢ وهي مكلفة بالبطاقة رقم

وبند التحقق رقم ١٩٢/ ١٧٦١ /١٢/٧/٥

وبما أن العقار غير مسموح بالبناء عليه

وبمطابقة التحققات مع القيد المالي

وبناء على القانون ٤٦/ لعام ٩٧١

والتعليمات رقم ٧٢/٦ لعام ٩٧٢

وموافقة رئيس قسم الواردات .

يقرر ما يلـــــــــي :

١- تثبيت اسم السيد جهان XXX بن والدته تولد ١٩٦٠ مالكا فعليا

على الدا ر اول ... جبو ك‍‍ القائمة على العقار رقم ١٧٦٤

من منطقة ... ...

والمقدرة بقيمة ٢٦٠٠ وريع ١٢٠٠ بدلا من

المالك السابق السيد XXX صر ٧ وذلك اعتبارا من أول ٥ ٢٠٠٥

٢- تعديل معطيات الحاسب بالبند رقم

٣- إبلاغ هذا القرار من يلزم لتنفيذه .

م‍‍ش دمشق ‍‍ا / / ٢٠٠

رئيس شعبة التحقق   رئيس الضرائب المباشرة   رئيس قسم الواردات   رمدير مالية محافظة دمشق

رياض عياش ,   محمد أنس مارديني   أمين كر‍‍‍ـــــي

نسخة إلى :

Fig. 3.3: Confirmation of name *(tathbit ism)*. (Translation opposite.)

Arab Republic of Syria / Ministry of Finance / Finance Directorate Governorate of Damascus

Order number *XXX* [0]

The Director of Finance of the Governorate of Damascus

[I] Following the [A] request presented by Mr. [1] *XXX* registered with the administrative Secretariat *(al-diwan al-idari)* under [2] number *XXX* dated *XXX* consisting of [3] *a request for confirmation* of the real property *(milkiya fa'aliyya)* of [4] an *apartment 85m² on the first floor south* located on parcel [5] *XXX* of district [6] *Shaghur Basatin* and listed on the financial register in the name of [7] *XXX*

[II] The examination showed the following:

[4] *Apartment 85m² on the first floor south* located on parcel [5] *XXX* of district [6] *Ch. Basatin* is assessed *(muqaddira)* at the value of [8] *26,000* and an interest of *1,300* by [B] first instance order / ~~appeals order~~ number [9] *XXX* dated *3/10/988* which is the property of [7] *XXX*

[C] Given the notarial documents /~~administrative order~~ number *XXX* dated *18/4/2004*

[D] In view of the annotation of [the administration] of the Property Commerce Department dated *XXX* stating the sale

[E] In view of the annotation of [the administration of] Tax Collection *(jibaya)* dated *XXX* indicating that no tax weighs *(bara' al-dhimma)* on [4] *the first floor apartment* mentioned above until the end of *2004* and subject to tax *(mukallaf)* by index number *XXX* and supervisory note number *blank*

[8] Although the parcel is not suitable for development

[F] In view of the conformity of the verifications with the financial statement;

In view of Law 46 of year 981 and instructions No. 73/1 of year 983 and the agreement of the Director of the Revenue Department,

[III] [The Director of Finance of Damascus governorate] orders the following :

[11] To confirm the name of Mr. [1] *XXX* son of *XXX* his mother *XXX* born *XXX* as real owner of the [4] *first floor apartment south* located on parcel No. [5] *XXX* of district [6] *Shaghur Basatin* and assessed at the sum of [8] *26,000* and an interest of *1,300* in place of the name of the previous owner Mr. [7] *XXX* and that as of *2005*

[12] To change computer data

[13] To notify those who enforce the decision

m. ch. Damascus *blank / blank / 2004*

[14] Head of the Verifications Office *(ra'is sha'bat al-tahaqquq)* *XXX* Director of direct taxes *(ra'is dara'ib al-mubashara)* *XXX* Director of the Department of Revenue *(ra'is qism al-waridat)* *XXX* Director of Finance of the Governorate of Damascus *XXX*

independent property for the Ministry of Finance. The fact that there is no building permit for the property has no effect on the registration procedure. The property is no longer defined by its illegal character *(mukhalif)*, but by the fact that it has been assessed by a commission *(mukhamman)* and is subject to taxation. This is made possible thanks to mechanisms I will now describe (Fig. 3.3).

This document sets up a *mechanism* which structures the successive elements of the procedure to organize the procedure's traceability and rationality and attest ownership. It is, at the same time, a statement, a list of mandatory documents to be checked, and a form to be completed by hand. Traceability is first ensured by (0) a reference number ascribed to the document itself. The document then presents the decision to confirm the change of name as a logical result of the process: the Finance Directorate of the Governorate of Damascus, based on a request by the buyer (1) and after verification of mandatory documents, orders the change of name. Thus, the document is divided in three parts. The first (I) recalls the content of the request. The second (II) states that the verifications have been carried out and compiles the list of documents and laws required to produce the confirmation document itself. The third part (III) responds to the request and orders the confirmation of the change of name. It is endorsed by the heads of the departments involved.

This document, which is a form, is produced as a guide for the employee who fills it in to facilitate cross-references and check the consistency of information between the requested document (A) and the following documents cited in the form of stamps/*visa*s (see page 77). These mandatory documents include: (B) the order of the Commission of First Instance that assessed the value of the property and described its current state *(wad' rahin)*, (C) a document proving ownership (the notarial document, that is, the power of attorney) with a reference number and date, confirming the ownership of the seller, (D) the sale statement registered by the Property Commerce Department, (E) the financial quietus from the Taxation Directorate, and (F) the financial statement. Some information is given several times. The description of the property (4), the number of the parcel and the district (6) are also repeated when referring to the request document, the order of the Commission of First Instance, the financial quietus of the Taxation Directorate, and the decision itself. The name of the previous owner (7) is also mentioned when referring to the request document, the order of the Commission of First Instance, and the decision to confirm the change of name. The value of the property is also given on two occasions: when referring to the order of the Commission of First Instance and the decision to confirm the change of name. This repetition shows that this document is organized in such a way as to be filled in using other documents whose compliance is checked.

In parallel with this list and connected to it, this document establishes logical links between the administrative documents mentioned and legal texts by means of introductory sections (*visas* in the French legal system) that set out the laws, or precedents in previous court cases, on which a new law or verdict is based. *Visas* can be identified by the fact that each of the reference texts is preceded by certain recurring phrases ("Following," "given," "in view of the fact that"). By doing so, the decision resulting from this *mechanism* is presented as its logical outcome. The fact that the property breaches the town planning regulations is marginal. What matters is that the property is registered with the Ministry of Finance, that it has been assessed by the Commission of First Instance, and that it is liable to tax. The tax base is indicated as well as the references to the decision of the Commission of First Instance which calculated the tax (7).

In conclusion, the order confirms that a property built on a parcel unsuitable for development can be the subject of property rights thanks to a set of references: the accuracy of the information on the property has been checked, and the law and how it is enforced are in conformity. The second part of the order confirms the name of the new owner and gives his/her civil status, (12) orders the name of the owner to be changed, and orders notification of the decision to the executive power. Finally, (14) the order is signed by the directors of the directorates concerned.

The creation of links between administrative documents and administrative bodies

I have shown how a property defined as an illegal construction is redefined as a property 'liable to taxation' and whose fiscal value has been assessed. I will now show how 'a property liable to taxation' becomes 'a property cleared of taxes' and how a tax clearance certificate *(shahadat bar'at al-dhimma)* is delivered through the sequencing and linkage of administrative documents referring to the nature of the property as liable to tax. I will describe in greater detail the four documents produced by the Finance Directorate of the Governorate of Damascus, and required by the notary public to certify the power of attorney for the sale of a property *(wakala li-bay' 'aqar)*. Three directorates of the Finance Directorate of the Governorate of Damascus (Da'irat al-Maliya, Muhafazat Dimashq) are involved:

the Indirect Taxes Directorate (Da'irat al-Dara'ib Ghayr al-Mubashira) under the Revenue Directorate (Qism al-Waridat) in charge of the annual property tax (ri' al-'aqarat, or trabia, in everyday language), the Property Commerce Directorate (Da'irat Tijarat al-'Aqarat) under the Income Directorate (Qism al-Dakhl) in charge of value-added property tax (dara'ib al-arbah), and the Taxation Directorate (Qism al-Jibaya) in charge of personal taxes. Documents certify that there are no unpaid taxes: on the property, concerning the transaction, or personal taxes. Obtaining one document depends on having obtained another. All share the characteristic of linking administrative documents and administrations to one another.

They include a financial statement (qayd mali) issued by the Registration Office (al-Sijl al-Asasi) (Fig. 3.4), a declaration of sale (bayan mabi') established by the Property Commerce Directorate (Fig. 3.5), a note (kitab tijarat al-'aqarat) from the Property Commerce Directorate (Fig. 3.6) indicating that the value-added property tax has been paid, and a financial clearance certificate (bara'at al-dhimma) delivered by the Taxation Directorate indicating that the seller has no unpaid taxes (Fig. 3.7). All procedures are aimed at the production of these documents, which refer to one another and ensure traceability: each document is drawn up with the aid of the others and contributes to associating financial terms with terms from the Land Registry.

The first document is a financial statement (Fig. 3.4) issued by the Registration Office. It is equivalent to the request for financial quietus. It is produced at the request of the owner of the property after he presents proof of ownership. It specifies (1) the governorate concerned, (2) the name of the person requesting the document, (3) the number of the parcel and its district, (4) the administrative body to which the financial statement is addressed (referred to as tawjih, in this case the notary public), (5) the reference number of the property with the Finance Directorate (miftah al-'aqar), (6) the tax base or value of interest (qayd 'aqari) (7) the references of the assessment order of the Commission of First Instance, (8) the name of the preceding owner (who took possession of the property, wad' al-yad), (9) the description of the property, and (10) the document's date of issue. The statement is first stamped by the Registration Office (11) at the very beginning of the procedure. The stamp stipulates that the document is not complete unless a financial clearance from the Property Commerce Directorate is provided with it. At the end of the procedure, the statement is also stamped by the Taxation Directorate (12). Stamps correspond to the successive steps of the procedure.

[1] The Arab Republic of Syria / Ministry of Finance / Damascus Directorate of Finance

[2] Following the request presented by Mr. XXX

[3] To obtain a financial statement for parcel XXX of Shaghur Basatin district

[4] To be presented to the notary public

[5] For lot *(al-maqsam)*: blank / Lot *(al-farz)*: 106 /

[6] Tax base *(al-qima al-ri')* 30,000 / 21,000 / [7] assessment order 06/10/1995 / m² of land and of parcel: 78 / annual tax was calculated *(sanat al-taklif)* : 1996

[8] took possession *(wad' al-yad)*: Intisar

[9] Financial description: house, first (floor) northwest consisting of a living room (…) 92m²

[10] The (financial) statement was published 15/5/2006

[11] Stamp: Do not accept the financial statement until the clearance of the Property Commerce Directorate indicated above is included

[12] Stamp: Herewith the partial financial clearance *(bara'at al-dhimma juz'iya)* No. XXX dated XXX

Fig. 3.4: Financial statement *(qayd mali)*. (Translation above.)

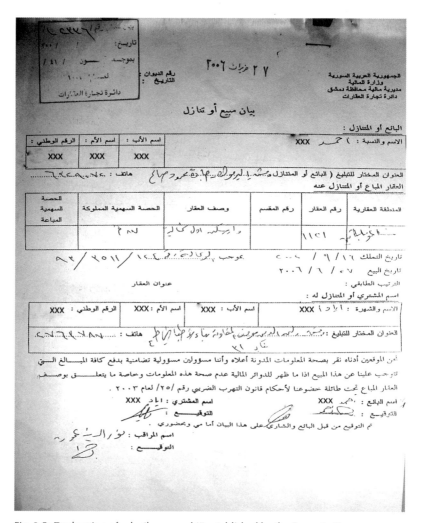

Fig. 3.5: Declaration of sale *(bayan mabi')* established by the Property Commerce Directorate (Mudiriyat Tijarat al-'Aqarat) under the Income Directorate (Qism al-Dakhl). (Translation opposite.)

[1] The Arab Republic of Syria / Ministry of Finance / Damascus Directorate of Finance / Property Commerce Directorate

[2] Diwan No. *XXX* / Date *blank*

[3] Declaration of sale or transfer

[4] The seller or the transferor: *XXX*

Address of *mukhtar* for notification *XXX*

[5] The parcel sold or transferred

Property district: *Shaghur Basatin*

Parcel No.: 1121

Lot *(al-maqsam)* No.: blank

Description of parcel: *house first (floor) north*

Percentage of share *(hussa sahmiyya)* owned: *87m²*

Percentage of share sold: blank

Date of possession *16/6/2002*

[6] According to: *power of attorney of notary No. XXX*

Date of sale: *XXX*

[7] Name of buyer or beneficiary : *XXX*

Address of mukhtar for notification *XXX*

[8] We, the signatories, declare the above information to be accurate and that we are jointly responsible for the entire payment of the sum due for this sale. Should the Directorate of Finances consider this information to be false, notably the description of the parcel, Law No. 25 2003 on tax fraud will be applied.

Name of seller / Signature / Name of buyer / Signature

[9] Seller and buyer have signed this declaration before me, in my presence / Supervisor's name / Signature

The declaration of sale (Fig. 3.5) is a declarative document signed by both the buyer and the seller that accounts for what happened. It is double sided; the front of the document comprises two parts: it is informative and indicates (1) the governorate concerned, (2) the number and registration date of the document with the administrative secretary *(diwan)*, (3) the title of the document, (4) the seller's civil status, (5) a description of the property sold, (6) the type of document certifying the property *(wathiqat al-thubutiya)*, and (7) the buyer's civil status. The second part consists of the declaration itself: (8) the seller and the buyer promise to pay property and transaction taxes, and (9) their declaration is certified by a financial officer *(muraqib)*. The back of the document is filled in by an officer from

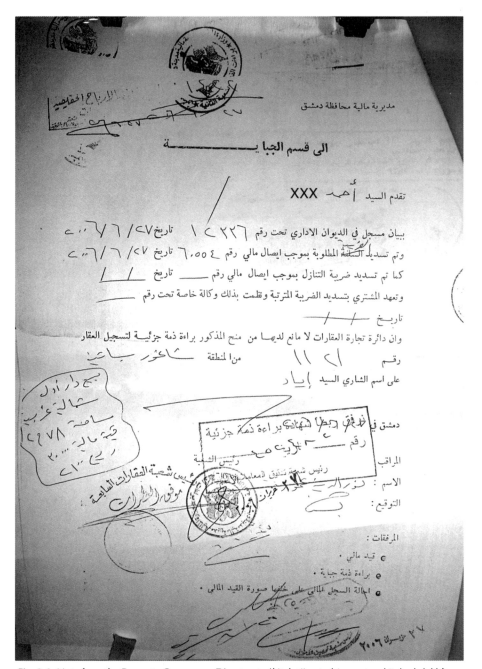

Fig. 3.6: Note from the Property Commerce Directorate (*kitab tijarat al-'aqarat* or *kitab al-dakhl*). (Translation opposite.)

Finance Directorate, Damascus Governorate
[1] To the Taxation Directorate
[2] Mr. *XXX* has presented
A declaration [3] No. *XXX* dated *27/6/2006* registered with the administrative bureau, ~~and an advance [on the tax]~~ the required *tax* has been paid, according to receipt No. *XXX*, dated *XXX*,
the tax on transfer/ cession according to receipt No. *blank* , dated *blank*
The buyer promised to pay the adherent tax and drew up for the purpose an exclusive power of attorney, No. *blank*, dated *blank*
The Property Commerce Directorate sees no objection preventing the above-mentioned person from obtaining a partial financial clearance to register [4] parcel No. *1121 of Shaghur Basatin* district [2] in the name of the buyer, Mr. *XXX*

[5] The house on the first (floor) northwest has a surface area of 78m², [6] its financial value is XXX, of which interest XXX

Damascus 27/6/2006
Supervisor / name / signature
[Documents] enclosed: financial statement, partial financial clearance, document addressed to the Registration Office and on the reverse side a copy of the financial statement

the Property Commerce Directorate who calculates the tax based on the value of interest *(ri' al-'aqarat)* written on the financial statement.

The third document is a note from the Property Commerce Directorate, the *kitab tijarat al-'aqarat*, also known by the term *kitab al-dakhl* (Fig. 3.6). It is the financial quietus of the value-added tax. The document is (1) addressed to the Taxation Directorate, informing it that the user has paid the tax and can be given a quietus. It sums up the procedure, indicating (2) the names of the parties, and (3) the reference number of their declaration of sale and its date. This note again gives (4) the parcel number on which the property stands and the name of the district, (5) a description of the property, and (6) the tax base. Unlike the financial statement and financial clearance, it states the names of the seller and buyer, thus providing information that does not appear on the other documents. It is filled in by an employee of the directorate based on the documents displayed by the dispatcher *(mu'aqib mu'amalat)* and summarizes information included in the declaration of sale, the financial statement, and the receipt proving the tax has been paid.

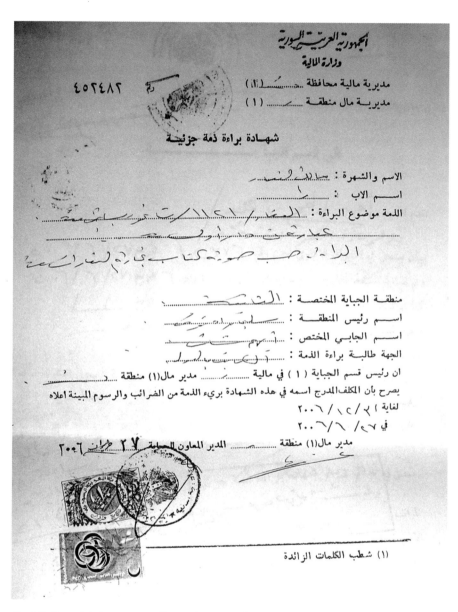

Fig. 3.7: Financial clearance certificate *(bara'at al-dhima)* issued by the Taxation Directorate. (Translation opposite.)

The Arab Republic of Syria / Ministry of Finance / Directorate of Finance of the Governorate of Damascus / No.

Certification of partial financial clearance [certificate]

[1] Name: *owner of the parcel*

Father's name: *blank*

[2] Object of the financial clearance : *parcel 1121 Shaghur Basatin consisting of a house on the first (floor)*

[3] *The financial clearance is in conformity with the copy of the Property Commerce note*

[4] District of the Tax Office *(jibaya)* in charge: *second*

Name of Head of district: *XXX*

Name of tax collector in charge: *XXX*

[5] Unit requesting the financial clearance : *notary*

[6] The Director of Taxation at the Finance [Directorate] of *blank* / The Director of the district of Damascus declares that the taxpayer whose name is registered on this attestation has paid the taxes indicated above up to *31/12/2006 on 27/6/2006.*

The director of Finance of the district *blank* / the assistant to the director of taxation *27 June 2006.*

The fourth document is a financial clearance certificate *(shahadat bara'at al-dhima)* stating that tax has been paid on the sale (Fig. 3.7). It indicates (1) the name of the owner and (2) describes the property, (3) it gives as a reference the note from the Property Commerce Directorate, (4) it specifies the office and the name of the supervisor who has followed the file as well as (5) the receiver of the financial clearance certificate (the notary public). Finally, (6) the document gives clearance to the owner of the property in a declarative formula signed by the director. This document is filled in by an officer *(muraqib)* using documents presented by the intermediary: the sale declaration, receipt, and the financial statement.

Interactions between employees and intermediaries

I will now describe how individuals involved in real-estate operations in informal neighborhoods cooperate to find ways to secure property in these neighborhoods. Various solutions are possible, among them the certification of a transaction by a notary public following registration with the Ministry of Finance. The form chosen is the result of transactions between administration professionals, either employees of the Finance Directorate or intermediaries *(muʿaqib muʿamalat)* temporarily employed by individuals to carry out administrative procedures for them. Their activities are closely linked and interdependent. Many live in informal neighborhoods themselves (including those who have responsibilities as directors in administrative bodies) and are aware of both the difficulties faced by the inhabitants of these neighborhoods in the securement of their property and of available solutions. They are often asked by inhabitants of their neighborhood to speed up their applications, in which case they can take it on themselves or send the person to an intermediary with whom they are in contact.

Thus, the documents mentioned in the first part of this chapter are produced thanks to practical interactions between employees of the Ministry of Finance and intermediaries, between employees themselves, and between intermediaries. Exchanges are carried out in such a way as to create a familiar, routine, and shared environment. Cooperation between these administration professionals takes place in various ways. I will begin by describing these administration professionals, in particular the intermediary. I will then show how each takes care to facilitate the other's work (whether successfully or not).

Administration professionals

Most of the people operating in the offices of the Directorate of Finance of the governorates of Damascus and Rural Damascus are administrative professionals, who are either employees or intermediaries. Nothing distinguishes one from the other except for a badge, which employees rarely wear, or the attaché case in which intermediaries keep their files. Individuals rarely enter administrative buildings: all administrative procedures begin by recruiting an intermediary. Generally speaking, the person who recruits the intermediary has been put in touch with him by the real-estate agency in charge of the transaction or by a lawyer. He is usually specialized in one neighborhood, most often the one he lives in, and/or in one administrative body (the Ministry of Finance, for example). An intermediary will use another intermediary (a notary public, for example) to pursue the procedure in another institution.

The intermediary is a key figure in the Syrian administrative process, and although individuals can carry out procedures themselves, they often prefer to call on a professional who knows the administrative body well. Administrative procedures are long, and recruiting an intermediary saves time and energy: the intermediary is a recognized figure. He is expected to be familiar with the administrative procedures which apply to the file he is in charge of, that is, to get the file qualified (see explanation of qualification process above). He presents himself as someone who has the know-how to solve the problems involved in registering a complex application (lahu ishkaliya)—someone who is familiar with the ins and outs of the administration and who has developed his own network of useful contacts. A good intermediary, referred to as a 'master' (mu'allim), 'will know how to manage' (bidabbir halu) and will be able to interact with the administration to discuss the procedure. Theoretically, these professionals are licensed by a training institute, but in fact many work without a license. Some have been trained by another intermediary, while others started out in the profession because a relative or employee of the administrative body suggested it to them.

Intermediaries will use all the employee's resources to speed up their applications. The contrary is also true: an employee can use the resources of an intermediary, or another employee, when the case he is personally in charge of (al-mu'amalla ilu) is blocked by a third party. Cooperation between employees is another essential aspect of these processes: besides soliciting advice from one another, employees can exchange forms and make use of forms already signed in other offices of the Finance Directorate, thus allowing them to speed up or even get around a procedure they have taken on privately.

Creating a shared, familiar environment

The intermediary's job is to facilitate the work of the employee and to understand the often complex cases he is in charge of. He must be able to explain the land-ownership position of a property, propose solutions to the employee when the problem is complex, and defend his client's case. He spends his time organizing and reorganizing his documents, pinning and unpinning small clips, and putting the relevant papers immediately at the disposal of the employee he is dealing with. He may also photocopy documents so that the employee will not have to request them from the Archives Service.

He often fills out administrative documents on the employee's behalf: thus he will use the buyer's and seller's identity cards and the power of attorney which serves as the seller's property deed to fill out the declaration of sale—the employee will only have to sign. Intermediaries must also facilitate the work of newly recruited employees who are as yet unfamiliar with their jobs. In some cases, intermediaries know more about regulations and the implementation of procedures than employees. An intermediary must be flexible and show good will. Sometimes he has to transmit a series of files to another office of the Finance Directorate. Intermediaries are more mobile than employees and can be used as internal mailmen.

While the intermediary's job is to facilitate the work of the employee, the latter must explain the correct procedure to follow, all the more so as the intermediary is experienced in these affairs and knows his way around. However, employees do this with varying degrees of willingness. Some make the effort to explain in detail how to proceed, before stopping to ask "you know how it goes, don't you?" *(ta'arif al-qisa, sah?)*, while others are less willing to help. One technique commonly used by employees is to put the intermediary in the position of an employee, as a way of informing him of the work being carried out by the administration. For example, an intermediary who insists on being given the reference number of a property under a certain name might be told to look it up for himself in the financial registers.

Showing competence

It is by showing his competence and by publicizing his experience that an intermediary will be authorized to get round certain demands of the property registration procedure. The employee will then make an effort to facilitate various steps or simplify the procedure *(yisahhil al-umur)*. The intermediary might thus be allowed to use the telephone, without necessarily asking for permission, in order to obtain information from another employee as to how to proceed. The fact that an employee allows someone to use a stamp shows that this person is recognized as a member of the profession, that he is trusted. It is by becoming a recognized member of the profession that an intermediary will be able to develop the arguments that will further his case. In particular, he can cite the way in which previous applications have been dealt with. He will have to be convincing with his case, so that the employee will decide to put through his file and order that it be dealt with *(yimashi al-umur)*. In this context, the intermediary always asks the same two questions: "what's the solution?" *(shu-l-hall?)* or "aren't there any other solutions?" *(ma fi hall thani?)*.

Employees and intermediaries are thus continually judging one another's work. One hears phrases like "he's a computer, he remembers everything," "he's an expert" *(huwa mu'allim)* or "he doesn't know his job," "this man doesn't know what he wants; they told him to come here, but he doesn't know what he's supposed to do."

Conclusion

As mentioned in the introduction to this chapter, the way to secure property may take different forms, including registration with the Land Registry, the notary public, the court and/or the Ministry of Finance. By looking at properties not registered before the Land Registry and qualified as 'breaches of the law' *(mukhalafat)* in situated contexts, this chapter set out to show how such properties may finally be secured thanks to re-qualification mechanisms, language games, and through tax payments.

Close observation of the procedures involved pointed to the fact that securing informal property is first made possible by the organization of categories as mechanisms of a broader category: that of 'joint tenancy property' *(musha')*. This category, rarely noted in writing, is the underlying conceptual framework of the registration process and guides it. Its use accounts for a change of frame of reference that makes property registration with the ministry possible. The property is not referred to as 'a breach of the law' but as part of a larger property. Shares *(hussa sahmiya)* may be sold once the Ministry of Finance has described their content and assessed their fiscal value. Thus, the property becomes an assessed property *(mukhamman* or *muqaddir)*, liable to taxation *(mukallaf)*. This re-qualification process is also made possible by a mechanism in which documents always refer to the Land Registry and its categories, thus establishing links between the two administrative bodies and building a shared language.

Secondly, the administrative documents analyzed in this paper constantly inscribe themselves formally within a broader mechanism by structuring the successive elements of the procedure and repeating certain pieces of information. The documents are interdependent; they constantly refer, implicitly or otherwise, to one another, thus ensuring traceability, establishing logical links, and demonstrating rationality. This well-structured administrative mechanism which links administrative decisions and services is ensured by close cooperation between administrative professionals, that is, employees from the ministry and intermediaries, who contribute to qualifying the nature of a property and allow it to acquire legal status.

Notes

1   The Land Registry Service (Property Office) is under the Ministry of Agriculture and Agricultural Reform and not the Ministry of Finance.
2   These documents belong to three different cases since the use of one single case appeared problematic.
3   The power of attorney allows the authorized person to carry out all the actions in regard to a property that an owner is entitled to carry out (see Chapter 2 in this volume).

4

Inhabitants' Daily Practices to Obtain Legal Status for Their Homes and Security of Tenure: Egypt

Marion Séjourné

Today, as in many developing cities, most urban fringes around Cairo are designated as illegal. This urbanization does not comply with at least one of the laws governing urban land development and building (planning codes, subdivision laws, land rights, and so on). Moreover, most of the transactions are not registered; constructions do not have building permits, and properties lack formal title deeds (Séjourné 2006). These forms of urbanization account for most of the expansion of Greater Cairo and house most of its population growth. Indeed, urban spread and population growth were very high from the 1950s until the late 1970s, mostly due to rural exodus. Paradoxically, whereas since the end of this period the growth trend of the metropolis has slowed down overall—the population of the Greater Cairo Region is growing at a rate only slightly faster than that of Egypt (2.1 percent per year versus 2.03 percent per year between 1996 and 2006)—illegal settlements continue to expand. Since the 1990s, informal areas have been the dominant mode of housing in Cairo: in 1998, they sheltered around 7 million people or more than half of the total population of Greater Cairo (12 million inhabitants) (Denis and Séjourné 2002). In 2006, this share increased to more than 65 percent, that is, 10.5 million inhabitants lived in those areas (Sims and Séjourné 2008).

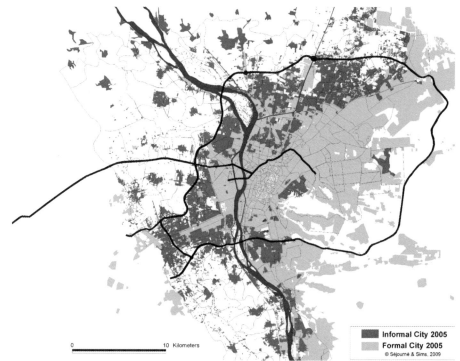

Fig. 4.1. Distribution of illegal settlements in Greater Cairo region in 2005 (© Séjourné and Sims, 2009).

This paper will set out the processes of illegal urbanization and especially practices and strategies implemented by owners who built their own properties (families and small entrepreneurs) to access a certain degree of 'legality' and to secure their tenure. I will look at all the extra-legal procedures, negotiations, strategies and 'fraudulent' practices (including bribery) used by inhabitants to gain official recognition, and sometimes legalization, or to obtain a building permit even if the land where they have built is officially prohibited for development. Finally, I will demonstrate that this form of urbanization is 'negotiated' and widely tolerated even though rarely legalized. It certainly constitutes an ordinary and commonplace mode of housing (Séjourné 2011).

Let us begin with a definition of what I consider to be informal settlements. I will start from the objective finding that illegal is, in essence, what is not legal. I take the dichotomy 'illegal city' versus 'legal city'—stressed especially by authorities and administrative officials—because it reflects realities on the ground. In other words, my definition is deliberately built according to the formal rights that prevail in Egypt (planning, subdivision and building regulations, laws protecting agricultural land, and so on). It does not prejudge the relevance of those laws nor their application or applicability. It does not pass judgment on people who build under those conditions. Finally, I take as a basis for the definition of illegality the land situation and regulations concerning building for domestic use.

In Cairo, illegality refers to two main situations: either settlements located on privately owned agricultural land (the plot might have been legally bought but construction has been strictly prohibited since the 1960s) or on public desert land, which belongs to the state domain (so called squatting). Squatting consists of appropriation and occupation of a plot (*wad' al-yad*, literally 'put a hand on') by an individual (inhabitant or entrepreneur) or, more rarely, a group, without the authorization of the true owner, in this case, the state.

The Legal Framework of Bringing About a Legally Recognized City

Starting from our basic position that 'illegal city' is opposed to 'legally recognized city,' I will highlight the two stages of the legal urbanization process. What are the major stages to obtain 'legality' of the land transaction, and then of the construction? Together, those processes make the 'legally recognized city.' First of all, I will shed light on the different ownership statuses in Egypt.

In Egypt, three forms of property exist according to the Civil Code (1948) and the 1971 Constitution: (a) private property (*mulk*); (b) public property (*miri*) subdivided into the state Public Domain and the state Private Domain; and (c) cooperative properties (for social use). Private and state Private Domain properties can be alienated and transferred, unlike state Public Domain properties, which are also not subject to prescription. They are generally used for public utility.

Means and procedures of legal acquisition of private land and/or state Private Domain plots and of obtaining the legal recognition of the construction

Acquiring a private plot of land is quite simple. The buyer and the seller must sign a preliminary contract (*'aqd ibtida'i*), which contains various details: size of the parcel, its location, price of sale, and so on. Two witnesses must sign the contract. Until the contract is registered with the *shahr al-'aqari* (Public Registry), the property is not considered officially legal.

To access state Private Domain land (agricultural land), the claimant must first inquire as to whom the plot belongs, because each type of land is handled by different public authorities (ministries of defence and of agriculture, governorates, and so on). For instance, governorates control and manage land located inside municipal administrative boundaries or inside the *ziman* (that is, boundaries of cultivated and uncultivated agricultural land, where land has been surveyed and is subject to property tax) and land located within a range of two kilometers outside the *ziman*. However, as El Kadi (1987) and Deboulet (1994) have shown, boundaries are not well known and often change. Thus, building permits are frequently issued by officials (who do not know the boundaries) although construction is prohibited. Only desert state Private Domain land can be assigned for urban use according to plans and projects made by the Ministry of Housing in accordance with the authorities and ministries that manage that land.

To transfer public land to private ownership, authorities to whom land belongs (often governorates) can implement two procedures: auctions or direct sale. Nevertheless, these procedures are extremely long and costly. In the case of auctions, the claimant of a subdivided plot will acquire it after following 125 administrative steps before 59 different agencies, which takes more than 286 days (ILD and ECES 2000, 40). In the case of direct sale, procedures include 110 administrative transactions with 38 agencies and 424 waiting days and the whole procedure costs LE25,000 (ILD and ECES 2000, 41) (which can be compared with the average annual salary in Cairo in 2000: LE4,445). Once those procedures have been completed, the claimant will be the owner of the plot; however, in order to be officially recognized, the property must be registered with the *shahr al-'aqari*.

Acquiring 'legality' of land transfer and registering a property: a Herculean task

As David Sims has shown, since 1946 (Law No. 114), all sales, purchases, and transfers of land must be registered with the *shahr al-'aqari* to ensure complete legal protection for the owner, but also to identify the property and allow property tax payment. The registration system involves two bodies: (a) the *shahr al-'aqari*, which comes under the Ministry of Justice (an office is located in each governorate and branches can be found in each district, or *hayy*), and (b) the Survey Authority (Hay'at al-Misaha), under the control of the Ministry of Irrigation and Water. Registering is a voluntary procedure initiated exclusively by owners.

If the property is not built on, there are two stages of registration. First, the owner goes to the local branch of the *shahr al-'aqari* to apply for registration. He must complete a file with many documents: an application form, primary contract *('urfi)*, and a receipt of property tax *(kashf al-mushtamalat)* which is paid by all owners, no matter what the status of tenure is. The official from the local *shahr al-'aqari* investigates the file, records the application in a special register, and forwards a copy of the file to the Survey Authority, in order to record the location, zone, and limits of the property. Through a field visit, a *misaha* official inspects the concerned site in order to collect and verify information on the location and surface area of the land. He then sends a report *(kashf kahdad)* with the results of the investigation to the *shahr al-'aqari*.

Next, the *shahr al-'aqari* looks at the legal aspects of the application and verifies that the property is really owned by the claimant. Once verifications are complete, the *shahr al-'aqari* approves the request, transfers the file to the claimant, and provides him with a provisional legal contract, which must be signed by the seller and the buyer before an official from the *shahr al-'aqari*. The contract must then be approved by the Syndicate of Lawyers and returned to the *shahr al-'aqari* for final ratification. Then the contract is finally eligible for registration.

The second step of the registration process concerns the registration of the primary contract itself by the claimant with the *shahr al-'aqari*. This marks the end of the procedures: property rights are officially approved. The owner receives a copy of his title deed *(hugga: proof, or blue paper)*, while the original will be stored at the *shahr al-'aqari*, in a specific department (Dar al-Mahfuzat). Only after completing these steps can the owner apply for a building permit.

The second case concerns registration of a built plot of land. The new owner (claimant) can register his property only if: (a) the building is in a zone where construction is permitted; and (b) the seller is registered with the *shahr al-'aqari* as the last owner. If not, the seller is not officially recognized as the owner and usually the buyer cannot proceed to the registration of his newly bought property. If the seller is registered, then the buyer must follow the same procedures as explained above (and also provide documents concerning the building: building permit, and so on).

It goes without saying that these procedures are costly and time consuming. It is extremely difficult for owners to register their property; they must be patient, have 'good connections' *(wasta)* and often pay financial 'compensation' *(ikramiyyat,* bribes) to officials in charge. A study showed that to officially register property, an owner follows 102 administrative steps with 34 official bodies, waits 198 days, and pays almost LE7,000 (ILD, ECES 2000), excluding legal fees and registration tax.[1]

Theoretically, to obtain a building permit or to subdivide a plot, land must have a formal title deed registered with the *shahr al-'aqari*. The plot must also be in a zone where construction is permitted, which, by law, excludes most agricultural land (Law No. 3 of the Urban Planning Act, 1982).

Urban planning was defined by the subdivision Law No. 52 of 1940 issued by the Ministry of Justice and was then completed by the Urban Act (Law No. 3) of 1982, which set quite high European standards for plot layouts: the requirement for there to be public spaces, the requirement that infrastructure be in place before plot sales can begin (Sims and Séjourné 2000), a minimum street width of ten meters, and that the length of buildings must not exceed 1.5 times the width of the street. In case of noncompliance with these regulations, the building might be demolished.

Before obtaining a building permit, the landowner must get authorization provided by the Planning Department of the district *(hayy)*, which ensures that the building plans meet land subdivision and building regulations. Once the department has given its approval, the applicant can apply for a building permit from the Engineering Department of the *hayy*. The completion of these steps is long, costly, and very complicated (as they involve many public and private agencies). For instance, in Cairo Governorate, to obtain documents and certificates required for a building permit an owner must follow 102 administrative procedures, wait 664 days (although the law stipulates that the whole process must be completed within thirty days), and it will cost him LE41,770 (ILD and ECES 2000, 54).

We have seen the main procedures to register a property title deed, subdivide a plot, and obtain a building permit. They are time-consuming, complicated, and costly. Moreover, before obtaining a building permit or subdividing a plot the land must first be registered, which implies that it is suitable for development, which, de facto, excludes most agricultural land. Furthermore, most desert areas belong to the state and obtaining a desert plot is particularly difficult.

Procedures for agricultural land located inside the urban zone also require documents and certificates that are hard to provide. Yet, all these procedures are necessary in order to legalize the city's housing. In short, the excessive regulations and formalities are so strict, complicated, and expensive that they prevent owners from obtaining legal status for their property. It is therefore not surprising that urbanization is mostly illegal.

Strategies and Practices of Inhabitants for Legalizing Their Residence or Accessing a Certain Degree of Legality

Faced with this judicial, legislative, and prescriptive system, inhabitants of illegal settlements take certain actions, implement strategies, and use certain practices—often considered fraudulent—to obtain official legitimacy (and, in rare cases, regularization of their situation), to obtain proof that they own their land and building, or to secure their tenure. These practices and strategies differ according to the location of the property (on agricultural land or desert land). The following section is based on four studies: ILD, ECES (2000), El-Shorbagi (2000), Sims (2002), and Séjourné (2006).

On privately owned agricultural land

Legally speaking, registration of property in the *shahr al-'aqari* is the only means to obtain full protection. However, as we have seen, in order to do so, the seller must be registered as the last owner. If one or more unregistered transactions have taken place before the last sale, which is very common, the new owner cannot register his property. However, inhabitants take procedures to bypass the problem or to obtain a document that gives them a certain degree of official recognition that is sufficient to prove their ownership.

The procedure of da'wa sihha wa nafadh

Owners can resort to a lawsuit called *da'wa sihha wa nafadh*, at the end of which the transfer of contract will be considered valid and will allow them to register their property with the *shahr al-'aqari*. Initially, as Monika El-Shorbagi explains, "the original purpose of a *da'wa saha wa nafadh* lawsuit is to rule in cases between the seller and the buyer after conclusion and before official registration of the provisional contract when the seller refuses to participate in the registration procedures. In this case, the buyer has to file a civil suit *(khusuma haqiqiya)* against the seller to obtain a court sentence that will force the seller to register the sales contract officially with the Public Registry" (El-Shorbagi 2000, 44). Today, this procedure is used as a first step in the registration process. The goal is to obtain a court judgment which proves that the seller is the real owner (El-Shorbagi 2000, 44). However, this procedure is unpredictable, complicated, and expensive. Nevertheless, for the buyer who completes the entire procedure, the document issued by the Court represents a strong proof of ownership. For some, it represents a kind of official recognition, almost like a title deed,

Fig. 4.2: View of Bashtil informal settlement, Cairo, 2008. Photograph by Marion Séjourné.

even though it is not recognized as such by the authorities, since registration of the property is the only way to obtain a proper title deed and true legal status.

Procedures to formalize sale contracts

In most informal property transactions, provisional contracts (*'urfi* or *'aqd ibtida'i*) are used. Until they are registered, they are considered as informal. Frequently, inhabitants resort to procedures in court or in the *shahr al-'aqari* to give their contract a certain form of legality, either by the attestation of the signature (*da'wa sihha wa tawqi'*) or confirmation of the date of sale (*ithbat tarikh*).

In the first procedure, called *da'wa sihha wa tawqi'*, the judge orders the seller to appear before the Court in order to verify his identity and signature on the contract. This procedure is easy to carry out. Moreover, it is relatively inexpensive (about LE100) and a few extra 'fees' (bribes) to employees will facilitate and expedite the process (El-Shorbagi 2000, 45). In the second procedure, *ithbat tarikh*, the buyer goes to the local Public Registrar and asks a civil servant to register the date of signature of his sale contract and affix a stamp on it to confirm that the date is registered.

Here again, neither of these documents is equivalent to an official property title deed, since the judge or the civil servant neither verifies the contents of the contract nor confirms them. So although these procedures do not amount to formal recognition of the property, they are used to support a file which ensures de facto security of tenure.

Legalization after occupying a plot without a title deed

An individual who occupies a plot of land without a title deed can initiate a legal procedure to obtain a judgment that declares that the claimant has a real property right based on the evidence of occupation. This right can be obtained if the claimant is able to prove that the *hiyaza* (possession of immovable/movable property without ownership) has been "peaceful, unchallenged and uninterrupted" for a period of fifteen years (Civil Code Nos. 131 and 969 of 1948). *Hiyaza* applies to private property. So it is a way to acquire ownership of a property through adverse possession. It also applies to properties belonging to the Private Domain of the state but never to the Public Domain (Civil Code No. 970 of 1948 and Law No. 100 of 1964).

The claimant has to produce for the Court all documents proving the occupation or possession of the property (electricity bills, sale contract, cadastral plan, and so on). Usually, evaluation of the evidence depends on experts commissioned by the Court. If the judge gives a positive answer, the occupant can register his property. However, this procedure is extremely long, sometimes taking up to eighteen years. The main obstacle facing the claimant is the difficulty of proving possession and occupation for fifteen years. This procedure is mostly used by those who do not have documents proving the land transaction and who, as such, cannot register their asset.

State Domain land

Possession and occupation of Public Domain land are normally strictly forbidden. However, inhabitants who already occupy this kind of land *(wad' al-yad)* upon which they have built their domicile can legally acquire this land after the event. Nevertheless, this method is only possible on state Private Domain land. It can only be implemented after the launching of a legalization campaign by the authorities or, less frequently, after a lawsuit.

Recognition of occupation of state Private Domain land

Squatters can obtain a property title even if the land they occupy belongs to the state. In order to do so, the authorities that control the land must approve the property transfer. In urban areas, the governor is usually the ultimate authority. Property transfer—land legalization *(taknin)*—might also be initiated by the president or prime minister, who must launch the opening of a State Domain land purchase process *(tamlik)* by official decree.

As a general rule, not all squatters can benefit from this procedure. In fact, in order to purchase a parcel they must have occupied it before the promulgation of Law No. 31 of 1984. This acquisition can be made by a direct sale which includes payment for the land and the payment of financial compensation to the state representing the use of this land for a period of five years before submitting the application. Under this law, the claimant must submit his application within six months following promulgation of the law. However, in certain governorates, such as those of Giza or Cairo, the governors implement programs of land regularization after this date. To do so, they apply article 28 of Law No. 43 of 1973 (called the Law of the Local Government) which gives them the right to manage, as they wish, land in their districts and land transfers.

When a regularization campaign is initiated, the governor forms a committee (consisting of various members of the agencies of the governorate) that is responsible for fixing the price to be paid for land (the amount of the initial deposit and the amount of the monthly installments).[2] This price is often calculated based on the location of the land in question but also on "the market value as of the date of possession and before the implementation of Law No. 31 of 1984" (Prime Ministerial Decree No. 857 of 1985). The claimant of a parcel (on which he has or has not built) must then approach the *shahr al-'aqari* to obtain a document detailing the history of the land on which the plot is located *(bahth tasalsul milkiyat al-'aqar)* (El-Shorbagi 2000, 39). After a period not exceeding thirty days, the *shahr al-'aqari* will publish a land certificate, confirming the real-estate transactions *(shahadat tasarufat 'aqariya)*, containing information concerning the current landowner and his predecessors (El-Shorbagi 2000, 39). If the land belongs to the state, this certificate will mention the name of the authority to which the land belongs (generally the governorate in urban areas). If the land has no owner, the *shahr al-'aqari* will supply a certificate *(istimarat awal ta'amul)* stipulating that the applicant is the first applicant in respect of the plot (which is extremely rare). The applicant can then register the plot directly in his name.

When land belongs to the state sector and when its administrator is the governorate, the applicant, after having filled in the application form for purchase of the land and having provided his certificate *(shahadat tasarufat 'aqariya)*, must go to the department of *amlak* (in charge of State Domain properties) of the district *(hayy)*, which deals with the implementation of the *tamlik*. Then he must bring a whole series of proofs of ownership of the property and/or occupation of the land (receipts showing the payment of property taxes *(kashf al-mushtamalat)*, water and electricity bills, a certificate attesting to the quality of the construction issued by an engineer from the district, and so on). All of this usually requires many long stages with various departments and the claimant must pay many fees, often with bribes. Then, various surveys are carried out by the departments in charge of the process (verification of required information, and so on). At the end of these checks, the person claiming ownership of the land must pay a deposit and will receive a temporary title deed, which stipulates that the land still belongs to the governorate. He will only obtain his final title deed once the monthly installments have been paid, generally after a period of fifteen years. A cessation of payment generally leads to the loss of the land. Moreover, modification of the construction and the use of the land is forbidden until the land fully belongs to the applicant.

On average, to obtain ownership of the land which he occupies, the claimant will make 72 transactions with 35 authorities, which will take him 262 days to complete and will cost him approximately LE10,000 (ILD and ECES 2000, 61). This is unquestionably the best means to secure their tenure and ensure the transmission of their property to their children, and to rule out the fear of demolition. Following this long process, which can take up to twenty years, the applicant can finally register his land with the *shahr al-'aqari*.

Appealing to the court as a means of regularizing land ownership
Sometimes the inhabitants of an illegal settlement appeal to the court to avoid the arbitrary demolition of their district and sometimes obtain its regularization. Such was the case in the district of 'Izbit Khayrallah, in southeast Cairo (El-Shorbagi 2000, 43). We assume that the procedures

followed for the regularization of the district were similar to those mentioned above. This kind of appeal is uncommon, and collective mobilization (lawyers acting on their own initiative or, sometimes, at the request of a group of inhabitants), such as that started in 'Izbit Khayrallah, is also uncommon.

Undeniably, the record of the practices and strategies implemented by inhabitants and developers of illegal urbanization, whether it is to circumvent the law or take advantage of it, is a unique register which records their competences (Deboulet 1994; Berry-Chikhaoui and Deboulet 2000; Florin 1999). Their aim is usually to protect them from arbitrary eviction, or from a dispute of their ownership of land and/or real estate, and to give them a certain 'degree' of legality (particularly those implemented by 'ordinary city-dwellers'). This usually entails extremely long, complicated, and very expensive procedures.

The Mechanisms Leading to de facto Securing of Tenure

For many inhabitants who have neither a legally recognized title deed, nor building permits, the security of tenure of the land on which they are settled is rarely a problem. They do not feel particularly threatened by the demolition of their domicile at the instigation of the authorities even if they have built on land unsuitable for development; nor are they concerned about expropriation, even if they occupy land in the State Domain. To what can we ascribe this feeling of relative security of tenure?

The progressive installation of equipment and services by the authorities: a guarantee of security of tenure

In practice, the Egyptian state shows much tolerance toward illegal districts. It even tends to grant them a certain de facto recognition. 'Unofficial' recognition is shown by the progressive integration of these districts into the rest of the city (whether they are located on agricultural land or on desert land), in particular by their connection to public service networks (electricity, sewage, drinking water), or by the setting-up of public utilities such as schools and police stations *(aqsam shurta)*, or by the installation of local regional administrative bodies (districts, *hayys*). The residents of illegal areas consider that once infrastructures or services are in place, their eviction or the demolition of their property will be almost impossible.

Moreover, although illegal districts are the first to suffer from the lack of infrastructure and services, they are not the only ones. Paradoxically, certain popular legalized districts (districts located in the old parts of the city, for instance) are indeed as poorly equipped with public utilities as many informal settlements. Moreover, public housing districts (built by the state) suffer from the same lack of infrastructure and basic services as certain illegal areas. Therefore, it seems that the status of the occupation of the land (illegal/legal) is less important than the size and the age (maturity) of these districts (Sims 2002, 95) when it comes to the installation of public services and infrastructure. The oldest illegal districts are indeed better equipped than the most recent, although both are illegal.

Protection by reason of the number of inhabitants
While the number of inhabitants in illegal districts is a sufficient condition for the authorities to gradually provide infrastructures and, consequently, grant them de facto recognition, the demographic 'critical mass' (Sims 2002, 95) that they represent is also seen by most of the residents as a guarantee which protects them from any attempted eviction.

Securing tenure by the acquisition (or possession) of 'official' documents
In application of the codes and regulations in force, construction on agricultural land and occupation of state-owned land (Public Domain) are strictly forbidden. Yet, paradoxically, many inhabitants in illegal areas pay taxes and property taxes. They also pay expenses relating to the use of service infrastructures (consumption of water, electricity, and so on) when they exist in the neighborhood. Payment for such utilities represents for them a strong sign of recognition on behalf of the authorities, although it is not a sign of legitimacy.

The payment of property taxes (al-'awa'id)
Many property owners in illegal districts pay property taxes (al-'awa'id). These are paid locally to a specific department under the Ministry of Finance, an office of which is located in the district (hayy), and are recharged to the ministry's central budget. These taxes are calculated from an estimate made by a committee which inspects land and buildings and writes reports containing all the information relating to the building unit and to the land (description of the asset, location, and so on). Thus, every property has a file that is kept in the tax department at the district office.

Property owners can obtain a copy (kashf al-mushtamalat) of this file from the department. This document is essential for their property to be connected up to the various public utilities when the government plans the installation of services in the district, whether or not the property is legal.

For inhabitants, this property tax document is also proof that the property belongs to them or that they occupy it. This document is also required by the authorities when they plan to launch a campaign of land and real-estate regularization in a district located on state-owned land. In such cases, it constitutes important proof of ownership of the property, and is often the only proof that residents of illegal districts hold. However, most of the inhabitants whom we questioned consider that paying these taxes guarantees them security and legitimacy of occupation of the property.

Electricity and water bills: a guarantee of 'legitimacy'

When electricity or water bills (for all the building) and the electric meter are recorded in the name of the owner of a building, it is highly unlikely that his ownership will be disputed (El-Shorbagi 2000, 34). As for the tenant, he can request the installation of a meter in his name, from the date when the owner cancels his meter rental agreement with the National Electricity (or Water) Company; bills will then be in his name. The electricity and water bills are thus documents that prove ownership of a property for the owner and its occupation for the owner and/or the tenant.

They play a particularly important role in the most recent (illegal) districts where owners cannot pay *awa'id* (taxes), since the statement of new properties is usually only prepared every ten years. From then on, these bills are often considered by the inhabitants as documentary evidence of a certain degree of 'legality.'

The infrequency of demolitions and evictions

Under current legislation in Egypt, only owners with a title deed which is duly registered with the *shahr al-'aqari* and with a proper building permit benefit from full and complete security of tenure and are guaranteed that their asset will never be subjected to arbitrary demolition.

Thus, from the legal aspect, parcels located on State Domain land can be taken back at any time by the authorities to whom they belong without squatters being either compensated or rehoused (Sims 2002, 93). Buildings built on private farmland can be demolished, but in such cases the owner receives compensation.

Nevertheless, unlike in certain African countries where demolition campaigns ('the bulldozer policy') of illegal districts and the 'eviction' of their inhabitants without compensation were carried out on a large scale during the years 1970–80 (Durand-Lasserve 1986; Massiah and Tribillon 1988; Legros 2003), in Egypt the cases of arbitrary demolition of districts

Fig. 4.3: Self-built housing in Manshiyat Nasir, Cairo, 2008. Photograph by Marion Séjourné.

constructed on privately owned land or on state-owned land are quite rare (El Kadi 1987; Sims 2002). The infrequent occurrence of arbitrary demolitions is due to the authorities' concern for the preservation of social order and fear of the potential political 'disturbance' that such tough action could provoke. This does not, however, prevent the authorities from occasionally using this threat as they did for example in Manshiyat Nasir (the biggest illegal district on state-owned land in Cairo)—by the minister of housing until 1999. Nor does it prevent them from occasionally demolishing property, as they did in the potters' district al-Fakhariya (in the governorate of Cairo) in January 1998.

In practice, the demolition of districts or parts of them is rare. When this does occur, it is generally for the construction of public projects (utilities, development projects, renovation of the district, and so on). In such cases, the government has a right of expropriation and can thus proceed with the demolition of houses. Nevertheless, the state must pay compensation to the inhabitants, whether or not they have a registered title (Sims 2002, 93). However, this compensation may also be linked to the fact that in Egypt there is a law (article 40 of Law No. 3 of 1982) which stipulates that in most cases, the owner or tenant of occupied property that is subject to a demolition order must receive compensation (if the property is unoccupied, the demolition can take place without compensation).

As a general rule, compensation takes the form of an apartment in one of the public housing programs, generally carried out by governorates or the Ministry of Housing. It applies to all residents, whether they live in districts built on agricultural land or are squatters on state-owned land. Apparently, the inhabitants are aware of this and consider that once occupied, their houses will not be destroyed without payment of compensation by the authorities. Certain inhabitants are even well informed of the case law concerning compulsory rehousing after a demolition order and thus mobilize various resources to press the authorities in order to obtain maximum compensation.

Furthermore, when projects of utility services, rehabilitation, or regularization are planned in a district, there is often a spate of construction activity. Such builders, who are generally private individuals, are aware that their actions are illegal and that their houses will certainly be destroyed if they are not occupied. Therefore they rush to build and especially to occupy buildings. They do so because they know that they will thus be very likely to get a replacement apartment in a public housing program. Thus, in Wadi Pharaon, a subdivision of Manshiyat Nasir, several hundred small houses and sometimes even simple shacks were rapidly built and inhabited when the governorate of Cairo and the GTZ (Deutsche Gesellschaft für Technische Zusammenarbeit GmbH) began to implement their project of rehabilitation and regularization of the district.

In the emergency divisions of Duweiqa, in Manshiyat Nasir, after the announcement of the opening of a rehousing program for families living there, apartments that were going to be built as part of the program were also resold at an inflated price, even though this practice was strictly forbidden because only the original beneficiaries are supposed to be rehoused. Indeed, in 2001, when the governorate of Cairo, via the district (hayy), published an announcement concerning the rehousing of the families of the emergency units via the public housing program of Duweiqa al-Gadida, the black market resale price of the units increased considerably. While the price of a unit did not exceed LE2,000 before then, it reached LE9,000 just after the announcement. This can be explained by the fact that the salesmen knew that the occupants of the units would be rehoused or 'compensated,' even if they were not the legal beneficiaries of the apartments to be demolished.

Thus, although in theory the registered title deed is the only means to be recognized and protected by the law, there are many other 'elements' that give inhabitants the impression of the relative security of their tenure or their occupation. On this topic, Omar Razzaz concluded about the illegal districts which he had studied in Jordan that "empirical evidence shows a security of tenure in illegal districts which depends less on the legal status than on the perception of the occupants concerning the probability of eviction and demolition" (Razzaz 1993, 349).

Conclusion

The 'success' of illegal forms of urbanization is linked to two main factors. Firstly, in spite of the occasionally violent declarations against their inhabitants, both squatters and private owners on farmland have benefited from a certain degree of tolerance for more than a quarter of a century. Secondly, except for squatters (who constitute a minority of 'illegal' inhabitants), the reality of the situation is paradoxical. Indeed, although agricultural land cannot legally have urban constructions for housing use (in which case it is *urbanization* that is illegal), land is purchased within a framework of 'normal' and legal transactions: the landowner receives payment for the parcel, either from the inhabitant himself or from a developer. This transaction is generally carried out within a traditional legal framework (the signing of a sale contract—often drafted by a lawyer—by both parties in the presence of two witnesses) that is completely legal, even though it cannot give the right to a building permit, as it cannot be registered first because the plot cannot be developed.

Nevertheless, inhabitants (whether they built their homes themselves, had their houses built for them, or bought an existing property) consider themselves to be the owner of their homes, and their ownership is generally undisputed. As a precautionary measure, they nevertheless try to obtain various documents by taking legal steps (which are sometimes fraudulent) that ensure a certain form of 'legality' of the property's transaction and construction.

The study of the practices and strategies implemented by 'ordinary city-dwellers,' previously undertaken by various researchers, highlight the skillfulness of residents of illegal districts (Deboulet 1994; Berry-Chikhaoui and Deboulet 2000; Florin 1999; El-Shorbagi 2000). They use these skills to overcome the 'restrictions' of the strict and prescriptive framework of 'legality,' which they are trying to enter into, either to resist, to 'make do' (De Certeau 1990), according to their resources, to their breathing space, or they try to bypass this framework of legality and to instrumentalize it.

These practices also prove inhabitants' aspirations to conform to 'legality' as far as possible. In other words, through these strategies of manipulation of the legal system, fraud, corruption, and so on, they are attempting to secure tenure of their domicile. Yet it is also a means to be integrated as far as possible into the 'legal' city and to acquire recognition from the authorities, "recognition by society as a whole" (Deboulet 1996, 152), and a "right to the city." They try to do this without political contestation or confrontation or "challenging the police" (Denis 1998, 90). The practices of "ordinary city-dwellers" sometimes enter the domain of politics but are mostly simple actions of "quiet encroachment."[3]

In spite of the rigidity and the severity of the legal and prescriptive framework (which is itself part of the spreading of land and real-estate illegality) that is imposed by the authorities and that defines a legal city, the Egyptian authorities are manifestly tolerant toward illegal settlements. This tolerance can be considered as de facto recognition thereof; however, it does not prevent these authorities from despising the inhabitants, sometimes threatening them, and regularly stigmatizing them.

Because of the expansion of these districts and their high population density, the utilities that they progressively obtain, and the very low number of demolitions, we can conclude that the authorities eventually accept this situation and try to meet social demand—at least to a minimal extent. Does this tolerance exist 'to calm people down' or is it a means of keeping voters happy? That is another issue. However, if the inhabitants and creators of these illegal areas are 'opposed' to the authorities by the fact that they violate established laws and standards (sometimes by choice but mostly because they cannot do otherwise), they certainly do not act alone. They generally benefit from the 'complicity' (imposed or deliberate) of officials (of the administrative and technical system in particular) and, more generally and tacitly, the 'complicity' of key authorities (who adopt a laissez-faire attitude). This 'complicity' is demonstrated by the tolerance from which they benefit and the very low number of evictions in illegal areas. The creation of these illegal areas in particular, and the city in general, is thus the result of a 'co-production' (Berry-Chikhaoui and Deboulet 2000, 16) between the inhabitants and the authorities. Indeed, everything happens as if it is a kind of 'negotiated' and 'tolerated' urbanization.

Notes

1 In the 1980s, registration tax represented 12 percent of land value. It decreased progressively to reach 3 percent in 2003. Since 2006, to encourage registration, the government issued a law stipulating that this tax must not exceed LE2,000.

2 The land cost and that of the compensation for the use of the land can be paid in one payment or in several installments. However, according to Decree No. 77 of 1995 promulgated by the Council of Governors, at least 10 percent of the land price must be paid at the beginning of the regularization process. The balance can be paid over a period of fifteen years at a 4 percent interest rate. However, sometimes the monthly installments can be spread out over a period of forty years with a 6 percent interest rate (ILD and ECES 2000, 60).

3 Asef Bayat defines "the quiet encroachment of the ordinary" as "a silent, patient, protracted and pervasive advancement of ordinary people over property owners and the powerful in order to survive hardships and better their lives. They are marked by quiet, atomized, and prolonged mobilization with episodic collective action—an open and fleeting struggle without clear leadership, ideology, or structured organization, one that produces significant gains for the actors, eventually placing them in counterpoint to the state" (Bayat 1997, 7–8).

References

Bayat, Assef. 1997. *Street Politics: Poor People Movement in Iran*. Cairo: American University in Cairo Press.

Berry-Chikhaoui, Isabelle, and Agnès Deboulet, eds. 2000. *Les compétences des citadins dans le Monde arabe. Penser, faire et transformer la ville*. Paris: Karthala.

Deboulet, Agnès. 1996. "Devenir citadin . . . ou partir à la conquête des droits urbains élémentaires: exemples tirés des faubourgs récents du Caire." In Michel Lussault and Pierre Signoles, eds., *La citadinité en questions*. Research booklet no. 29, 141–57. Tours: URBAMA.

———. 1994. "Vers un urbanisme d'émanation populaire, compétences et réalisations des citadins, l'exemple du Caire." PhD diss., University Paris XII, Institut d'urbanisme de Paris.

De Certeau, Michel. 1990. *L'invention du quotidien*. Vol. 1. *Arts de faire*. Paris: Gallimard (Folio-Essais).

Denis, Eric. 1998. "De de Certeau à de Soto ou quand l'emphase sur la débrouillardise rejoint l'argumentaire des partisans du laisser-faire ajusté." In *Lettre d'Information de L'observatoire Urbain du Caire Contemporain* (OUCC), no. 48, 90–93.

Denis, Eric, and Marion Séjourné. 2002. "Information System for Informal Settlements (ISIS): First Assessment." Unpublished Policy Discussion Paper, Participatory Urban Management Programme, Egyptian Ministry of Planning, under GTZ-CEDEJ joint project. Cairo.

Durand-Lasserve, Alain. 1986. *L'exclusion des pauvres dans les villes du tiers monde, l'Harmattan.* Paris: Villes et Entreprises.

Florin, Bénédicte. 1999. "Itinéraires citadins au Caire. Mobilités et territorialités dans une métropole du monde arabe." PhD diss., Université François-Rabelais, Tours.

ILD, ECES (Institute of Liberty and Democracy, Egyptian Center for Economic Studies). 2000. "Formalization of Egypt's Urban Informal Real Estate Sector, Institutional Reengineering Stage, Situational Analysis." Unpublished report, Cairo.

El Kadi, Galila. 1987. *L'urbanisation spontanée au Caire.* Research booklet no. 18. Tours: Centre d'etudes et de recherches URBAMA.

Legros Olivier. 2003. "Le gouvernement des quartiers populaires. Production de l'espace et régulation politique dans les quartiers non réglementaires de Dakar (Sénégal) et de Tunis (Tunisie)." PhD diss., Université François-Rabelais, Tours.

Massiah, Gustave, and Jean-François Tribillon. 1988. *Villes en développement. Essai sur les politiques urbaines dans le Tiers Monde.* Paris: La Découverte.

Razzaz, Omar. 1993. "Examining Property Rights and Investments in Informal Settlements: The Case of Jordan." *Land Economics* 69:341–55.

Séjourné, Marion. 2011. "Loin de la marginalité, la "banalité" d'une urbanisation illégale aujourd'hui majoritaire d'habitat en Égypte." In Vincent Battesti and François Ireton, eds., *L'Égypte au présent. Inventaire d'une société avant la révolution.* Paris: Actes Sud.

———. 2006. "Les politiques récentes de traitement de l'urbanisation illégale au Caire: Nouveaux enjeux et configuration du système d'acteurs?" PhD diss., Université François-Rabelais, Tours.

El-Shorbagi, Monika. 2000. "Real Estate and Informal Practices in Greater Cairo." Unpublished report on the findings of Team 1 for the Institute of Liberty and Democracy, Cairo.

Sims, David. 2002. "What is Secure Tenure in Urban Egypt? "In Geoffrey K. Payne, ed., *Land, Rights and Innovation: Improving Tenure Security for the Urban Poor,* 79–99. London: ITDG Publishing.

Sims, David, and Marion Séjourné. 2008. *The Dynamics of Peri-urban Areas around Greater Cairo: A Preliminary Reconnaissance.* Washington, D.C.: World Bank.

———. 2000. "Residential Informality in Greater Cairo: Typologies, Representative Areas, Quantification, Valuation and Causal Factors." Unpublished report, Egyptian Center for Economic Studies (ECES), Institute of Liberty and Democracy (ILD), Cairo.

5

Vertical Versus Horizontal: Constraints of Modern Living Conditions in Informal Settlements and the Reality of Construction

Franziska Laue

U rban Syria is one of numerous examples worldwide of a city deal- ing with the issue of rapid urbanization, as well as urban formal and uncontrolled informal growth.[1] Alarmingly, this contributes to ever increasing 'costs' in terms of land consumption, environmental damage, and infrastructural needs. Syrian cities are continuously expand- ing, mainly at their urban fringes. Besides demographic growth and rural–urban migration, Syria's larger cities are growing while rural areas are gradually losing their population. With the rate of urbanization increasing from 51 percent to 61 percent in the next twenty-five years (Meinert 2007), projections for municipal development suggest that Syria's urban population will increase from 12.1 million (2010) to 18.3 million (2025) people (UN-Habitat 2006). Due to a current average pop- ulation growth of 2.5 percent, and the Syrian state's near-total monop- oly on public real-estate and housing programs, the country faces a demand of about 120 thousand flats per year (Seifan 2010). So far, the state cannot provide sufficient compensation for the increasing demands of a growing population. The two cities most affected by rapid urban- ization and informal growth are Damascus (rural and urban) and Aleppo. Other, medium-sized cities, such as Homs, Latakia, and Tartous are also facing a similar process.

The existence of informal settlements in Syria is not a recent phenomenon; it dates back to the first half of the twentieth century, as described by Klaus Dettmann (1969) and René Danger (1936) among others. Today, informal settlements alone currently account for about 45–50 percent of the existing urban space in Damascus and Aleppo. While Syria has the lowest percentage of 'slum' population in the Arab region, at only 10 percent, it also has to contend with a high annual growth rate in its slum population (3.2 percent, 1990–2001, according to UN Habitat 2006). Informal settlements in particular are experiencing shortcomings in technical infrastructure and social services, which place an extra burden on people's incomes and living conditions. The phenomenon of moving and settling in cities together with the economic pressures that have multiple effects on those same trends have become a growing area of interest for researchers of different scientific disciplines.

In this chapter I will discuss the issue of urban informality as a spatial and built result of complex global and local processes from an architectural point of view. Here Damascus is the focus. As the subject of informal settlements is a very complex one, I focus mainly on technical aspects of the creation of new informal housing and its characteristics by describing the built transformation over approximately seven years. More precisely, current prevalent types of housing and constructions out of concrete will be analyzed through a selected neighborhood in the Syrian capital called Jeramana.

Background and Research

This article discusses an extract from a comparative study analyzing urban informality in the capitals of Bangladesh, Burkina Faso, and Syria. For each city, ten different sites were chosen in order to analyze and contrast the different cases within the area of informality in a spatial and architectural context. The comparative study helped to create an overview of different aspects of urban informality in the sphere of housing and construction, from essential needs for shelter to higher standard housing causing law violations.

In the study, categories have been developed covering the observations in the three cities with the help of a systematized structure of analysis (technical and social) to find common criteria to help define informality within a global context. The findings have been compared with each other in order to elaborate an understanding of solutions and innovations undertaken by the new urban population on different levels and in different contexts, especially in the field of construction and spatial organization and mutual negotiation.

Case Studies in Damascus

Despite a great number of similarities across cities, urban informality varies not only from country to country but from city to city within the same country. Certain characteristics of informal settlements in Damascus might not necessarily be applicable to those of other Syrian cities.

In 2006, an analysis by Dirasat[2] estimated that there were thirty-one informal settlements in Damascus.[3] At that time, qualitative and quantitative categorizations had not been identified.

Therefore, for the purposes of our research, eight areas were visited and analyzed with different degrees of intensity and at different times in order to illustrate the differing characteristics of informal settlements within Damascus, be it on public land through squatting or on private land through the subdivision of agricultural land. All these settlements, which differ in terms of urban pattern, density, social and ethnic structure, building height, size, and so on, are: Qassiun area, al-Qaboun, Bustan al-Ruz in Dummar, Tabala and Dweila, Kafr Sousseh, and northeast of Yarmouk.

In addition, informal code violations that take place in areas within the central old and new city are analyzed.[4] This helped to gain an overview of the diverse informal activities surrounding individual construction work. These code violations relate to the creation of additional stories, transforming garage spaces into shops, and so on. One relevant lesson deriving from this comparative study is that urban informality in Syria is not limited to the poor segments of society but also includes middle-class groups. Urban informality describes an ongoing phenomenon in which various factors contribute to a form of urban development that increasingly takes place informally, and often arising from the discrepancy between the growing demand for land and housing and the insufficient supply by the authorities. The case of the Jeramana neighborhood reveals this noncompliance despite its moderate, yet diversified social structure.

Focal Study Area: Jeramana

This section describes the built environment in one specific part of a Damascene town, Jeramana, on whose fringe an ongoing informal densification is taking place. Specifically, the covered area of two streets was observed over a period of seven years (2003–2010), and will serve as the basis of analysis for the discussion that follows. While other settlements might represent more 'dramatic' features of urban informality, the selected area in Jeramana proved, however, to be an interesting example of the recent expansion at the fringes of Damascus's urban sphere and the transformation of land use. Beginning in 2003, the area has been picked to illustrate the mechanisms of informal urban growth in Syria. A team of ten architecture students, supervised by Dr. Sonja Nebel from the Habitat Unit at the Technical University of Berlin (TUB), undertook a week of fieldwork there, which included measuring the area, conducting interviews, and carrying out an analysis of the town's social, technical, and economic infrastructure. A representative street was selected in order to illustrate the following: stages of construction and densification, mechanisms of vertical and horizontal development and transformation, density of living space, and analysis regarding priorities regarding space, privacy, and relation to the neighborhood.

Jeramana: An Example of Urbanizing Damascus

New settlements in Damascus are typically created in one of four categories:
1. The development inside the administrational borders of the city, filling vacant land.
2. At the urban periphery up to twenty kilometers from the city center. In this case, agricultural borders date back to land reform decisions taken in 1958.
3. The horizontal expansion and vertical densification of existing urban quarters, that is, Muhajirin neighboorhood, Midan, and so on.
4. The expansion of existing villages in 'Rif Dimashq,' transforming and sealing the fertile land in favor of new habitable ground, as the case of Jeramana reveals.

The selected research area of Jeramana represents the type of urban expansion which consists of consolidated informal construction on illegally subdivided agricultural land. Its legal status arises from an informality "resulting from non-compliance of land-use and planning regulations, including a lack of consideration of urban boundaries" (Fernandes 2008).

Jeramana, originally a village, is located about twenty kilometers southeast of the city center, surrounded by the fertile oasis Ghouta (Fig. 5.2).[5] The area now contains the main con-urban corridor, which is dramatically converting agricultural lands for residential and industrial use. As is evident on maps from the first half of the twentieth century,[6] Jeramana was not originally a part of the urban agglomeration of Damascus, but

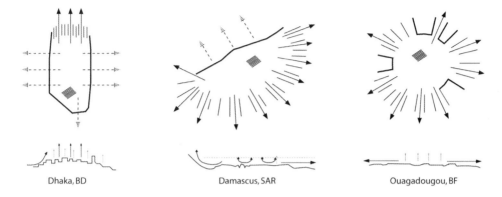

Fig. 5.1: Expansion schemes of of three capitals. Illustrations by Mareike Boller and Franziska Laue, 2007.

over the last fifty to sixty years the space between the village and the city fringes has been continuously filled with new settlements.[7]

As a result of the establishment of the Jeramana refugee camp in 1948, and its growth toward the fertile land in the south, an increasing densification has taken place at the borders from both sides since the 1950s. The city and the village developed to become continuously larger over the years until they finally merged together.

The original inhabitants belonged mainly to the Druze community and increasingly they have been joined by more Druze from parts of southern Syria, such as Suweida. In addition, Jeramana has traditionally attracted mixed groups of residents, including Christians, Muslims, young families, and students who are in search of affordable housing, whether they are moving within the urban sphere (from Bab Sharqi, Bab Touma, Tabala, and Dweila), or moving long distance (from Suweida, Latakia, and so on). At least 80 percent of the house owners are originally from Suweida and its environs, and rent their flats out. Today, Greater Jeramana hosts one of the largest Christian communities in Damascus. Since 2007, a growing number of Iraqi refugees, initially on the lookout for short-term accommodation (Dorai 2007),[8] have contributed to further growth beyond the borders of modern Jeramana and other fringe areas. This caused rents in Jeramana to rise by more than 40 percent.[9] As the current political situation is not stable in Iraq, many refugee families end up postponing their

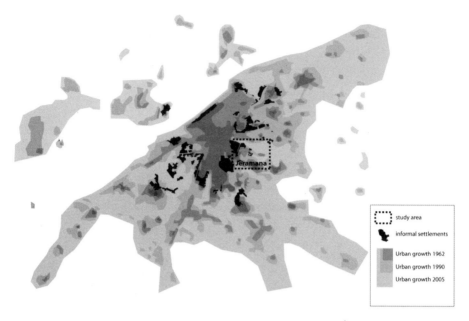

study area

informal settlements

Urban growth 1962

Urban growth 1990

Urban growth 2005

Fig. 5.2: Stages of urban development in Damascus and location of informal settlements.
Map by Mareike Boller and Franziska Laue, 2007 (after Balanche 2006).

return to their places of origin to an unknown date, becoming another
group of inhabitants in Jeramana.

While the rate of Jeramana's population growth rose from 0.47 percent in 1981–94 to 4.52 percent in1994–98 (Nebel 2003), the growth rate
of the specific region under study reached about 5.3 percent per annum
(1994–2004). Jeramana is now considered to be one of Damascus's outlying settlements, with a population growth that is higher than the average
growth rate for Syria as a whole. Despite the fact that the area has reached
an urbanization ratio of 100 percent, its settlements will have a continuing urbanization potential due to an accelerating population growth trend
(JICA 2007).

The spatial, architectural, and social situation of Greater Jeramana is
complex. Different factors, including social and regional origin, the time
and motivation available for setting up houses and apartments, as well as
the resulting spatial architectural and urban organization can be discerned
through the following: (1) the original village that is located about eight
kilometers from the city's administrative border, (2) the refugee camp as
an extension of urban structures, and (3) the gradual densification of space
between village and camp.

In contrast to the design and system of urban fabric for the 'ville nouvelle',[10] which was created and developed during and after the French mandate, the guiding principle for these new urban patterns is now based on the existing natural borders of farmland, especially for those parts of the city that are currently 'planned' or under construction beyond the parameters of official agreements. The general effect for the city is fatal: the continuous sealing of ground, as it can be observed around Jeramana, is threatening the provision of national natural resources such as fertile land for crops, vegetables, fruits, and timber.

Long Term Observation of Jeramana (2003–2010)

The neighborhood of Jeramana was subject to observations and analysis for over seven years. Each year, updates concerning physical change, spatial growth, and vertical additions were made. In 2003, the area was subject to field research with a focus on on two streets: Gurban Street and Kashkul Street, which marked the end of the built settlement at that time, verging on the fields of Damascus's oasis (Ghouta). In 2004 and 2006, I revisited and reviewed the site,[11] and registered changes and extensions to add to the overall research data gathered thus far. At that time, this particular area did not face any significant horizontal expansion toward arable land, except for a small number of newly built blocks. However, one remarkable innovation was the phenomenon of basements being added to the new constructions or foundation pits.

Another field visit in 2008 revealed increased building activities on both sides of the main road. The most significant progress was the creation of a newly constructed block layer moving toward the fertile land of the Ghouta. Some constructions from 2003 have now been complemented with additional floors and have been subjected to a range of transformations to their façades. The street has since been paved. In 2010, the neighborhood around the two streets became consolidated and densified as an urban area to such an extent that the Ghouta's proximity is no longer noticeable. Five visits over the years allowed a medium-term observation of this area as a built and social environment. This observation not only represents common changes in construction methods and tendencies within the formal and informal building sector in Syria, it also reveals legal changes and the people's ability to adapt to them. The details of the changing construction methods will be discussed on the following pages.

Zooming into the Study Area

Thus, the case of Jeramana reveals the nature of the changes and adaptation that have taken place on several levels. An area of about one square kilometer was observed for its continuous densification and for the changes in construction methods that had occurred in the area after follow-up visits each year (Fig. 5.3). This area, located northwest of the original village, represents the third type of densification on agricultural ground. The illegal subdivision of the fertile land makes this neighborhood an informal part of the Jeramana neighborhood, while the construction of the houses follows a general consensus among the different stakeholders regarding the building process. This rather small part of the whole township, called Harat al-Abu Mazer, which developed in the late 1990s, caused an increased pace of construction activity in the neighborhood as well as speculation within the broader surrounding area. This part of the informal area developed along smaller roads following the borders of former fields (Figs. 5.3 and 5.6). However, it is an integrated part of the "Plan for General Organization of the Jeramana Community for 2020" (Jermana Municipality 2003). It started out with self-help architecture and real-estate-developer-based multistory-blocks built directly adjacent to each other, a pattern still visible today. The single-story houses, though, tend to be replaced by the more profitable multistory buildings as can be seen in the 3-D illustrated growth study (Fig. 5.4).

Built space   Streets

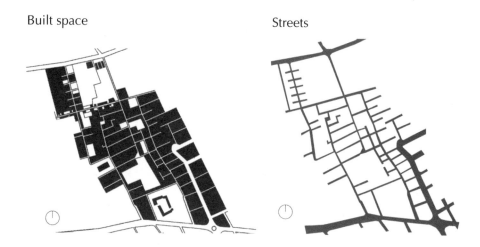

Fig. 5.3: Urban patterns and organization of a site in Jeramana. Illustrations by Mareike Boller and Franziska Laue, 2006 (after TU Berlin, Habitat Unit seminar on Urban Upgrading in Jermana, 2003).

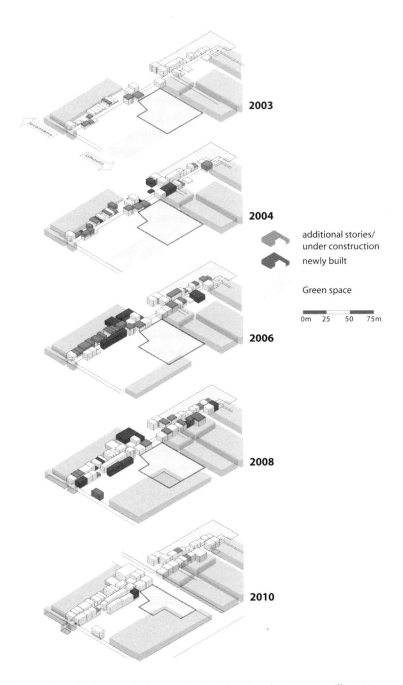

2003

2004

additional stories/
under construction

newly built

Green space

0m   25   50   75m

2006

2008

2010

Fig. 5.4: Growth study of a street in Jeramana (Harat Abu Mazer) 2003–2010. Illustrations
by Mareike Boller, Franziska Laue, and Anas Mohammad, 2010.

Spatial and Technical Features of the Study Area

As observed on site and within the site's broader neighboring areas, the prevailing trend is of maximum use of the purchased land in order to maximize the enclosed interior space. Privacy is an issue for house-builders and this manifests itself in building trends that favor interior, private space as opposed to public ones. This not only has a tendency to lead to the construction of buildings that can be vertically extendable, but also results in an enormous reduction of open spaces between buildings. In most cases, people's informal negotiations lead to compromises, which contribute to minimal forms of vacant outlets for the provision of ventilation and some lighting for the lower stories in the event of the gradual construction of buildings adjacent to each other.

This case study clearly attests to a strong demand for flexibility from inhabitants and developers to adapt to new and everchanging situations in high-densifying areas. Free lots exist side by side with buildings. A 3-D growth study has been prepared to illustrate this fact over several years (2003–2010) (see Fig. 5.4).

Constraints Versus Flexibility

There are several constraints that affect the creation of new settlements as well as the quality of housing, especially in informal settlements; these are technical, political, social, financial, mental, and cultural in nature. There is a growing tendency for young families to choose to live in separate, smaller social groups, as this has become more affordable, especially in newer parts of the city such as Jeramana. Nevertheless, despite the trend toward individualism in Syrian society, family ties are still very strong. Families prefer to keep their members as a part of their households or at least within the neighborhood. They do this by reserving space in their houses or premises, such as providing an additional floor above existing apartments. This reservation of space is based on mid-term and long-term planning considerations such as transforming the ground floor or basement into a commercial area or a new apartment for other family members.

As interviews (Laue and Boller 2006/2007) in the observation area in Jeramana revealed in 2003,[12] the financial circumstances of house owners are a major constraint strongly affecting the built structure. This factor varies regionally, locally, and, in this particular area, even from household to household. This forces house-builders to take decisions and set priorities for how their buildings should be constructed, by whom, and within which period of time, causing families to keep their homes open to further extension within any given space. Still, in each case a household's income as the basis of purchase and finance can be influenced by other factors that make decision-making more flexible. One such factor is a social one, as when households enter into negotiations with other potential stakeholders, extended family members, and so on, in order to bolster their finances.

In terms of the choice and availability of materials, constraints arise mainly from landowners and the manufacturers of different goods. There are local differences regarding the availability, quantity, and quality of raw materials for use on the construction site and the distance from producers is also an important issue for house builders. While the existence of natural stone such as basalt or limestone in other regions can reduce the costs of producing concrete blocks, Damascus relies heavily on their manufacture on site. One sign of flexibility is the movement of production sites for different construction items in tandem with the expanding urban areas. These reduce transport costs, since the use of concrete blocks and reinforced frame construction building materials for the housing sector is quite similar within the wider Arab world. Its production is optimized and large amounts can be manufactured in a considerably short period of time. Similarly, merchants trading in supportive parts such as doors and windows, frames, fences, and so on, also set up shop in these expanding neighborhoods. In this regard, new construction sites become sources of economic activity providing opportunities for additional household income through job opportunities, such as the need for day labor.

Another constraint arises from the principle of frame construction, which is based on a rigid rectangular system (Fig. 5.5). In combination with concrete blocks as filling materials, it allows for only limited architectural shapes and simple cubature. Nevertheless, the use of simple and stable grid structures based on rectangular principles, easily conceptualized by the naked eye, simplifies construction and technical sequences, thereby shortening the time period required for construction and providing an additional flexibility of its own. Another source of flexibility evident in this construction method is the technical freedom it awards the builder to add new stories in several phases on constructively solid floors, and the freedom to organize and reorganize interior space contained within the frame construction. This is easily done through the subsequent shifting of walls and openings (windows, doors, courtyards, loggias, and so on) and the flexible reorganization of the exterior surface such as openings and cantilevers.

Constraints arising from plot shapes are a result of the nature of the subdivision of farmland. In Jeramana, constraints of urban arrangement are created by the boundaries of agricultural fields, traditional and modern roads, and of the courses of rivers that traverse the region (Fig. 5.6). On the one hand this works to prevent the optimal use of ground space due to residual areas that have triangular or semicircular shapes. On the other hand, in order to be flexible, constructors developed the concept of constructing frames out of concrete, allowing buildings to adjust to almost any irregular shape, as long as the techniques and dimensions allow for spatial usage (Fig. 5.5).

Another constraint is climate, which in turn leads to the adaptive use of openings, open space, and materials, which goes hand in hand with the other kinds of flexibility mentioned above. The tendency to construct vertically and to use industrially produced rather than naturally occurring materials is dominant in present building activities in nearly all Damascene quarters. In modern building processes, steel, concrete,[13] cement, aluminum, and other synthetic materials have replaced traditional materials such as clay, timber, stone, and lime for single- and multistory houses. Despite house-builders' preference for lightweight concrete blocks these houses generally lack appropriate insulation from the exterior climate. As a result, modern facilities for heating and cooling are needed to compensate for the walls' energy inefficiency, where traditional building materials such as clay would have a greater capacity to preserve heat during winter months and let it out in the summer.

The approach to technical construction so described can be regarded as one that applies to the entire city—whether in formal or informal districts. Nonetheless, there are considerable variations in the quality of the final buildings—in terms of the amounts and correct combinations of building substances, manufacturing quality, assembly, and so on. In the case of the

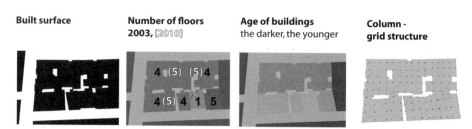

Graphs by Mareike Boller, Franziska Laue, 2010,(based on Szubert/Becker/Laue 2003)

Fig. 5.5: Plans of construction of a built example in Jeramana. Illustrations by Mareike Boller, Franziska Laue, 2010.

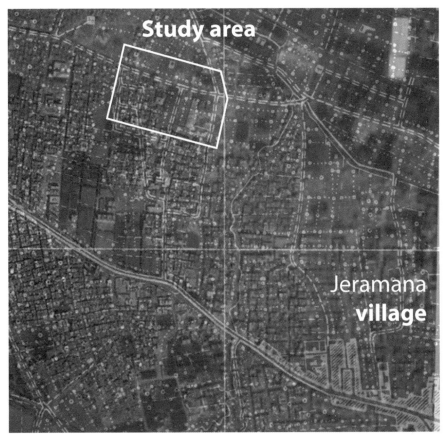

Fig. 5.6: Study area and overlapping of farm borders of Jeramana. Map by Mareike Boller and Franziska Laue, 2007.

Jeramana study area, there is a considerable mix of high-quality construction (especially construction which is not based merely on the urgent need for housing, but on real-estate speculation by developers as well) alongside low-quality, self-help modes of construction. Thus, informal construction is not necessarily a sign of poverty, although a general lack of resources is widespread. The case of Jeramana represents this increasing use of modern, affordable technologies and methodologies by those households with lower- and medium-income levels.

An interim observation resulting from the long-term study of the Jeramana neighborhood is that gradual densification and physical development aside, the quality of construction, infrastructure, and general appearance of the neighborhood has improved as well—in terms of paved streets, social and technical infrastructure, and diversification of building-material and land use. It has clearly become an integrated urban area, leaving the urban fringe well behind.

Horizontal Versus Vertical

The instrument of comparative research is generally helpful in providing different views on a specific subject. In the case of informal settlements, comparative research makes sense at both the local and regional levels. Further, research at the global level provides insight into superordinated mechanisms related to informal housing actitivities, ones detached from local contexts.

National comparison

As already stated above, local comparisons among Syrian cities, for example, Aleppo, Homs, or Latakia provide an immediate understanding of national and local mechanisms and issues. Taking the case of Aleppo, the second largest city in Syria after Damascus, significant differences arise, especially in terms of construction heights, the use of building and finishing materials, informally grown urban patterns, spatial distribution and segregation, social affiliation, and population density. In Aleppo, construction methods differ in terms of quality within informal settlements as much as they do in Damascus—one can find well-constructed houses on large plots with good infrastructure, as well as high-density areas with poor construction safety and all ranges in between. Land subdivision takes place on a larger scale than in Damascus, creating land plots with regular grid structures. The municipal area of Aleppo has a total of twenty-eight areas that are classified as informal. A recent study, undertaken by the Municipality of Aleppo, supported by the Gesellschaft für Technische Zusammenarbeit GmbH (GTZ), placed informal settlements within three categories of density—high (six settlements), medium (fourteen settlements), and low (eight settlements) (GTZ 2009). Furthermore, they have been categorized in four groups (Wakely 2008): upper income and illegal (Type 1), safe medium density (Type 2), unsafe high density (Type 3), mixed safe and unsafe (Type 4). One significant difference from Damascus is the common use of natural stone as solid building material (rubble masonry) or as façade cladding. The material is affordable and is transported from stone pits. Another significant characteristic is the existence of high-rise buildings with low-quality construction (Type 3). The absence of any structural reinforcements makes the construction highly unstable.

International comparison

In the comparative research between the capitals of Bangladesh, Burkina Faso, and Syria two overall types of housing construction have been defined: (a) temporary and (b) permanent. During the course of our research it became clear that the meaning of these two characteristics varied considerably across regions. These two opposites refer not only to materials used in construction but also to the use made of the built structures and their surroundings. In Syria, low-income house builders tend to use permanent building materials, such as concrete, brick, stone, timber, and so on, which is also the case in Burkina Faso. However, urban inhabitants on lower incomes in Bangladesh rarely have access to any affordable solid building materials such as stone, timber, or bricks. It is the combination of solid building materials and viable construction method that enables the house owner to expand vertically. In this regard there is also a significant difference between Burkina Faso and Syria. The use of load-bearing frames with foundations for self-help housing purposes is more widespread in Syria. As already discussed, it enables a more secure vertical extension such as the addition of another story, but it is also based on the traditional building of several stories, as seen in the historical cities of Syria. In Damascus, for example, multistory housing is a result of both high densification and a common organization of space that has been used over centuries by households from different social levels.

In contrast, house owners in Burkina Faso rarely use frame construction to create multistory construction. Self-help housing as well as some of the housing that is built as part of a project are mainly oriented toward horizontal development and extension. The spatial constraints that would otherwise compel house-builders to expand vertically are nonexistent, as a result of a seemingly endless supply of land and few natural and topographical borders. Moreover, the form of urban evolution has been traditionally single-story oriented. The equal value and adjacent structuring of private open space and enclosed private space within one compound creates a spatial and territorial entity and this is supported by virtue of its separation from the public open space through a wall. This system is predominant all over the city of Ouagadougou, which, for centuries, was the traditional urban cradle of the Mossi kingdom.

The urban reality in Bangladesh is even more extreme. The ability of lower-income groups to construct vertically depends very much on their access to land of an appropriate size. Dhaka is an extremely densified city, surrounded by natural borders such as rivers and deltas that prevent the city from expanding horizontally. Further urban development has prevailingly been vertically oriented, causing enormous land speculation. This becomes visible in the extremely dense historic city center of Dhaka; with plots sized at 40 m² holding six-story buildings (Laue and Boller 2006/2007). The lack of free, legal, and habitable land for the new settlers in Dhaka causes them to seek any available land space, even if it is illegal. These people have neither the financial capacity to construct solid housing nor the requisite geographical urban environment that would allow them to settle down as fully respected citizens. Furthermore, the use and affordability of solid building materials are very limited as the threat of eviction toward settlers is extremely high.

Nevertheless, the principle of frame constructions filled with brickwork is used in all three capital cities. Moreover, this type of construction can be found internationally in many developing countries, as it provides a very simple yet flexible way of creating vertical housing in a short period of time using globally accessible materials with internationalized cubatures. The main difference across countries tends to be with respect to the affordability of materials and therefore the extent to which different income groups can access them. Another difference concerns the type of the brickwork used: concrete blocks in Syria and Burkina Faso, fired bricks in Bangladesh, and pressed bricks in Burkina Faso. Furthermore, inhabitants of informal settlements in Ouagadougou construct mainly single-story houses, using clay bricks, which are increasingly being replaced by lightweight concrete blocks. In Dhaka, however, inhabitants of lower income areas and slum clusters use burned clay bricks, often in combination with a wide range of different nonsolid materials.

The principle, however, that can be found in all regions is the use of brick construction, with or without a load-bearing frame. Low-income groups in Burkina Faso and Bangladesh also tend to employ rural spatial techniques when creating housing in the city. Brick construction can be regarded as the lowest affordable level of solid housing construction. Technically speaking, access to a load-bearing frame construction is dependent on its general acceptance and affordability within different levels of the society. The use of frame construction still remains inaccessible to lower income groups in Bangladesh and Burkina Faso, remaining the sole preserve of upper income groups and the private and public construction sectors. Additionally, the lack of effective family networks capable of pooling together financial resources could also be a factor preventing its use in both countries.

In contrast, the case of Syria shows that a broader range of society has access to this construction type, including the inhabitants of informal settlements. It allows for flexibility in terms of self-regulated construction according to climate, adaptation to different topographical locations, and further expansion. The combination of affordability, tradition, and high densification is what is at stake for the cities of Bangladesh and Syria. In conclusion, raising the height of existing buildings only represents affordability in those countries and regions where construction methods have been traditionally predisposed to multistory buildings, high rates of densification therefore telling only part of the story. Thus, in Burkina Faso, multistory buildings are simply not a tradition, whereas in Bangladesh and Syria they have been developed over centuries.

Standards Versus Consensus

The informal urbanization process in Syria definitely includes the vertical growth of buildings. If financially capable, within one or several construction phases, house owners tend to build their houses with a view to future floor and room extensions as described above. This leads to the question of standards within the context of informal housing construction, especially that which is carried out by house-builders on lower incomes. Standards basically describe the technical and spatial guidelines that identify how a manufactured product, a material, and consequently a building with its urban surroundings should be planned, produced, and used. As soon as guidelines are formulated, they give rise to conflicts over what should be the minimum requirements of building standards and how regulations should be implemented. It is necessary to distinguish between relevant national or international standards in terms of construction and a regional consensus over building habits, and 'objective versus subjective' aspects. Multistory housing may demonstrate fusions of international or national standards, older building traditions, and more recently developed, locally specific habits.

Nonetheless, there are similarities of construction methods worldwide, based on a mix of identical methods that can easily be implemented, even with limited financial resources. Similar methods may draw on pragmatic or consensual decision-making, or compromises over how buildings should be built in the regional or local context, while respecting certain aspects relating to openings, social codes, the use of materials, and so on.

However, standards should be flexible and must relate to the local context, particularly with respect to materials used, spatial conception, and safe construction methods. The relevance of each component may vary—according to the capacities and financial background of the constructor, the technical needs of the location (earthquake, floods, storms, and so on), the minimum required standard of constructive, and therefore physical, stability, and the social climate. This may lead to rules that do not necessarily have to be defined as general standards. This creation of standards is useful in the sense of guaranteeing an environment for controlled construction and densification, to ensure an enhanced quality of living and even encourage a debate about what is 'legal' and 'illegal.'

Informal standards and compromises become important for the creation of a 'minimum' of an optimum construction for lower income households and the maintenance of buildings for lasting and secure use and inhabitation.

In the discussion surrounding the creation of acceptable living habitats, even the least demanding standards tend to exclude certain groups. Usually defined as low income, they do not have the financial, human, and economic resources to meet theoretical obligations due to a strong limitations to their ability to construct adequate housing. For example, it is not possible to speak of standards in relation to many of the single-story buildings that can be found in the informal peripheries of the city. In areas of Damascus, where there are lower levels of financial tolerance and flexibility, builders tend to provide the most basic and fastest methods of construction. The technical aspects, style, and appearance of the constructions are the pragmatic outcome of trial and failure, of optimized working and construction processes. Single-story blockhouses are one of the cheapest and most flexible construction types possible and can easily be replicated and transferred to any plot size.

A discussion of standards covering the entire range of existing housing is therefore difficult, especially in areas where limited resources are accompanied by the use of less durable and alternative materials, namely carton, plastic bags, bamboo, and so on (Fig. 5.7). Hence on the one hand, it makes sense to discuss standards on a global level, because urban growth is a global phenomenon. On the other hand, standards always have to be weighed alongside the reality of the accessibility of resources in each country or region. Can the load-bearing frame structure be a basis for a minimum criterion for standards for safe housing? What are the minimum demands for this version of frame construction? How can this be made more affordable within the local context and especially for lower income parts of society?

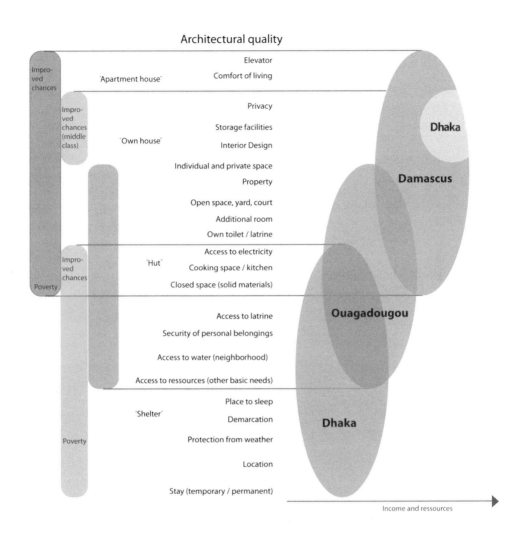

Architectural quality

Improved chances

Improved chances (middle class)

Improved chances

Poverty

Poverty

"Apartment house"

"Own house"

"Hut"

"Shelter"

Elevator
Comfort of living

Privacy

Storage facilities

Interior Design

Individual and private space

Property

Open space, yard, court

Additional room

Own toilet / latrine

Access to electricity

Cooking space / kitchen

Closed space (solid materials)

Access to latrine

Security of personal belongings

Access to water (neighborhood)

Access to ressources (other basic needs)

Place to sleep

Demarcation

Protection from weather

Location

Stay (temporary / permanent)

Dhaka

Damascus

Ouagadougou

Dhaka

Income and ressources

Fig. 5.7: Definition of architectural quality (based on observations). Illustrated by Mareike Boller and Franziska Laue, 2007.

Thus, the challenges for architects are enormous. They must reconcile a host of conflicting and competing issues: top-down planning schemes, bottom-up community participation, upgrading or beautification and enhancement, and basic human needs in the dwelling unit and on theoretical levels.

The Architect's Role and Informality

Today, the public is still ambivalent about the role of architects and engineers in society, partly because architects and engineers are *themselves* ambivalent about their commitment or otherwise to their precise role—as contributors with creative solutions, as members of the society, as technical consultants, and so on. Basically, architects are expected to use their knowledge and skills in order to provide house dwellers with their basic needs, balanced with the idea of a healthy habitat, optimized space, and a sound urban environment.

In terms of construction alone, engineers and architects are currently only partly involved in the entire building process in informal settlements on the professional level. In the case of Jeramana they function as informal consultants to the construction process. House builders replace them by drawing on a common knowledge of typical construction methods and adapting existing plans according to plot sizes and heights, physical accessibility, and so on, of already built examples provided by family members or neighbors. Plans and details end up being drawn to scales of between 1:100 and 1:50, thereby lacking essential details and information, as was the case in the study area in Jeramana. Implementation is carried out mainly according to experience.

From the technical point of view and in respect of the urgent need for intervention, architects and civil engineers (in both the private and public sectors) in particular have a role to play in raising awareness, by acting as advisors on plans, materials, calculation, and timetables, since they have practical knowledge regarding materials, building techniques, engineering methods, acoustics, climate control, statics, and so on. Given the fact that the modern-day realities of urban growth are not subject to master plans or any other static planning tool, the role of engineers, architects, and urban planners demands reconsideration on many levels. It is not sufficient that they work merely on new planning tools at the ministerial or central government level:[14] Engineers should be regarded as persons worthy of trust and must be involved in the work of local authorities, as well as that of neighborhood councils or broader regional advisory committees, preferably free of charge or supported by the local administration. Since dealing with informal settlements is new to engineers in local administrations, it is crucial to raise awareness of informal housing areas within the public sector.

In 2008, the Municipality of Aleppo became the first local administration in Syria to establish an informal settlements department. The department's engineers currently receive specialized training in the areas of adaptive planning and management and consultancy methods for informal settlements. At the political level, informal settlements have increasingly become the subject in recent years of discussions relating to proactive and reactive urban management. It has become obvious that ministries, international and local institutions, city councils, and so forth must be essential interactive stakeholders. For example, the Syrian Ministry for Local Administration (MLA), in cooperation with GTZ, began discussing recommendations for planning standards and codes within a sustainable urban development project for all Syria in 2008. Recommendations have also been made by the European Union's Municipal Administration and Modernization Programme (MAM) to not only enable transformations of national policy (laws) and establish special agencies within municipalities but also to involve the private sector and planning firms and consultancies in the process of transformative planning methodologies and strategies (MAM 2008).

At the moment, however, the gap for these professionals—between healthy urban growth and the provision of good, affordable housing for a growing urban population on low incomes—is a wide one. Hence, well-functioning social and local policies and strategies based on transparent research can help experts to react flexibly to the realities of urban growth and of existing social structures.

Conclusion

There is no question that informal settlements in Syria are increasingly the subject of scientific and strategic analyses and research in various disciplines. These studies should contribute to ongoing and future discussions and solutions, especially as the phenomenon of informal and uncontrolled urban growth will remain a major global challenge for the foreseeable future. This chapter sought to highlight the built and spatial constraints affecting the growth of informal settlements but also the opportunities created by the construction methods used in such an environment.

As long-term observation of Jeramana reveals, neighborhoods react to legal, urban, and demographic changes by flexibly adapting to their built environment. Concrete is a flexible and increasingly affordable source of building material for the basic structures of multistory buildings. On the one hand, this means the replacement by concrete of more traditional and ecologically efficient building materials. On the other hand, the use of concrete allows for a more flexible grid structure, since cement is affordable and associated labor costs reasonable. In this way even low-income areas can benefit from the enhancement of basic physical structures with the help of systematic and pragmatic solutions for housing, despite initial legal insecurity. As this type of construction allows for further upgrading within the given space at a later stage, so the bracing can be replaced with ecologically more effective materials. As described in the case of Jeramana, private constructors adjust their housing and construction methods over time and invest in enhancements despite demonstrable time pressures at the outset.

Urban sprawl will continue and thus there should be a common understanding and steering of the correct and sustainable use of these analyzed building techniques and materials in order to avoid unsafe buildings at city fringes. Even informal or illegal construction should provide physically secure shelter for its inhabitants. The question then arises as to whether the creation of guidelines can help avoid insecure informal housing in practical terms, particularly as building construction must take account of a complex web of interlocking political, legal, social, and economic constraints. This raises a further question in turn: who should be in charge of raising knowledge of careful but affordable construction in low-income areas? What is needed is an efficient and trustworthy urban administration, and responsive and effective planning. Time will tell if public bodies, with or without the collaboration of other public or private parties, will be able to find adequate management tools. Particularly in low-income informal settlements, wise and sustainable solutions should be elaborated—ones that find a balance between economic and administrative efficiency, socially inclusive management, and spatial and built planning services, on paper as well as on site.

Notes

1 With contributions by Mareike Boller and Anas Mohammad.
2 Dirasat, also called GCEC (General Company for Engineering Studies and Consulting), was founded in 1980. It is a state agency for real-estate planning and development, with one office in each governorate in Syria. The headquarters are in Damascus.
3 In 1995, a first analysis by Ziad Muhanna estimated a number of thirty-six informal settlements in Damascus. In 2006, the number had decreased by the merging of neighboring areas.
4 The study discussed ten areas, including parts of the planned city, such as Baghdad Street, as well as Old City quarters like Naqqashat.
5 Planners such as Écochard and Banshoya originally estimated the area of Ghouta to be in the region of 850 km². It was inhabited and farmed by

about 200,000 persons in 1960. At that time the rate of population growth in the Ghouta area was roughly in line with that of Damascus, leading to a growth to 450,000 inhabitants in Ghouta by 1984.

6   The plan is titled "Plan de Bureau Topographique des Troupes Françaises du levant, 1937: Plan de l'Institut Géographique International, France" and was drawn up in 1941.

7   Until 1977 the prohibition of building on irrigated fertile land was respected. In the following years an increase in the urban population placed a high demand on new housing space expanded the peripheries of the city, mainly in the Ghouta.

8   In 2005, 16,000 Iraqis lived in Jeramana; in 2008, 27,161 refugees had been counted by the UNHCR (Dorai, 2009).

9   "Syria: Iraqis Have Rough Ride, but Reluctant to Return. www.irinnews.org/Report/62538/SYRIA-Iraqis-have-rough-ride-but-reluctant-to-return; In-depth: The Long Journey Home: An IRIN In-Depth on the Challenge of Refugee Return and Reintegration." www.irinnews.org/InDepthMain.aspx?Country=Yes&InDepthId=16&ReportId=62538

10 R. Danger and M. Ecochard developed the urban master plan in the 1930s. Entire new neighborhoods were created and contrasted with the 'existing urban fabric.' One major aim of the plan was the complete reorganization of the infrastructure in favor of optimized traffic flow (Stockhammer 2009).

11 I visited the site in 2003, 2004, and 2006 together with Mareike Boller, Sonja Nebel, and Anas Mohammad; I conducted the visits of 2008 and 2010 with Anas Mohammad alone.

12 During the field visit in 2003, a systematic interview sheet was prepared. The interviews, though, were conducted in a casual and conversational style.

13 Following fast-growing industrialization after 1946, Syria became self-sufficient in the production of steel and concrete blocks.

14 Since 2008, activities have been undertaken by EU-MAM and GTZ's Urban Development program with the Municipality of Aleppo, and in the next phase will take place with the Ministry for Local Administration and Environment.

References

Balanche, Fabrice. 2006. "Damas la tentaculaire." *Villes et Territoires du Moyen Orient* no. 2, revue electronique de l'IFPO. http://www.ifporient.org/OU/VTMO.

Dahman, Fatima. 1999. "Informelle Siedlungsstrukturen und Wohnungstypologien: Selbsthilfe-Wohnungsbau in Aleppo und Mexiko-Stadt im Vergleich." PhD diss., University of Stuttgart.

Dettmann, Klaus. 1969. *Damaskus: Eine orientalische Stadt zwischen Tradition u. Moderne. Erlangen.* Erlanger geogr. Arbeiten, 26. Erlangen: Palm & Enke in Komm.

Dorai, Kamel. 2009. "L'exil irakien à Damas—Modes d'insertion urbaine et reconfiguration des réseaux migratoires." http://echogeo.revues.org.

———. 2007. "Iraqi refugees in Syria." http://www.aucegypt.edu/GAPP/cmrs/Documents/MohamedDorai.pdf.

The Economist Intelligence Unit Limited. 2007. *Syria—Country Profile 2007.*

ETH Studio Basel. 2009. "The French Mandate City." Draft paper by Wild Stockhammer. http://www.studio-basel.com/projects/beirut/damascus/student-work/the-french-mandate-city-(damascus).html.

Fernandes, Edesio. 2008. *Informal Settlements in Syria: A General Framework for Understanding and Controlling the Phenomenon.* Damascus: EU-MAM.

GTZ (Gesellschaft für Technische Zusammenarbeit GmbH), Aleppo Informal settlements task force. 2009. *Informal Settlements in Aleppo—Rapid Profile of All Informal Settlements in Aleppo.* Aleppo: GTZ.

Jermana Municipality. 2003. "Plan for General Organiztion of the Jermana Community for 2020." Unpublished municipal development plan, Damascus.

JICA (Japan International Cooperation Agency). 2010. *Project for Urban Planning and Development of Damascus Metropolitan Area in the Syrian Arab Republic*—Project Progress Report 1. Damascus: JICA.

———. 2007. *The Study on Urban Planning for Sustainable Development of Damascus Metropolitan Area in the Syrian Arab Republic*—Interim Report. Damascus: JICA.

———. 2003. *Country Profile Study on Poverty.* Planning and evaluation department. Damascus: JICA.

Laue, Franziska, and Mareike Boller. 2006/2007. "Stadt und Informalität—Urbane Studien in drei Hauptstädten." TU-Berlin diploma graduation paper, Habitat Unit.

MAM (Municipal Administration Modernisation). 2008. "Issues and Options Paper: Toward an Urban Transformation Law." Damascus. http://www.mamsy.org/userfiles/file/AP9/Urban%20Transformation%20&%20Regeneration%20Law%20review.pdf

Meinert, Günter. 2007. Minutes, Start-up Conference for GTZ-UDP. Rida Said Center, Damascus.

Mouhanna, Ziad. 2002. "The Informal Housing Areas in Damascus and Its Surroundings 'Problems and Solutions." Unpublished paper, Faculty of Architecture, Damascus University.

Nebel, Badwan. 2003. "Damaskus—Oase und Urbanisierung Über den Umgang mit knappen Ressources." In "Stadt und Wüste," *Trialog*, no. 76, 10–14.

Ranger, René, and Michel Écochard. 1936. "Damas: Rapport d'enquête mono-graphie sur la ville 1936." Unpublished copy in library, IPFO, Damascus.

Serageldin, Mona, and William Doebele. 1980. "Land Tenure Systems and Development Controls in the Arab Countries of the Middle East." In *Housing: Process and Physical Form*, 75–88. Geneva: Aga Khan Award for Architecture.

UNDP (United Nations Development Programme). 2007. *Human Development Report 2007/2008.* http://hdr.undp.org/en/media/HDR_20072008_EN_Complete.pdf.

UN-Habitat. 2006. *State of the World's Cities Report 2006/2007.* Nairobi: United Nations Human Settlements Programme.

UN Population Division. 2005. *World Urbanization Prospects: The 2005 Revision.* New York: United Nations. http://www.un.org/esa/population/publications/WUP2005/2005wup.htm.

Seifan, Samir. 2010. Interview by *Baladna English*, no. 216, 14 October.

Wakely, Patrick. 2008. *Informal Settlements in Aleppo.* Aleppo: Gesellschaft für Technische Zusammenarbeit GmbH (GTZ)–Aleppo Urban Development Project (UDP).

6

The Politics of Sacred Space in Downtown Beirut
(1853–2008)

Ward Vloeberghs

Beautiful or not, the Muhammad al-Amin Mosque (Fig. 6.1) is Lebanon's largest mosque. The view of its characteristically blue dome dominates the Beirut city center, and its construction of this mosque arguably marks the magnum opus of the late Rafiq Hariri, the former Lebanese prime minister assassinated in 2005. This new structure, in a pervasive way, transforms the immediate urban environment and embodies a politically meaningful evolution of the city's skyline.

This chapter will show how a prestigious building like this mosque, in its actual form, is the result of a confrontation with a number of norms that imposed themselves upon the built fabric. In other words, we will illustrate how various (legal, administrative, aesthetic, legal, religious) norms affected the (architectural and urban) form of the edifice. At the same time, we will also document the ways in which the physical form of the Muhammad al-Amin Mosque has impacted the environment that hosts it.

At first sight, the construction of this monumental mosque may appear to have little to do with informal building. Urban informality in Beirut, as any occasional visitor will probably argue, can be found across several areas and neighborhoods of this eastern Mediterranean port city but not within its nucleus, the Beirut Central District. Nevertheless, if we look into the details of this project's origins we find that several formal and informal

Fig. 6.1: General view of Muhammad al-Amin Mosque with Hariri's gravesite in front of it. Photograph by Ward Vloeberghs, 2009.

(legal) practices went into acquiring, claiming, and appropriating the land that accompanied the construction process and thus contributed to shaping the edifice into what it has become today: an intended benchmark of Islamic architecture in a symbolically most valuable part of Beirut.

By analyzing five different phases of this mosque's history,[1] I seek to show how this apparently extremely formal settlement has been the outcome of subtle negotiations relating to what at one point appeared to be no more than undeveloped and residual (although central) urban space. It is also my objective to illustrate how legality has been treated throughout a dynamic and surprising trajectory as a flexible given that could be accommodated according to the needs of the situation or as a function of the preferences of the respective actors. These five phases can be seen as five instances where sacred space is being negotiated. Throughout this overview, we will highlight the flexible and pragmatic attitude adopted by most of the actors involved toward legality as a set of fixed laws.

It is important and useful to clarify some of the title's terminology. First, by 'genesis of a mosque' I mean to indicate that I will be talking about the creation of a mosque. This covers the mosque's formation in a wide sense, from conception through to construction, inauguration, and use. In choosing the term 'negotiation' of space I wish to stress the fact that acquiring, defining, and appropriating urban space is an ongoing, dynamic process that involves more than a mere moment of price bargaining. The term 'sacred' is used in a broad sense and does not mean that the space under analysis is related exclusively to the realm of spirituality or religion. On the contrary, as we will show, although the mosque may seem to be a religious edifice, a great deal of political, judicial, and sociological dynamics are associated with its construction. Finally, 'downtown Beirut' refers to the specific part of the Lebanese capital in which the mosque has been built.

From *Zawiya* to *Jami'*: From Abu Nasr to Muhammad al-Amin (1853–1975)

The mosque's history dates back to at least 1933, since a document[2] recalls the presence of a *zawiya*,[3] named Zawiyat Abi Nasr, on a plot of land registered with the real-estate administration of Beirut in the sector of al-Marfa' (the Port). Little more is known about this place of worship related to Abu Nasr except that it had been operating since 1853 when the Ottoman sultan entrusted the land to Sheikh Muhammad Abu Nasr al-Yafi, as a gift to the Muslims of Beirut and in counterbalance to another plot he had presented to Lazarist nuns (Oger Liban 2008).[4]

Several sources mention commercial activity of a different nature on the same site. Chehab Eddine speaks explicitly of a "Suq Abu Nasr," also known as the Souk al-Moutran, where one could buy "colours, spices and oriental sweets" (Chehab Eddine 1960, 257). Other residents recall a so-called *qahwat al-izaz* (glass café) on the site where the mosque now stands.[5]

In the early-twentieth century several Sunni Beiruti families joined forces with the aim of establishing a place of worship at this location. From then on, the mosque project lived throughout several generations of Beirut's community of Sunni Muslims as a communal dream; it lived among the inhabitants in their collective imagination, in terms of spoken references and collection boxes where everyone could deposit his or her contribution to the project.

In order to grasp the significance and the impact of this project, it may be helpful to sketch the historical context in which Zawiyat Abi Nasr and the subsequent plans for the mosque emerged. This seems all the more relevant since discussions with Beirutis suggest that the attempt to establish a Sunni place of worship in this part of Beirut may have been a reaction against what many non-Christian Beirutis (and they were predominantly Sunni at the time) felt was an invasion of this emerging city by newly arrived missionaries during the second half of the nineteenth century.[6] Such an interpretation may be a bit one-sided but it is an undeniable fact that the arrival of western missionaries and their activities had a considerable impact on the daily lives of Beirut residents, and influenced, among other things, the existing power relations among elites of Beirut in the last quarter of the nineteenth century (Kassir 2004, Johnson 1986).

This historical context is important to bear in mind because it allows us to describe the construction of the mosque within a long-term perspective. However, this is certainly not the only dynamic at play, as the recorded history of the project suggests that the project was also caught up in an internal contest between different factions of Beirut's Sunni community. The identified document prepared by Dar al-Fatwa (an umbrella organization headed by the Mufti of the Lebanese Republic which represents the head of the Sunni administrative hierarchy) is crystal-clear about the mosque's origin, as it states explicitly that the Muhammad al-Amin Mosque was founded in the year 1933 under the name "Zawiyat Abu Nasr" on part 6 of parcel number 323 of the real-estate sector al-Marfa'.

Things are, however, less transparent when attempts are made to determine who exactly took which initiative in order to transform the existing *zawiya*, a *waqf* (religious endowment) administered by descendants of the Abu Nasr family,[7] into a full-fledged mosque.

A legal document provides us with more helpful information. On 26 Jumada II 1327/ 5 May 1948, the Sunni Supreme Court of Appeal of Beirut adjudicated the transfer of the tutelage of the mosque and the aforementioned *waqf* to the Directorate General of the Islamic Awqaf (DGIA). The very existence of such a ruling suggests that a dispute had ensued between the administrators of the *waqf* and the DGIA.

At this point, it is important to note that the document produced by the Dar al-Fatwa claims that in the years following the ruling of the tribunal, the Directorate General of Islamic Awqaf formed a committee "to care for and supervise matters related to the mosque."[8] According to the same document, this committee decided to found a "Muhammad al-Amin Association," which later obtained a permit from the Ministry of Interior and worked for the acquisition of plots adjacent to part 6 and on which the

DGIA intended to build "a large and appropriate mosque." The text then goes on to make a reproachful remark:

> the Association, however, proceeded to register the parts that it acquired with the contributions of the Muslims in the name of the Association instead of registering them in the name of the Directorate General of Islamic Awqaf.

Clearly, the text condemns the behavior of the Association and considers that its actions were the start of a problem that accounts for much of the delay in construction during the following decades. Nevertheless, the presentation made in the Dar al-Fatwa document is but one version of a more complex reality.

Another explanation for the inertia that hit the project seems to reside in a battle for influence between various factions of Beirut's Sunni community. It appears that the Muhammad al-Amin committee was founded in the early 1940s, and later (most likely around 1965) evolved into an 'association.'

This body consisted of members of several influential families within the Beirut Sunni establishment[9] and was indeed set up with the objective of raising funds for the acquisition of neighboring plots. However, crucially, it considered itself autonomous and, as such, acted independently from the DGIA—which it viewed as a rival institution.

As a consequence, the verdict by the Sunni Supreme Court of Appeal did not settle the dispute that had ensued between the Association and the DGIA. On the contrary, the Association contested the legality of the 1948 ruling in favor of the DGIA. It continued to pursue its own activities and had its newly acquired properties registered in its own name, which, as we have seen, was considered illegal by the DGIA on the grounds that it alone was the authority with the legitimacy to administer what it called "Muslim contributions."

Relations between the two bodies remained strained,[10] with both sides rallying for political backing from local and regional actors—thus worsening the situation rather than paving the way for a settlement of the dispute. Notwithstanding (or probably because of) the involvement of a vast network of local, national, and even international donors (including Egyptian president Gamal Abdel Nasser and King Faisal of Saudi Arabia, among other royal eminencies) the project did not materialize. A look at the *ifada 'aqariya* (real-estate notification) of parcel 323 attests to this bickering between 1966 and 2002.[11] That is not to say that plans were not elaborated; on the contrary, architectural schemes had been drawn up by the mid-1960s, and a billboard placed on the site made explicit the ambition to build a mosque there.

However, if during the 1960s the Muhammad al-Amin Association appeared to have been dominated by local political chiefs and clientelistic patrons in Beirut, during the last two decades of the twentieth century the Association—reflecting a wider trend among Muslim institutions—was reported to have been subject to growing Islamization (Mermier 2009; Rougier 2007).

Thus, as the second millennium drew to a close, few Beirutis could have guessed that a breakthrough in this ambitious project was near. This critical point was in fact arrived at through an accumulation of various factors.

The Controversy over Beirut Central District (1975–90)[12]
The birth of a company

A first, important, and quite spectacular factor that influenced the construction of the mosque was the development of the area surrounding it. That area is the Beirut city center, known as Beirut Central District (BCD). Although the city center comes across today as a homogenous neighborhood dominated by the sandstone color of its buildings, and may, as a consequence, provide the occasional visitor with a feeling of natural uniformity, the BCD is in fact the artificial result of a huge enterprise that entailed uncountable rounds of formal and informal negotiations at a multitude of levels.

As Nabil Beyhum (1992) and others have shown, all of these plans were—each in their own way—the expression of how the urban engineers intended to react to the socio-political alterations and the physical transformations brought about by the successive waves of hostilities arising from the fifteen-year-long Lebanese civil war.[13]

It is no coincidence that the mosque arose on its actual location; there are historical reasons for this choice. Moreover, this corner of Martyrs Square in downtown Beirut is a prime location in itself because of the special place it occupies in Lebanese historiography, as Najem maintains:

> the Beirut Central District is the most prized piece of property in Lebanon. During Lebanon's prosperous years (1950–1975) the city center was not only the heart of the country's economic, cultural and bureaucratic establishment, but it was also the financial and commercial center of the Middle East. It might even be argued that the center's prosperity confirmed Lebanon's success as a country (Najem 2000, 163).

It should come as no surprise, therefore, that as soon as the violence appeared to calm down in the early 1990s major efforts were deployed to bring this central part of the capital back to life. The reconstruction became a highly important issue that attracted much attention and was, at times, heavily debated by many different actors. Tom Pierre Najem puts it well, when he describes the political dimension of the reconstruction effort as follows:

> From a symbolic standpoint, rebuilding a center accessible to persons of all faiths would help to signify an end to the divisions in Lebanese society. . . . There has been a continuing belief among many observers of the Lebanese scene that those who dominate the city center will also dominate the rest of the country (Najem 2000, 164).

Among the figures who promoted such reconstruction plans, one was increasingly present on the Lebanese political scene—even though he remained out of the spotlight for the most part. That man, Rafiq Hariri, while mediating between belligerent factions with a mandate from the Saudi king Fahd bin Abdul Aziz Al Saud, had nourished his own vision of Beirut and dreamed of making the city rise up once again from the ashes. Years before the warfare had stopped, he had offered his logistical support to help clear the capital's rubble (Verdeil 2001). At the time, protests emerged to contest this contribution, arguing that the bulldozers were destroying valuable architecture rather than helping to clear the debris. The project to rebuild Beirut had, however, been in Hariri's mind since the early 1980s (Blanford 2006, 41).

A Lebanese entrepreneur, Hariri was the founder of a flourishing conglomerate with construction activities as its core business. He was determined to propose his services as well as his vast network of powerful friends for the purpose of rebuilding the Lebanese capital and had proved his skills and ambitions in his hometown of Sidon (Bonne 1995). Najem recalls that :

> the degree of Hariri's personal interest in the BCD's reconstruction was such that critics have suggested that it was one of the main factors behind his decision to make himself available as a candidate for the office of prime minister (Najem 2000, 164).

One of the main obstacles concerning reconstruction initiatives was the management of the property rights of the ruined, and in some cases partly abandoned, quarters of central Beirut. To deal with this problem, Solidere, The Lebanese Company for the Development and Reconstruction of Beirut Central District s.a.l., was set up in 1994, almost two years after Hariri became prime minister.[14] The purpose of this privately owned, real-estate company was to return Beirut to its prewar glory and to firmly re-establish the city as an attractive international center for the finance, business, culture, and tourist industries. The mere task of identifying property owners and documenting property certificates was a daunting one that led to fierce debate and contestation, particularly because of Hariri's simultaneously dominant position, in both the reconstruction project and in Lebanese politics.[15]

A contested transaction
The project proposed by Solidere for the rebuilding of the Beirut Central Disctrict[16] was not to the liking of several Lebanese, who did not hesitate to formulate their objections. In fact, from the very beginning, Solidere's proposal to compensate property owners in the form of shares in a new private company encountered much criticism. Two kinds of contestation emerged. The first was based on factual grounds (condemning urban anni-hilation and contesting ownership rights), while the second was a more ideological type of criticism.

To start with, a considerable and valuable part of the old city has been lost in what amounts, according to some, to an operation of major destruction:

> the demolition of three hundred buildings in the old city center, without determining whether they could be salvaged, generated a contrary feeling. What the fighting had not managed to destroy of the urban memory and the national heritage, the bulldozers of those reconstructing the city destroyed far more radically (Beyhum 1992, 52).

Furthermore, the opponents maintained that the appropriation of real estate by Solidere as well as the expropriation was "highly illegal,"[17] and a violation of the democratic rights of the owners and tenants of property because they had not been consulted or even been given the right to opt out.

The proponents of the plan defended the decision by saying it was the only feasible solution to enable reconstruction—a view that was once again contested by the critics of Solidere on the grounds that identical constraints had not prevented development elsewhere in Beirut.

These legal arguments laid bare a more philosophical kind of criticism about the ways in which reconstruction should be conceived:

If the objective is to transcend the war, then it must reverse the profound sociological changes caused by the war . . . . Reconstruction does not simply imply rebuilding but also includes social processes; . . . it is a process taking into account time, and is not merely a transformation of space. Reconstruction must act to regenerate urban society (Beyhum 1992, 44).[18]

Moreover, notwithstanding the conveniently altruistic meaning of its French homophone (*solidaire*), much of Solidere's actions suggest that its raison d'être is essentially commercial: to maximize profit for its shareholders. The privately owned real-estate company indeed soon turned profitable, and today its shares trade on the stock exchanges of Beirut, London, and Kuwait.

Since Hariri was involved in the project on both the public and private levels, suspicions of a conflict of interest seemed not completely unjustified. Hariri was wearing two hats: first, as supposedly impartial decision-maker on the political level and second as that of an investor in a private company. Crucially, this company was involved in many of the projects he had to take decisions on in his capacity as a politician. Therefore, several close observers of events expressed their concern at so ambiguous an arrangement.

The contradiction between the project's theory and praxis was problematic. Conceived of as an island of wealth and power, the city center would no longer play a centralizing role in the country as a whole, but would instead become an island like all the other urban islands that arose during the civil war (Beyhum 1992).

At the time of writing, the appropriation procedures used by Hariri have become a well-known and substantially documented fact. The opposition to Solidere is ongoing and a committee of defendants continues to organize activities aimed at denouncing what has taken place and continues to take place.[19] This did not, however, prevent Solidere from acquiring a comfortable bargaining position, since the company has solidly imposed itself as an unavoidable actor and global reference in terms of the urban reconstruction of Beirut's historic heart. We have chosen to highlight some of these reconstruction efforts in Beirut during the aftermath of the civil war because they provide interesting examples of property transactions and legal practices in a period of countrywide economic renewal.

Political Rivalry as a Catalyst (1990–2003)

As much as in the years before the Lebanese civil war, the history of the mosque in the war's aftermath was rife with political rivalry. However, whereas during the war this competition had brought the project to a standstill, similar antagonisms after the war served to accelerate the mosque's planned evolution. It is therefore useful, for the sake of argument, to look at two periods: The first period runs from 1976 to 1996 and explores the restructuring of Beirut's Sunni community, while the second period unravels the sudden boost to the mosque's construction that took place between 1996 and 2003.

One significant factor in the development of the mosque was the reconfiguration of the Sunni political scene in Beirut, a process that had begun several decades earlier. From the mid-twentieth century, the Sunni religious authorities had initiated a gradual and laborious expansion of their influence over the traditional communal leaders *(zu'ama)* of Beirut's Sunni community. This dynamic had become explicit with the 1951 inauguration of the Dar al-Fatwa complex in the Musaytbeh area of West Beirut and continued, with ups and downs, under the tenure (1966–89) of the charismatic Mufti Hassan Khaled during the civil war in Lebanon.[20]

After the Sunni militias were jeopardised or defeated because of their alliance with the Palestinian fedayeen, radical Islamism gained some measure of popularity in the 1980s. With the gradual disintegration of the Lebanese state, the importance of Sunni religious institutions in the community's religious and political affairs increased, and more pronounced communal identities became the norm. At the same time, the traditional leadership of the *zu'ama* came under pressure, if only because they had growing trouble providing their constituencies with the patronage of state administrations and charities, such as the Maqasid–which increasingly came under the (financial) control of Saudi Arabia and its Lebanese proxies.

While some of the established leaders, such as the Salam family, adapted to this situation, others tried to exploit it. Among them, Mufti Khaled gained so much political influence that he grew too powerful and was assassinated in 1989. By this time, new actors had emerged on the scene.

Rafiq Hariri, for one, had systematically established a patronage network that was not linked to traditional Sunni religious institutions, thus overcoming the principal weakness of the Salam family. On the other hand, because of his apparent moderation and cross-communitarian alliances and partnerships, he was generally regarded with suspicion by the more radical Islamist groups, some of whom were rumored to have infiltrated the Muhammad al-Amin Association, which was still overseeing the development of the mosque on the ground.

Regarding the physical evolution of the mosque during these decades, only an advertising board of sorts, installed on the plot in question, indicated the intention of building a mosque there. Unsurprisingly, this signboard did not survive the war. However, according to eyewitness accounts, as informal a structure as a tent was set up on the site. It is unclear, however, who exactly placed it there and who actually used this tent and how frequently, but it appears that the tent was meant to allow local laborers to pray when on duty.[21] This tent was virtually the only thing that could be seen on the mosque's plot by the time a forest of cranes had transformed Beirut's city center into a huge, continuously evolving construction site.

It was the strategic alliance between Rafiq Hariri as prime minister and Sheikh Muhammad Rashid Qabbani as head of the Dar al-Fatwa on a number of issues, alongside the rapid development of the urban area surrounding the planned mosque, that thrust the project for the mosque into a new period of accelerated development between 1996 and 2003. This alliance, however, was not simply a result of the previously described transformations permeating the Sunni community of Beirut during the 1976–96 period.

Alongside the development of the urban area surrounding the planned mosque, another important factor was to bolster the mosque project: the new duo's aim to overcome the tutelage issue by excluding the Muhammad al-Amin Association from being an actor in the mosque's construction.

The enthusiasm of Dar al-Fatwa, embodied in the will of the Mufti of the Lebanese Republic, Sheikh Qabbani, appears to have been fueled by a number of factors. First, there was the explicit willingness to go on with the project of building the Muhammad al-Amin Mosque and to turn it into a beacon of Sunni Islami in Beirut. The following statement from Dar al-Fatwa is clear testimony to this ambition:

Dar al-Fatwa . . . took upon its shoulders, together with the DGIA, the work of realizing this hope to allow this mosque to become a landmark among the landmarks of Islamic civilization in Lebanon and more specifically in the capital, Beirut.[22]

There are three additional factors bearing consideration: First, according to a longstanding tradition in Lebanon and not unlike common practice in other Middle Eastern countries, leaders of religious communities yield considerable influence over political affairs (Khuri 1991; Eickelman and Piscatori 2004; Koutroubas 2006). Thus, as the leader and representative of a major religious community, the Mufti of the Lebanese Republic is a senior political actor and, as such, eager to strengthen his legitimacy. Widely seen as the candidate championed by Hariri, the Mufti had been elected to office on 28 December 1996, hours after an item of institutional reform—masterminded by advisers close to Hariri—had modified the voting procedure (Rougier 2007, 130).[23] As a newly appointed leader in search of credibility, the Mufti had to earn his credentials among his constituency and, in this respect, the construction of a mosque was a welcome opportunity to do so.

Moreover, both Hariri and the Mufti seem to have viewed the construction of the mosque as a means of epitomizing the regained political strength of the Sunni community in post-war Lebanon, and this landmark mosque can be understood as the symbolic crown on the work of those members of the Sunni community who had labored long and hard for more influence within the Lebanese political system.[24]

Besides, another factor had come to influence Hariri's position regarding the mosque. For, until then, Samir Kassir recalls Hariri as having been opposed to building a mosque on this prime location. According to Kassir, Hariri's opposition was inspired by two reasons: The first was the fact that, as a Muslim who considered himself to be pious but moderate, Hariri did not want religious markers "on the postcard of Beirut."[25] The second reason for his opposition was that, as a businessman, Hariri did not want to sacrifice one of the most expensive parcels of Solidere to a mosque, a building unlikely to generate any added value.

So, what was the trigger that caused Rafiq Hariri to review his position toward the plans for the Muhammad al-Amin Mosque? In order to answer this question, it is important to recall the—by now legendary—friction and strained relationship between Hariri and Emile Lahoud, then commander-in-chief of the Lebanese Army. Hariri unsuccessfully tried to prevent Lahoud from becoming president of the republic in 1998. This animosity between the country's two most powerful officials had been a paralyzing factor for countless political issues in Lebanon,[26] and affected the construction of the Muhammad al-Amin Mosque as well.

President Lahoud, a secular and military-minded figure and a Maronite Christian, saw an opportunity to weaken the position of his political opponent on his own territory, that is, within the Sunni community of Beirut. President Lahoud reportedly invited Al-Waleed bin Talal, the well-known Saudi prince and one of the world's richest men with alleged ambitions in Lebanese politics, to participate in the financing of the mosque. In 2001, Al-Waleed, whose Lebanese mother, Mona al-Solh, is the daughter of the late Riad al-Solh, donated two million dollars toward the purchase of parts of the land parcel.[27]

If, until this point, Rafiq Hariri's attitude had been one of disinterest or even opposition to the building of the mosque, from that point, he found himself in a position where circumstances forced him to act. Hariri could not consider withholding financial contributions, therefore allowing himself to be perceived as parsimonious or sidelined by a rival on a major project in his own backyard. Neither could he limit himself to making a symbolic contribution since this would be seen as merely endorsing an initiative taken by notable political competitors.

Hariri reacted decisively: in a style true to his image and reputation he pledged to fund the project entirely and, from then on, he became closely involved in every phase of its operations. He personally oversaw each and every step in the construction process, thus clearly putting his mark on the project. This gradual move toward the appropriation—through financial means and networking—of the mosque project was a striking development in Hariri's association with the mosque.

This shift in Hariri's position can be explained by several factors. First, this is a good illustration of Hariri's double-sided but not per se contradictory position as a Lebanese and Sunni politician. On the one hand he carefully nourished his image as being that of a truly Lebanese statesman, a consensual leader who enjoyed massive, trans-communitarian support, as his popularity among the Christian bourgeoisie attested. On the other hand, given that he occupied the highest public office available to a Lebanese Sunni Muslim, he was eager to actively uphold his reputation as a devout and practicing Muslim, assets essential to the role of a true *za'im* (communal leader).

Second, one should be careful not to exaggerate Hariri's opposition to the Muhammad al-Amin project, however. For two reasons at least, it seems that Hariri's revised position was more an opportunistic reconsideration than a volte face. For one, the rivalry between Hariri and Al-Waleed, who share business interests and a similar personal background, should not be overestimated (Sakr 2002: 73f). Besides, and perhaps crucially, Hariri's attitude to the plans for a mosque may have been more one of lukewarm disinterest than one of outright opposition. In fact, it appears that Hariri had been looking for some time for a suitable place to erect a major mosque in Beirut.[28] When that project failed to materialize, the opportunity of pulling off a breakthrough in the long deadlocked Muhammad al-Amin project suddenly became more alluring.

One may wonder, therefore, whether Hariri's trajectory concerning the Muhammad al-Amin Mosque was not more one of consciously crafted gradual involvement (and later appropriation) based on personal (electoral) interests rather than one of a radical U-turn in response to a threat from of one of his perceived competitors—one whose areas of interest range far beyond tiny Lebanon anyhow.

Be that as it may, less than one year after the contribution made by Al-Waleed bin Talal, the alliance between Hariri and the Mufti paid off. The prime minister was able to obtain, with the backing of Dar al-Fatwa, the ministerial signature to decree number 8572, by both the minister of interior, Elias al-Murr, and President Lahoud. This decree, published in the Official Gazette on 31 August 2002,[29] declared the Muhammad al-Amin Association to be illegal and dissolved by virtue of the law, thus removing perhaps the biggest obstacle to the mosque's actual construction.

The Actual Construction (2003–2005)

In this section we will focus on a selected number of actors and issues involved in the relatively short phase of actual construction of the mosque, in order to highlight how different interests clashed and how several norms upheld by the various stakeholders affected and regulated the final form of the mosque.

Now that he had established himself as the project's principal sponsor, Hariri was able to have a determining impact on its plans. This was greatly facilitated by the fact that he commissioned Oger Liban, his own contracting company, to carry out this new, valuable contract.

One of the issues raised in the case of the Muhammad al-Amin Mosque concerned the Roman remnants, laid bare merely weeks after digging works for the foundations had started, in 2002. These ruins were of particular interest to archaeologists and historians of ancient Beirut, who yearned for the opportunity to investigate them. Thus, a bargaining process started between contractors and developers of the site, who pressed for a swift continuation of building activities, on the one hand, and archaeologists and the

Directorate-General of Antiquities (DGA), who devoted all available energy to their quest for the time and money to allow for more serious excavations under optimal circumstances, on the other. Permission and funding was finally obtained and excavations onsite started in late October 2002,[30] but only for a limited period of time and under strict conditions since no more than a handful of researchers were allowed onsite.[31]

It should be recalled that Oger Liban was the final supervisor and coordinator of the works onsite. The firm outsourced many of the construction activities to subcontractors.[32] At Oger Liban, the architectural planning of the mosque was in the hands of a team of engineers under the expertise and leadership of Azmi Fakhouri, an architectural engineer by training who had gained his credentials while working on several other projects for Hariri, including the Hind Hijazi Mosque and the Bahaeddine Hariri Mosque in Sidon.[33]

The first stone of the Muhammad al-Amin Mosque was laid on the first day of Ramadan (6 November) 2002, by both Sheikh Qabbani, the mufti, and Hariri, then prime minister. The first concrete for the foundations was poured on 3 October 2003, and by March 2005 the raw construction of the whole building, including the 65-meter-high minarets and the 48-meter-high dome, had been finalized. The total surface covered almost 4,000 square meters and the built-up area covered over 11,000 square meters. The calculated surface per worshiper (0.75 m²) provides space for more than 7,000 attendants, including a mezzanine for 800 female worshipers.

The stone used for the Ottoman-inspired[34] scheme came from Riyadh, while the studios of the Saudi Sheikh Uthman Taha prepared the calligraphy. The design of the mosque's interior was in the hands of Nabil Dada, a Lebanese decorator who had worked for Hariri on previous occasions. As for the characteristically blue color of the dome, it was a composition chosen by Hariri himself out of a selection of blues compiled by an Italian laboratory after almost a year of experiments. The total cost of the project was estimated to be in the region of $30 million.

Before as well as during the construction work, the engineers at Oger Liban were confronted with a great number of technical challenges. Let us now look at some of the more informal practices involved in negotiating space, one that influenced the final form of the mosque. Indeed, Oger Liban had to translate the wishes and directives of all the actors involved into a feasible building within budgetary and spatial limits. However, the interests and intentions of the actors involved were not always compatible.

To be more explicit, Solidere was initially opposed to the construction of a monumental mosque and did everything possible to downscale the project so as to make it fit into the urban context and projects surrounding the mosque. In fact it favored an alternative scheme for the mosque, devised by the Jordanian architect Rasem Badran. For its part, Dar al-Fatwa had clearly expressed its ambition to turn the Muhammad al-Amin Mosque into a landmark of Islamic civilization in Lebanon. Rafiq Hariri, once involved, had come to consider the construction of this mosque as one of the cornerstones of his reconstruction efforts in the BCD and one which put his prestige and reputation at stake. Oger Liban, from its side, faced technical and budgetary constraints and wanted the project to be completed as efficiently as possible. These actors were the ones with decision-making power; others, such as neighboring locals, archaeologists, and residents of Beirut were all directly or indirectly concerned, but had very limited means at their disposal to influence decisions. This diversity of objectives among the various actors is important to take into account because it is here that one discovers the political maneuvering behind the construction of a religious building.

One example of these potentially conflicting objectives and the ordinary practices that surrounded the actual construction on a daily basis became clear through a dispute that arose in the northwestern corner of the land parcel. The problem was that this corner was not, initially, part of the lands acquired for the construction of the mosque but was in fact part of Solidere land committed by the latter to another project, namely the Garden of Forgiveness. The trouble was considerable since the orientation of the main entrance was scheduled to be exactly on this plot of land, in the direction of this northwestern corner (Fig. 6.3), facing the heart of BCD—the Nejmeh Square—and thus completing, in a way, one of the two missing radii that depart from the square. Early drafts of the more than three hundred and twenty schemes prepared by Mr. Fakhouri's team at Oger Liban as well as several maps published by Solidere, clearly indicate the intention of orienting the main entrance of the mosque toward the northwestern corner (Fig. 6.2).

The problem was all the more serious because the 2.3-hectare Garden of Forgiveness project was a high-profile initiative destined to become a "paragon of social integration" for the purpose of offering "an important neutral location with a multi-communal history" and serving as "a meeting point for Lebanon's many communities." Solidere had encountered considerable difficulty in finding a suitable location for the project, which was

Fig. 6.2: The original Oger Liban design for the northwestern corner of Muhammad al-Amin Mosque, with the main entrance facing Nejmeh Square; Martyr's Square is to the left of the photograph. Courtesy Oger Liban.

closely monitored by international NGOs because of the unique opportunity it offered to commit a public space in reconstructed Beirut to the sensitive issue of sectarian reconciliation. Its brochure spoke in glowing terms of using "foundations of the past to build foundations for the future" and of providing "a place for individuals to reflect on their collective memory" with the hope of nurturing a "renewed sense of common identity" among the Lebanese.[35]

Solidere insisted on securing a passage between the mosque and the cathedral that would allow visitors to the Garden to connect Rue Weygand with Rue Emir Beshir. However, it came under pressure twice to sell more land. For Oger Liban, the problem was significant because not including this part would have major effects on building stability and force the relocation of the main entrance. This problem turned out to be the biggest challenge for Fakhouri's team of architects and they had to muster all their talent to find a solution. In the end, a compromise was struck which allowed both projects to go ahead with minimal nuisance.

Nevertheless, a permanent visual reference to all this bargaining remains.

The solution involved Solidere giving up an additional plot of land to accomodate what Fakhouri calls "the mosque's umbrella," a vaulted structure covering the northwestern corner at the level of the first elevation (Fig. 6.3). This creates an unhindered passage for visitors to the Garden while at the same time accommodating a secondary entrance to the mosque.

In doing so, the trapezoidal form of the parcel and the stability of the original plan were secured, but the mosque's main entrance was now transferred beneath another vaulted hall, to the northeastern corner of the parcel, which gave direct access to Martyrs Square and no longer to Nejmeh Square.

We have highlighted this rather technical problem because it reveals how the different parties negotiated and finally settled a dispute about a plot of land. It illustrates how negotiating over space leaves physical marks. Another example of clashing interests and actors can be found in the reaction of the ecclesiastic leadership in charge of the Saint George Maronite Cathedral, located just next to the mosque.

The constant interactions between different communities, sometimes harmonious, sometimes confrontational, sometimes occurring along intra-confessional lines, at other times transgressing confessional boundaries, is an essential feature of Lebanese society—be it in times of peace or war. As

Fig. 6.3: The northwestern corner of the Muhammad al-Amin mosque, showing the 'mosque's umbrella,' which guarantees a covered passage to all. Photograph by Ward Vloeberghs, 2006.

such, the interplay with other buildings in the surroundings of the Muhammad al-Amin Mosque, and especially with the religious architecture in its vicinity, greatly affected the construction and use of the mosque and continues to do so.

The Saint George Maronite Cathedral, based upon the Basilica Maria Maggiore in Rome, was built to replace a church of the same name which had become too small for the growing Maronite community. Archbishop Debs (r. 1872–1907), who had decided to increase the visibility of the Maronite community in Beirut, inaugurated the cathedral in 1894.[36]

Exactly a century later, the cathedral was restored (at a cost of $8 million) at the behest of the archbishop of Beirut "because it had not been used for twenty-five years and wild herbs had invaded the cathedral during the war." To emphasize the importance of the cathedral "which is to Maronites of Lebanon what the Notre Dame is to the Catholics of France," the inauguration ceremony of the restored cathedral, in 2000, was presided over by Patriarch Sfeir "in the presence of President Hariri and Cardinal Lustiger of Paris."[37]

The "gargantuan" mosque literally dominates and "dwarfs"[38] the adjacent cathedral in such a way that many visitors (including residents and non-residents irrespective of their faith) perceived it as a form of provocation. The least that can be said is that the hegemonic ambition of the Muhammad al-Amin Mosque went neither unnoticed nor without criticism.

Archbishop Matar, eager to respond to the construction of the mosque regardless of political conjunctures, ordered the design of a visible reply to the new mosque. He commissioned a well-known architect to draw up plans for a campanile that would "not reach higher but attain the same height" as the minarets. As a result, detailed plans (Fig. 6.4) have been finalized and the construction of the new campanile is now well underway. It will take the form of a high clock tower on the street side, to the west of the cathedral, where it will replace an existing building (Fig. 6.5). Archbishop Matar explains how, shortly before the construction of the mosque:

> Hariri came to see me and tell me that they would build a mosque there. He told me that it would be the height of the cathedral, "but what more do you want, in Islam the domes are high." But they created a monumental structure that conceals the cathedral and the Maronite presence. In fact, they wanted a presence on Martyrs' Square. So, in response we will construct the campanile.

Fig. 6.4: Plans for the new campanile, as prepared by the studio of Pierre el-Khoury (1930–2005). Said J. Bitar eventually took over the project. Photograph by Ward Vloeberghs, 2006.

The prelate goes on to describe the campanile's appearance:

I have asked Sheikh Pierre El Khoury[39] to prepare the plans by looking at Saint Marc in Venice and the Pisa Tower for inspiration. The campanile will be sixty-five meters high, not higher than but the same height as the minarets. In fact, I do not reproach Hariri for having built a mosque, but I do reproach him for having built a mosque that is disproportionate in relation to the city. . . . This is a kind of showing off, to attract attention. By the way, from an architectural point of view, this is not a big success; Solidere never photographed it and actually tries to avoid displaying it in their promotion brochures. It is a bit like the Tour Montparnasse in Paris; everyone wants to be inside in order not to see it.

According to some, this step must be understood in the context of a contest for visibility by mosques and churches in the downtown area.[40]

Fig. 6.5: A view from Amir Bashir Street depicting Muhammad al-Amin Mosque, the Maronite cathedral, and the building that is to be replaced by a 65-meter campanile—see plans in Fig. 6.4 opposite. Photograph by Ward Vloeberghs, 2006.

Competition arises not only as to which monument has the highest minaret or church tower but also which call to prayer is loudest, that of the *adhan* or ringing church bells.

The Installation of the *Darih* (Tomb) Next to the Mosque and Its Effects (2005–2008)

Quite dramatically, much of this competition and rivalry was forgotten during the dramatic events that followed Hariri's assassination. On Monday 14 February 2005, a massive explosion shook the city of Beirut, one which changed the course of the country's political history. As Hariri's impressive motorcade passed the Saint George Hotel in Ayn al-Mraysseh,[41] around a ton of TNT was detonated, killing more than twenty people, including Hariri.

On Wednesday 16 February, hundreds of thousands of Lebanese joined the funeral procession from Hariri's residence in Qoraytem to the Muhammad al-Amin Mosque and the subsequent funeral ceremony to which President Lahoud was not invited.

Hariri's family subsequently decided to bury Hariri and his bodyguards on a plot of land bordering the Muhammad al-Amin Mosque on Martyrs Square. The decision to install Hariri's tomb in Beirut was taken overnight and, like the decision to turn his funeral into an anti-Syrian event, the decision to lay the martyred president to rest in Beirut amounted to a political statement.

Virtually from the very first moment of Rafiq Hariri's burial in Martyrs Square, vast numbers of people amassed at the improvised tomb, and soon the site became a popular attraction. Indeed, as a consequence of his accomplishments and his international renown, combined with the shocking violence of his assassination but also as careful planning, political maneuvring, and a dose of well-aimed propaganda, Rafiq Hariri acquired the status of a mythical martyr, *al-ra'is al-shahid* (the martyr president) whose tomb has evolved into an improvised shrine, complete with large lifesize portraits, flowers, and candles (Fig. 6.6).

As a consequence, and because of the events that followed, this newly created sanctuary soon acquired a prominent place in Lebanese public life. Scenes of Lebanese[42] and foreign[43] dignitaries paying their respect, or a local football team celebrating a championship,[44] at Hariri's tomb are particularly significant in this respect. These visits by celebrities as well as ordinary people have contributed to shaping the character of the *darih* which has de facto evolved into a modern pilgrimage site.[45]

Just as the mosque can be said to have started under a tent, so too did the mausoleum develop out of a tent. A more permanent structure—to be co-designed by one of Hariri's sons—is destined to replace the actual, temporary large hall created by the tent structure. What is more important is that the mosque has become inextricably linked to the tomb. This is not only the result of the extreme physical proximity between mosque and emerging mausoleum, but also because Hariri's spectacular death has affected the mosque in a profound way. If before 14 February 2005 some Christians felt outspokenly humiliated by the mosque, the installation of the *darih* and the dramatic events during the month following the assassination have had an attenuating effect: all of a sudden, the Muhammad al-Amin Mosque appeared to lose some of its dominant and provocative characteristics and found itself transformed into a symbol of unity and understanding.[46] At that moment, the mosque and grave ceased to be a site of contestation and appeared to be embraced, even by some outspoken Maronites. In later years, however, the site took on more markedly confessional connotations, especially after the July 2006 War (see below).[47]

Fig. 6.6: A man contemplating Hariri's tomb. Photograph by Ward Vloeberghs, 2009.

At the same time, because of its high popularity, the *darih* became a use-ful tool for communication and a convenient tool in the political liturgy for members close to Hariri. As such, the tomb only added to the mosque's importance and turned it de facto into one big sanctuary devoted to the cult of the slain president. Hariri's family and sympathizers have assi-duously reinforced Hariri's connection to the mosque through the *darih*. One example of this is the display, at the burial site, of a special series of postage stamps, issued in commemoration of his death, on which Hariri is featured four times; one stamp bears Hariri's portrait next to an image of a minaret and a church tower of the same height, all collated next to the well-known statue of the martyrs, while another stamp shows a small portrait next to the large Muhammad al-Amin Mosque (Liban Post 2005).

It must be noted, however, that soon after Hariri's assassination, two broad political coalitions emerged: the 8th March group (in reference to an enormous pro-Syrian demonstration organized by Hezbollah)[48] and the 14th March group (in reference to an even bigger demonstration orga-nized to commemorate the first month after Hariri's assassination). Both of these camps evolved considerably as the weeks and months went by, eventually becoming the two main new political actors of the post-Hariri era in Lebanon. The gap between these two opposing currents widened during 2005, worsened after the July 2006 war, and developed into deep mistrust during the economic and socio-political deadlock of 2007. That same year saw both camps, each with their respective international allies, pitched even more fiercely against each other over the highly problematic issues of electing a successor to Emile Lahoud and finding an acceptable, power-sharing formula in government, a problem that lasted well into 2008 and culminated in the traumatizing armed takeover of Sunni neighborhoods in Beirut by Shi'i militias on 7 May 2008.

Spectacularly, this political cleavage has had spatial repercussions which have affected both the gravesite and the mosque. Quite revealingly, if Hariri's tomb, during one (brief) moment[49]—that is, immediately after his assassination—seemed to have had the potential to develop into a national mausoleum that could attract visitors of almost all confessions, the gradual degeneration of the political situation soon prevented this. As time passed, an opposite dynamic surfaced, one which transformed[50] the *darih* and the neighboring mosque into a space clearly belonging to the 14th March camp.[51]

By December 2006, the 8th March camp[52] had confirmed this dynamic of spatialization of power by launching a major sit-in *(i'tisam)*[53] in the central squares of Beirut and by organizing a subsequent 'siege' of the downtown area—from the Grand Serail (the prime minister's offices) to the Muhammad al-Amin Mosque. In contesting '14th March space,' the 8th March supporters chose to occupy rival space and turn it into a clearly marked political space of their own.[54] Thus, the stalemate acquired visible expression and, on the occasion of the second annual commemoration of Hariri's assassination, on 14 February 2007, the mosque was surrounded by barbed wire, as a safety measure.

From then on, one literally had to choose sides in order to access the city center; either entering through the tent camp[55] installed by the supporters of 8th March or by passing the *darih*, thus paying respects to the 14th March camp. Thus, the mosque had been politically hijacked even before its inauguration.

It was not until the political climate in Lebanon had cooled and the suffocating sit-in had been lifted in June 2008, that the solemn inauguration ceremony could finally take place. On 17 and 18 October 2008, an impressive array of international guests, among them the Mufti of Egypt and the Shaykh of al-Azhar, participated in a Friday prayer accompanied by a crowd of thousands.[56] After a century and a half of accumulated efforts, the Muhammad al-Amin Mosque had finally been brought to life.

This brief overview of the genesis of Lebanon's most prestigious Sunni place of worship shows how its gradual elaboration consisted of numerous small and often quotidian stages of planning, adjusting, and readjusting by a multitude of ambitious actors. As such, the mosque's history is not only the history of a community through the decades but also the illustration of a good deal of appropriation as well as contestation of sacred space. This chapter has documented how intended acts can have unintended consequences and how the constraints of various stakeholders can leave physical traces on the built fabric. In other words, besides being the outcome of a communal aspiration of power, the Muhammad al-Amin Mosque can also be seen as an example of how urban form is produced and accomplished in both formal and informal ways.

Notes

1   The five phases selected here are of unequal length and were not picked based on any specific rationale other than the practical and didactical, that is, to focus on practices of acquiring and claiming land and of titling a settlement.

2   Dar al-Fatwa, "Masjid Muhammad al-Amin salla Allah 'alayhi wa sallam, Beirut." The document is undated. However, repeated inquiries made of the Mufti's administration allowed for the retrieval of the date of publication, which was given as 28 August 2004.

3   A zawiya (pl. zawaya) is a space closely associated with Sufism and can take extremely diverse physical forms. For more discussion of the term, see Kane 1995.

4   See also: al-Hadeer 2007 and Hallaq 2008.

5   This café was a commercial outlet where one could order drinks and food or enjoy a water pipe. Ridwan al-Sayyid, for example, remembers having breakfast at the coffee house "for 25 piasters." Interview, Beirut, 27 June 2006.

6   In addition to the construction of a Lazarist convent on the plot of land mentioned earlier (located just opposite the entrance to the zawiya), one of the most tangible testimonies to the missionaries' activities is the opening of universities such as the Syrian Protestant College in 1866 (later the American University of Beirut). The convent was subsequently replaced by a 1953 design by André Leconte, which is the complex that stands to this day.

7   The document mentions Sheikh Muhammad Abu Nasr, Sheikh Abdel Karim Abu Nasr, and Sayyid Subhi Abu Nasr.

8   Dar al-Fatwa, n.d.

9 On the membership of this association, see Taha al-Wali 1973, 111–12, and al-Hut 1966, 16–17.

10 This was not an unusual situation; other mosques were also hampered by poor relations with the religious authorities. See Charara 1989, which also contains some information on the Muhammad al-Amin project.

11 The copy obtained by the author from the Directorate-General for Property Issues (Ministry of Finance) dates from 29 March 2006.

12 Since this episode is replete with instances of legal practices and contestations, we are compelled to include a discussion of the controversy here. However, the story of Beirut's reconstruction has been the object of numerous studies and for that reason we will keep this discussion as brief as possible. In addition to the works refered to throughout this chapter, more elaborate analysis can be found in Rowe and Sarkis 1998. For another dimension of the same issue, see Kögler 2005. In addition to the works cited in this chapter, more elaborate analysis can be in found in Rowe and Sarkis 1998, Najem 2000, Schmid 2002, Kögler 2005, Fawaz 2007, and Harb 2010.

13 A first plan was elaborated and presented in 1977–78 and dealt exclusively with the renovation of the city center, destroyed during the civil war violence of 1975–76. The second, more inclusive and ambitious plan of 1983 covered the entire Metropolitan Beirut; and, finally, the 1991 plan was unveiled, which once again covered only the Beirut city center.

14 A French acronym for 'Société libanaise de développement et de reconstruction de Beyrouth.' See http://www.solidere.com. It should be noted that adoption of Law No. 117 of 1991 (the preparation of which had been heavily influenced by those close to Hariri) had cleared the way for the establishment of a private company to carry out the reconstruction.

15 Marwan Iskandar (2006, 59) maintains that Hariri's participation in Solidere amounted to $183 million, thereby covering "the capped 10 percent shareholding by any individual, institution or group." Extensive details of the complex history of the birth of Solidere and the respective actors and stakes involved are well described by Najem 2000, 163–73. It is important to note that the attribution of A-shares was a complicated matter, since several owners claimed to own the same property.

16 For a presentation of Solidere's core project by a senior advisor to Solidere, see Gavin and Maluf 1996.

17 Paul Mourani and Assem Salam, quoted in Najem 2000, 165.

18 For another critical analysis of Solidere's reconstruction practices see Makdisi 1997.

19 See, for example, the articles in *The Daily Star* of 11 March 2004, 18 July 2007, and 6 August 2007, which show that the property-owners committee is still active under the presidency of members of the Daouq family. Some sources have put the number of "citizens with legal entitlements" in the city

center at as much as 120,000. See Assem Salam, interview, Beirut, 20 July 2007. Verdeil 2002 cites this same figure, whereas Najem (2000) puts the number of "property owners" at 40,000.

20 For more details on the transformations of the Sunni community, see Johnson 1986 and Skovgaard-Petersen 1998.

21 The idea of an informal mosque in a tent may appear to be a strange one, especially given the fact that several other mosques are available in the surroundings, but one should not forget that the nearest mosques, the Amir Assaf and the Omari mosques, were themselves under construction in the 1990s. At least one article confirms the presence of a tent; see "Group Agrees on How to Build New Mosque," in *The Daily Star*, 3 December 1999. According to Azmi Fakhouri (interview, Beirut, 18 July 2007) the tent did not correctly face the qibla.

22 The use of the word *ma'lam* (landmark) is important here because of its associated meanings. The most basic significations of the root *ayn–lam–mim* are linked to concepts such as 'teaching' or 'knowing,' examples being the words *'ilm* (knowledge) or *'alam* (banner). The word *ma'lam* therefore embodies several messages within it, one of which is: to teach, implying that 'this' [mosque] is part of a rich Islamic civilization. The language used stress this implied meaning through use of the plural form *(ma'alim)*, a common rhetorical technique.

23 Sheikh Muhammad Rashid Qabbani had been interim mufti since the assassination of his predecessor, Sheikh Hassan Khaled, on 16 May 1989. This means that Sheikh Qabbani and Rafiq Hariri rose to political prominence in Lebanon at around the same time, that is, by the end of the 1980s. On the assassination of Hassan Khaled, see Harris 1997, 255.

24 Marwan Iskandar, in an avowedly partisan biography, documents Hariri's contribution to this effort to empower the Sunni Muslims by playing a "pro-active role of acute political awareness" for them as well as creating community "participation that would contribute to the rebirth of Lebanon." In what Iskandar calls "an uphill struggle to restore Sunni credibility," Hariri contributed his own "perseverance, as well as substantial resources provided by the Saudis." See Iskandar 2006, 163–64. Indeed, one of the major shifts since the Taif Agreement (1989) is the enhancement in the prerogatives of the prime minister at the expense of the those of the president of the republic.

25 "Il (RH) ne voulait pas d'emblème religieux sur la place des martyrs, sur la carte postale de Beyrouth." Samir Kassir, in an interview featured by "Le kiosque arabe" on Radio France Inernationale (RFI), 8 April 2005.

26 For a detailed account of this process, see Corm 2006, especially chapter 11, 267–92. Alternatively, turn to the somewhat partisan but revealing Blanford 2006, especially chapter 4, 71–99.

27 See "Milyunay dular min al-Walid bin Talal li-masjid Muhammad al-Amin," *an-Nahar*, 6 December 2001, 5. See also Khan 2005, 318. This book is the tycoon's authorized biography. Blanford (2006, 85) qualifies Bin Talal as an outspoken supporter of President Emile Lahoud.

28 Saad Khaled (Director-General of Urbanism between 1993 and 1999 and a close adviser to Hariri on urban planning affairs) maintains that several sites were seriously considered for this project. Interview, Beirut, 16 April 2009. For more details on this, see Vloeberghs 2010.

29 *al-Jarida al-rasmiya*, no. 49, 31 August 2002, p. 5807; *al-Jarida al-rasmiya* (the Official Gazette) is a public journal in which laws and governmental decrees are published before they come into effect.

30 *al-Mustaqbal*, 28 October 2002, 5.

31 Interview with Montaha Saghiye, Beirut, 23 March 2006. The excavations nevertheless resulted in the discovery of high-quality material that shed new light on the alignment of Beirut's Roman streets. At the time, the DGA and Solidere even held brainstorming sessions about the feasibility of developing a public access to an underground gallery that would allow visits to the unearthed *decumanus*.

32 As many as thirty-five external contracting companies were involved, according to an interview with Azmi Fakhouri, Beirut, 5 July 2006. It should be noted that Oger Liban stepped into the execution of the project after substantial parts of the architectural planning had been accomplished by a collaboration of the Egyptian architect and scholar Saleh Lamei and the Sidon-based Office for Engineering Studies of the Hariri Foundation.

33 These mosques had been commissioned by Rafiq Hariri in honor of his mother (d. 1995) and father (d. 1999) respectively; they were inaugurated in 1999 and 2006.

34 Although the architect insists on the fact that a wide variety of other influences are manifestly present as well.

35 Quotations are from the Solidere brochure outlining the project—*Hadiqat al-Samah* (Solidere, Beirut, 2004).

36 On the cathedral and its history, see Abi 'Ad 2000.

37 All quotes in this paragraph are from an interview with Archbishop Boulos Matar, Beirut, 27 July 2007.

38 Both adjectives are quotations from: Khalaf 2006, 31.

39 Pierre El Khoury is a Maronite Lebanese architect who has designed several highly visible buildings in Lebanon, including a monumental church on Mount Harissa and the emblematic UN House in central Beirut. He died in 2005. See for example El Khoury 2000.

40 Angus Gavin, Beirut, 16 March 2006.

41 Ironically enough, this hotel is an iconic building that had not been restored to its prewar glory, due to a conflict between its owner, Fadi

Khoury, on the one hand, and Hariri and Solidere, on the other, about property rights. In fact, the Saint George Hotel was among the most visible symbols of the contestations surrounding Solidere's activities in BCD. See for example Warren Singh-Bartlett, "St. George and Solidere do battle over soul BCD," *The Daily Star*, 23 February 2001.

42 Sayyid Hassan Nasrallah, secretary general of Hezbollah, came to pay his respects, together with member of parliament Saad al-Hariri, after the second day of the 'National Dialogue.' See *al-Sharq al-awsat*, 4 March 2006, 5.

43 The most well-known example is of President Jacques Chirac but dignitaries such as Kofi Annan (*al-Liwa*, 29 August 2006) and others feature as well.

44 As reported in *al-Liwa*, 15 May 2006. Syndicates came to visit the mosque on the eve of their strike in a move designed to bolster their action.

45 People of all ages visited the site: newlyweds, youngsters, parents taking their children on a trip, the elderly, and tourists. For more details on the development of Hariri's tomb, see Vloeberghs 2012.

46 Such as on the occasion of 14 March 2005, when a million people seemed to transform the mosque into a forceful symbol of national unity. See the book published by Dar an-Nahar on the occasion of what has been called "the Beirut Spring," "Independence05," or the "Cedar Revolution." See *The Beirut Spring. Independence 05* (Beirut: Dar an-Nahar and Quantum Communications, 2005).

47 One Lebanese Maronite Christian we interviewed told us that "before [2005], the mosque would arouse my anger; I didn't like the way the mosque was imposed next to the cathedral. But now [March 2006], all of this is forgotten; it's almost as if I don't see the mosque anymore."

48 In reference to 8 March 1963, which is the day the Ba'th Party came to power in Syria.

49 See for example the high-spirited document: *L'espoir en lettres de sang... 14 février 2005-14 février 2006, la Révolution du Cèdre en marche*. Supplement of *L'Orient-Le Jour*, 13 February 2006.

50 For example, when a significant step toward the establishment of the UN Special Tribunal for Lebanon was taken, this was regarded as a political victory and a small, framed copper plate was therefore installed at the tomb to celebrate this.

51 Mainly consisting of Hariri's Future Bloc, Jumblatt's Progressive Socialist Party (PSP), and the remnants of the Qornet Shehwan Gathering.

52 Mainly: Hezbollah, Aoun's Free Patriotic Movement (FPM), Amal, and the Marada.

53 The *i'tisam* can be understood as a contestation of Hariri's appropriation of space in Beirut. The connotations of the term *i'tisam* (safeguarding, resistance, preservation) are therefore meaningful in this regard.

54 The opposition launched the sit-in on 1 December 2006 for an unspecified period of time, in order to obtain a government of national unity that would replace the Siniora government—labeled as illegal.

55 I am grateful to Zouhair Ghazzal for insightful comments on how the tent camp of 8th March was itself divided: in a grouping of tents belonging to the Aoun-led Free Patriotic Movement and the 'Qawmi' (on the eastern side of the sit-in) and a grouping of tents staffed mainly with militants from Amal and Hezballah installed more to the west, on Riad Solh Square.

56 See *al-Liwa* of 17, 18, and 20 October 2008.

References

Abi 'Ad, Tubiya. 2000. *Katidra'iyat Mar Jirjis al-Maruniya*. Beirut: Chahine Printing Press.

Bennani-Chraïbi, Mounia, and Olivier Filleuleeds. 2003. *Résistances et protestations dans les sociétés musulmanes*. Paris: Presses de Science Po.

Beyhum, Nabil. 1992. "The Crisis of Urban Culture: The Three Reconstruction Plans for Beirut." *The Beirut Review* 4 (Fall): 43–61.

Blanford, Nicholas. 2006. *Killing Mr Lebanon. The Assassination of Rafik Hariri and its impact on the Middle East*. London: I.B. Tauris.

Bonne, Emmanuel. 1995. *Vie publique, patronage et clientèle. Rafic Hariri à Saïda*. Beirut: Centre d'Etudes et de Recherches sur le Moyen-Orient Contemporain (CERMOC).

Cattedra, Raffaele, and M'Hammed Janati. 2003. "Espace du religieux, espace de citadinité, espace de mouvement: les territoires des mosquées au Maroc." In Mounia Bennani-Chraïbi and Olivier Filleuleeds. *Résistances et protestations dans les sociétés musulmanes* (Paris: Presses de Science Po, 2003), 127–75.

Charara, Waddah. 1989. "Mosquée et quartier: une 'pratique du paysage sociale.' Une enquête sur un comité de mosquée." *Monde arabe, Maghreb, Machrek* 123 (January–March): 96–107.

Chehab Eddine, Saïd. 1960. *Géographie humaine de Beyrouth. Avec une étude sommaire sur les deux villes de Damas et de Bagdad*. Beirut: Imprimerie Calfat.

Corm, Georges. 2006. *Le Liban contemporain. Histoire et société*. Paris: La Découverte.

Dar al-Fatwa. n.d. "Masjid Muhammad al-Amin. Beirut." Official statement issued by Dar al-Fatwa.

Eickelman, Dale, and James Piscatori. 2004. *Muslim Politics*. Princeton, NJ: Princeton University Press.

"L'espoir en lettres de sang… 14 février 2005–14 février 2006, la Révolution du Cèdre en marche." 2006. Supplement of *L'Orient le jour*, February 13.

Fawaz, Mona, 2007. "Beirut: The City as a Body Politic." *ISIM Review* 20 (Autumn): 22–23.

Gavin, Angus, and Ramez Maluf. 1996. *Beirut Reborn: The Restoration and Development of the Central District*. London: Academy Editions.

al-Hadeer. 2007. *al-Jami': Masajid Bayrut fi-l-alafiya al-thalitha*. Beirut: al-Hadeer.

Hallaq, Hassan. 2008 "Ba'd intidhar dama khamsin 'aman al-ra'is akhraj al-mashru' al-hulm ila hayyiz al-tanfidh." *al-Liwa al-islami*, October 17.

Harb, Mona. 2003. "al-Dahiye de Beyrouth: parcours d'une stigmatisation urbaine, consolidation d'un territoire politique." *Genèses* 51 (June): 70–91.

Harris, William W. 1997. *Faces of Lebanon. Sects, War and Global Extensions*. Princeton, NJ: Markus Wiener.

al-Hut, Abd al-Rahman. 1966. *al-Jawami' wa-l-masajid al-sharifa fi Bayrut*. N.p.: n.p.

Iskandar, Marwan. 2006. *Rafik Hariri and the Fate of Lebanon*. London, Beirut: Saqi.

Johnson, Michael. 1986. *Class and Client in Beirut: The Sunni Muslim Community and the Lebanese State 1840–1985*. Reading: Ithaca Press.

Kane, Ousmane. 1995. "Zawiyah." In John L. Esposito, ed., *Oxford Encyclopedia of the Modern Islamic World*, 370–73. New York: Oxford University Press.

Kassir, Samir. 2004. *Histoire de Beyrouth*. Paris: Fayard.

Khalaf, Samir. 2006. *Heart of Beirut. Reclaiming the Burj*. London: Saqi.

Khan, Riz. 2005. *Alwaleed. Businessman, Billionaire, Prince*. New York: William Morrow.

El Khoury, Pierre. 2000. *Pierre El Khoury Architecture 1959–1999*. Beirut: Dar al-Nahar.

Khuri, Fuad Ishak. 1991. *Imams and Emirs. State, Religion and Sects in Islam*. London: Saqi, 1991.

Kögler, Oliver. 2005. "Der Umgang mit dem urbanen Kulturerbe im Nachkriegslibanon." PhD diss., University of Heidelberg.

Koutroubas, Theodoros. 2006. *L'action politique et diplomatique du Saint Siège au Moyen-Orient 1978–1992*. Louvain-la-Neuve: Presses Universitaires de Louvain.

Makdisi, Saree. 1997. "Laying Claim to Beirut: Urban Narrative and Spatial Identity in the Age of Solidere." *Critical Inquiry* 23 (3) (Spring): 661–705.

Mermier, Franck. 2009. "La mosquée Muhammad al-Amîn à Beyrouth: mausolée involontaire de Rafic Hariri." *REMMM* 125:176–96.

Najem, Tom Pierre. 2000. *Lebanon's Renaissance: The Political Economy of Reconstruction*. Reading: Ithaca Press.

Oger Liban. 2008. *Jami' Muhammad al-Amin: al-Hariri yuhaqqiq hulm Bayrut*. Beirut: Oger Liban.

Rougier, Bernard. 2007. *Everyday Jihad. The Rise of Militant Among Palestinians in Lebanon*. Cambridge, MA: Harvard University Press.

Rowe, Peter, and Hashim Sarkis, eds. 1998. *Projecting Beirut: Episodes in the Construction and Reconstruction of a Modern City*. Munich: Prestel.

Sakr, Naomi. 2002. *Satellite Realms: Transnational Television, Globalization and the Middle East*. London: I.B. Tauris.

Schmid, Heiko. 2002. *Der Wiederaufbau des Beiruter Stadtzentrums: Ein Beitrag zur handlungsorientierten politisch-geographischen Konfliktforschung*. Heidelberg: Heidelberger Geographische Arbeiten.

Skovgaard-Petersen, Jakob. 1998. "The Sunni Religious Scene in Beirut." *Mediterranean Politics* 3 (1): 69–80.

Taha al-Wali, Taha. 1973. *Tarikh al-masajid wa-l-jawami' al-sharifa fi Bayrut*. Beirut: Matba'at Dar al-Kutub.

Tueni, Ghassan, and Ilyas Khuri, eds. 2005. *The Beirut Spring. Independence 05*. Beirut: Dar an-Nahar and Quantum Communications.

Verdeil, Éric. 2002. "Une ville et ses urbanistes. Beyrouth en reconstruction." PhD diss., Université de Paris I Sorbonne.

———. 2001. "Reconstruction manquées à Beyrouth. La poursuite de la guerre par le projet urbain." *Les Annales de la recherche urbaine* 91 (December): 65–73.

Vloeberghs, Ward. 2012. "Worshipping the Martyr President: The Darih of Rafiq al-Hariri in Beirut." In T. Pierret, P. Pinto, and B. Dupret, eds., *Ethnographies of Islam: Performances and Interactions in Muslim Contexts*. Edinburgh: Edinburgh University Press.

———. 2010. "A Building of Might and Faith: Rafiq al-Hariri and the Muhammad al-Amin Mosque: On the Political Dimensions of Religious Architecture in Contemporary Beirut." PhD diss., Université catholique de Louvain (UCL).

Yacoub, Gebran. 2003. *Dictionnaire de l'architecture au Liban au XXème siècle*. Beirut: Alphamédia.

7

Shared Social and Juridical Meanings as Observed in an Aleppo 'Marginal' Neighborhood

Zouhair Ghazzal

S yria's main cities, beginning with Damascus and Aleppo, are padded with neighborhoods whose housing, design, and sewage facilities are the products of the residents themselves. Known in the common official dictum as "the zones of illicit habitat," such neighborhoods have been built from scratch by the inhabitants themselves, defying all kinds of rules and regulations imposed by state and municipal authorities.

This chapter focuses on one such 'illicit' neighborhood in Aleppo on three interrelated levels. First, it examines the norms of the habitat created by the inhabitants themselves, who have to take planning decisions not only with regard to their own homes, but also to public infrastructure and services, such as roads and pavements, water, electricity, telecommunication, and sewerage facilities. Second, it analyzes the contractual norms that lie behind the exchange and sale of properties. Since such neighborhoods fall outside state regulations, the users must create their own contractual norms to exchange property, in such a way that contracts can eventually become 'legal' once endorsed by state officials. Third, we examine the private and public norms that help construct the space for a 'society of individuals.' Taking into consideration Erving Goffman's motto that "the street is a society," we follow actors in their face-to-face situated encounters, paving the way for the dialogical structures that make the existence of a 'society' possible.[1]

Normalizing the Illegal:
the Unmitigated Disaster of Aleppo's Illicit Neighborhoods

Three interrelated levels of analysis come to mind when analyzing Aleppo's illicit neighborhoods, all of which center on the establishment of regulated norms and normative values.

The first set of norms is related to the habitat. Broadly speaking, what are commonly referred to in the official jargon as 'illicit' neighborhoods (or specific illegitimate informal zones within legitimate neighborhoods) are usually no more than informal trespassing zones, where actors have illegally built either on their own properties or on those of others. Let us assume for the sake of simplicity the existence of vacant plots of land at the city's outskirts, all located within the urban 'regulated planned area' under *al-mukhattat al-tanzimi* (master plan), which could be either private or public (state property). Before issuing any construction permits, the municipality should in principle first create a neighborhood plan, partition *(farz)* all plots in order to determine their boundaries vis-à-vis the public space (pavements, roads, schools, and parks), and determine infrastructural needs (water, electricity, and telecommunications). Construction permits are then issued either for residential buildings or commercial properties. Prior to receiving a permit, however, landowners should have their properties legalized at the municipality's cadastre, in order to receive the much needed *tabu akhdar* (lit. 'the green cadastral deed'; it was referred to in Ottoman times as *tapu*), the 'green form' officializing ownership.

The whole problem of the 'illicit zones' *(manatiq al-mukhalafat* and *al-sakan al-'ashwa'i)* is twofold. First, the areas did not receive any formal infrastructural plan from the municipality prior to construction, which pushed residents of other areas or from the countryside to improvise their own plans and go ahead with construction at their own risk. Second, ownership of individual plots of land has not, in most instances, been officialized either, nor have permits been issued prior to construction. Consequently, the trade in ownership tends to be custom-based, with all kinds of properties changing hands on the basis of trust and custom. That users invest so much in property and construction outside the bounds of legal norms is indeed staggering, but, as I point out below, this is the outcome of historical, political, and social shortcomings that have been accumulating since at least the mid-1970s. Third, the new residents would improvise their own plans, including decision-making regulating water pipes, sewerage, and electricity grids, as well as the installation of land lines (the broad availability of cell phones has eased such concerns). Finally, constructed properties, whether residential or commercial, are 'illegally' exchanged, based on 'legal norms' sanctified by the users themselves.

'Norms' are thus constructed at three interrelated levels. First of all, users, once they seize a property, whether legally or illegally, have to plan their own homes, decide which materials to use, and even allocate portions of 'their' space for public use. Even though such matters do not represent any 'collective' action per se, and are be the outcome of individual (if not poorly planned) actions, the outcome is ultimately one of collectively sanctioned normative values that regulate the habitat, while determining its contours in the absence of an officially sanctioned 'legal' framework.

Second, considering that the bulk of those properties have been 'illegally' owned and transmitted, the mode of illegal transmission itself becomes a 'legalized' norm of transmitting properties through the use of quasi-official or officially sanctioned documents and procedures. The present chapter is mostly concerned with elaborating this crucial issue.

Thirdly, we now approach the most fundamental aspect of the problem, that of the creation of social norms specific to illicit neighborhoods. Individuals and families from different backgrounds, ranging from nomadic tribes to rural peasant families from the nearby countryside and impoverished urban middle-class families who relocate to the outskirts, all come together in peripheral urban spaces, searching for labor and cheaper alternatives to inflated real-estate prices. That's the most intriguing aspect of those neighborhoods, whether old or new, and certainly the most difficult to pin down for researchers: How can we, as researchers, document the formation of norms in private and public spaces? Since direct observation proves the most crucial element, what is the role of situated encounters in such an experience?

The Lingering Regional and Economic Imbalances in Syrian History

In 1949, six years after Syrian independence from French rule, Husni al-Za'im, a Kurdish officer, led a coup d'état, ushering in a whole era of militarized politics for the country. Even though Za'im's rule lasted a mere six months, and was followed by a series of further coups leading up to 1953, the coming of the military to the Syrian political scene had not yet affected the *ancien régime* created under the auspices of the French mandate. In effect, from 1943 up to 1958, when Nasser became the president of the newly created United Arab Republic (U.A.R.), the system of elite and middle-class control of the country' upper echelons that took shape in the aftermath of the dismemberment of the Ottoman Empire, had been pretty much well preserved. Syria's 'first republic,' as it is often called, maintained the characteristics of the liberal spirit of the mandate, an ethos that even the military, once they had come to power, found hard to dislodge. In a strange way, the military even contributed to the further liberalization of a repressed Ottoman elite. Thus, Za'im, in spite of his short-lived rule, managed to promulgate the bulk of Syria's modern civil laws, beginning with the civil code and the penal code in 1949, while Adib Shishakli came up with the no-less-impressive code of personal status in 1953. The important point for our purposes here is that the advent of the military to politics neither dislodged traditional class equilibriums nor strained rural and urban relations, as the cities were able to absorb rural migrations without disrupting bourgeois middle-class life.

Such equilibriums would begin their *longue durée* disruptive cycles starting in 1958, when Syria entered into formal political union with Egypt to form what became known as the United Arab Republic. In effect, it was shortly after the brief military interlude of 1949–53 that the bourgeoisie, composed mostly of the old Ottoman notables class (under the aegis of president Shukri Quwwatli), lost its imagination and gave up on Syrian politics, giving full power to the corrupting influences of Nasser's bureaucratic regime.[2] In what would become Syria's 'second republic,' covering the period between 1958 and 1970, the coming of the Ba'th to power in 1963 appears, in hindsight, to be the single event that capitalized on and benefited the most from the unfortunate Union. It was at this stage that the middle class felt deeply threatened. Not only had its financial institutions and manufacturing properties been for the most part nationalized, but gradually the bulk of its rural properties was lost to small- and medium-sized peasant families during the agrarian reforms of the 1960s. It was the change in the status of agrarian properties that would eventually trigger the decisive change in Syrian urban–rural relationships.

Even though 'building on the properties of others' *(al-bina' 'ala aradi al-ghayr)* was 'promoted' by peasants and small landowners, who received their fair share of property in the wake of agrarian reforms, migration toward urban areas had not yet affected the cities in the 1960s. In the three decades after the mandate, the standard of living was in step with inflation, providing enough opportunities for tenants and landowners alike. More importantly, breaking the law when building on the properties of others, or building on your own land without prior permit, were no easy matters. Cities grew out of an Ottoman tradition where the rule of law mattered to the urban elites that kept it alive through the sharia court system. That same system was further liberalized throughout the mandate and gradually adapted to the needs of an ever-expanding professional middle class. It was then the early postcolonial military regimes that pushed further the liberalization of the law through the formalization of codes and procedures.

That was set to change dramatically in the 1970s. When Asad came to power in 1970, then confirmed in a national referendum in 1971, Syria already had a reputation for being politically unstable. Not only had it, like Egypt, suffered the massive defeat of the 1967 war,[3] but, more importantly, the Ba'th's statist policies were a big disappointment for society at large. Thus, while for the well-rooted professional (and 'secular') middle classes such policies represented a reversal of the liberal trends that had been painstakingly acquired during the mandate, for the popular classes and rural populations, not to mention the 'Alawis of the mountains, they were too little too late.

Asad's genius consisted precisely in his ability to quickly seize on his predecessors' shortcomings. Unsurprisingly, however, his method was not to eschew 1960s statist policies in favor of liberalization and the enhancement of the rule of law; rather, he opted for populist strategies that enhanced confessional and regional *'asabiya*s ('group feeling'). It is indeed that kind of change, which occurred in the mid- to late-1970s, that is of interest to the subject here, namely that of understanding the unlimited expansion of illicit neighborhoods in the cities of Syria. Such an expansion was the outcome of three interrelated factors. First, the rapid growth of state apparatuses, whether in their civil branches (state bureaucracy, public education, and the Ba'th Party, in addition to multiple 'youth' movements), or the military (the army and a mixture of privatized 'presidential' militias), not to mention a diversification of intelligence agencies (*amn al-dawla* [state security], and the various *mukhabarat* [intelligence] arms). Second, with that kind of numerical push for a combination of civil and military jobs, the number of state employees soared to over 50 percent of the total workforce (compared to just 20 percent in the 1950s). Therein lies the heart of the problem when it comes to the rapid urban growth and the popular neighborhoods that locked the outskirts of most Syrian cities: all kinds of individuals and families, hoping to benefit from the newly expanded statism, migrated to the cities, and with the galloping inflation, the loss in real wages, and the rise in real-estate prices, they had no other choice but to opt for the ever-expanding illicit neighborhoods. Finally, the state, rather than proceeding with well-thought-out urban plans, opted for all kinds of piecemeal (if not suspicious) policies, laws, rules, and regulations that clogged the real-estate market, making it even more difficult to exchange property legally, not to mention introducing all kinds of impediments to the obtaining of legalized building permits. To summarize, the state's reaction to urban growth was slow and clumsy at best, and littered with a proliferation of ineffective laws and regulations whose only aim was to foster counterproductive relations with private property, thus benefiting speculators, bureaucrats, and party officials, while placing landowners at the mercy of municipal and local (regional) committees.

Before we move on to the normative rules that regulate the legalization of illegal properties, we need to expand a bit more on the three factors, outlined above, that eventually led to the massive urban crisis the Syrians are witnessing today.[4]

To begin with, the present urban crisis cannot be properly understood without coming to terms with a major truth, namely, that construction initiated by private individuals has become extremely costly, due to rigid zoning laws, the hassles (caused by bureaucratic slowness and corruption and high legitimate or illegitimate fees) that one would typically encounter when obtaining the appropriate construction permits, and inconsistent state laws and municipal regulations, mostly aimed at 'deregulating' private property. In short, not only is inflation rampant, and the basic building materials (manufactured mostly by the state) not always available, but, more importantly, real-estate transaction costs have grown considerably since the late 1970s, pushing users toward more affordable solutions, beginning with an outright aversion to construction permits.

Do-it-yourself Illicit Practices

The influx of migrants to the city suburbs, combined with high inflation, wage stagnation, inefficient bureaucratic norms, and rigid zoning plans, all contributed therefore to the situation of irreversible crisis that the Syrian cities find themselves in at present. But then it would be unwise not to underscore, albeit very briefly, the legal implications of it all. In effect, the urban and property laws, which for the most part were promulgated in the mid- and late-1970s, reinforced in a series of amendments in the 1980s or later, and which led to the present crisis, could be read as attempts to 'deregulate' private property, with a covert endeavor to weaken even further the propertied urban groups.[5] Consider for instance Law No. 60 of 1979, whose purpose was initially to 'take care' of urban expansion, but which did just the reverse, allowing all kinds of municipal and regional councils to confiscate land at will in preparation for a five-year urban plan.

But even the amendment that came twenty-one years later (in the form of Law No. 26 of 2000), despite placing limits on abusive confiscation, did little to regulate that awkward phenomenon of abusive confiscation, as it is still perceived as a coerced 'selling' of the properties of the well-to-do at prices far below their market value. Added to this is the fact that in 1976 propertied groups were hit hard by Law No. 3 of the same year, which forbade the buying and selling of properties on an open competitive basis.

The users were therefore left with a do-it-all-yourself situation where they had to create their own 'laws' for 'seizing' properties, constructing neighborhoods, and exchanging properties and rents. We should pause for a moment to examine what 'legal' and 'illegal' really mean under such conditions. Or, rather, is 'legality' the main issue at stake here? In other words, should the bulk of properties in the 'anarchic' neighborhoods *('ashwa'iyat)* be looked upon as 'illegal' or 'illicit'?

They certainly are from the viewpoint of the official authorities who describe such areas as 'zones of collective transgression' *(manatiq al-mukhalafat al-jama'iya)*. Within that perspective, the 'illegality' of constructions in slum neighborhoods is the outcome of four interrelated transgressions: the absence of a construction permit; building on the properties of others (private or public, including *waqf*s; lack of an ownership contract ('the green form,' *tabu akhdar*); or the absence of a legal tenancy or sale contract.

It should be noted that usurpation and the violation of the rights of others do not have to go through all four levels. For instance, it is possible that an actor without a construction permit is nevertheless violating state and municipal laws on his/her own land: that is, the ownership is legal but not the construction project. In reality, it is quite common for users to decide to forgo the construction permit even though they already own the land. There are various reasons behind such illegitimate actions: (1) the area in question is not yet within 'the master plan' *(al-mukhattat al-tanzimi)*,[6] or else it is, but the neighborhood in question has yet to be partitioned *(farz)* and various spaces delimited *(tahdid)* for public use (pavements and roads, mosques, parks, schools, and hospitals); (2) the neighborhood has been partitioned, but receiving the appropriate building permits proves a hazardous task, due to high fees (which even if users could afford they nonetheless decide to override) and bureaucratic slowness and corruption; (3) it is much cheaper and affordable to bypass the law; (4) residents can come up with their own architectural designs and styles, often borrowed from the rural areas that they have moved from.

Legalizing 'Illegal' Ownership

When a private property is used for the sake of an 'illicit' construction, the property itself may either be owned by the person proceeding with the construction, or else it may belong to someone else. In the latter case, de facto settlements with the landowner can follow suit, either immediately (during the various construction stages) or much later (sometimes years later). It has been reported to me by some residents that it has become more and more difficult to build on 'the lands of others.' Apparently such violations were the rule back in the 1960s, when the phenomenon of 'illicit neighborhoods' had only just seen the light, and when much of the terrains outside Aleppo were owned by some of the 'big families' who had inherited their properties from Ottoman times. Those families, which for the most part lived either in the city's old neighborhoods or in modern homes outside the old city, kept farms (*mazariʿ*) on lands acquired in Ottoman times. With the decline of the agricultural sector, the professionalization of the middle classes, inflation, and the decline in real wages, the value of land itself became much more lucrative than that of its agricultural produce. Naturally, farmers living in those areas or in the countryside were the prime purchasers. Soon, however, the original owners realized that those new owners were not only illegally constructing on the lands they had just purchased, but even expanding their constructions on lands they did not own. Today, however, unconstructed land outside the city's limits belongs mostly to peasant and nomadic families, tribal sheikhs, or the nouveaux riches, who have benefited since the 1970s from all kinds of lucrative deals. "It is very difficult to build on someone else's territory," said one of the residents of a slum neighborhood east of Aleppo, "as some of these properties belong to residents in the neighborhood, or to their relatives in villages further east, or to tribal sheikhs, or to people in the city. That's the big change from the 1960s when those lands were owned by a few families from the city, who had no contact at all with the aliens who grabbed their lands and violated their rights."

Given, then, that residents are building on their 'own' lands—or at least opting for de facto settlements—how do they manage their leases and property transfers? We enter here into lawless territory, where the inhabitants themselves create their own norms and laws. Not only do residents have to design their homes and manage enough space for pavements, roads, alleys, water pipes, sewage facilities, electricity, and telephone cables (and now fiber-optic equipment), but they must also make an assessment of the 'legality' or otherwise of the whole business of settling in such neighborhoods.

Because they have no access to legalized contracts, the residents create their own sets of legalized—albeit 'illegal'—contracts. What this implies is that in spite of the grossly illegal nature of all transactions—lack of proper permits, planning, and contracts—life goes on as normal, and residents have to live by that reality. Considering that obtaining the green form is a near impossibility, residents have to opt for what comes closest to fully legalized ownership, namely, contractual settlements that grew in parallel to those imposed by the state. In themselves such contracts are neither legal nor illegal. At one level, they do what all contracts do: describe an exchange relationship between two or more parties. The problem here, however, is that the property that is the subject of exchange has not been legalized, and sometimes even the land upon which the building has been erected has an illegal status (for instance, because it is public property, or is a *waqf* territory, and hence belongs to the Ministry of Awqaf). A language therefore has to be devised to construct a terminology of exchange that would attempt to bypass the illegality of all transactions. If we see things 'through the eyes of the state,' the whole process looks like a complete aberration. But seen from the perspective of the actors themselves, the contractual settlements make sense. The process is simple enough for the layman to understand, and one should add that, *mutatis mutandis*, it is even simpler than state procedures. In effect, had the residents followed the normalized state procedures, not only would the costs (on their side) have been higher, but the bureaucratic procedures would have been more complex. From the example outlined below, it turns out that the residents, while working out sets of procedures parallel to the legitimate ones, use state institutions to endorse their own 'illegitimate' procedures. Yet, taken at face value, what the residents' documents are claiming is authentic, in the sense that each document describes what was happening to the property: x purchased from y the following property, as described, for a specified sum; or x rented from y the following property, as described, for a specified monthly rent. But even though the information provided was (in most instances, we presume) 'correct,' it lacked 'credibility' because of the information it fails to spell out, namely, that the area on which the property stands has not been partitioned *(farz)* by the municipality, nor has the landowner sought a permit to proceed with the construction.

Suppose, as with our first case below, that the building was illegally erected back in 1990 without a prior construction permit on a property that belonged to the same person who had initiated the construction. The landlord then sold his property in 1991 through a 'procedural fiction' type of contract where buyer and seller exchange (false) claims that the seller sold his property, received part of the payment, and then refused to deliver (more on such procedures below). The same property was subsequently transferred from one owner to the next through similar procedures. What is remarkable, then, is that residents would routinely use various state agencies—in particular the 'settlement courts,' *mahakim al-sulh*—to proceed with their transactions—even if each one of those contracts was rooted in an 'illegal' act. In effect, a settlement court would take over contracts while knowing beforehand that the entire property subject to the act of exchange (either sale or rent) was illegally constructed, without any prior permit, while possibly trespassing on someone else's property. Most of those contracts are therefore attempting to legalize either a single or double violation, or in other words, each contract sits on a single or double violation.

Hasan 'Abd is presently a state employee at the Ministry of Petroleum, having served in its Aleppo branch for close to a decade. His BA degree in social sciences from Aleppo University (which he received in 2005), and various salary increases since 2000, when Bashar al-Assad came to power, have boosted his salary to above SYP10,000 a month ($200). A father of seven, he belongs to the Walda tribe, and more precisely to its al-Sa'ab clan branch. He shuttles weekly between his native village east of Aleppo, where his parents and extended family still live, and his neighborhood of Karm al-Muyassar where he has been settled since the early 1990s with his cousin-wife and seven children.

The Karm al-Muyassar ('Olive Yard of Muyassar') originally belonged to notable families *(a'yan)* who had inherited their properties in Ottoman times, and probably in this case dominated by the Muyassars themselves. Such families controlled the city's suburbs through a system of farmed lands, which in some instances served as a buffer zone to the properties that they owned in remote villages. Only under the agrarian reforms, initiated by Nasser during the Union under the pretext of property distribution but with the real aim of building political support among the peasantry, and then by the Ba'th protagonists in 1963–65, did land ownership begin to change hands. It does seem that it was the shifting of ownership of some of the lands in Aleppo's suburbs from the big families to small and medium farmers which had initially prompted the illegal movement of construction within agricultural zones. Thus, small to medium farmers, who all of a sudden became owners thanks to the agrarian reforms, preferred to build on rather than farm the newly acquired plots

Fig. 7.1: View of Karm al-Muyassar in July 2007. Floors are added to the original infra-structure as needed, without official authorization. Photograph by Zouhair Ghazzal.

of land: apparently these were too small and too fragmented to be worth the effort of farming. The movement accelerated in the 1970s with the state recalcitrantly playing the role of the nation's largest employer.

"When I used to come to Karm al-Muyassar as a teenager back in the 1980s," says Hasan, "it was to play football. Most of the terrains were olive yards, and there was very little construction around. I never would have dreamed that I'd become an owner in that same area fifteen years later." How do you become an 'owner' in an area like that?

The process of ownership involves a two-step procedure, which, pre-dictably, is much simpler than what state bureaucracies would have required. The first step involves a 'procedural fiction,' where buyer and seller claim that the property has been purchased but that the seller refused to deliver. Procedural fictions have been common since at least Ottoman times (for further elaboration on this subject, see chapter 2 in Ghazzal 2007), and they mainly serve to confirm and establish the validity of acts of sale or rent which under normal circumstances would be hard to acknowl-edge. In our case here, the construction was probably completed in 1989–90, on land that seems to have been owned by the same person; hence there was no trespassing involved. Having, however, constructed in an area that had no partition plan (*ghayr mufraz*), and with no construction permit in

Fig. 7.2: Water meters are designed by the inhabitants themselves and are in public view. Photograph by Zouhair Ghazzal.

hand, the original owner, whenever he wanted to rent or sell his property, had to opt for a contractual settlement through a procedural fiction.

Today the areas of Karm al-Muyassar that had been initially partitioned *(mufraz)* by the municipality, and those that still are not *(ghayr mufraz)*, are separated by a wide boulevard, which at night shines with yellowish fluorescent bulbs. Hasan's home is located only a few blocks east of the demarcation zone. What distinguishes the two zones—the legal from the illegal—is the quality of construction, rather than the standard of living. While the partitioned areas are ripe with five- to six-floor high-rises, shops, boutiques, and small manufactures, illegal areas have mainly one-to two-level constructions, euphemistically referred to as 'Arab homes' *(hosh 'arabi)*, for the simple reason that their epicenter consists of an inner 'courtyard,' which these days is more of a covered staircase than an inner yard per se. What is characteristic of these 'Arab homes' is their insistence on regarding the inner space of the home as something totally 'private,' where no eye could peek through its outside walls and windows. Even Hasan's terrace on the top floor, which he added to the lower two floors only recently, after ten years of hard work and a couple of loans from state agencies, is completely walled to the exterior, blocking the panoramic view of the neighborhood and the city's endless eastern expansion. "I really need my privacy. When I sit with my wife and kids on our terrace in the summer nights, we need to breathe some air, and we don't want anyone prying at us." This desire for 'privacy'—or rather the fear of intrusion—explains the unusual absence of pavements: instead, the main doors are protected by means of an angular stoned wall which acts like a massive curtain that blocks any inside view.

But the big difference between the two areas lies in ownership titles. Thus, while the partitioned western areas of the Karm have all been planned by the municipality prior to construction, and hence each property (home, shop, or manufacture) can—at least in principle—be identified using its green form, the eastern part of the neighborhood lacks such luxuries. If your property is legal—meaning both land and construction have received the green form—then you transfer it through a regular sale contract, and the new owner receives his or her green form, in turn. The residents located in the eastern zones of the Karm have to operate differently. The first step would have to be a procedural fiction where buyer and seller exchange claims, and where a judge rules in favor of the buyer, followed, much later, and only if necessary, by a quasi-regular sale contract. But even if the two steps are successfully completed in a court of law, with a judge's full endorsement, the lucky owners still do not receive the illustrious green form.

Let us first look closely at the procedural fiction. The one-page handwritten document was signed by a *qadi sulh* ('peace judge') in Aleppo's seventh civil court on 2 May 1994, when Hasan decided to 'own' the property and transfer it to himself. Knowing that this was one of those homes 'illegally' completed around 1989–90 (even though the original terrain *may* have been legally transferred through a green form, but that remains uncertain), he knew beforehand that the property, which was transferred to several successive owners between 1990 and 1994, could be 'legally' owned under his own name only through a procedural fiction.

The main purpose of a procedural fiction is to facilitate a process that cannot be dealt with through regular channels. In the particular case here, Hasan knew that the entire neighborhood, having received no partition plans, was 'illegal,' and that his own property, having not been originally granted a construction permit, is also 'illegal.' In a civil court in Aleppo he poses as a plaintiff in a lawsuit against the then 'owner.'

Fig. 7.3: A typical fictitious contract of sale whereby the sale is posed as a fictitious litigation between a seller who failed to deliver and a buyer who is claiming his property, which is ratified in an official Aleppo civil court in the Palace of Justice. For a complete translation, see Appendix on page 199. Photograph by Zouhair Ghazzal.

Section one of the lawsuit reads as follows:

In the lawsuit dated 17 January 1994 the plaintiff claimed that he purchased from the defendant the totality of 14 shares [ashum][7] from property number 2900, in Aleppo's tenth residential district, for a sum that the two parties had agreed upon, and which the defendant had received in total. The defendant owns the aforementioned property thanks to a court's ruling number 451/4967 in 1993, but still has not transferred [faragh] the property to the plaintiff.

We therefore request that:

a notice [ishara] be inscribed on the property's form [sahifat al-'aqar];

to notify the defendant of the litigation;

to confirm the sale in his presence;

to remove the litigation's notice once the property has been transferred;

to have all fees and expenses paid by the defendant.

The first thing to note is that the plaintiff and defendant were situated within a 'friendly' litigation that they had *both* initiated, even though the court's ruling does not state that fact overtly. Herein lies the essence of procedural fictions: the litigation is not to be taken as 'real,' but only as a procedure to confirm a transaction, which in this case is an act of sale. Why not then go directly for an act of sale? Precisely because the property in question is illegitimate, so a direct act of sale would not work. Since the property has neither a partition number nor the requisite green form, it would not be eligible for sale through a regular sale contract. The procedural fiction, which in this case transforms the handicap into a litigation between plaintiff and defendant, totally bypasses the 'legal' issue of the property's ownership.

Second, the judge's ruling notes that the defendant had owned the property since 1993, and we should add that the ownership was also an outcome of a fictitious litigation from a previous 'owner.' Which means that between 1990 and 1994 the property went through at least two acts of sale, both as fictitious litigations conducted in a court of law. Obviously, judges *know* very well what is behind such contracts, and that users seek the litigation *(khusuma)* form precisely because they have to appear in front of a judge in a civil court. In effect, centring around the notion of 'litigation,' procedural fictions (often referred to as *hiyal* in the old Hanafi manuals) are common since Ottoman times (if not before) for the precise reason that their formula entitled the litigants to receive a ruling in the presence of a judge. Since a judge's ruling would in most instances be irrevocable, an act of sale through a fictitious litigation would carry more weight than a regular act of sale.

The second part of the lawsuit reads as follows:

> In the open court hearings, the plaintiff reiterated his claims and, accordingly, requested a hearing in his favor. The defendant also acknowledged his opponent's rights in their totality, and had no objection to a ruling in favor of the plaintiff on the basis that the latter would assume all fees and expenses. The two parties agreed on that.
>
> Considering that acknowledgment [iqrar] is at the root of evidence [sayyid al-adilla], and it has the status of contract for the acknowledger [huwa hujja 'ala al-muqirr];
>
> Considering that the notice of the litigation [isharat al-da'wa] has been inscribed on the property's form based on contract number 373/1994;
>
> Considering that the court has sought the opinion of professional expertise, a visit to the place has revealed that it is composed of an Arab home [dar 'arabiya] whose main door is oriented toward the west, with two rooms, a living room, a staircase that leads to the top floor. The house, constructed in concrete, is made for residential living, and the expert estimated that it was twenty years old;
>
> Considering that from the ruling that the defendant 'Abdul-Karim has brought with him to court, he owns 14 shares of property number 2900, based on a previous civil court ruling number 451/4967, issued on 31 August 1993;
>
> And based on articles 62, 132, 200, and follow up articles 99–100, and articles 148, 386, and 826 of the civil code;
>
> It was decided:
>
> Confirm the present act of sale between the plaintiff Hasan 'Abd and the defendant 'Abdul-Karim Zayn on the fourteen shares of property number 2900 in Aleppo's tenth residential district, and the transfer and registration of the shares in the plaintiff's name in the city's cadastral registers.
>
> Retract the lawsuit's notice as soon as the ruling takes place.
>
> Payments of fees and expenses are on the defendant.
>
> Signed on Saturday 9 April 1994 by the judge and his assistant.

What is remarkable in this document, which issued from a civil court, is that it totally avoids the 'illegitimate' *(mukhalif)* nature of the building in question. Moreover, it gives the wrong impression that the construction is perfectly legal, has a specific number allocated to it in the city's cadastral records, and that it has been standing as it is now for at least twenty years. Of course, none of that is true. To begin with, we know for certain that the fourteen shares (of a total of twenty-four) allocated to the building are neither officially recorded in the city's cadastral records nor carry the celebrated 'green form' for that matter. Furthermore, since the entire area has not even been partitioned *(lam tufraz)* by the municipality, the latter cannot provide maps that would delimit each property with the number allocated to it. In effect, and based on my informers' knowledge of the area, I was told that until 2007 the municipality had yet to prepare topographic layouts for the area at large. In other words, the municipality is left with the only choice of acknowledging such a slum neighborhood as a fait accompli. The other possibility is a partial or complete reconstruction through a mixture of state, private, and foreign investment funds (more on that later). For the moment, however, the neighborhood lacks adequate maps, sewage facilities, water, electricity, and telecommunication infrastructures.

So the number 2900, which the suit claims was assigned to the property, is therefore totally bogus. The property's current owner, Hasan 'Abd (the plaintiff), told me when I visited him in July 2007, that the number 2900 must refer to the "entire area"—and even that was open to speculation (which area? which boundaries?)—and not to his "own" property. Moreover, and contrary to the court expert's claim that the property must have been at least twenty years old, Hasan told me that he is almost certain that the foundations and first floor could not have been completed prior to 1989–90. In short, and at the margin of the fictitious litigation itself, lie several other 'fictions,' beginning with the property's alleged number and its age. Finally, and this is in itself a remarkable omission, considering how important it is, we never know from the document what the *value* of the property is. Such 'omissions' are characteristic of procedural fictions in general. Had the plaintiff specified a *specific* sum for the transaction, the judge would have summoned him to furnish evidence: for instance, the value of the transaction and methods of payment. But that is not the purpose of a fictitious civil lawsuit: the aim here is *solely to confirm the act of sale*, not the value of the property and the methods of payment. It is therefore common in fictitious litigations that either no sale price is mentioned, or at best the sale price is so minimal—or 'symbolic'—that the judge would not even bother with evidence. As we will see in a moment, the sale price becomes important only once the contract of sale is formalized.

Overall, then, the civil courts tend to be quite soft with their 'illegal' owners (or tenants). Not only the formal 'illegal' status of the property is never mentioned, but the judge seems to be playing the "shared meanings" of his actors (Žižek 2006, 51–52). To be more precise, the language strategies displayed by the actors (judge, plaintiff, and defendant) are a combination of formalized procedures that borrow from so many sources that they look like a bricolage puzzle. Thus, elements of the civil code are there for sure (quoted in terms of their specific codes), and also the formal routine of a litigation (the plaintiff–defendant duo), in addition to the judge's ruling. An essential element of the language game is what the formalized litigation 'hides': mainly, the original 'illegal' status of the property, and the fact that this court of law is *legalizing a transaction on an illegal property*. The court also makes the bogus claim that the property was assigned a specific number, giving the false impression that the area and street in question, which include the litigious property, have been partitioned *(mufraz)* and the properties have received their green forms. Moreover, the court, through its expert, claimed that the property must have been at least twenty years old, which I was assured by the owner himself, is not the case. Needless to say, the court plays in favor of its disputants, accepting their language games at face value, while leaving behind the 'genuine' status of the property.

We are therefore in an unusual situation, characteristic of such illicit neighborhoods, where several state agencies are working independently of one another. On the one hand, there are institutions such as the city's council and municipality, which are always 'late' and cannot keep up their services with the high level of demand. Planning lags behind, the fees are high, and the bureaucratic routine is merciless. On the other hand, even though users violate every law on the ground, they nevertheless come to courts that are user-friendly in order to process their litigations. These courts provide them with a substitute for the green form.

Rethinking Context
In order to understand what at first glance appear to be bipolar contradictions—the legal and the illegal, the legitimate and illegitimate, and the legalization of the illegal in civil courts—we have to contemplate *how actors work their language games within specific contexts* (or "frames," as Erving

Goffman would call them) (Joseph 1998). Within each situated encounter, actors enter into active procedures that help them define the situation at hand. Thus, for every situated encounter, actors would contexualize their actions by indexing them in relation to a shared meaning that is taken for granted. What therefore appear at face value to be irrational bureaucratic procedures—for instance, a civil court ratifies a sale contract that lacks the proper 'legal' endorsements when it comes to property rights (the green form)—could be sociologically looked upon as *contextual rites of passage*. The social actors are constantly moving from one context to another, and for each context active procedures are deployed to define the situation at hand. When, for instance, buyer and seller are on their own, the 'illegality' of their situation can be overtly stated without the need for euphemisms: they both know beforehand that the property lacks the proper green form, and that it does not have a registration number with the city's municipality. When they are both in court, as plaintiff and defendant, for the purpose of ratifying their sale contract, the judge knows beforehand of the property's 'illegal' status, and that such properties can be 'legalized,' without benefit of the proper green form, through procedural fictions. Had the property been legal in the first place, the two parties would have directly opted for a regular sale contract (see below), and then the buyer would have received a green form from the municipality's cadastral offices in his own name. The irony here is that a regular legal sale contract could take as much as a year to be completed (until the reception of the green form by the buyer), or even more, particularly if the property has a sign *(ishara)* attached to it from a previous lawsuit, while an illegal contract can be settled in a civil court in two weeks.

For our purposes we will distinguish here between two operative levels of contextualization.

The ethnographic context consists in this case of the *legal* expertise, which consists of the expertise of the civil courts, and that of the actors outside the system, such as buyer and seller, who in court assumes the role of plaintiff (buyer) and defendant (seller). Actors mobilize their communicative resources in respect to a specifically situated context, and they *account* for their actions in respect to that same context.

The conversational context and its negotiated order. We have dealt above with a typical contractual settlement where buyer and seller negotiate with a civil judge over the possibility of a litigation-cum-contract where the 'illegal' status of the property is precisely resolved by *not* evoking it. Granted that the judge had gone through the same kind of settlement many times before, and that he was, on that occasion, only applying a 'formula' that would legalize the selling of an illegal property, he nevertheless had to deploy his 'contractual competence' for the task at hand.

Courts therefore do not simply come up with rules, regulations, and norms ready to be applied. Had courts proceeded that way the illicit neighborhoods and their contractual settlements would have been left entirely out of their adjudicative system—at least until new legislation could come to their rescue.

Another Sale Contract

With his 1994 contractual settlement Hasan 'Abd had secured the ownership of his new home. But he was still without the regular water, electricity, and telecommunications facilities provided by the state, and, needless to say, the entire area lacked sewage utilities. It is indeed common for illicit neighborhoods to remain without state-run utilities for several years, or for over a decade. Residents typically proceed with illicit utility connections from neighbors 'on the other side,' that is, with those areas that are profiting from the state's benevolence. As hacked electricity and phone cables are visible all over such areas, the thin metallic water pipes are for their part barely noticeable. Residents learn how to 'share' electricity and phone lines with the more fortunate residents of neighboring areas. Then, once the illicit area has fully 'matured'—which, in most instances, implies that the vacant areas have shrunk considerably, and the density of the population is comparable to other crowded areas—the utilities companies step in and install their services. In other words, planning is always piecemeal and the outcome of circumstances on the ground, rather than the product of conscious urban planning.

But to receive the services of the electricity company, which residents look upon as a top priority, a contract of sale is needed. The document that we discussed above was more of a contractual settlement that confirmed the buyer's ownership through a fictitious litigation than a regular sale contract. It is therefore not the kind of ownership contract that the electricity company would accept for the purposes of consigning a meter specifically to the house. Under normal circumstances, the green form would have served nicely for that purpose. When the form is not there the alternative is a less glorious form of ownership: a regular contract of sale.

Hasan 'Abd concluded a formal contract of sale only in 2002. Even though the earlier 1994 sale confirmation through a fictitious litigation was enough for all intents and purposes, by 2002 regular state electricity had become available, and a formal sale contract was needed in lieu of the green form, which was unobtainable, for an electricity meter to be installed.

The 2002 contract is much simpler than the one concluded in 1994. To begin with, it is printed on a form to be filled in by the two parties. Only two witnesses sign the contract, side-by-side with the buyer and seller. The form itself is printed at a regular commercial press, and is not an official state document, even though it does for practical purposes serve as one.

Article 1 of the sale contract specifies the names of the buyer and seller, the location of the property and its number, and a brief description of the construction. Article 2 specifies that the sale value was SYP350,000 ($7,000). Article 3 notes that the buyer paid the seller SYP50,000 ($1,000) as an 'advance payment' or deposit (ra'bun), which would serve as a damage compensation in case the buyer defaults. Article 4 states that the seller has promised to pay all taxes and fees attached to the property and complete all the necessary repairs by September 2002. Article 5 states that the buyer has made up his mind after carefully examining the property and all its annexes. Article 6 states that the seller has agreed to transfer (faragh) the property to the buyer within a two-month period, and in case the seller has failed to deliver, his failure would be looked upon as a deliberate decision not to sell, and he would pay the buyer the sum of SYP50,000 ($1,000) as damages, without the need for any warning or prior request. The buyer would then have the right to receive back his 'advance payment' and put an end to the contract. My understanding of the text is that in case the seller defaults, the buyer would receive back in addition to his 'advance payment,' an amount equal to the original, or a total of SYP100,000 ($2,000).

Article 7 states that if the buyer defaults, in addition to losing his deposit, he would pay the seller damages equal to SYP50,000 ($1,000). The seller would be given the option to annul the contract, or to confirm it, or to pursue the buyer in court. The final articles, 8 to 11, are concerned with fees and expenses.

The 1994 and 2002 contracts obviously represent different language games. The two had to be devised either separately or in combination in lieu of the green form, which was impossible to obtain. Thus, while the 1994 contractual settlement was explicitly devised—in the form of a fictitious litigation—to confirm the act of sale, the 2002 contract was more straightforward, and its sole purpose was to make the owner eligible for basic state utilities (electricity, water, and phone services). The fictitious litigation in the 1994 contract prompted a court hearing and a judge's ruling—hence its importance—while the regular 2002 sale contract did not—hence its value is more formal. Indeed, as the judge's ruling carries the mark of authority and is hard to revoke, users opt for such a prestigious and more reliable cachet over a regular sale contract.

A Grammar for a Microsociology of Neighborhoods

We have now reached the most emblematic level—that of understanding the norms that guide social relations in such neighborhoods. When asked about what guides them in their daily lives, residents would place the 'tribal factor' *(al-'amil al-'asha'iri)* at the top of their list. But what exactly are tribal norms or values, and how do they affect such an urban environment? The well-established residents of Aleppo's old, middle-class neighborhoods typically deride claims that popular neighborhoods have anything 'urban' about them, as it is commonly assumed that their new residents bring with them 'tribal values' from their villages and previous, nomadic lifestyles.

The so-called tribal factor ought to be taken seriously by researchers for a variety of reasons. To begin with, the residents of the peripheral popular neighborhoods maintain strong ties with their villages and tribes, as a nexus of economic relations grows between city, periphery, and neighboring villages. As visits to the village tend to be frequent, their significance is more than economic, since it fosters the traditional values associated with the countryside and the nomadic life.

Second, as family relations are taken seriously, marriages tend to mimic kinship relations within the family or tribe, which accords predominance to the paternal cousin's marriage, to the *mahr* (as a way to discourage multiple marriages), which could be worth the price of an apartment and is based on the value of gold vis-à-vis the Syrian Pound, and finally, to 'customary marriage contracts,' which are officially obtained only once couples need them (to allow their children to be admitted into public schools, for example). Moreover, when migrating to the city, the tendency is to choose a neighborhood where some of "our kin are already there." However, even though some of those neighborhoods are dominated by specific tribal affiliations, urban settings are too complicated and economically non-compliant to allow for a continuous juxtaposition of tribal affiliations, in reality scattering kin members all around the urban peripheries. Residents tend to map the territory in terms of their various kin affiliations.

Third, kinship relations can be strong enough to regulate public behavior. During my last visit to Hasan's neighborhood in July 2007, a young man had been stabbed to death a couple of nights before following a fight with a small youth gang in the same neighborhood. Apparently, the elders from each clan took rapid control of the situation, and within twenty-four hours handed in the culprit to the police; the latter were informed of the killing only *after* all inter-clan disputes had been settled. Hasan transformed this event into an anecdote, as evidence of the strength of conventional clan ties over state institutions, beginning with the police. It would be fair to say that in some instances clan ties take over or replace the tasks of state institutions: in this particular example, the police were only involved after the alleged culprit had been identified and the decision had been taken to turn him over to the police. Sometimes a minor is delivered as the 'culprit,' on the assumption that penal laws will try him under mitigating circumstances. At every level, therefore, there exists a flimsy tension between weak pre-existing state infrastructures, ever prepared to expand further into the lives of individuals, and the local practices of neighborhoods.

Fourth, clan relations can be useful in the job market. Residents have either to find jobs in the neighborhood itself or in neighborhoods close by, or else in the city at large. Many of the new peripheral neighborhoods, such as Karm al-Muyassar, unlike the northern Kurdish neighborhoods with their small to medium-sized textile and shoe export-oriented manufacturing facilities,[8] generally lack decent manufacturing hubs. Instead, available jobs tend to be oriented toward the immediate neighborhood's needs (construction, carpeting, carpentering, and car repairs and maintenance), a high percetange of which are occupied by male teenagers. As clan relations tend to make a difference in the hunt for local neighborhood jobs, or even for the other close neighborhoods where the clan has some presence, so they are generally irrelevant to the city at large, particularly when it comes to state employment, or employment in the manufacturing zones (Kallaseh, 'Arqub, 'Ayn al-Tall, Shaykh Khudr, Hulluk, Bustan al-Basha, and the industrial zone). Some small to medium manufactures, located in the northwest of Aleppo, have larger proportions of Kurds than average, due mostly to their proximity to Kurdish neighborhoods, and because of the superior skills of Kurdish young men and women. Kurdish women, due to weaker religious and clan pressures, enjoy higher employment rates.

Fifth, clan relations have some influence on the routines of daily life. That is the most difficult level to pin down and understand. I would like to propose a preliminary set of sociological categories, situated within the sociology of action that would eventually serve for more thorough research in this area.

Frame. Harold Garfinkel (2005, 106) quirkily stated in his early work (which was only published in 2005) that an actor acts based on a "cognitive style" that allows him or her to assess, understand, and react to a specific situated encounter (see also Goffman 1986). By assigning the "actor" (or "member") to a specific situation, Garfinkel attempts to delineate the "actor" from the (philosophical) "person" or "individual," while showing that the actor's cognitive framework is only geared toward *that* situation. The notion of "frame," which was introduced by Erving Goffman in one of his latest and most compelling works, *Frame Analysis* (1986), assumes a "cognitive style" through which actors would practically understand and organize their social experiences. A frame thus helps actors to orient themselves while interpreting and evaluating a specific situation.

The notion of the frame could be crucial to a multilayered understanding of illicit neighborhoods. We have already noted the importance of what actors describe as the 'clan factor.' Because it is 'all over,' the tendency among researchers would be to develop a general regulating matrix where the 'clan factor' would be everywhere: from marriage, the habitat, neighborhood life, and recreation, to securing a job in the labor market. The notion of frame, by contrast, avoids reducing actions to a general regulating matrix of sorts, be it the clan or the economy, as it situates the cognitive capacities of actors within situated encounters. We have seen, for instance, how, in the absence of state regulation (due to the 'illegitimate' labeling that has fallen on such neighborhoods), residents have to 'legalize' their 'ownerships' (or tenancy rights) through a number of contractual settlements that require actors to interpret the situation at hand. Thus, in the absence of a green form, users could opt for a 'regular' 'illegitimate' contract (the second type of contract analyzed above) that would work perfectly well under some circumstances (for example, to receive basic state utilities, if available), but would be looked upon as a 'weak' 'proof of ownership'—hence the usefulness of a fictitious litigation (the first type of contract analyzed above). Actors therefore learn which type of contract to use, based on the frame that would determine which contract would be relevant at a particular juncture.

Context. A specific context is determined by the available resources within a frame, which users assess based on the indices of the situation. When users come, for example, to a civil court to ratify a contract of sale (the first type of contract), they know beforehand that their home is situated in an 'illegal' zone, and that the building itself is therefore 'illegal.' They nevertheless do come to a court of law, knowing that the act of sale would be legalized through a fictitious litigation. Thus when the user poses as a 'plaintiff' he knows that he is not one per se, but he indexes his action within the frame of the 'legal context' of the civil court. 'Legalizing the illegal therefore achieves a more meaningful strategy once understood within the notions of frame and context: the users are simply 'legalizing' an action that transfers the property from seller to buyer, while avoiding, however, any mention of the non-availability of a green form for the property that has just been transferred.

Involvement, commitment. Actors become involved and committed once they assume a 'role' within their 'communities.' The degree of intensity of involvement and its significance will vary considerably from one framed context to another. Let us assume, for instance, that some individuals, whether young or old, assume the dubious role of 'clan coordinators' in their own neighborhoods. They could thus intervene and offer their services for things as diverse as a contractual settlement, a sewage problem, or a fight that has erupted among a group of teenagers. As those are different situations, which would obviously need the mobilization of different resources, the same actor would not participate with the same kind of involvement and commitment, even if the 'clan context' is present in each of these situations. Moreover, the 'clan context' would in all likelihood have little significance, if at all, once the actor moves outside the neighborhood, say, for his daily job in the state bureaucracy: his involvement there would be limited to the bureaucratic context, which generally assumes different resources than that of neighborhood interactions.

Face. This is the social value that a person claims through the line of action that he adopted during a situated encounter. To stick to our example above, when a neighborhood resident adopts the role of 'clan coordinator,' it is not enough for him, in the context of a situated encounter, to simply claim that he 'belongs to clan X, and is only acting as coordinator for the benefit of the community.' Such a claim would constitute the 'social value' at work in an encounter, but since the 'face' is located neither inside nor outside an individual, nor in what actors overtly state or claim, but in the flux of events within a specifically framed context, which determine the 'value' at stake, the social value (face) is never stated once and for all, but is always in a state of flux. In other words, there is neither an identity nor a norm to which actors can simply abide. The shared meaning emerges once actors cut through the impasse of endless probing by simply taking for granted what they 'mean' to be doing in a particular situated encounter. That is to say, there is a 'leap of faith' that is profoundly anti-normative, in that it cannot be ascribed in language once and for all, since it precisely attempts to bypass the deadlocks of accepted norms by enabling a form of fictional communication whereby 'we accept what we are doing simply because we mean the same thing.'

Face-work. The common expression "to save one's face" implies that, during a situated encounter, one has to adopt a certain posture, as a protective gesture, and to come to terms with possible dangers in a particular situation. The 'clan coordinator' can adopt tough or soft stances, and his posture must find the right equilibrium based on the situation in which he finds himself. Again, and in relation to traditional kinship sociology, microsociology does not operate within a broad notion of kinship that would absorb all the daily strategies of day to day life. It instead follows actors in their situated encounters, pointing to the postures that they adopt and the maneuvers that ensue.

Interaction. The reciprocated actions that the protagonists exchange as individuals, teams, or as groups, and which can be located in public (the street) or in private (at home), are in themselves either focalized interactions—involving direct conversations and face-to-face work—or non-focalized, for instance, street interactions. The latter are particularly common in poorer neighborhoods, as streets and empty lots (parks and public recreational spaces tend to be absent) are filled with youth 'buddy teams' (even though age is not necessarily the determining factor). But while male teams can be present at every street corner, pavement, or empty lot, complete with mats, chairs, narghiles, *tawla* sets (Tictracs) and food and drinks, women are more private and tend to sit together in public only at the main entrances to their homes. Children, who are everywhere, play the go-between between different age groups, men and women, homes and families, and neighborhood zones and their clan divisions. Children pose easily for photographs; they even pursue the photographer until their photograph is taken—and with digital cameras, they insist on seeing the snapshot at once. Men consider that posing in public in front of a camera is something that only they can do and is therefore a provocation that women cannot afford. Indeed, men often challenge the photographer with 'provocative' poses and by calling them directly: it is the *anonymity of the encounter* that is at stake here, the kind of anonymity that a woman cannot afford—not even with a female photographer. In contrast, girls of up to a certain age, when they still don't wear scarves or veils, behave like boys and men. By the time they reach the ages of twelve to fourteen, however, the culture of shame steps in, confining them to their households. Bedouin women usually do not veil themselves—only urban women do—and their attire tends to be more vibrantly colorful.

A 'foreigner'—or someone *perceived* as such due to body language and attire—is like an 'intruder,' who is shamelessly looked at by everyone in the street: men, women, and children. As that whimsical feeling of 'foreignness' is instantaneously bestowed on the bearer, he or she could be openly asked questions about their origins (*nasab* or *nisba*), nationality (if suspected to be non-Syrian or non-Arab), whereabouts, current residency, profession, and the reasons for being in a shanty neighborhood "like this one." Such an overt *openness* is indeed characteristic of such neighborhoods, as 'privacy' refers more to 'the inner space of the home,' than that of a private (bourgeois) individual with rights and duties toward himself and others. In other words, the notion of a *public privacy* is here practically nonexistent. As a decent percentage of the men has worked in Lebanon, either as laborers or in the military (or both), in the last thirty years, the *anonymous individualism* of the people in the street is what strikes them the most over there: "that you walk around, and no one—no one—looks at you, is what's most amazing in Beirut," said a young man, while comparing the attitude of people in his own Aleppo neighborhood. However, gazing at a woman from the neighborhood is inappropriate, as it can even be looked upon as a deliberate act of provocation. But a woman 'from the outside' is another story, in particular if the 'outside' is further from home. In a similar vein, looking at your neighbor's home from the inner privacy of your own home—or worse, from your veranda—is more than inappropriate. Indeed, there is a parallel between the sacredness of woman-as-*hirma*,[9] and that of the inner space of the home: as the latter is perceived as feminine, it is de facto the space of honor, and if trespassed, then that 'honor must be washed' (*ghasl al-'ar*), for instance, through an honor crime, which in Syria is acknowledged by the courts as such. 'Private,' if it means anything, is therefore that of the 'interior' feminine space of the home, and is certainly not associated with an abstract right of individual privacy.[10]

Public order. This is an order that is founded on the right to look (*droit de regard*), which implies that others give us that privileged right to look at them and to react accordingly. What Goffman labeled as "the presentation of the self in everyday life" (Goffmann 1959) is an outcome of the right to look and looking back at one's self, or, in other words, how the self constructs (an image of) itself through the looks of others.

Not looking at a woman of the neighborhood, and not gazing at the inside of a neighbor's home, are instances of public order. In such instances there is no notion of 'self' that would be 'universal' enough to be abstracted from the common concerns of clan honor, trespassing on a woman's virtue, and the dynamisms of tribe and clan, and their urban–rural connections. As the self has a hard time distancing itself from the group at large, team behavior dominates, particularly among men. Men in teams of all ages—a phenomenon referred to as 'office'-work, *maktab*—occupy street corners and empty lots, home and shop entrances, mosques and Sufi orders (if available), enjoying that *endless* right to look in public (Totah 2007). Their tendency to congregate in teams (sing. *fariq*, pl. *furaqa'*) of sorts is a combination of kinship and labor factors: shopkeepers, for instance, use their shops—or, rather, the front pavement—as meeting spots for men, whether employed or not. As lots of young men are either employed with very low salaries, or benefiting from sporadic employment, or have been unemployed for years, the *maktab* has become their favourite place for gossip and street observation.

Creating an 'autonomous' private and public self, independent of the group at large, could therefore prove an arduous task. Hasan told me how a man he had known for some time began regular visits to their home, only to show an interest in his eldest, eighteen-year-old daughter who had just passed her baccalaureate, and soon after asked for her hand in marriage. But as his daughter did not show any interest, he decided not to pressure her: "For my generation, marrying one's paternal cousin, as I myself did, was imperative. But I am not alone in thinking that none of my seven children will go in that direction; they will take time and make their own choices. I won't force them into anything—not even the girls." Although Hasan's daughter has more physical space to herself than her mother did, she still has a long way to go before she achieves that autonomous space of her own, since much of the public order does not yet see individuals in terms of their private rights.

Recent news reports have indicated that the Syrian government has, for the 121 or so illicit zones throughout the country and their estimated 11,000 hectares of illegally constructed areas, struck a deal with a private Saudi company totalling $440 million. The General Habitat Company (al-Mu'assasa al-'Amma li-l-Iskan), regarded as Syria's prime public company, is the main beneficiary of the joint venture that the government worked out with al-Ula ('The First'), a private real-estate Saudi company. Of the $440 million that would set up the new real-estate joint company,

30 percent would go for the Mu'assasa and the remaining 70 percent would be in the hands of al-Ula. It remains to be seen, however, how the newly established joint Syrian and Saudi public–private venture will work in reality. Considering that zones labeled as *mukhalafat* are illegal from the state's point of view, the Iskan could, for instance, propose new plans for each one of the illegitimate 121 zones, which could imply either a partial or total destruction of the built areas for the purpose of infrastructural rehabilitation *(ta'hil)*. It remains unclear, however, whether the residents themselves would have any voice at all: Would they be simply 'fairly' compensated and then asked to leave? Would there be compensation settlements where both parties—the tenant-owner and the new joint venture—would compromise for a fair price *(bi-l-taradi)*? How will the compensation schemes work out concretely, and who will decide what are fair and unfair policies?

There might be several reasons behind the government's policy shifts, assuming that the aforementioned joint venture will see the light as planned. First, great reviews in the last decade—and more and more are published on online web services—have indicated that the slum cities that strangle the main urban areas are nothing but time-bombs waiting to explode. Damascus itself has 38 illegal zones (out of the estimated 121 on the national scale), whose projected area ranges from 30 to 50 percent of the capital's urban neighborhoods. Second, as 85 percent of construction sites are in private hands, and as the state seems to be slowly withdrawing from its old socialist policies of the 1960s and 1970s, the tendency would be to look for a 'solution' to illicit neighborhoods among private investors. Third, considering how close they are to the legitimate zones, some of the illegal areas have become financially quite lucrative, prompting official authorities and private financiers alike to regard them as zones of capitalist investment, rather than social drawbacks. The official authorities may thus have opted to open those areas to local, Arab, and foreign investors, hoping that in the meantime the illegal tenant-owner would move to other areas, which in itself would reinitiate the infernal cycle of constructing in agrarian areas without prior authorization.

As the nation-state is a never-ending enterprise, even in the most advanced liberal societies, always expanding in all directions, while attempting to control lives and territories, social actors have to fill in the gaps on their own, through their daily practices. When it comes to the societies of the eastern Mediterranean, however, due to the brisk transition from an Ottoman imperial administration to colonial and postcolonial state formations, the historical weaknesses of the nation-state are particularly visible. In this instance, users of a particular space—namely, those inhabiting the marginal neighborhoods in big urban agglomerations—not only *create* their own space, but more importantly, have to establish normative values that would otherwise be part of the overarching structure of state enterprises. What is therefore remarkable is that users tend to mimic the now remote state infrastructures as best as they can, creating their own living spaces through tempered negotiations with state administrative and juridical institutions, in particular the civil courts. What emerges in this process are *negotiable norms*, which sooner or later become integrated within the larger framework of a nation-in-progress, and of spaces where power relations are determined more by what is materializing on the ground and less by the historical weaknesses of the authoritarian regimes in question.

During the last decade not only has there been little improvement in the quality of life and in terms of the legalization of illegal contracts in the *'ashwa'iyat* zones, but, more importantly, since the beginning of the Syrian uprising in March 2011, such zones have become the most prosperous economic havens in town. Indeed, observers have been baffled at how much Aleppo and its province (totaling over four million inhabitants) have been quiet during the uprising, such numbness being attributed to a combination of political and economic factors: the presence of strong Christian and Kurdish minorities; Aleppo's preponderant role in the national economy (20 to 25 percent of the private investments); and the role of families in controlling neighborhood violence. But what has been overlooked is that the uncontrolled expansion of the *'ashwa'iyat* is in itself a stabilizing factor: left on their own, without the usual (mostly corrupt) police intervention, social actors are building at an ever more frantic pace. These factors bring an urgency to the questions posed in this study: whatever the nature of the future government in Damascus, what kind of organization is it possible to envisage for the *'ashwa'iyat* zones, which, by all accounts, have become uncontrollable?

Appendix
Translation of sale contract in Figure 7.3.

In the name of the Syrian people
[Names of judge, assistant, plaintiff, defendant, and representatives]

Subject of the lawsuit: sale confirmation
I. The lawsuit
In the lawsuit dated 17 January 1994 the plaintiff [Hasan Abd] claimed that he purchased from the defendant the totality of 14 shares *(sahm)* from property number 2900, in Aleppo's tenth residential district, for a sum that the two parties had agreed upon, and which the defendant had received in total. The defendant owns the aforementioned property thanks to a court's ruling number 451/4967 in 1993, but still has not transferred *(faragh)* the property to the plaintiff.

We therefore request that:
a notice *(ishara)* be inscribed on the property's form *(sahifat al-'aqar);*
to notify the defendant of the litigation;
to confirm the sale in his presence;
to remove the litigation's notice once the property has been transferred;
to have all fees and expenses paid by the defendant.

II. Verdict
In the open court hearings, the plaintiff reiterated his claims and, accordingly, requested a hearing in his favor. The defendant also acknowledged his opponent's rights in their totality, and had no objection to a ruling in favor of the plaintiff on the basis that the latter would assume all fees and expenses. The two parties agreed on that.

Considering that acknowledgment *(iqrar)* is at the root of evidence *(sayyid al-adilla)*, and it has the status of contract for the acknowledger *(huwa hujja 'ala al-muqirr);*

Considering that the notice of the litigation *(isharat al-da'wa)* has been inscribed on the property's form based on contract number 373/1994;

Considering that the court has sought the opinion of professional expertise, a visitation to the place has revealed that it is composed of an Arab home *(dar 'arabiya)* whose main door is oriented toward the west, with two rooms, a living room, a staircase that leads to the top floor. The house, constructed in concrete, is made for residential living, and the expert estimated that it was twenty years old;

Considering that from the ruling that the defendant 'Abdul-Karim Zayn has brought with him to court, he owns fourteen shares of property number 2900, based on a previous civil court ruling number 451/4967, issued on 31 August 1993;

And based on articles 62, 132, 200, and follow up articles 99–100, and articles 148, 386, and 826 of the civil code;

It was decided to:

Confirm the present act of sale between the plaintiff Hasan 'Abd and the defendant 'Abdul-Karim Zayn on the 14 shares of property number 2900 in Aleppo's tenth residential district, and the transfer and registration of the shares in the plaintiff's name in the city's cadastral registers.

Retract the lawsuit's notice as soon as the ruling takes place.

Payments of fees and expenses are on the defendant.

Signed on Saturday 9 April 1994 by the judge and his assistant.

Notes

1 After a dearth of urban studies, some recently emerged publications show greater attention to the daily lives of ordinary urban inhabitants, in particular, Balanche 2006; Ababsa 2009; Ismail 2006; Elyachar 2005; Tuğal 2009.

2 The Union introduced a series of practices that the Baath would later capitalize on once it took power in 1963, for example, the politicization of the police force; the promotion of intelligence services to the dubious role of controlling the population at large; the abrogation from the civil code of articles that permit voluntary associations and cooperatives; the dismantlement of waqfs through the promotion of the direct sale of their properties rather than going through the strict regulations of 'exchange' demanded by the Hanafi school of law; and all kinds of economic measures (for example, the nationalization and confiscation of private enterprises and funds) that severely restrained free enterprises.

3 While the 1948–49 so-called war of independence created a massive influx of Palestinian refugees—close to a million—into neighboring Arab countries, giving Syria its fair share of what became known as 'temporary camps,' which translated into de facto slum neighborhoods outside the traditional city peripheries, the consequences of the 1967 war proved even more dramatic, as over 150,000 inhabitants of the Golan Heights moved to safer areas (including the outskirts of Damascus) within a three-day period, creating the largest population influx in Syrian history.

4 An anonymous article, edited and published in the online daily Akhbar al-Sharq (14 November 2007) by Tarif al-Sayyid 'Isa, digresses on some

of the reasons that led to all forms of illegal urban expansion in contemporary Syria.

5 Even though most properties are owned by individuals, and are registered under individual names, property ownership in Syria, as in the rest of the eastern Mediterranean, tends to be status- and family-oriented. Many rural properties in particular were collectively owned as musha' (or shuyu', meaning collectively owned property), while urban properties, in order to keep up with the family ethos, would be registered under more than one name. Needless to say, the state largely benefited from such collective-cum-family ownership, as it knows full well that decision-making among family members slows down considerably under such conditions. Thus, abusive confiscation of properties for the 'public good' became the norm, encouraged by all kinds of laws and regulations, leaving family owners totally helpless in most instances in the face of labyrinthine court procedures.

6 The purpose of such plans is to delimit 'urban' and 'rural' zones, in order to protect the latter from excessive abuse.

7 Twenty-four shares of a property represent its totality, that is, the full 100 percent.

8 In Kurdish neighborhoods, where clan relations have broken down, prostitution is on the rise. That is particularly true of Shaykh Maqsud, considered as the hub of prostitution and drug trafficking. The northern Kurdish neighborhoods have strong connections with the region of 'Ifrin, a conglomerate of 366 villages.

9 From *haram*, what is sacred.

10 See Pierre Bourdieu's structural analysis of the house of the Kabyles in Esquisse d'une théorie de la pratique (Geneva: Droz, 1972).

References

Ababsa, Myriam. 2009. *Raqqa: territoires et pratiques sociales d'une ville syrienne*. Beirut: Institut Français du Proche–Orient.

Balanche, Fabrice. 2006. *La région alaouite et le pouvoir syrien*. Paris: Karthala.

Bourdieu, Pierre. 1972. *Esquisse d'une théorie de la pratique*. Geneva: Droz.

Elyachar, Julia. 2005. *Markets of Dispossession: NGOs, Economic Development, and the State in Cairo*. Durham, NC: Duke University Press.

Garfinkel, Harold. 2005. *Seeing Sociologically: The Routine Grounds of Social Action*. Boulder, CO: Paradigm Publishers.

Ghazzal, Zouhair. 2007. *The Grammars of Adjudication: The Economics of Judicial Decision Making in fin-de-siècle Ottoman Beirut and Damascus*. Beirut: Institut Français du Proche-Orient (IFPO).

Goffman, Erving. 1959. The *Presentation of the Self in Everyday Life*. Garden City, NY: Doubleday Anchor.

————. 1986. *Frame Analysis: An Essay on the Organization of Experience.* Boston: Northeastern University Press.

Ismail, Salwa. 2006. *Political Life in Cairo's New Quarters: Encountering the Everyday State.* Minnesota: University of Minnesota Press.

Joseph, Isaac. 1998. *Erving Goffman et la microsociologie.* Paris: Presses Universitaires de France.

Singerman, Diane. 1996. *Avenues of Participation : Family, Politics, and Networks in Urban Quarters of Cairo.* Princeton: Princeton University Press.

Totah, Faedah. 2007. "Maktab." In Baudouin Dupret, Zouhair Ghazzal, Youssef Courbage, and Mohammed Al-Dbiyat, eds., *La Syrie au présent.* Paris: Sindbad—Acte Sud.

Tuğal, Cihan. 2009. *Passive Revolution: Absorbing the Islamic Challenge to Capitalism*, California: Stanford University Press.

Žižek, Slavoj. 2006. *The Parallax View.* Cambridge, MA: Massachusetts Institute of Technology.

8

Secure Land Tenure? Stakes and Contradictions of Land Titling and Upgrading Policies in the Global Middle East and Egypt

Agnès Deboulet

Over the last decade, the percentage of the urban population living in slums has decreased dramatically in the developing world: it has dropped from 39 percent in 2000 to 33 percent in 2010 . . . . Despite this the number of slum dwellers is increasing in absolute terms . . . . The progress made by the development goal on slums is inadequate" (UN DESA 2010, 62). Precarious urbanization is separate from economic growth and is reinforced by difficulties in finding decent housing in urban areas where speculative mechanisms, weak or disengaged states, and inadequate standards deny an increasing proportion of the population access to decent housing, including those whose incomes have increased (Mitlin 2008).

Almost half a century after experts and researchers began to draw the authorities' attention to social issues in Arab countries and cities of the south, the Millennium Development Goals[1] and the Cities without Slums projects have helped raise awareness of the challenges posed by the large-scale presence of housing with unrecognized land tenure. Paradoxically, many projects develop without consideration to any redistribution of resources, yet it is possible to study the changes in discourse and public policy that have begun to recognize so-called informal neighborhoods.

Recent shifts in these worldwide policies must therefore be examined from two perspectives. On the one hand, one must try to discern what now anchors the intellectual and operational structure of the transformation of vulnerable settlements. We will address this complex issue by making formal and discursive links between slums and informal settlements. This study of semantics leads us directly to decision-making and to an understanding of the evolution of the political agenda. Secondly, this article investigates paths and models of legalization and regularization from the Habitat I conference, which took place in Vancouver in 1976, until the late 1990s. The last decade (2000–2010) also been marked by the increasing importance of urban renewal issues in the context of international urban competition. These include many discrepancies and contradictions. The extent and variety of topics covered by unplanned settlements in the cities of the south require us to focus on certain recurrent measures in the treatment of social and spatial issues in owner-built neighborhoods. For this study, the Arab world will be used to illustrate some of the ways in which to take account of legality and illegality in the treatment of poor neighborhoods.

A Historic Turning Point: Consensus on the Eradication of Slums

Today, we can consider that the legalization of informal neighborhoods has failed in many aspects. It is usually only regarded by evaluators as successful in pilot programs, but rarely widens to a larger scale of intervention, through individual projects in specific defined areas.[2] Dozens of researchers are now working on producing a critical corpus of legalization. We will use their work as an element with which to highlight the treatment of illegality in the Arab world and especially in Egypt. But first we shall focus on the vocabulary of social issues in cities of the south. Legalization, restructuring, and also eradication are supposed to put a stop to the proliferation of squatter settlements, which are substandard, called shantytowns in North Africa, and are now known as slums on the international agenda. The change of lexical register, with the generalization of the term 'slum,' pervades all institutions, old and new (especially UN-Habitat) that seek legitimacy (Gilbert 2007) and provides new operational frameworks for states to combat one of the worst aspects of poverty. Thus the policy of slum clearance is in full swing: in Morocco the Cities Without Slums program is supported by several bilateral cooperation agencies and the World Bank (Le Tellier and Iraki 2009). In the Middle East it is now possible to truly legalize and/or improve or restructure certain neighborhoods; this has been the case in Syria since

2008, with the new GTZ (Gesellschaft für Technische Zusammenarbeit GmbH) programs. Recently in Egypt all housing more commonly called *'ashwa'i* or 'random' in Arabic (Bayat and Denis 2000) is subsumed under the term 'slum.' This new international term for public action draws a new line between the international injunction to eliminate slums (and consequently relocate inhabitants) and the consolidation of existing insecure tenements, thereby opening a way for action that did not exist previously. This new policy orientation distinguishes between actions to be taken regarding squatter settlements—the new equivalent of slums—and unplanned areas, or illegal subdivisions.

In addition to an increasing awareness by international institutions, policy regarding shantytowns has adopted stronger technical measures, whereby the 'upgrading' of all slums is considered necessary. Risk was the benchmark for typology of housing, the urban environment, and thus of public action. This new categorization largely overlaps with that of squats and former slums, now clearly targeted for action.

In Duweiqa, a district in Manshiyat Nasir, one of Cairo's largest squatter areas, had already been identified as vulnerable to rock slides in the wake of various accidents that had followed the massive urbanization of this unrecognized neighborhood. But in 2008, a major accident caused the death of 119 people. Replacement dwellings were erected but occupied by people other than those threatened by a future rock collapse. The scandal was such that within three monthes a new national agency, the Informal Settlements Development Fund (ISDF), was set up with the aim of redeveloping high-risk informal areas in Egypt. The ISDF distinguishes unsafe areas *(gheir amina)*, which the Fund's director describes as the "equivalent of slums," from unplanned settlements *(gheir mukhattata)*. The demolition of so-called unsafe areas falls within the ambit of the Ministry of Housing and the General Organization for Physical Planning, which are also responsible for the improvement of unplanned settlements. Their categorization aims to restructure the UN-Habitat definition of slums according to a new risk-related scale. High-risk areas are to be demolished as a priority (category 1), closely followed by unsafe housing (shacks, or *'ishash*). Categories 3 (areas with hygiene or public health problems) and 4 (areas with insecure land tenure) therefore become low-priority areas for eradication. Presumably category 3 areas will be upgraded in situ and category 4 accorded land ownership regularization. For the ISDF, which is under the direct control of the prime minister, the solution is the eradication of slums (or unsafe housing) and the relocation of slum inhabitants to new towns. In Cairo, the ISDF has identified sixteen urban areas out of fifty-three as unsafe (that is, category 1 areas). They will not all be awarded the same level of priority for demolition, however (Interview with the ISDF in December 2010; UN-Habitat 2010). Risk is used to legitimize the erasure of parts of squatter settlements where eviction had long been considered impossible for fear of the social consequences that might ensue. Government agencies are also more likely to demolish areas with greater financial potential than areas that cannot be developed again. Considerations of risk therefore allow the authorities to justify the demolition of areas, paving the way for a regeneration strategy by offering new stretches of land to developers. Since the 25 January 2011 revolution, the ISDF has been keen to show that this hidden strategy should not be allowed to take place.

Identify the Problem Before Trying to Solve It

Many recent publications, especially Mike Davis's pamphlet (2006), reiterate the findings of UNCHS reports (UN-Habitat). They stress that a third of urban dwellers live in slums. The category of slum now used by transnational UN institutions is defined by: a lack of sustainable housing, insufficient living space, poor access to safe drinking water and sanitation, and insecurity of tenure (UNPFA 2007, 16). Internationally, it thus partly replaces the older term 'informal settlement.' However, the category of 'slum' has connotations that combine different perceptions and physical realities of habitats: indeed, slums are historically depressed areas, including run-down historic town centers. The term first appeared in Victorian England (Faure 2003; Gilbert 2007) and spread to India to designate run-down inner city slums as well as newly created shantytowns.

The term 'slum' also covers all informal areas, regardless of their legal status: occupation of land, illegal subdivisions, and minor infringements of the law. Mona Fawaz (2007) notes for example that the first generation of developers of Hayy al-Selloum, an illegal subdivision located to the south of Beirut, had divided the land quite legally because at that time the municipality did not have a master plan. In addition, all land was registered in the land register (*katib 'adil*) and taxes were paid. Therefore the criterion of legality, although important, is not sufficient to define these neighborhoods.

Another aspect obscured by the systematic use of the word 'slum' is the nature of the built environment. Common use of the term 'slum' encourages officials and the media to consider informal settlements as shantytowns or worthless areas due to both the precarious nature of the constructions and the allegedly unplanned nature of the urban fabric. Yet, with the exception of Morocco, Arab countries are characterized by a strengthening of the tenure of the built environment, including in informal districts, and a low prevalence of shantytowns built with scrap materials. This is supported by legislation that sanctions constructions when the roof slab has been cast. The buildings of these neighborhoods are considered stable because they are built in solid materials, and are therefore less at risk of demolition. This is especially true for illegal subdivisions on private land (often agricultural), much less so for squats on public land (often desert). The status of land ownership is all-important here. Countries of the Middle East and North Africa, except for Morocco, are thus characterised by 'informal' housing with a structure of fairly good quality, but that still often suffers discriminatory treatment in access to infrastructure.

Insecurity and Legality: Squatted Land

Using Michel Agier's (2005) terminology or the definition of 'slum' adopted by Fawaz and Peillen (2002), I prefer to talk about insecure settlements, thus focusing the following discussion on the vulnerability of squatter settlements with regard to their differential treatment. Indeed, although demolitions are infrequent (yet sometimes occur on a massive scale when large economic interests are involved, as in Luxor for tourism), the consequences of insecure tenure are evident in squatter settlements. These threats prevent the consolidation of residential areas. They deprive neighborhoods of the substantial improvements that residents could make if they felt less threatened.

The term 'owner-built neighborhoods' is less stigmatizing and takes into account the process of creation. The issue of legalization of land ownership therefore only arises for squatted state land, or as it is known in Egypt, housing established by *wad' al-yad* (taking possession/occupation) of the land, which accounts for about 17 percent of all informal settlements (Sims 2011, 88) in the Greater Cairo area. Conversely, the land status of illegal subdivisions is clearer, but individual buildings and all settlements of this type require full regularization. Illegal subdivisions on agricultural land are like a southern version of Parisian "failed housing developments" of the interwar period. They are regularized on a case-by-case basis by recognition or by the purchase of a planning and subdivision permit, which encourages corruption. However, the entire neighborhood is not regularized, that is, recognized as being able to develop, have rights, and therefore be equipped with urban amenities. In practice, uncertainty and unclear status do not prevent de facto legalization via the provision of facilities (Clerc 2010). We must remember that squatting on public land is more strongly punished than squatting on private land, especially if it belongs to a small farmer. There is considerable heterogeneity of land status, ranging from unrecognized squatting to the ownership of a lot in a recognized illegal subdivision.[3]

In countries where the state has largely disengaged from the direct production of public housing, owner-built housing is an escape valve. It allows construction at virtually no cost for public authorities and a total transfer of responsibility to occupant-builders. Only Morocco has a very ambitious program to eradicate 'insalubrious' housing. The terminology for the clearance of informal settlements always sounds military or hygienist, particularly for the resettlement of slums (Navez-Bouchanine 2002; Navez-Bouchanine forthcoming; Le Tellier 2009).

Legalization and Regularization Projects: The Aims of Pilot Neighborhoods

This section builds on the two-phase study of the restructuring of the suburb of Kilo 2, in Ismailiya. This initiative was studied in the late 1990s and again in 2007; it was followed by a project in two other neighborhoods (al-Halus and al-Bahtimi) and was addressed in terms of its participatory dimension (Deboulet 2007). A follow-up visit in December 2010 assessed the upgrading of al-Halus. Before going into the details of this case study, let us define the terms used and try to decipher their specificities.

Operational practice generally distinguishes between regularization, legalization in the form of physical intervention, in situ upgrading, and restructuring. The table below attempts to show the scope of these terms.

Legalization	Distribution of legal titles or securitization
Regularization	Securing land by various means including legalization; providing collective land rights.
Upgrading in situ	Provision of basic amenities (water and sanitation)
Restructuring	Transformation of parcels and/or of the road system

Legalization and regularization programs are confined to areas where land tenure is not validated by public authorities, that is, land occupied without a land title; in the Arab world this is usually public or state land. In the case of the projects implemented in Egypt since the mid-1980s: in Aswan, Cairo (the Helwan area), and more recently Manshiyat Nasir and Ismailiya, legalization is the central framework to which are added physical improvements and the provision of services and amenities. Based on various studies and research projects (including Dorman 2009), Carolin Runkel (2009) shows that in Aswan in 2006, 45 percent of lots in the Nasriya neighborhood had been purchased through the project, whereas land acquisition in Helwan was uncertain.

To understand the significance of these projects in the long term, it must be stressed that all are based on a formal principle of physical rectification of plots and the urban fabric. They are also rooted in the legalistic and market principle that occupiers without land titles must prove their ownership for the right to stay put and benefit from urban services. In theory, legalization must precede the provision of new services. Legalization is thus linked to urban restructuring and dependent on it.

A 'successful' precedent in the district of Hayy al-Salam gave Ismailiya a headstart in terms of regularization (Davidson and Payne 2000). The legalization of 5,548 lots was conducted in parallel with the construction of many facilities. Above all, this project was partly funded by subsidies linked to the sale of land available in an adjacent area to outside bodies (UNDP 2006).

However, the context of interventions changed radically in the twenty years from the late 1980s to the late 2000s. In particular the expansion of the city has been accompanied by the rapid vertical growth of housing in poor suburbs. Yet the city has many unrecognized and under-serviced districts. Moreover, legalization and new amenities accelerate densification, causing new management challenges. A 2008 study showed that the peri-urban district of al-Hallus (with the administrative status of a village), which in 1998 consisted mainly of single-story houses in *tin* (earth, mud), now has mostly multistory buildings. Meanwhile, its population has increased by one third. Between 2008 and 2010, of the 640 buildings counted, Bérangère Deluc noted 210 with one or two additional floors; indicative of growth due to an increase in value thanks to sanitation coverage.[4]

Monetization and legalization

Another element of change, the dogma of cost recovery, has been entrenched in the institutional landscape, although there are difficulties in implementation (El-Batran 1999). Squatters who wish to obtain a legal title deed for the land they occupy must pay the governorate, and not the project officers. And this is often where difficulties arise, as with other projects in Egypt or elsewhere. The unclear status of the land and the unreliability of the cadastre complicate matters. Claimants are subject to countless steps, as in Kilo 2, Ismailiya. That project was abandoned partly because of the failure of the legalization process. Similarly, Marion Séjourné (2006), citing a report by the Institute for Liberty and Democracy led by Hernarndo de Soto (2000), reported seventy-two transactions needed for registration and legalization *(tamlik)* in Cairo.

Let us review the reasons for failure: (1) the number of steps required for legalization, (2) the process facilitates corruption in countries where low-ranking officials cannot live on their salary alone, (3) the fragility of accompanying legal measures, especially the registration system, does not guarantee sustainability and real security for the purchaser, and (4) the high costs of legalization often make it inaccessible to buyers. The issue of costs is now the subject of controversy both internationally and in the Middle East. Citing Lanjouw and Levy (1988), Alan Gilbert (2002) shows that in Ecuador, the cost of land acquisition is 102 percent of annual household consumption. Other authors (Bolivar 1995) have stressed that ownership puts a burden on household budgets because of property taxes and other taxes that must be paid. Thus, legalization and impartiality do not necessarily go hand in hand.

In Cairo and Ismailiya, the creators and directors of projects disagree over the issue of costs. To cover legal costs and pay the fees to buy illegally occupied state land, those in charge of the GTZ project agree on the payment of a reasonable 10 percent of the land's market value. Thus in Manshiyat Nasir, the cost of *tamlik*, or land ownership, in the governorate in 2010 ranged between LE100 and LE200 per square meter depending on the location.

Lots closest to main roads have the highest value. In Ismailiya, the *tamlik* has increased considerably since the installation of sanitation and a water supply. Since Law No. 148 of 2008, the cost of legalization is reviewed by a committee of the governorate working with several departments including the Department of Agriculture. What are the origins of these variations? Prices established before 2006 vary depending on the size of the road that runs alongside the house: LE6, LE8, and LE16 respectively for property located on a cul-de-sac, a small road, or a main road. Since the installation of a sanitation system, the market price and public price have risen sharply, initially between LE30 and LE50, then in a range from LE45 to LE85. Do these prices multiplied by 5 (upper range) and 8 (lower range) take into account the fact that if the property is not resold, occupants of a 100 m² plot cannot easily afford such a sum, which represents a laborer's annual salary.[5] In these circumstances, the reopening of the process after a two-year freeze by the governorate was only partially successful. Only 200 households out of 1,100 (11 percent of which were tenants in 2006) received titles. From 2006 to 2008 the prime minister rejected all requests for regularization, creating a dispute between the project's officers and the governorate.

However, the aim should be to enable secure real-estate transactions and residential stability in particular. Alan Gilbert (2002) demonstrated with the case of Bogota that large-scale titling is driven by economic objectives. The government hopes thereby to dispense with infrastructure provision, which is far more expensive. In the Egyptian case, it is meant to accompany or precede the provision of amenities. The work of the Institute for Liberty and Democracy around the ideology of 'dead capital' showed the monetary value of informal housing stock, which would amount to $74 billion in Egypt. This financial aspect is the main argument.

Over the past thirty years, local authorities have only allowed legalization in localized areas. The Participatory Urban Management Program, which began in 1998, was the first example of a multi-level approach, and also covered Manshiyat Nasir. Piloted by the GTZ in collaboration with Egyptian ministries, it appears to be successful in the provision of services, job-creating activities, and the upgrading of the largest squatted settlement (Manshiyat Nasir) estimated to have 900,000 inhabitants (as well as Bulaq al-Dakrur). In contrast, the legalization program has been at a standstill for fifteen years,[6] with long periods awaiting the signing of the decree to initiate legalization by the governorate, followed by limited implementation with unknown results. In 'Izbit Bekhit (Runkel 2009) 10 percent of applicants were successful.[7] The program was reinstated following the disaster in Duweiqa. However, as elsewhere, legalization was considered a prerequisite. In Hilwan, Nadia Taher (2001) shows the impact of disagreements between the United States Agency for International Development (USAID) and the Ministry of Housing; conflicts between ministries and the Governorate of Cairo impeded the realization of the program.

When legalization takes place, its territorialization pits the legal against the illegal. It perpetuates the denial of "recognition" (Durand-Lasserve and Tribillon 2001, 73), by allowing the harassment of those who are not regularized, in other words, most occupants. What is needed is a form of social ownership, which would provide "social equivalents of private property" (Castel 2003, 31) like pension schemes in companies, or collective regularization. This would go beyond an approach based on profitability, and favor realistic solutions, such as the provision of amenities with an official announcement of regularization (Runkel 2009). A clear announcement of the regularization of an entire neighborhood can also produce very significant effects in terms of recognition (De La Saussaie 2009); we must avoid subjecting grass-roots rights systems to rigid and dysfunctional legal systems.

Legalization and restructuring projects: reconciliation and adaptation

The programs in Ismailiya fall under the Sustainable Ismailiya Governorate Project (SIGP), a pilot project supported by the UNDP and UNCHS with various forms of bilateral cooperation, and initiated in 1993. The project was resumed in 2003 and aims to upgrade two slums. With support from UNDP and UNCHS, it focuses on the participatory dimension. This Participatory Slum Upgrading in al-Hallus and al-Bahtini, or PSUHB, seeks to provide more economic intervention and education. During the SIGP phase, we studied the implementation of the legalization and upgrading program in Kilo 2, followed by research in al-Hallus before and during the PSUHB.

Let us begin by considering the buy-back procedure and its costs. In previous situations such as in Kilo 2, legalization schemes failed because dwellers were supposed to justify the fact that occupied land was not agricultural (but desert and thus public). But in Ismailiya, as in all cities on the margins of the Nile Delta, most agricultural land has been reclaimed from desert land, roughly since the opening of the Suez Canal, and this process continues to this day. Thus land status is often unclear as desert land has often exchanged hands among Bedouin populations, without benefit of formal contracts. Another shortfall is often exemplified by the growing sale and purchase of squatted land. Many large cities host a growing number of squatters, who, because of a lack of availability of free land, have had to pay informal land brokers in order to squat on a plot of land. This situation can be seen in 'Izbit Khayrallah and Stabl 'Antar in Cairo, where since the mid-1990s, access to land has been determined through the marketplace. During the early years of the settlements, one simply paid someone a symbolic lump sum to buy a plot; it was even possible to occupy land directly. This ability to squat by *wad' al-yad* became restricted due to the scarcity of available public land and land-grabbing by intermediaries. In cities where competition for land is fiercer, the markets for squatting land were largely monopolized by local land mafia or mafia networks, which put additional pressure on buyers by making them pay for land several times over. How can one justify the price of legalization—especially if it is fixed on the market price—if the squatted land has already been purchased from a so-called owner? This inequity is often emphasized in Cairo in informal neighborhoods. Since the 1990s, squatters have not benefited from free land.

In Ismailiya, regularization has been halted since 2007 after a disagreement between the PSUHB and the governorate concerning the provision of infrastructure and the terms of legalization. Taking advantage of its comfortable budget, the PSUHB was however able to pre-finance the health infrastructure, without waiting for a hypothetical solution to the issue of land ownership. It is this realization, combined with microcredit and social facilities, that has substantially improved the quality of life of inhabitants.[8] This confirms the initial survey of residents at the outset of the first project. The five priorities identified during meetings did not include legalization, but did mention, successively, the very poor condition of schools (especially the toilets, which caused many girls to skip school); rodents; the lack of sanitation; lack of health services; and the absence of waste collection.

The upgrading undertaken by the PSUHB is based on a set of urban standards that begin with road straightening and widening. Thus the right to occupy disputed land is combined with the straightening of roads and the redefinition of rights to plots. The scheme plans to make all roads over six meters in width suitable for vehicles, which *in principle* involves the demolition of all or part of buildings that encroach on the future public right-of-way. This demolition, which must be carried out by the occupier himself, only applies to homes built with materials considered worthless and is designed to spare concrete houses. This program is supported by the urban upgrading strategy advocated by UN-Habitat. Since "unplanned areas generally suffer from narrow streets and a lack of BUS (basic urban services) they need: security of tenure; a lower degree of densification helped by street widening, and the provision of BUS . . . to encourage the contribution of civil society" (UN-Habitat 2010).

The low level of street alignment undertaken by plot settlers themselves confirms the observation made by John Turner in 1968. He linked the failures of urban planning with the lack of understanding of the settlement processes and an integrated definition of housing based on the relationships between location and accessibility, tenure, and services. Therefore, the chief characteristic of good housing for residents is its capacity to provide attachment, that is, affordability and compatibility with social and economic practices, such as informal street activities or production. The priority for first-generation settlers and low-income residents has always been employment and the securement of a living, not street layout and enlargement, a reality frequently overlooked by urban restructuring schemes.

In practice, the principles of this upgrading were so poorly accepted that property was frozen rather than demolished. In this 'model' project, decisions concerning buildings could not be made without negotiations. The residents of Kilo 2 were not officially recognized as interlocutors in this arbitrary system with its ever-changing rules (Deboulet 2000); however, they managed to influence standardization by explaining to local officials that it would be financially difficult for them to demolish a wall of their home. Plagued by a series of unrealistic urban standards, the project was considered a failure by its proponents, who abandoned it.

Al-Hallus has the same urban regulations: the technical team decided to widen a number of roads without prior assessment of the use of the roads or the traffic needs of the population, 99 percent of which does have a vehicle (UNDP 2006). This is in line with the straight roads and traffic systems that are the basis of most urban plans. While some of these widenings are considered indispensable by residents for the avoidance of moral stigma (especially when dead bodies have to be carried to the road), they are not accepted without prior negotiations. In order to bring about "small modifications" (Hamdi 2004) one must show the project's technicians that their demands are unrealistic and that the paradoxes of planning contradict the objective of helping residents out of poverty. Only very few houses encroaching on a busy road have been partially demolished. Infrastructure has finally been provided without having to adopt the originally planned alignment (except along the road leading to the school).

These discrepancies between rules and their implementation come about because there is room for negotiation. This pilot project reflects an acknowledgment, if not formally but at least in practice, of the difficulty of applying strict planning standards that conflict with the objective of reducing vulnerability. These adjustments are the product of a mediating technical team and of a 'local committee' of 'voluntary' residents. They must be taken into account to transmit problems to a steering committee composed of local officials and officials with international expertise.

The upgrading program originally planned was therefore never implemented. The few demolitions were negotiated on a case-by-case basis with the residents concerned and 'community leaders,' mostly women. The Manshiyat Nasir program anticipated these negotiations by discussing required retreats and alignments with residents. This dialogue shows consideration for the ability of people to express their individual and general interests by starting group discussions on the topics of urban standards and traffic systems.

Tenants: those who are overlooked by regularization

However, differential treatment is part of a vision shared by all local and national professionals. The public health approach sees that problems of "accessibility are caused by . . . narrow streets and lane widths and very close buildings. This also reflects the bad health conditions of the area . . . the narrow roads prevent the community from having proper wind circulation and sun exposure and therefore this physical problem has environmental implications" (UNDP 2006, 22–23).

These schemes also anticipate and encourage the removal of adobe houses, considered unfit for habitation and vertical extension. Thus, concrete structures are unaffected by the alignment scheme, partly because their compensation would be much more costly. Studies ignore the fact that these very basic adobe dwellings primarily house the poorest residents, who bear the brunt of this urban model. Legalization programs generally show no concern for tenants and the poorest residents, and ignore the vulnerability caused by the project for households unable to meet expenses. Professionals in charge of these programs are not always aware of or equipped to anticipate such unintended effects of policies in order to integrate issues of vulnerability.

Over ten years, the landscape of al-Hallus has indeed changed dramatically. A survey of all dwellings made of *tin* (mud) bricks in 2007 shows the extent of the transformation. During the first visit, almost all houses were first generation, that is, built of slabs of dry mud or adobe. The combined effect of demographic and social pressure caused these structures to be rapidly demolished by their owners or occupants or abandoned.[9] Most of those that remain house tenants. Comprising one main room with no running water, these homes also house large families lacking opportunities, often fishermen from Fayoum. This is because the future lies in vertical expansion resulting in five- to six-story buildings that are halfway between investment property and multi-generational homes on the patrilineal model (*al-beit al-kebir*). This context of socially and functionally obsolete housing is reinforced by the indifference of local and foreign professionals as to the genetic code and heterogeneity of its population. Moreover, this social discredit due to building materials is reinforced by the UNDP building report: constructions in *tin* and *debsch* (limestone), that is, adobe and limestone bricks, make up 23.3 percent of all buildings, whereas the program encourages construction in reinforced concrete. Concrete is equated with progress, while densification and speculation are overlooked aspects of regularization.

The association of legalization with urban regeneration or restructuring (the former involves the installation of amenities and the latter also includes improvements, especially of the road network) therefore also leads to unanticipated social problems. Studies of World Bank projects of the 1980s to the most recent work on projects that combine legalization and regeneration are quite critical of two main points. Firstly, the beneficiaries are often the most well-off among average-income households; secondly, because they are very limited geographically and improve living conditions, these programs put additional pressure on the poorest and most vulnerable sections of the population. Indeed, they encourage speculation from slum lords (in India, wealthy or powerful individuals who charge rents for land that does not belong to them) or minor landowners who see the opportunity to rent under more favorable terms (Kantor and Nair 2005; Huchzermeyer and Karam 2006). While this is hardly a case of gentrification, the rising value of land and property is an unanticipated consequence of operational practice. It results in the upsurge of evictions carried out by the private sector (Durand-Lasserve 2006) in order to select tenants or buy cheap plots with the potential for high profits in legalized or well-equipped neighborhoods. With no protection for tenants or the occupants of plots, the pressure of rising rents and the temptation of expulsion are associated with and reinforced by the rising value of land and property related to legalization, regularization, or upgrading in situ when possible. This is true in Cairo, where the search for available land has become a major target for public authorities and developers (Barthel 2010).

Twenty-five years after the beginning of regularization programs, which are sometimes accompanied by building upgrades, the serious risk of discrimination against the poor remains high. The lack of first-hand knowledge of revenues and the capabilities of households, poor social support, except in Morocco with Maître d'Ouvrage Sociale (MOS) programs followed up by the Agency for Social Development, improves the finances of some households but also the vulnerability of others because of discrepancies between income and land and property values. The very detailed study by Kantor and Nair (2005) shows that within a restructured slum in Lucknow (India), the vulnerability perceived by residents is expressed through the combination of socio-demographic characteristics and the stage of the lifecycle. Thus, large families, a high ratio of girls to boys, and a high number of adolescents and households headed by women are all identified factors of vulnerability. But in the event of an economic shock due to restructuring, the vulnerability of these specific groups can be explained by the difficulty large families face in coping with family responsibilities; both material and symbolic (in particular, ritual costs). The difficulty of bouncing back following increased housing costs or the risks of eviction is exacerbated by women being forced into labor because of social norms and expectations of female behavior.

Quasi-rights and Impossible Legalization

Land-use practices in owner-built neighborhoods are little known. While they are original and adapt well to living conditions, they are barely taken into account by developers when securing tenure. However, researchers have already demonstrated that what matters most to occupants is not ownership, but secure land tenure (Razzaz 1991).

In the Middle East, this relates to the lack of recognition of the variety of rights and active systems and quasi-legal and customary practices based on collective ownership. Balamir and Payne (2001) note that in the nineteenth century the system of Islamic law was based on the recognition of occupation or possession by residents or neighbors. Similarly, systems of communal ownership of land have been shelved by legal measures inherited from colonial powers and independence, erasing local rights (Comby 2007). To avoid a process of legalization and land registration that would be extremely costly for both the government and occupants in sub-Saharan Africa, there is a need for a simplified system of adverse possession (in Brazil, a resident must have occupied a property for five years before he or she can gain some kind of legal entitlement to ownership). We must emphasize that this system exists under Egyptian law and mainly concerns plots occupied and developed in good faith. It is essentially a "reversal of the land tenure system." The point is to clearly introduce peaceful and continued possession as the origin of ownership (Comby 2007, 13) based on the existence of a 'customary market'; in essence, an updated popular market. Besides the possibility of signing before a notary, as is the case in

Morocco, also cited by Comby, one can rely on the principle of continuity of occupation based on testimonial evidence and verbal agreements. Neighbors and real-estate intermediaries or informal agencies, *samasra* (sing. *simsar*), can also become recognized parties for this validation of land titles.

Quasi-rights or grass-roots rights in the Arab world are very well described in the pioneering work of Omar Razzaz (1991). It shows the nature of land disputes between the state of Jordan and the Bedouins to determine the use or ownership of land on the poor outskirts of Amman. It becomes very difficult to determine the sole owner of a piece of property when previous owners claim rights to it based on their own perception of ownership. As Razzaz writes, there is a need to distinguish between legal claims and legal rights. But these potential conflicts are also present, though rarely mentioned, in other areas like assisted desert sectors, such as the neighborhoods of Arab Rashed and the neighboring areas on the outskirts of Helwan, south of Cairo (Taher 2001).

In Cairo's squatter areas, intermediary land rights validate and secure transactions. Secondary markets highlight the' fact that land is already developed in order to circumvent the ban on selling the land of others. In the mid-1990s in Stabl 'Antar, documents show that ruins *(anqad)* were sold on state land. As well as this type of title, electricity and water bills can be used as the basis of legitimacy of tenure. In the late 1980s, a trial pitted the residents' committee of 'Izbit Khayrallah and the Governorate of Cairo against the Maadi Company,[10] which claimed ownership of the land, and in the days before Google Earth changed the means of establishing proof, utility bills were used to justify the presence of many residents.

Finally, it must be accepted that illegal occupation always reflects the failure of government structures not only to provide building land but also to efficiently manage land. In the Middle East, squatted land is always located in disputed areas, with ownership that is uncertain and often the subject of conflict prior to occupation. This aspect should be taken as seriously as legalization (cf. Soares Gonçalves 2010).

It is useful to study the convergence between an analysis of informal economies based on trust and honor (Tarrius 2002) and the functioning of land and property markets. Therefore in considering the forms of access to a legal framework, social hierarchy should be borne in mind as well as the systems of interaction and norms that underlie land exchanges. Specifically, the operation of parallel markets based on social rules shared by all parties is based on the legitimacy of developers in the local sphere: whether in Beirut or Cairo, they reinvest in a symbolic economy or euergetism (building schools and mosques) and try to be considered as notables (Fawaz 2008; Haenni 2005).

The existence of new rights produced by the population, which reinvent traditional practices with the aim of providing security, is even more visible in squatted areas. Indeed, only personal protection can offset the total uncertainty of occupation. In 'Izbit Khayrallah in Cairo, the casual developers who began urbanization act as agents capable of identifying ownership and boundaries. The frequent presence in squat neighborhoods of individuals who are legitimized by all or part of the population shows that subdivision and the settlement of conflicts go well together, yet new locally acknowledged authorities have appeared in the 1990s in self-developed popular areas, in the form of the *sheikh al-balad*, or neighborhood leader, whose work combines land regulation, social networking, and organizing projects in neighborhood associations *(gam'iyat)*. Local knowledge and connections, the social capital of associated parties, and honest practices set apart associations that are deep-rooted, protective, and protected from those that are doomed to disappear sooner or later. These bodies should be used as a base for a multifaceted production of rights while avoiding the cumbersome and penalizing nature of legalization. This form of organization is to be compared with the re-emergence of popular committees against the backdrop of working-class tradition, as in Imbaba where a group of residents linked to a leftist party worked for four years from 2008 to counter expropriations due to road-widening projects.

Recognition and autonomy of civil society

While a few examples of mass access to ownership have been possible in some countries (such as Mexico), it remains fairly exceptional. In Egypt, the momentum in response to opportunities created by the ILD led to successive refusals to open the file of extensive legalization. Runkel (2009, 65–66) reports that an organization for the formalization of ownership (Real Estate Formalization Organization), which should also have been in charge of the formalization of title deeds (95 percent of residents do not have valid titles) was never started. In cases with worse housing conditions, solutions such as 'land sharing' were established, for example, in 1985 in Thailand, giving land use rights to squatters with long-term leases paid by cooperatives and self-help organizations to private owners and even supporting onsite reconstruction programs (Angel and Boonyabancha 1988). Solutions other than legalization, whether or not coupled with regularization, are possible. But these examples also highlight the fact that a process that is completely 'managed' by local authorities, which are generally de-legit-imized, has little chance of succeeding. For over twenty years, researchers have stressed that the key to substantial improvement in the quality of life in informal settlements does not lie in massive relocation programs, which are often too expensive, but in social innovations based on the acceptance of a grass-roots approach (Hardoy and Satterthwaite 1989). Complemen-tarity is essential between residents, associations, and government.

I believe that the true strength of the regularization program of al-Hal-lus and al-Bahtini resides in the relative margin of freedom permitted by the high level of trust between volunteers who are heavily involved in neighborhood issues and technicians and project leaders who take their skills into account (rather than their grievances). Yet the solutions pro-posed hardly take account of local rights and actual patterns of land use. The legitimacy of the project manager allowed him to ignore the process of legalization, which he considered inadequate, and to bypass the conflict with the governorate by dissociating legalization and regularization. But this was only possible thanks to the relative political autonomy and finan-cial independence of this project, which was financed by the debt swap mechanism.[11] Indeed, all the regularization programs in Egypt are wholly or partly funded by international cooperation. Local governments can no longer cope with growing demand for sanitation and a more decent envi-ronment. Since almost all urban residents, whether legal or not, have access to drinking water, by legal or informal supply, it is very difficult for local officials to maintain large differences in access to the sanitation net-work. And it is through that infrastructure that security of tenure is auto-matically accorded. All experts are now trying to demonstrate the need to strengthen areas where the state has already invested, going as far as affirming, like Partha Chatterjee, the need to distinguish a "natural" right from a "legal" one (Chatterjee 2009).

Conclusion: The Case for Legality in Global Land Competition

Recent developments in imported styles of urbanization and tourism have also shown that legitimacy of existence in these areas can also be called into question when patrimonial or neo-patrimonial interests (Denis 2006), or local or global interests, are challenged by the presence of a habitat deemed sub-standard. This is the case in Luxor, around archaelogical sites, where the demolition of homes that are sometimes centuries old contin-ues on the grounds that such houses are incompatible with the surround-ing archaeological landscape and therefore degrade the site. A series of demolitions was justified by the route taken by the Avenue of the Sphinx, a tourism project. Another project concerned housing located between the Valley of the Kings and the Valley of the Queens: residents were rehoused in the new area of al-Tarif, even though surveys conducted by students on these various peri-urban villages show that the buildings were not well adapted to the site.[12]

While legalization proves ineffective and does not take into account the urban resources of residents, new challenges are emerging in large cities. At this stage of urbanization, it is a case of supporting the growth and densification of these neighborhoods. In situ upgrading and affordable recognition of the existence of squatter settlements continue to be demanded as the only means for vulnerable residents to continue their lives. Yet we are witnessing a new form of stratification of forms of public intervention and thus a separate discourse for owner-built neighborhoods. De facto legalization, leading to full recognition in illegal subdivisions coincides with the relocation of some sections of neighborhoods with a view to urban renewal (such as in Imbaba).

It therefore appears that a simplification of procedures and a more pragmatic approach would address the challenges of security of tenure for inhabitants with unstable income. This would also limit evictions, which are encouraged by urban competition in South Mediterranean cities, and which ignore the strong demand for equity.

Notes

1 A United Nations project to reduce poverty, launched in 2000.
2 This was the case in Egypt, in particular, until the national program for urban restructuring was initiated in 1992: urban policies until the 1990s mainly treated informal land squatter areas as specialized phenomena, either focusing on particular pockets that exhibited slum characteristics, or simply redressing the shortfall in urban services in larger informal agglomerations. Donor-supported upgrading projects in Helwan, Ismailiya, and Nasriya remained isolated pilots and 'islands of excellence,' Cities Alliance 2008, 12.
3 Including the status of tenant and owner, tenure rights in ascending order are: tenant of a squat, unregularized squatter 'owner,' tenant in an unauthorized subdivision, regularized squatter 'owner,' owner of an unauthorized (non-regulatory) lot, owner of an unauthorized construction, tenant with a contract—to full owner. Adapted from G. Payne (2000), Urban land tenure policy options in Runkel 2009, 19.

4	Observation and surveys conducted by Bérangère Deluc.
5	The breakdown of household income obtained during a survey published in 2006 (UNDP) is as follows: 33 percent have incomes below LE250, 57 percent earn between LE250 and LE500, 10 percent of households have incomes above LE750.
6	Besides an interview about Manshiyat Nasir with the former and current project manager (2010) and interviews with local officials and communication officers from GTZ (since 2005), this is also based on the work of El-Shorbagi and Sims (2003), and Séjourné 2006. For a recent review of legalization, see Runkel (2009).
7	Interview with K. Chaat, Cairo.
8	Interviews between 2007 and 2010 with residents and project leaders, and with a project leader who became the director of urban development. The 2010 survey was also conducted by Bérangère Deluc.
9	Noted by Gregory Földi and Agathe Santos, students of the Ecole Nationale Superieure d'Architecture de Paris-la Villette, "Projet urbain en situation de développement," 2007, and presented in 2008.
10	Neighborhood whose NGO Kheir wa Baraka estimated that the population was between 500,000 and 750,000 inhabitants, without any process of land tenure security. However the governorate of Cairo is in the process of installing a sewer system.
11	Respectively LE18,744 million and LE3 million from the Egyptian government, interview with H. Eid, 2007.
12	In January 2007, two groups of students from a Masters in Architecture program (directed by Philippe Revault and Agnès Deboulet) studied working-class and informal habitats in Egypt; one group studied Ismailiya, the other Luxor. For more information on this work, see www.centresud.info.

References

Agier, Michel. 2005. "Faire ville, aujourd'hui, demain. Réflexions sur le désert, le monde et les espaces précaires." In Capron Guénola, Cortes Geneviève and Hélène Guétat-Bernard, eds., *Liens et lieux de la mobilité-Ces autres territoires*, 167–78. Paris: Belin.

Angel, Shlomo, and Somsook Boonyabancha. 1988. "Land-sharing as an Alternative to Eviction—the Bangkok Experience." *Third World Planning Review* 10 (2): 107–27.

Balamir, Murat, and Geoffrey Payne. 2001. "Legality and Legitimacy in Urban Tenure Issues." Paper presented at the Communication au Séminaire international seminar, ESF/N-Aerus Louvain, May 23–28.

Barthel, Pierre-Arnaud. 2010. "Relire le Grand Caire au miroir de la densité." *Confluences* no. 75 (Autumn). http://www.cairn.info/revue-confluences-mediterranee-2010-4.htm

El-Batran, Manal. 2000. "Tenure Upgrading and Security of Tenure Policies in the Cairo Metropolitan Region." Unpublished paper, International Workshop on Security of Tenure Policies, Johannesburg, July 1999.

Bayat, Asef, and Eric Denis. 2000. "Who is Afraid of Achwaiyyat? Urban Change and Politics in Egypt. *Environment and Urbanization* 12 (2): 185–99.

Bolivar, Teolinda. 1995. "Construction et reconnaissance des *barrios* urbains du Vénézuela." *Les Annales de la Recherche Urbaine*, no. 66, 81–87.

Castel, Robert. 2003. *L'insécurité sociale-qu'est-ce qu'être protégé?* Paris: Seuil.

Chatterjee, Partha. 2009. *Politique des gouvernés: Réflexions sur la politique populaire dans la majeure partie du monde*. Paris: Editions Amsterdam.

Cities Alliance. 2008. *Slum Upgrading Up Close: Experience of Six Cities*. http://www.citiesalliance.org/sites/citiesalliance.org/files/su-up-close_0.pdf.

Clerc, Valérie. 2010. "Du formel à l'informel dans la fabrique de la ville. Politiques foncières et marchés immobiliers à Phnom Penh." *Espaces et Sociétés*, nos. 4–143, 63–79.

CNUEH (UN-Habitat). 2003. *Global Report on Human Settlements: The Challenge of Slums*. London: Earthscan.

Comby, Joseph. 2007. "Reconnaître et sécuriser la propriété coutumière moderne." Unpublished paper, World Bank Symposium, Washington, D.C. http://www.comby-foncier.com.

Davidson, Forbes, and Geoffrey Payne. 2000. *Urban Projects Manual: A Guide to Preparing, Upgrading and New Development Projects Accessible to Low Income Groups*. 2nd ed. Liverpool: Liverpool University Press.

Davis, Mike. 2006. *La planète des bidonvilles*. Paris: La Découverte.

Deboulet, Agnès. 2011. "Contrer la précarité par la sécurisation foncière et la légalisation Enjeux et opportunités dans le Monde arabe et en Egypte." *Revue Tiers-Monde* 206 (2): 74–94.

———. 2007. "Re-développement de quartiers précaires: l'évaluation des 'best practices.'" *Espaces et Sociétés* 4 (131): 67–83.

———. 2000, "Apprendre à faire la ville-les compétences à l'épreuve de la restructuration urbaine (Ismailiya, Egypte)." In Isabelle Berry-Chikhaoui and Agnès Deboulet, eds., *Les compétences des citadins dans le monde arabe-penser, faire et transformer la ville*. Paris: Karthala.

———. 1995. "Régularisation foncière, propriété et espace urbanisé." *Egypte-Monde Arabe*, no. 23, 57–75.

De La Saussaie, Simon. 2009. "Régulariser sans titriser," Agence Française de Développement, division collectivités locales et développement urbain. http://www.afd.fr/jahia/webdav/site/afd/users/administrateur/public/Portail percent20Dvpt percent20Urbain/doc/Regularizer-sans-titriser-Simon-de-la-Saussey.pdf.

Deluc, Bérangère. 2010. "Observation réalisées par Bérangère Deluc, mission d'étude Centre SUD-CEDEJ." December.

Dorman, W.J. 2009. "Of Demolitions and Donors: The Problematics of State Intervention in Informal Cairo." In Diane Singerman, ed., *Cairo Contested: Governance, Urban Space, and Global Modernity*, 269–90. Cairo: American University in Cairo Press.

Durand-Lasserve, Alain. 2006. "Market-driven Evictions and Displacements: Implications for the Perpetuation of Informal Settlements in Developing Cities." In Marie Huchzermeyer and Aly Karam, eds. *Informal Settlements: A Perpetual Challenge?*, 207–27. Cape Town: University of Cape Town Press.

Durand-Lasserve, Alain, and Lauren Royston. 2002. *Holding Their Ground: Secure Land for the Urban Poor in Developing Countries*. London: Earthscan.

Durand-Lasserve, Alain, and Jean-François Tribillon. 2001. "Pays en développement, la loi ou la ville?" *Urbanisme*, no. 318 (May/June): 72–77.

Faure, Alain. 2003. "Un faubourg, des banlieues, ou la déclinaison du rejet ?" *Genèses*, nos. 51–52, 48–69.

Fawaz, Mona. 2008. "An Unusual Clique of City-makers: Social Networks in the Production of a Neighborhood in Beirut (1950–1975)." *International Journal of Urban and Regional Research* 32 (3): 565–85.

———. 2007. "Apogée et déclin d'une nouvelle classe de citadins: les lotisseurs dans une banlieue irrégulière de Beyrouth." In Berry-Chikhaoui Isabelle, Deboulet, Agnès, and Laurence Roulleau-Berger, eds., *Villes internationales-entre tensions et réactions des habitants,"* 223–41. Paris: La Découverte.

Fawaz, Mona, and Isabelle Peillen. 2002. "The Slums of Beirut, Lebanon." Report UN-Habitat.

Gilbert, Alan. 2007. "The Return of the Slum: Does Language Matter ?" *International Journal of Urban and Regional Research* 31 (4): 697–713.

———. 2002. "On the Mystery of Capital and the Myths of Hernando de Soto: What Difference Does Legal Title Make?" *International Development Planning Review*, no. 24, 1–19.

Haenni, Patrick. 2005. *L'ordre des caïds. Conjurer la dissidence urbaine au Caire*. Paris: Karthala.

Hamdi, Nabeel. 2004. *Small Change: About the Art of Practice and the Limits of Planning in Cities*. London: Earthscan.

Hardoy, Jorge, and David Satterthwaite, 1989. *Squatter Citizen: Life in the Urban Third World*. London: Earthscan.

Huchzermeyer, Marie, and Aly Karam. 2006. *Informal Settlements: A Perpetual Challenge?*. Cape Town: University of Cape Town Press.

Kantor Paula, and Padmaja Nair. 2005. "Vulnerability among Slum Dwellers in Lucknow, India." *International Development Planning Review* 27 (3): 333–58.

Khor, Martin, and Lim Li Lin, eds. 2001. Good Practices and Innovative Experiences in the South. London: Zed Books.

Le Tellier, Julien, and Aziz Iraki. 2009. Habitat social au Maghreb et au Sénégal. Gouvernance urbaine et participation en questions. Paris: L'Harmattan.

Matteuci, Claudio. 2006. "Long-term Evaluation of an Urban Development Project: The Case of Hai el-Salam." Unpublished paper presented at N-AERUS conference, Darmstadt.

Mitlin, Diana. 2008. "With and Beyond the State: Co-production as a Route to Political Influence, Power and Transformation for Grassroots Organizations." *Environment and Urbanization* 20 (2): 339–60.

Navez-Bouchanine, Françoise. Forthcoming. *Effets sociaux des politiques urbaines*. Paris: Karhala.

———. 2002. *Les interventions en bidonville au Maroc-une évaluation sociale*. Rabat: Agence nationale contre l'habitat insalubre (ANHI).

Razzaz, Omar. 1991. "Law, Urban Land Tenure, and Property Disputes in Contested Settlements: The Case of Jordan." PhD diss., Harvard University.

Runkel, Carolin. 2009. "The Role of Urban Land Titling in Slum Improvement: The Case of Cairo." Diploma, Institut for Stadt-und Regionalplanung, TU, Berlin.

Séjourné, Marion. 2006. "Les politiques récentes de 'traitement' des quartiers illégaux au Caire: Nouveaux enjeux et configurations du système d'acteurs?" PhD diss., Université de Tours, France.

Shehayeb, Dina. 2009. "Advantages of Living Areas." In Regina Kipper and Marion Fischer, eds., *Cairo's Informal Areas: Between Urban Challenges and Hidden Potentials*. Cairo: GTZ-PDP.

El-Shorbagi, Monika. 2000. "Real Estate and Informal Practices in Greater Cairo and Alexandria." Report submitted to the Institute for Liberty and Democracy.

Sims, David. 2011. *Understanding Cairo: The Logic of a City Out of Control*. Cairo: American University in Cairo Press.

Sims, David, with Marion Séjourné and Monika El-Shorbagi. 2003. "The Case of Cairo." In *Understanding Slums*. London: Earthscan.

Sims, David, and Monika El-Shorbagi. 2006. "Slums and Eco-health in the Middle East and North Africa: Report on Approaches and Opportunities." Unpublished report for the International Development Centre, Canada.

Soares Gonçalves, Rafaël. 2010. *Les favelas de Rio de Janeiro. Histoire et droit XIXè et XXe siècles*. Paris: L'Harmattan.

Taher, Nadia. 2001. "In the Shadow of Politics: USAID–Government of Egypt Relations and Urban Housing Intervention." *Environment and Urbanization* 13 (1): 61–76.

Tarrius, Alain. 2002. *La mondialisation par le bas. Les nouveaux nomades de l'économie souterraine*. Paris, Balland.

Turner, John. 1968. "Housing Priorities, Settlement Patterns, and Urban Development in Modernizing Countries." *Journal of the American Institute of Planners*, no. 34 (November): 355–60.

UN DESA. 2010. "Objectifs du Millénaire pour le développement (OMD)." New York: United Nations Department of Economic and Social Affairs (UN DESA)

UN-Habitat. 2010. *Egyptian Experience: Strategy for Intervention in Informal Areas*. Cairo: UN-Habitat.

UNDP-Cooperazione Italiana-UN-Habitat. 2006. "Participatory Slum Upgrading in El-Hallous and El-Bahtini. Ismailiya-Egypt. Process, Results and Lessons." Unpublished paper, fifth draft.

UNFPA (United Nations Population Fund). 2007. "Rapport sur la population dans le monde." Unpublished paper.

9

The Commodification of the *Ashwa'iyyat*: Urban Land, Housing Market Unification, and de Soto's Interventions in Egypt

Eric Denis

The Neoliberal Land Reform Approach in Action

From 1997 to 2002, I followed the intervention of the Institute for Liberty and Democracy (ILD) in the framework of experimental urban rehabilitation in Egypt. At that time I was involved with the GTZ (Gesellschaft für Technische Zusammenarbeit GmbH) in a study regarding the extent and dynamics of irregular settlements in Cairo. The work of the ILD aims at formalizing so-called 'illegal' popular ownership, with the strong hypothesis that these secured ownership acts allow for more transparent transactions and popular and generalized access to mortgage loans aimed at stimulating a more inclusive economy. Hernando de Soto, Director of the ILD, calls this the rehabilitation of *dead capital*.

Deciphering the effects of such a reform entails more than evaluating results by the yardstick of ambitions announced at the outset. This does not make sense, in the same way as it does not make sense when a legal text is commented on without account for judicial practices, legal precedents, and especially the embedding of the text in a bundle of rules, customs, and interpretations. In other words, there are successive negotiations and arrangements in the reform dynamics.

Reform is legitimized through actions, in the encoding of norms to be imposed on the relevant parties—in this case, the majority of inhabitants of working-class areas, whose accommodation is never completely respectful of the laws on construction and town planning. Reform can also be understood in terms of the follow-up to the relationships between inhabitants and local civil servants, who have to integrate new rules that have already been adapted by the services of the concerned ministries.

The initial statement of intent is usually an intentionally negotiable one, and the program result often has little to do with the intentions proclaimed in a forceful and dogmatic manner at the outset, since the purpose is to obtain funding from the relevant international institutions. The project addresses itself to potential financial backers, using in-vogue terminologies, creeds, and keywords. These pre-action formulations are similar to the amplifications on which marketing principles are based. Implementation, on the other hand, must be negotiated, even in order to obtain the support of competent authorities, let alone the numerous concessions that have to be made on the spot. The impacts therefore obviously differ from the original objectives.

Timothy Mitchell (2007) articulates this in his preamble to the examination of Hernando de Soto's intervention in Egypt: "To understand the performativity of economics, it is not enough to look for economics at work in the economy; one must also stop understanding it simply as (mis)representation. The effectiveness of economics rests on what it does, not on what it says. It does not work alone. It operates together with other techniques, sets of information, arrangements, and agencies, with different strengths and resources."

The preliminary studies on the situation of illegal housing in Cairo led by de Soto's team, have served as guidelines for initiating a reform process, or at the very least for initiating a series of announcements that speak of the intention to reform, backed up by the competent ministries: the justice and finance ministries first and foremost, followed later by the ministries of housing and agriculture. The conclusions of these studies on Egypt are at the heart of the arguments revealed in his book *The Mystery of Capital* (2000), which is still a much-debated reference. *The Mystery of Capital* was translated into more than ten languages and brandished as a powerful global lobbying tool, leading President Bill Clinton to refer to de Soto in 2003 as "the greatest living economist." This media strategy allowed de Soto, at the end of 2008, to publicly claim that the key to deliverance from the global financial crisis lay in "legalising the property of poor people."[1]

While my colleagues, Alain Durand-Lasserve, Harris Selod, and Geoffrey Payne, and also in part Timothy Mitchell, have decided, maybe too early and from too far away, on the failure of and the deadlock surrounding de Soto's project, which aims at formally legalizing working-class ownership in Egypt and elsewhere,[2] I show here that the spirit of the reform proposed by de Soto is now integrated in the operating methods of competent civil servants, in the same way as it has been integrated by the inhabitants' into their practices and daily lives. The spirit of his reform now effectively sustains operating methods of public agencies, as it structures forms of resistance to them. Not that de Soto has personally set it up, nor even that his NGO, the Institute for Liberty and Democracy (ILD),[3] has been especially present, but they are at the heart of a reformist movement of neoliberal inspiration which came to dominate mainstream economic thinking in Egypt at the behest of several governments from the early 1990s onward. I do not wish to confuse the observation of this dynamic with the evaluation of 'results' expressed in terms of 'more land security for the poor' or even 'the better functioning of land and property markets.' I simply take note of, and describe, locate, and specify the nature and the conditions for the implementation of these groups of convergent actions, which weigh heavily on daily operating methods in Cairo where the acts of acquiring, allotting, selling, and maybe even mortgaging plots of land are concerned.

In other words, the only way to describe the intervention of the ILD in order to better assess its impact, without prior assumption, is to look at how, in the field, in neighborhoods, as well as in the mechanisms of the competent bodies, the principles aiming to transform the poor people who live on the margins of society in illegal housing, into happy entrepreneurs integrated in the market, have been applied.

But first let us see these large working-class areas, where more than half of the inhabitants of Cairo live: the so-called 'ashwa'iyyat.

A Domain Outside the Law

It is January 2005 and Hajj Ahmed has had some difficulties in reaching the building site of his private school in Bashtil, in the northwest of Giza. His Mercedes *zalamuka* got stuck twice on the way.[4] Septic tanks have overflown in several places because of leaks in the water system caused by the sewerage system's working machinery, signs that the neighborhood is developing, which reinforces Hajj Ahmed's vision of a bright future for his investment—eight classes, a playground, and a three-story building. He is returning from a meeting held at the Ministry of Education for the registration of his school, which some inspectors will come and visit next month. On his way, he met an inspector of the Imbaba neighborhood, who was evaluating the alignment of his building with that of the road—no problems there, but everything else could be contested, and a number of permits are missing. Thereafter follows a brief, friendly discussion; some promises are made as to the acceptance of a cousin at the school, and a visit is arranged to a local café, where he promises to pay for the tea (the baksheesh). The conversation does not go any further.

Like all the construction that surrounds it, and like 90 percent of new constructions in Cairo, Hajj Ahmed's violates several rules and laws. The de facto subdivision of a plot and the construction of floors before receipt of a building permit, are illegal. Such activities violate the Urban Planning Land Act (Law No. 3 of 1982), the Building Code (Law No. 106 of 1976), and the Status Law (Military Decree No. 7 of 1996). Moreover, construction on land that has been subdivided constitutes two "offenses against society": it becomes an illegal division of land and a construction without prior permission. The situation worsens if it happens to be agricultural land. In this case, two new offenses are committed: the sterilization of arable soil and construction without prior permission (Law No. 53 of 1966 and Military Order No. 1 of 1996). The sentences for these violations and offenses are extremely severe: they range from fines that can amount to the value of the construction itself, to the demolition of the building, and even the incarceration of the owner and the builder for up to seven years. Hajj Ahmed's school is also in total breach of a plethora of construction and security rules pertaining to a private establishment that is made open to the public, not to mention earthquake-resistant norms.

But Hajj Ahmed has other worries. Was it a good idea for him to have invested all his savings in this project, the result of fifteen years of relentless work in Saudia Arabia during which he ran a small cement and gravel slab business? Will he earn enough? The idea that legal objections would be raised to his building site never worried him; neither did it worry his neighbors. Demolitions and evictions have never been all that frequent. They reflect a time when living in unauthorized buildings was less common, before everyone, including civil servants, policemen, and judges, lived in them; a time when the government still built local authority housing, well before the 1990s.

Today, Hajj Ahmed may even hope to have his construction legalized in a simple way. The newspapers talk about it almost every day. The finance minister and the housing minister have apparently given their approval. In Manshiyat Nasir, it seems that a campaign has already started.

The 1996 military decree, meant to harden the prohibition on rural land construction, had the paradoxical effect of securing the illegal constructions that were present before it was promulgated. From that time, the demands of the *baladiya* (local council) civil servants, became less severe when confronted with a building obviously constructed in breach of a series of decrees and laws, but well integrated in a densely built-up area. The revocation of fines related to undeniable infractions subsequently cost a great deal less.

Yet this military decree (No. 1 of 1996) was meant to be a serious reinforcement of Law No. 116 of 1983, reaffirming the prohibition on constructions on rural land. It permitted the rapid destruction of illegal constructions and hardened the imprisonment penalties. However, no one in Hajj Ahmed's quarter, nor elsewhere, has ever heard of its application in practice. It was even repealed in October 2003, after the national meeting of the National Democractic Party (NDP)—the ruling party of President Hosni Mubarak—and the decision was promoted personally by the president's son, Gamal. The repeal falls within a whole body of transformations favorable to the recognition of the powerful informal and popular dynamics of construction.

The Opportune Moment of the ILD's Intervention

The first conference led by Hernando de Soto in Egypt and entitled "Dead Capital and the Poor," was held in the presence of entrepreneurs, deputies, and ministers, notably the ministers of finance and housing, on 24 September 1997. It was organized by the Egyptian Centre for Economic Studies (ECES),[5] an Egyptian think-tank then with an influential board member, the executive director of Med Invest Associates, London, the son of the president, Gamal Mubarak. In a grand show, de Soto presented the first conclusions of the study evaluating the extension of the informal sector in Egypt—a study funded by the United States Agency for International Development (USAID). On 9 September 1997, ahead of the conference, the Egyptian minister of finance had explained in the columns of the most widely read national daily, *al-Ahram*, that "if the ILD project is accepted, the doors of history will open up for Egypt." The conference press release elaborated this point:

> For him [de Soto], the starting point is that the aim of the reforms is to create a market economy and, if the majority of the population is to bear the costs of these reforms and be supportive, they must also reap

the benefits. This objective can be achieved in part by bringing the dead capital owned by the poor to life. Interestingly enough, few are aware that the less privileged in developing countries may already possess most of the land and businesses in the country, but lack the kind of formal property rights over these assets that could raise their value and convert them into capital. Assets of the poor cannot be used in efficient and legally secured market transactions, because ownership cannot be readily traced and validated, and exchanges cannot be governed by a legally recognized set of rules. Their property is, in effect, 'dead capital.' In a pioneering effort, de Soto's institute in Peru has in fact conducted such a process, with the direct support of President Fujimori. A similar attempt has been made in Haiti, with the direct involvement of President Preval and former President Aristide. This experience can be brought to bear in Egypt. What it takes is conviction on the part of those who believe in market economy systems to realize that carrying out successful macroeconomic transformations, like those taking place in Egypt today, should be complemented by efforts to bridge the informal–formal divide, overcome the institutional constraints that impede the majority, especially the poorest, from increasing the value and productivity of their assets.[6]

In Egypt, as elsewhere (Peru, Haiti, Indonesia, Tanzania, and Ethiopia), the inscribing of de Soto's land-law regularization program as an interministerial priority of the state reform process is an absolute priority for the ILD. The NGO relies on rock-solid support from international UN institutions and on American aid for its work. De Soto's approach is understood by them as being a tool for implementing the adjustment and good governance reforms, while perfectly fitting the Millennium Goals Perspective and poverty reduction programs.[7] These institutions therefore favor the ILD, of course through financial support, but also by setting de Soto up as a prestigious mediator and by providing him with direct access to the then head of the state notably the president, through think-tanks and affluent individuals. This principle of the de Soto method, established as fundamental, allows the ILD, especially in authoritarian regimes, to avoid the wheels of bureaucracy of the competent ministries. That is why none of his interventions are made within an invitation for tender. "More than twenty heads of state in developing and former Soviet nations have called on the ILD to help them implement the model of reform that they have created," he explains, thereby justifying this approach:

Most titling programs in the developing world are purely technical endeavours, contracted by lower echelon government surveying, mapping, and recording organizations. Alone, such home-grown technocratic efforts are in no position to achieve the kinds of reforms necessary to make a market economy work. That is why in each country where it works, the ILD partners with the head of state. Otherwise, major reform would be doomed from the outset. Only the head of state and his immediate entourage can command the attention of resistant elites and garner the overwhelming political support required to wipe out the wilful inertia of the status quo. Also, it is only the head of state who has the power to prevent the bureaucratic infighting that inevitably paralyzes legal reform. Clearly, a decision as far-reaching as creating a market-based system by reforming the legal property system, which will in turn redistribute a nation's wealth and emancipate the poor, is essentially political and should be put in the hands of the head of state right from the start.[8]

At the World Trade Center in Cairo, on the banks of the river Nile, de Soto pointed out that the state no longer had the means to house the poor, while economic liberalization did not automatically reduce poverty: "There is increasing recognition that waiting for the benefits of growth to trickle down to the poor does not work. Nor do social safety nets address wide-scale poverty." Power must therefore be given to the poor; they have to be removed from the fringes of society; we have to recognize their capabilities for managing the land and real-estate capital that they have raised.

In Egypt, the security issue—terrorist and insurrectionary threats—played its part in the government's willingness to reverse these perspectives and quickly progress from ignoring most popular settlements and maintaining their status as illegal to regularization. These neglected working-class areas situated on the city's outskirts, and not even mentioned on maps, became, from 1992 to 1996, the seat of violent protests of an Islam-related nature, and easy targets for the strengthening of a close network of social and activist activities, effectively replacing deficient state services; healthcare and education notably, but also policing and justice (Denis 1994; Denis and Bayat 2000; Haenni 2005). The earthquake that shook Cairo in 1992 revealed the power of Islamic charities in the *'ashwa'iyyat*, particularly as they were the first and practically only outside source of succor to afflicted families. From that time on, it appeared essential to the regime and its public apparatus to roll back these illegitimate margins, and essential not to oppose their development through reluctance to provide them with services. The National Program for Urban Upgrading was thereby launched in 1993. It was deployed over a ten-year period with investments estimated at LE4 billion.

The Ministry of Local Administration's 1994 report identified 904 informal settlements in Egypt. It determined the terms of their rehabilitation and their provision with services, and, very rarely, of their eradication (thirty-two zones only), while considering ways of re-accommodating their inhabitants. Illegality was accepted as the most common way of living in Egyptian cities.[9] A demonstration of the sea change in political perspective that occurred during the 1990s can be seen in the fact that one of the most active planners in the sector of illegal habitat development, Mustafa Madbouli, was Chairman of the General Organization for Physical Planning (GOPP) at the Ministry of Housing in 2008.

De Soto and his ideas therefore came into play in a context already predisposed to the de-marginalization of working-class areas. His arrival coincided with that of other European aid agencies, that of the British Department for International Development (DFID) and the German Gesellschaft für Technische Zusammenarbeit GmbH (GTZ). These other agencies are different insofar as they support equipment projects, access to services, and the securing of tenure, rather than the formalization of property. Thus, a latent opposition appeared in the functioning methods, between the European approach on the one hand and the American approach, as adopted by the UN agencies, on the other.

De Soto himself considered the issue of terrorism, especially after 11 September 2001. His first book, *The Other Path* (1989), subsequently had its subtitle changed for its second edition in 2002 from *The Invisible Revolution in the Third World* to *The Economic Answer to Terrorism*. In an article published by the *New York Times* immediately after September 11,[10] de Soto explained that "in order to keep the poor at bay from terrorist sirens, the United States and its allies must call on the entrepreneurial capabilities of these people. It is not sufficient to satisfy the stomachs of the poor." In November 2001, during a REALTOR conference in Chicago, de Soto also stated that "recognising through titles, the interests of poor people in property and businesses, is a key element in the global war against terrorism . . . . The recruitment pockets of terrorists are the slums of the Third World, where radicals, fundamentalists, and other militants prowl on the impressionable youth, frustrated by limited opportunities."[11] He led the *Washington Post* to say in 2004 that "Hernando de Soto offered an alternative vision of Peru's poor. Rather than see them as the proletariat, he showed that they were in fact budding entrepreneurs whose greatest desire was not to bring down the market economy but to join it." De Soto thereby established as a principle for intervention, the popular formula according to which small owners do not revolt.[12] He therefore proposed to transform developing countries into nations of owners—in a sort of neoliberal reversal of the agrarian revolutions that aimed to redistribute property to the public. AlSayyad notes in this respect, and very rightly so, that in Egypt, the massive increase in the number of working-class areas was the result of the land redistributions of the post-1952 agrarian reform, which allowed a multitude of small land owners to subdivide and individually sell their parcels on the urban fringes (1993).

This new outlook was facilitated because in Egypt service provision in districts is unrelated to the legality of their status. David Sims (2002) notes that "the provision in urban Egypt of basic infrastructure and public services to residential areas has only the most tenuous link to the type or degree of formality of tenure. Comparisons of service levels across different parts of Egyptian cities show that it is the age of a settlement and its sheer size in terms of population which are the main determining factors." Moreover, the inhabitants are not fooled; they feel that no possible dispute can arise with regard to their settlement: a very large majority, 94.4 percent of households surveyed in 2007 in Greater Cairo, do not feel at all threatened by the possibility of eviction, while 2.2 percent are blissfully unaware that eviction is a possibility in the first place, and only 3.4 percent think that it could happen to them (Aziz et al. 2007, 18).

From the 1990s onward, the efficiency targets to which public services were forced to comply no longer allowed the banning of administrative connections. Also, the development of the private sector, spearhead of economic liberalisation, now comes through the dominant market of popular para-legal habitat. Thus, Ahmed Ezz, in 1998, during one of the first meetings of the Future Generation Foundation,[13] the lobbying tool of Egyptian businessmen led by Gamal Mubarak, explained that the illegal construction market was essential to the reinforced concrete sector. Ahmed Ezz, the CEO of Al Ezz Steel Rebars, is a tycoon who largely benefited from privatisations in the steel sector—he controlled 70 percent of the steel market and 50 percent of the ceramics market, and was also formerly deputy of Egypt's ruling National Democratic Party (NDP). He wanted para-legal districts to be recognized. Their increasingly effective legitimacy nevertheless remains tied to a para-legal principle of tolerance:

the legislative reform of the construction and urban planning code, embodied in Law No. 119 of 2008 maintains in article 62 that it is forbidden to connect illegally built buildings to the water and electricity networks, and all other services.

In reality, those who can pay do have access to these basic services. The private growth of wireless telephone systems has allowed the generalization of access to telecommunications. And here again, for those companies that are among the most powerful in Egypt, such as Orascom (Egypt's biggest stock market capitalization), it is a fruitful market that no state service would care to hinder. The growth in private transport by microbus, and, more recently still, by Indian-made tricycles, Bajaj Tuk-tuks, allows excellent accessibility to these working-class areas. They are attractive and close to potential job opportunities. They remain, on this point, much more attractive than the new outlying cities in the desert.

Consequently, the question now focuses on the financial promotion of these districts. The de facto securing of land, the extension of networked services, experience and announcements with regard to the distribution of title deeds, fully accepted by inhabitants, owners, sellers, tenants, and buyers, tend to increase prices. Therefore social selection is already in place, according to the accessibility and integration of these areas. The areas along major roads or in close proximity to mass transportation networks such as the subway, are already in their third generation of construction. Such areas have ten-story buildings equipped with elevators. These plot developments, which are still considered unlawful by the law on property registration and even more so by the law on construction, are nevertheless accompanied by a considerable rise in the prices of land and real-estate, as well as rents.

Studies carried out by the ILD never address the issues of the status and the future of tenants. De Soto does not deal with this topic,[14] even though no less than 40 percent of the inhabitants of illegal neighborhoods in Egypt are tenants.[15] Between 2001 and 2006, 82.2 percent of access to accommodation within Greater Cairo was made in the form of tenancy contracts. These contracts are 20 percent higher for constructions duly registered at the public department for property registration (*al-shahr al-'aqari*), which is only one of the first steps in the never-ending quest for full legality with regards to property and construction.

What is more, a great majority of tenants have, for many years, and even after the first law of 1996 on the liberalization of rents in new constructions, paid a lump sum upfront on arrrival at an apartment. They move into a place which is usually only a concrete slab with a frail beam structure and brick partitions; and all the finishing touches are made at their expense, including the door, the window frames, and the plumbing. In other words, the tenants participate considerably in the improvements made to the building. Yet, the formalization of property effectively excludes this type of possession. Without being able to say exactly how this dynamic will change, we can note that in 2006 the prices of housing in the formal sector were 74 percent higher than a comparable illegal habitat unit (Aziz et al. 2007).

In this transformation, one can see the potential consolidation of the socioeconomic fracture between owners of property and tenants, with all that entails in matters of access to mortgages and inter-generational transmission. This is just one example of the risks that the shortcuts involved, in what Hesseling and Le Roy (1990) call the continuum of the law of practice or "the multiple pathways and arrangements" around custom, responsibility, and property.[16]

The Pertinence of the ILD Diagnosis
The ILD study, started in 1997 and published in 2000 by the ECES, shows that 53 percent of developed land is illegal (49 percent in Alexandria and 25 percent in Tanta). Neighborhoods referred to as 'ashwa'iyyat have been divided into plots, 83 percent of them on private agricultural lands. In 2007, 62 percent of the population of Cairo was living there, which amounts to nearly eight million people.

This much-publicized statistic served as a lever with which to obtain new funds in order to promote active phases of reform, and continue studies, by tackling the regularization of informal profitable activities (2000–2005).

The impact of the studies in Cairo was such that it led Bill Clinton to remark in 1994 that

We have a project in Africa and Ghana with the great Peruvian Economist Hernando de Soto . . . . I saw a map the other day of old Cairo that de Soto had prepared that showed that 85 percent of the small businesses in the old part of the city were not in the legal system. Not because the owners did not wish to pay taxes but because it takes an average 700 days to legalize a business, if you go through every bureaucratic step in the old system and most people don't have that kind of time and money. So anyway, it's a fascinating thing and I thought you would be interested in it because of what you do for a living. . . . De Soto is convinced that America grew rich more quickly than it otherwise would have and more quickly than virtually any other country in the world because we had a simple way of vesting title to property and people that could then be used as collateral for loans. And so we're trying to do this in Africa. It's very interesting.[17]

The diagnosis doesn't end here; it includes a formalistic judicial assessment, underlining the impossible course to legality, but also integrating (and this is a first in Egypt and probably in the Arab world) a subtle anthropological approach to daily practices, allowing the securing of tenure, and the construction and insuring of transactions. The divide between formal and informal reveals itself as it should be, that it is never complete. Between popular practices or neo-customary practices, and the rules of positive law, the continuities are as obvious in daily practices, transactions, and inheritances, as they are in the references to rights invoked in tribunals in the case of conflicts (El-Shorbagi 2000).

The cunning in de Soto's approach lies in his ability to incorporate the gains of judicial pluralism as an argument in favor of his neoliberal views. Generally speaking, pluralist approaches to the analysis of judicial practices related to land law in urban environments moved from Latin America in the middle of the 1980s, to Africa and economies in transition at the beginning of 1990, then onward to the Arab world and Asia in the mid- to late 1990s. They accompanied, and sometimes slightly preceded, the neoliberal reforms that they served to promote. Creative destructions aiming at individualizing property with a view to market expansion, and academic research promoting "the competence of ordinary city-dwellers" (Berry-Chikhaoui and Deboulet 2000) joined forces. It also comes through the cannibalization of the benefits of judicial pluralism. From then on, it becomes a normative tool. Self-help and contractual adjustments are promoted as neoliberal values. What was 'illegal' becomes the 'vanguard' of the free market. Klift (2003) points out that "the strength of ILD work is to enable governments to understand and evaluate their informal sector in order to elaborate a strategy of change. What they do not see yet is that the poor are already in a free market, although extra-legal and very fragmented."

The study first shows that the legal registration for the transfer of private property requires 102 administrative transactions in 34 different offices and that it takes, on average, 198 days. It costs around 23 times the average monthly salary. The procedures concerning the subdivision of lots or the transfer by inheritance are no less lengthy. The account of all these administrative procedures helps explain generalized illegality, and serves as a very convincing argument for the ILD to plead in favor of the simplification of procedures and the campaigns to regularize property that cannot achieve this state of positive legality.

Obtaining a building permit is equally impossible. The procedure depends on the district's administration *(hayy)* and varies from one district to another. The study has listed 102 administrative procedures, which equate to 64 working days, for an average cost equivalent to 139 times the average salary. Having access through legal means to public (but not more accessible) land requires 106 administrative steps and 130 days!

We will not detail here the growing number of decrees and laws that govern private property *(mulk)*, as defined in the 1971 constitution and the 1948 civil code. The study initiated by the ILD team summarizes these issues perfectly (see Chapter 4 in this volume by Marion Séjourné). In any case, neither the contradictions between the successive laws and decrees that are supposed to contribute to the protection of agricultural lands (like those governing the subdivision of parcels), nor the complexity of laws governing the concession and sale of the public domain or the code of urbanism, are important. What matters are the customs and the exploitation of internal contradictions that are used on a daily basis by real-estate agents, families, buyers, and sellers, as well as the *qadis* (judges) in tribunals. How do these courts refer to the law? To which rules and case laws do they refer? In what way do they refer to Islamic law *(shari'a)*, which in Egypt had evolved from "a source" of legislation according to a provision in the 1971 constitution to "a principal source" by 1980? This reference to the Islamic corpus of law and jurisprudence favors tolerance and simplifications. It assures a good security of the tenure in working-class areas. Moreover, lawsuits related to neighborhoods, property, boundary marking, or construction disputes, even in the absence of full registration, an up-to-date land-use plan, as well as of a building permit, are usually easily solved. In this regard, tribunals appear as fundamental mediators in the relationship with state services. They guarantee the legitimacy of property with regards to customary law and set a precedent that ensures a de facto break in the never-ending chain of laws governing the legality of formal property and legal construction. Article 42 of Law No. 119 of 2008 on the revision of the town planning code, itself reaffirms the legality of tacit permits.

Monika El-Shorbagi's basic summary (2000) for the ILD, and Marion Séjourné's brilliant thesis (2006), which corroborates the diagnosis of the ILD, have very clearly defined the contours of the daily negotiation of the obviously pluralistic systems for the securing of property, transactions, and construction, as well as renting. Let us simply underline that in the never-ending process of legal registration, when, in the presence of two witnesses and possibly a lawyer, buyer and seller have established a sales agreement, a preliminary contract ('aqd ibtida'i), or an act governed by customary law ('urfi), the new owner must voluntarily have the transaction validated by two distinct bodies placed under the control of two ministries: he must register it at the local branch delegated by the district administration (hayy) of the public department for registration of property (al-shahr al-'aqari), which is under the control of the Ministry of Justice; he must then obtain the authorization of the land registry (Hay'at al-Misaha, or Egyptian Survey Authority), which is under the control of the Ministry of Irrigation and Water Resources. The procedure also involves the Ministry of Finance, to whom the owner should prove that he has settled the property tax (kashf al-mushtamalat). He must therefore go to the local office of the tax authority—and this even before the registration. Once the registration has been completed, the file is submitted to the misaha (land registry), which must then inspect the land. As this chain of procedures 'progresses,' more specific cases and possible obstacles appear, which need wastas (direct connections with civil servants), which allow the applicant to clear or bypass each step, and to save time. In the end, the full procedure is never followed, especially if we include the painstaking steps required for the obtaining of building permits, and those related to the conformity to town planning rules. This last point is very interesting in practical terms, because it involves adapting the construction to the neighboring environment regarding road width and respect for accessibility to all plots as well as correct alignment.

De Soto himself would effectively understand these practices, without any divide between de jure and para-legal legitimacy. He assesses the potential of ordinary practices to produce structured cities and to assure a circulation of property without property disputes, which would otherwise constantly require the intervention of tribunals.

Multiple Ways of Implementing the Hernando de Soto Program

Today, de Soto publicly declares that his program is the origin of profound changes, particularly in Egypt. On his website,[18] at the end of 2007, one could read: "Both the Egyptian and Filipino governments have reportedly continued to press for or initiate reforms influenced by the ILD's work and reform proposals."

Of course, we could start by pointing out that, in effect, regularization remains the least easy thing to do, and that progress in this field is as weak as elsewhere.[19] De Soto's program, which had no locally applicable constituent, has not, in itself, generated any effect with regards to formal registration in any given district.

The GTZ program in Manshiyat Nasir, situated to the east of the medieval center of Cairo, in 'Izbit Bakhit, was among the most efficient with respect to concerted rehabilitation and land securing since its launch in 1998. Yet, at the end of 2007, the people in charge of the project were reluctant to give any figures, even in private, on formal regularization. According to our sources, by the end of 2008, this did not amount to more than a few dozen titles.[20] We are facing a well known, but totally unpublicized syndrome: land regularization can never be carried out at the same speed as the renovation or redevelopment of districts, nor even remain as an objective, one which will never be completed once the project has exhausted its financial resources. It works as an ideal. The timing of urban intervention and compliance to formal judicial norms are not adjustable.

De Soto is not fooled by this limit. That is why he aims for a convergence that allows flexibility, which means that he pleads as much for the rehabilitation and recognition of informal rules as he does for total formalization even after having simplified the judicial framework. The regularization, announced as a major ambition, equates to company marketing; simple principles that appeal to the public are announced with much determination, but application is not necessarily an objective for de Soto's consultancy and study enterprise. Klift (2003) in an article to the International Monetary Fund (IMF) promoting the ILD's approach, explains that "he travels much more than heads of companies, and uses the competence and techniques of a marketing expert to sell his theory."

Other intervention projects carried out in Egypt have incorporated a regularization element, which is very distinctly inspired by the program announced by de Soto: the initiative of the World Bank in Alexandria declares it openly, as well as the strategic plan for Greater Cairo led by the Japan International Cooperation Agency (JICA) on behalf of the Egyptian Ministry of Housing.[21] Regularization has become a component to be reckoned with, much like community participation in development, as a determining factor of eligiblity for international funding.

In Egypt, de Soto also proposed a type of institutional reform that must go hand in hand with the program on regularization of land and real-estate ("real-estate formalization program").[22] In it, he pleads for the creation of a body whose mission is to regularize tenures, and which must collaborate with the public department of property registration *(al-shahr al-'aqari)*.

By 2007, one had to acknowledge that the lobbying was successful. Even though governmental measures do not stick to the plan proposed by the ILD, nor even make explicit reference to it, they proceed in rapid succession with an array of options favorable to the registration and legitimization of illegal construction. Reforms, notably of the judicial kind, were indeed applied from the arrival of the reforming government of Ahmed Nazif in 2004. The 1997–2004 period, beginning with de Soto's first conference in Egypt in 1997, did not lead anyone to hastily conclude that the project should be abandoned. The year 2004 also marked a new line of thinking within the NDP itself. In September, its secretary general had approved a policy paper entitled "Agricultural Land Preservation and Urban Growth Management in Egypt," which concluded that it was no longer possible to stick to the imperious defense of cultivated lands, which has clearly shown its limits. This was a conceptual revolution for Egypt. The report pleads in favor of relaxing the rules on the extension of urban areas, and, consequently, legitmizes working-class settlements, thereby opening a radically new pro-urban perspective.

From as early as 2001, the law on mortgages (Law No. 148 of 2001) was ratified by parliament and little by little put into practice with the appropriate financial and banking instruments. It clearly establishes the principles of sequestration of property, of failure to make a claim within the statutory time limit, and non-payment. Before being applied, it was amended in 2002 and 2004, notably to establish the General Authority for Real Estate Mortgage Affairs. The Ministry for Investment, in coordination with the Mortgage Finance Authority (MFA) proceeded by introducing the Insurance Supervisory Authority (EISA) and a mortgage insurance fund (Egyptian Company for Mortgage Refinancing) in order to protect the market from unpaid debts, and create a secondary market for mortgages, with the aim of favoring credit access for owners with the lowest repayment abilities.[23] This very system, which makes securities out of mortgage credit, showed its limits in North America in 2008.

According to the law ratified in 2001, the repayments of mortgage credits cannot exceed 25 percent of the owner's monthly revenue. Multiple forms of international support, far from limiting themselves to the ILD,[24] have been involved. By 2006, only two banks had obtained the accreditation from the Egyptian Central Bank to launch themselves on the mortgage market: the Egyptian Housing Finance Company and the Taamir

Mortgage Company. North American international firms and petroleum monarchies such as Codwell Banker and Century 21 are starting to take an interest in the Egyptian market. In 2007, the Ministry of Finance and the Central Bank gave their support to the creation of a national credit bureau, Estealam, a private organization that rates credit seekers and gives access to their financial history. It has even started carrying out private cadastre operations in order to establish, in the case of a mortgage, a mapped guarantee of the existence of the property along with public registration.

At the same time and in order to cope with the major problem limiting the growth of mortgage credit, but also the generalization of land and real-estate taxation, that is, the shortfall in registered property, the registration fees paid to the *shahr al-'aqari* were significantly decreased: in the 1980s, they were equivalent to 12 percent of the value of the property. This rate then fell to 6 percent in 1991, then to 4.5 percent at the beginning of the 2000s, to finally reach 3 percent in 2003. Since July 2006, these fees cannot exceed LE2,000. In certain districts, localized operations of free registration were even carried out.

In 2008, a government bill put into motion the current property taxation rate, which is presently fixed at between 10 percent to 20 percent, or 42 percent to 46 percent, depending on the age of the property and the rental value, which was fixed in the 1960s to a single rate of 10 percent, according to an updated and revisable rental value. This value takes into account the level of services in the district. The funds thereby collected must as a priority be spent on improving local services, school material, transport networks, and so on. The registration of property in working-class areas is therefore also essential in order to increase the tax base of land and real-estate taxes, which currently only concern old buildings in and around the town center, most of which have fixed rents and for which the tax rate is among the lowest. More than half of the urban constructions in Greater Cairo are not affected by property taxes.

A unified and simplified law on construction (town planning code) has also been published. It replaces Law No. 3 of 1982, which regulates urban planning and construction. Its aim is to re-evaluate the role of local government, to highlight community participation in development, and to review current standards in order to better integrate the norms of popular construction.

The de-marginalization of popular construction also implies the relaxing of 'containment' rules, or *takhzim*, which limit the extension of built-up zones and their related public facilities on agricultural land, beyond a precisely defined radius around towns, *kurdun* (from the English 'cordon') *al-madina*. This particularly concerns areas that are cultivated and surrounded by constructions, *mutakhallat*. Regulation thereby becomes more realistic. It adapts itself to the reality of construction dynamics and integrates them. For villages, the removal of controls on their expansion is even more advanced, with the widening of the area suitable for development, *al-hayz al-'umrani*. The General Organization for Physical Planning (GOPP) of the Ministry of Housing, in coordination with the local authorities through special committees, has prepared local plans that increase the possibility of legally constructed sprawl around villages by 20 to 25 percent. The owners of agricultural parcels are allowed, without the control of the Ministry of Agriculture, to divide and sell their lands, even for building purposes. Plans were made for 1,700 villages out of a total of 4,500, and 1,000 of them were approved by ministerial decree, from as early as 2007. In fact, many of these 'villages' are big market towns, or even small towns often numbering more than 30,000 inhabitants. Sometimes, they simply merge with the build-up of bigger cities. In other words, the true popular urban dynamic is, de facto, little by little, being integrated into the administered metropolis.

In 2001, Presidential Decree No. 153 unified and legitimized the multiple forms of privatizing public land. It instituted The National Center for Planning State Land Uses, for the purpose of managing and preparing for the privatization of the private state domain. It structured the already well-initiated dynamic dating from the beginning of the 1990s, of lifting the prohibitions on settlement on state-controlled desert lands.

The monitoring of the ILD intervention in Egypt does not allow me to confirm Timothy Mitchell's statement (2005) that de Soto requested a monopoly on the implementation of land titling reform in Egypt. Admittedly, only one diagnosis has been made without an invitation for tender. On the other hand, these reforms have been implemented by numerous agents and backers, without necessarily referring to the ILD study, or following its recommendations. De Soto was merely an initiator with an incomparable lobbying force.

Liberalization and Reinforcement of the Centralized State

In effect, regularization through the formalization of property is progressing in Egypt. Announced at the beginning of 2007, the free registration of 850,000 housing units started in the fall of that same year. It was the first phase of a six-phase project. In the long run, it should enable the reintegration of 25 million homes.

Nevertheless, in November 2007 this registration trend met with unprecedented resistance from civil servants working in the land-tax department. It had been at least thirty years since Egypt had last faced such a public sector strike—three thousand employees took turns, day and night, for over a week, to camp in front of the Finance Ministry. Surprisingly, the forces of law and order did not intervene to break up the protesters. The employees finally won their case for most of their demands: the revision of their salary scale, profit-sharing, and their reinstatement in the Finance Ministry.[25] This was necessary to the continuity of the reform process.

Since 1974, the 50,000 agents in charge of registering property had been regarded as local authority employees, earning much lower salaries than those of the civil servants at the Ministry of Finance. The tax reform on built and unfinished properties was therefore a strategic moment for these regional civil servants, who were becoming the architects of a new fiscal windfall. The immense work ahead that regularization entails and the ministerial reforms that it requires, need a strong mobilization of these officials. Besides their reinstatement in the Finance Ministry, the negotiations also focused on profit-sharing schemes. Herein lies a major limit to the simplification of registration. It presupposes a radical change in the rhythm and ways of working. In addition, these officials have been benefiting from the para-legal system: they ensure the necessary *wasta*s in the procedures undertaken by city-dwellers to have their property recognized, or even put pressure on offenders by questioning them. Yet these 'bonuses' are threatened by the reforms. This was also what motivated this strike. It questions the state as to if and how civil servants are going to benefit from this de-marginalization of ordinary citizens.

Whereas it has become conceivable to acknowledge the capabilities of ordinary city-dwellers to construct their accommodation and district, the state services are nevertheless still in charge of a number of projects as direct developers. In 2005, the National Housing Policy Report (Ministry of Housing and New Communities, internal report) planned the construction over six years of 500,000 public housing units for populations with limited revenues. In 2007, the Ministry of Housing established the Core Housing Project and the Site and Services program, which aim at offering (as in the 1980s) renovated housing units in desert lands for the most impoverished and displaced families. These projects are associated with a reduction in construction norms, within the framework of the revision of the town-planning code and the simplification of the preconditions for acquisitions in the context of the Beit al-'Eila (Family House) and Ibni Beitak (Build Your Own House) programs.

These trends, without necessarily being radically contradictory, nevertheless indicate that the regime (itself a compromise between power struggles and contradictory visions as to the exercise of power), still wants to exercise close control over the ways populations settle and integrate in the city. Despite the adjustment, it also wants to control the production of habitats, and therefore garner legitimacy and support through redistributions of property that benefit building entrepreneurs as well as the recipients of these homes.

In this context, the adoption of the reforms advocated by the ILD entails negotiations and adjustments among contradictory approaches. De Soto's options do not radically change the economy of relations to land property and construction in a unique and self-regulated market. De Soto's options remain embedded in multiple social and symbolic ties to the land.

Conclusion: Property and Poverty on the Nile

What emerges from this report on the recognition of illegal property in Egypt in which Hernando de Soto took an interest, is that property and most illegal construction have not yet become any more legal with respect to, de jure, positive law; they are no more founded on all the necessary land registry documents, notarial deeds, and building permits than they were before. On the other hand, the intervention shows a trend toward de facto recognition in the field. To all occupants of illegal land and construction subdivisions, this confers increased security with regards to settling and possession.

Of course, the formal reform aimed at granting property titles to all parcels in illegal districts (no less than half of all accommodation in Cairo and Egypt) is unachievable. It is a neoliberal utopia, but plays a role in the gathering and harmonization of data concerning the registration of multiple forms of property and transactions. In particular, it contributed to a gradual dissolution of the sense of dichotomy between the legal and illegal markets.

The difficulty that the numerous, often very negative, critical analyses of de Soto's theories have to face, is that they question the principles announced at the outset, but not the multiple changes that the dogma is subjected to during implementation through negotiation and contextual adaptation, while the number of actors (public agencies, contractors, and inhabitants) is increasing.[26]

The evaluations of the programs launched by de Soto, in Peru notably, stick to the programs led directly by him and his NGO. Yet, the ILD's main strength is that of a formidable lobbying cabinet that draws on the engagement of a wide range of global actors, both individual and institutional, so that its programs are taken up by a multitude of agents that bend laws and practices at all levels, in favor of the trends defended by de Soto.

With his ability to make his ideas known at high levels, de Soto is seen as the architect of the "post-Washington consensus" (Sgard 2005), that is, a powerful voice in favor of the integration of the most impoverished into economic liberalization.

In Egypt, his intervention expects, rather than counteracts, the monopolization by a few businessmen of public land reserves rather than the prospect of the emergence of popular capitalism. Those businessmen were favored by the discretionary methods employed in the system of auctioning property belonging to the private state domain and by access to terms of credit that were highly advantageous to them.

The circumstances plead in favor of the promotion of popular capitalism, of support for and securing of small family property and small businesses, as well as the promotion of microcredit. The fundamental underlying principle is that property rights are the basis of individual liberty. It reflects the concept that "the emancipation of individuals, in order to be achieved, must come through that of property because it is a determining and therefore priority factor" (Capitan 2000). Thus, *Forbes* magazine, commenting in February 2004 on the intervention of de Soto in Egypt, explained it would "dramatically transform its economy into a wealth-creating, wealth-distributing dynamo that will lead millions of Egyptians into a vibrant, increasingly democratic middle class."

The idea of the post-Washington consensus emerges from the works of Rajan and Zingales (2003) according to whom "the disappointing results of the liberal reforms are due to the fact that insiders control the institutions and the access to markets: they therefore stand in the way of new entrepreneurs, or, more generally, of social innovators capable of questioning their economic means and their political privileges" (Sgard 2005). It is thus not the liberal principles as such that create problems, nor their insufficient implementation on the 'macro-reforms' level. The problem would seem to lie in the monopolization of the new institutions and the potential benefits of the reforms by private economic elites closest to the highest levels of state. Egypt is pragmatic in this respect, particularly since the entry of businessmen into the political arena—into the ranks of the NDP, into parliament, and then, in the mid-1990s, into the government itself—was presented as the integration of civil society in politics, and therefore as proof of the democratization of the regime. Do the reforms actually introduced after the intervention of de Soto in Egypt have the characteristics of an effective economic de-marginalisation? Rather, are we not witnessing, with a flood of popular property entering a unified market, the exclusive securing of property by developers, while the value of land in popular areas is increased tenfold by legislation? It is probably too early to make such an assertion. It is far too early to evaluate the correlation of these reforms to democratization. However, as demonstrated by Polanyi (1983 [1944]), reducing land simply to a form of exchangeable merchandise that is tradeable on a market never led to democracy, but much more to dictatorship, because of the authoritative regulation required to prolong an unjust regime between landowners and landless citizens.

Under these conditions, should we return to the analysis proposed by Auguste Walras in 1848 ([1848] 1997, 49), which differs from that of Hobbes on the question of exclusive property: "Individual land ownership strips beforehand and denies of their rights, all those whose fathers had never been land owners or stopped being so . . . . The citizen makes the individual free. The collective government of land, the public ownership of soil, ensures the legitimacy of one's own ownership, which here is considered secondary: the objective is not only to better enjoy your properties, but to benefit from a status that guarantees the exercise of liberty."

The debate on the association between land and democracy is not new: It was not initiated with the land reforms, or after 2002 with the emergence of the Middle East Partnership Initiative (MEPI), or with the imposition of aid conditionality in respect of the implementation of legal reform.

Market forces are powerful. The main actors are thereby involved, with the support of lobbyists like de Soto, and are able to incorporate the reforms aimed at reinforcing the capacities of the most impoverished. De Soto's intervention has contributed by transforming into supposed entrepreneurial skills, the survival and adaptation abilities of ordinary citizens. As with the acquired benefits of judicial pluralism, the aptitudes of citizens have become levers for extending land supply.

In the end, land is made available. This is the major issue of these reforms: to fill the market with land investment opportunities and through the simplification of regulations, to favor those who own capital, while creating higher fiscal revenues. In practice, the issue of democratization and the reduction in inequalities is secondary. The same applies to popular access to mortgages. The global financial crisis that started with the bursting of the American speculative subprime bubble at the end of 2008 clearly shows the limits of such a possibility, even if it were implemented on a large scale, such as in Egypt, which is far from being the case so far (Struyk 2007)!

When this intervention paradigm of regularization is applied, it does not appear as an end in itself, but as a transactional tool for land liberalization and the increase of land supply.

Notes

1   Hernando de Soto: "We must make poor people's wealth grow," in *Le Monde*, 10 October 2008, and this, at a time when the trigger itself for the crisis is the securitized mortgage over-indebtedness of the North American working classes.

2   The failure of some nationwide titling programmes (for example, in Egypt) can be attributed to the "deficiency of land administration" (Durand-Lasserve and Selod 2007) or "in addition, lessons from abandoned or cancelled titling programmes such as the programme jointly initiated by the Institute for Liberty and Democracy and the Egyptian Centre for Economic Studies in Egypt" (Durand-Lasserve, Payne and Rakodi 2007), assessments I had long shared with these authors before realizing, at least in the field in Cairo and in Egypt at large, that the dynamic of reform was in fact pursued with multiple actors engaged in convergent actions.

3   www.ild.org.pe

4   Refering to the W124 car model of Mercedes-Benz available from 1985 to 1995, where *zalamuka* is a familiar expression in Egyptian colloquial Arabic meaning 'duck's backside.'

5   www.eces.org.eg

6   Press release, "Dead Capital and the Poor," Egyptian Centre for Economic Studies, 24 September 1997, Cairo.

7   In 2000, 189 nations, including Egypt, made a promise to free people from extreme poverty and multiple deprivations. This pledge became the eight Millennium Development Goals, to be achieved by 2015. In September 2010, the nations recommitted themselves to accelerating progress toward these goals.

8   "The Other Path, The Economic Answer to Terrorism," report to the conference sponsored by the Centre for International Private Enterprise, April 2003: http://www.cipe.org/publications/overseas/pdf/otherpath.pdf

9   The follow-up projects to the program initiated in 1993 were launched from 2005 onward. In 2006 they received the support of several UN agencies. This coincided with the generic renaming of 'urban upgrading' to 'slum upgrading,' a usage more appropriate to the terminology and

objectives of these agencies. In Egypt, the term 'slum' applies to both dilapidated housing and to housing constructed in violation of legislation related to the subdivision of land, land use, construction, or registration of property. Housing constructed in violation of legislation related to registration of property is commonly referred to with the generic 'informal settlements,' or housing. Informal settlements usually lack basic infrastructure such as paved roads, sewerage, schools, and health facilities as a result of non-recognition by the government.

Following the National Slum Upgrading Policy, defined between 2005 and 2006, a project entitled "Integrated and Participatory Slum Upgrading in Egypt" was set up. It was initiated by the Ministry of Housing, Utilities and Urban Development, as well as the Ministry of International Cooperation, the governor of the Upper Egyptian governorate of Minya, and six UN agencies. These agencies are: UN-Habitat, the United Nations Development Programme (UNDP), United Nations for Population Affairs (UNFPA), the International Labour Organisation (ILO), the United Nations International Fund for Women (UNIFEM), and the UN Children's Fund (UNICEF). The National Slum Upgrading Policy identified 1,221 zones, home to 24 percent of all Egyptians, and 40 percent of urban dwellers, and some 8 million people in rural areas (mostly peri-urbans). It located 81 zones in the Greater Cairo region—of these, it planned to destroy and displace the populations of only 21 zones.

10 "The Constituency of Terror," *New York Times*, 15 October 2001.

11 A conference reported in the Global Perspective in Real Estate report, Realtor, second quarter, 2002. Realtor is an association founded in 1908. It brings together agents from the North American real-estate sector. Its objective is to "unite the real-estate men of America for the purpose of effectively exerting a combined influence upon matters affecting real-estate interest" (www.realtor.org). This is another example of the logic of land globalization, the opening up of new real-estate markets clearly being behind the desire to promote capital ownership among ordinary families of developing cities.

12 In an eight-page brochure issued in 2003 by the International Centre for Private Enterprise promoting The Other Path, the word 'terrorism' appears no less than twenty-three times! Francis Fukuyama therein explains that "the ILD has really brought about a major conceptual revolution in the way we think about questions of poverty and problems in the world that really stretch from poverty to terrorism"; Ali Jalali, Afghanistan's interior minister, points out that "the ILD has said that if war against terrorism is to succeed, we have to talk to the excluded, the people. We believe this is right: with community and economic development, we will be able to fight more effectively against terrorism and to

legitimize trade in our country"; Brian Atwood, a former administrator of USAID, states that "[if] we are going to deal effectively with terrorism, we can't just use our military, we can't just use our diplomats. We have to use creative ideas in development assistance such as that of the ILD."

13 http://www.fgf.org.eg/.

14 In fact, de Soto never replies to critics; we have seen this in several meetings in Cairo. He follows a logic of product promotion, not of debate, although he persistently glorifies himself based on his strongly mediated status as the world's greatest economist and the numerous awards he has received: in 1999, *TIME* magazine named him as one of the twentieth century's five greatest innovators hailing from the Latin American continent; *Forbes* magazine chose him as one of the fifteen personalities "who will re-invent your future"; *The New York Times Magazine* wrote that "To the leaders of poor countries, de Soto's economic gospel is one of the most hopeful things they have heard in years"; *The Economist* identified the ILD as one of the two most affluent think-tanks in the world. He received intellectual support from two winners of the Bank of Sweden prize, otherwise known as the Nobel Prize for Economics, namely, Ronald Coase and Milton Friedman, but also from Francis Fukuyama; he himself received the Milton Friedman Prize for Advancing Liberty, delivered by the Cato Institute of Washington, spearhead of the neo-conservatives (or 'neocons'), but also the Compass Award for Strategic Direction from *Forbes* magazine, the Adam Smith Award, and the Goldwater Award; political figures such as Bill Clinton, Tony Blair, and Margaret Thatcher have praised him. The World Bank assigned to the ILD a $37 million program for Peru in 1997; the International Labour Organization appointed him to its World Commission on Globalization; the UNDP supported the establishment of the Commission on the Legal Empowerment of the Poor (active from 2005 to 2008), co-chaired by de Soto and Madeleine Albright. His familiarity with international institutions and influential and powerful world figures is not only a function of the pertinence of his words and the performance of the reforms that he has helped implement, but also of his family's well-connectedness. According to Klift (2003), "his father, a lawyer, was working for the International Labour Organization in Geneva, and his brother, Alvaro, is the Under Secretary General to the United Nations [he was a special coordinator for the peace process in the Middle East, from May 2005 to June 2007]. He himself worked briefly, at the beginning of his career, at the GATT, the organization that preceded the WTO, and was later President of the inter-governmental Council of copper-exporting countries. He was also at some point of a time, Governor of the Peruvian Central Bank."

15 In Greater Cairo, tenants represent 50.4 percent of inhabitants, of which 41.7 percent depend on the previous law (with frozen rents and the possible inheritance of leases) and 8.7 percent come under the law that came into force in 1996 on the renting of new constructions (Aziz et al. 2007, 2).

16 On this issue, see the truly pioneering work carried out by Jamal Akbar (1988) with respect to the Arab world: he helps formalize the specific place of collective property and its management, with an eye to the different local customs of Muslim law in the Arab world.

17 Bill Clinton, "Speech: Remarks at CB Richard Ellis 18th Annual Market Forecast Meeting," 9 March 2004, Foundation Clinton, http://www.clintonfoundation.org/030904-sp-cf-hs-ai-ee-sbi-gn-gl-usa-ind-zaf-per-qat-irq-isr-uga-sp-remarks-at-cb-richard-ellis-18th-annual-market-forecast-meeting.htm

18 http://www.ild.org.pe/en/influence (2007)

19 The first study that aimed to draw up a program of land regularization, long before the intervention of ILD in Egypt, was published by El-Messiri (1989), but no concrete measure followed.

20 The project, in its initial formulation, stated among its major objectives (ILD 1999) that "it is recommended that the Project establish an office in Ezbet Bekhit to facilitate the ownership process in coordination with the Amlak department of the Governorate and the Survey Authority, and that a representative of the Amlak be stationed in the District to Oversee the operation. The opening of the process for building permits should also be announced and established by the District, available to those who have completed land ownership procedures."

21 Alexandria Development Project (World Bank 2007): "The project makes a deliberate focus on removing constraints to private-sector-led growth and enabling the creation of sustainable economic opportunities to all city residents, including the urban poor. In response to the argument that the trickledown effect of growth-focused interventions may be somewhat limited, at least relative to expectations, this project includes direct poverty alleviation interventions targeted at the city's poorest areas—squatter settlements, which would constitute a critical complement to the project's growth focus and greatly improve the likelihood of an effective poverty alleviation impact. This approach is supported by an increasing body of research which argues that limited efforts for the socioeconomic inclusion of the poor can have damaging effects on overall growth due to increased social unrest" (JICA 2007, 9).

22 ILD 2001a and ILD 2001b.

23 The mortgage industry received a boost in 2007 due to the launching of the Egyptian Company for Mortgage Refinancing (ECMR), a joint venture between the Central Bank of Egypt and twenty-four public and private

financial institutions. ECMR will provide twenty-year secured loans to banks, which will in turn lend this money to individuals at an interest rate of 11 per cent. Existing mortgage companies offer only ten-year loans with an interest rate of 12–14 percent (*Al-Ahram Weekly*, 27 December 2007–2 January 2008).

24 A project, valued at $500,000, was funded through the Canadian International Development Agency (CIDA) and the Egyptian government to allow the Canada Mortgage and Housing Corporation (CMHC) and its Egyptian partner, the General Organization for Physical Planning (GOPP), to create the National Urban Observatory.

25 This movement coincided with and benefited from a general period of strong social unrest, during which major strikes were being staged in the public textile industry in al-Mahalla al-Kubra, a large city located in Egypt's Nile Delta.

26 Notably, Gilbert (2002) and for a recent critic related to the subprimes crisis, G. Payne (2008).

References

Akbar, Jamal. 1988. *Crisis in the Built Environment: The Case of the Muslim City*. Singapore: Judith Shaw.

AlSayyad, Nezar. 1993. "Informal Housing in a Comparative Perspective: On Squatting, Culture, and Development in a Latin American and a Middle Eastern Context." *Review of Urban and Regional Development Studies* 5 (1): 3–18.

Arnold, Craig Anthony. 2002. "The Reconstitution of Property: Property as a Web of Interests." *Harvard Environmental Law Review*, no. 26, 281–364.

Assaad, Ragui. 2007. *Labor Supply, Employment and Unemployment in the Egyptian Economy*, 1998–2006, Working Paper 0701. Cairo: Economic Research Forum.

Aziz, Suzette, Selim Kamal, Serageldin Hany, and Kamal Hazem. 2007. "Housing Demand Study for Greater Cairo." Unpublished report for the United States Agency for International Development, Technical Assistance for Policy Reform.

Berry-Chikhaoui, Isabelle, and Agnès Deboulet, eds. 2000. *Les compétences des citadins dans le monde arabe-penser, faire et transformer la ville*. Paris: Karthala.

Bourdeau, Vincent. 2006. "Les républicains du 19e siècle étaient-ils des libertariens de gauche? L'exemple d'Auguste et Léon Walras." *Raisons politiques* 3 (23): 93–108.

Bukhari, Saleem. 1982. "Squatting and the Use of Islamic Law. A Case Study of Land Occupation in Madinah Munawara, Saudi Arabia." *Habitat International* 6 (5–6): 555–63.

Capitan, Colette. 2000. "Propriété privée et individu-sujet-de-droits. La genèse historique de la notion de citoyenneté." *L'Homme*, no. 153 (January–March). http://lhomme.revues.org/document4.html.

Culpepper, Roy. 2002. "Demystifying Hernando de Soto: A Review of the Mystery of Capital." http://www.nsi-ins.ca/ensi/pdf/deSoto.pdf.

Denis, Eric. 2008. "Cairo, between Traces and Liberalization." In Renata Holod, Salma, Jayyusi, Attilio Petruccioli, and André. Raymond, eds., *The City in the Islamic World*. Leiden: Brill.

————. 2006. "From the Walled City to the Walled Community: Spectres of Risk, Enclaves of Affluence in Neoliberal Cairo. In Diane Singerman and Paula Amar, eds., *Cairo Cosmopolitan: Politics, Culture, and Urban Space in the New Middle East*, 41–71. Cairo: American University in Cairo Press.

————. 1994. "La mise en scène des 'ashwaiyyât-s (des quartiers spontanés). Premier acte Imbâba, décembre 1992," *Égypte, Monde Arabe*, no. 20, 107–16.

Denis, Eric, and Assef Bayat. 2000. "Who is Afraid of Ashwaiyyat? Urban Change and Politics in Egypt." *Environment and Urbanization* 12 (2): 185–99.

Denis, Eric, and Marion Séjourné. 2002. *ISIS: Information System for Informal Settlements* (Report). http://hal.archives-ouvertes.fr/hal-00198975/fr/.

de Soto, Hernando. 2000. *The Mystery of Capital: Why Capitalism Triumphs in the West and Fails Everywhere Else*. New York: Basic Books.

————. 2002. *The Other Path: The Economic Answer to Terrorism*. New York: Books Group.

————. 1989. *The Other Path: The Invisible Revolution in the Third World*. New York: HarperCollins.

de Soto, Hernando, and Francis Cheneval. 2006. *Realizing Property Rights*. Zurich: Ruffer and Rub.

Dorman, W. Judson. 2007. "The Politics of Neglect: The Egyptian state in Cairo, 1974–98." PhD diss., School of Oriental and African Studies, University of London.https://eprints.soas.ac.uk/155/1/Dorman_Politics_of_Neglect.pdf.

————. 2002. "Authoritarianism and Sustainability in Cairo: What Failed Urban Development Projects Tell us about Egyptian Politics." In Roger Zetter and Rodney R. White, eds., *Planning in Cities Sustainability and Growth the Developing World*. London: ITDG Publishing.

Durand-Lasserve, Alain. 2006. "Market-driven Evictions and Displacements: Implications for the Perpetuation of Informal Settlements in Developing Cities." In Marie Huchzermeyer and Aly Karam, eds., *Informal Settlements: A Perpetual Challenge?* Cape Town: University of Cape Town Press.

Durand-Lasserve, Alain, and Harris Selod. 2007. "The Formalisation of Urban Land Tenure in Developing Countries." Paper presented at "Urban Land Use and Land Markets" Urban Network Symposium, World Bank, Washington D.C.

Durand-Lasserve Alain, Payne Geoffrey, and Carole Rakodi. 2007. "Social and Economic Impacts of Land Titling Programmes in Urban and Peri-urban Areas: A Review of the Literature." Paper presented at "Urban Land Use and Land Markets" Urban Network Symposium, World Bank, Washington D.C.

Erbas, S. Nuri, and Frank E. Nothaft. 2005. "Mortgage Markets in Middle East and North African Countries: Market Development, Poverty Reduction, and Growth." *Journal of Housing Economics* 14:212–14.

Everbart, Stephen, Berta Heybey, and Patrick Carleton. 2006. "Egypt: Overview of the Housing Sector." *Housing Finance International*, June, 9–13. http://www.housingfinance.org/uploads/Publicationsmanager/0606_Egy.pdf.

Fahmi, Wael, and Sutton Keith. 2008. "Greater Cairo's Housing Crisis: Contested Spaces from Inner City Areas to New Communities." *Cities* 25 (5): 277–97.

Gilbert, Alan. 2002. "On the Mystery of Capital and the Myths of Hernando de Soto: What Difference Does Legal Title Make?" *International Development Planning Review* 24:1–19.

Granovetter, Mark. 1994. "Les Institutions Economiques comme Constructions Sociales: un Cadre d'Analyse." In André Orléan, ed., *Analyse Economique des Conventions*, 79–94. Paris: PUF.

———. 1985. "Economic Action and Social Structure: The Problem of Embeddedness." *American Journal of Sociology* 91 (3): 481–510.

Haenni, Patrick. 2005. *L'ordre des caïds: conjurer la dissidence urbaine au Caire*. Paris: Karthala.

Hesseling, Gerti, and Etienne Le Roy. 1990. "Le droit et ses pratiques." *Politique africaine*, no. 40, 2–11.

Hollingsworth, Rogers, and Boyer Robert. 1999. *Contemporary Capitalism: The Embeddedness of Institutions*. Cambridge, UK: Cambridge University Press.

ILD. 2001a. "Executive Regulations for the Real Estate Formalization Program and the Registration at the Special Section of the Real Estate Public Registry." Unpublished report, Cairo.

———. 2001b. "Proposal of a Presidential Decree for the Promulgation of the Proposed Law for the Creation of the Real Estate Formalization Program." Unpublished report, Cairo.

———. 1999. "Ezbet Bekhit Planning Workshop." Unpublished report, Cairo.

Japan International Cooperation Agency (JICA). 2007. "The Strategic Urban Development and Master Plan Study for Sustainable Development of the Greater Cairo Region." Final report, vol. 1: Summary, Master Plan.

El Kadi, Galila. 1988. "Market Mechanisms and Spontaneous Urbanization in Egypt: The Cairo Case." *International Journal of Urban and Regional Research* 12 (1): 22–37.

———. 1987. "L'articulation de deux circuits de gestion foncière au Caire en Egypte—Recompositions." *Peuples méditerranéens*, nos. 41–42, 167–79.

Keivani, Ramin, and Mattingly Michael. 2007. "The Interface of Globalization and Peripheral Land in the Cities of the South: Implications for Urban Governance and Local Economic Development." *International Journal of Urban and Regional Research* 31 (2): 459–74.

Klift, Jeremy. 2003. "Écouter les chiens qui aboient. Entretien avec H. de Soto." *Finances and Développement* 40 (4): 8–11.

Lavigne Delville, Philippe. 2005. "Quelques mystères de l'approche de Hernando de Soto." *L'Économie Politique* 28 (4): 92–106.

Le Velly, Ronan. 2007. "Le problème du désencastrement." In *Avec Karl Polanyi, contre la société du tout-marchand*, 213–56. Paris: La Découverte/MAUSS.

Meinzen-Dick, Ruth, and Esther Mwangi. 2007, "Cutting the Web of Interests: Pitfalls of Formalizing Property Rights." *Land Use Policy* 26 (1): 36–43.

El-Messiri, Sawsan. 1989. *Regularization of Land Titles for Informal Communities in Cairo: An Analysis and Proposed Approach*. Washington, D.C.: Cooperative Housing Foundation, USAID.

Ministry of Housing and New Communities. 2005. National Housing Policy Report. Internal report.

Mitchell, Timothy. 2007. "The Properties of Markets." In Donald MacKensie, Fabian Muniesa, Lucia Siu, eds., *Do Economics Make Markets? On the Performativity of Economics*. Princeton, NJ: Princeton University Press.

———. 2005. "The Work of Economics: How a Discipline Makes its World." *European Journal of Sociology* 47 (2): 297–320.

———. 2002. *Rule of Experts: Egypt, Techno-Politics, Modernity*. Berkeley: University of California Press.

Panaritis, Elena. 2001. "Do Property Rights Matter? An Urban Case Study from Peru." *Global Outlook: International Urban Research Monitor*, no. 1 (April): 20–22. Woodrow Wilson International Center for Scholars and United States Department of Housing and Urban Development, Washington, D.C.

Payne, Geoffrey. 2008. "Beware of Sub-prime Housing Policies in Developing Countries." Proceedings of the Institution of Civil Engineers. *Urban Design and Planning* 161 (3): 93–95.

Polanyi, Karl. 1983 (1944). *La grande transformation, aux origines politiques et économiques de notre temps*. Paris: Gallimard.

Rajan, Raghuram, and Luigi Zingales. 2003a. "The Emergence of Strong Property Rights: Speculation from History." *NBER Working Papers* no. 9478. National Bureau of Economic Research, Cambridge, Massachusetts.

———. 2003b. *Saving Capitalism from the Capitalists*. New York: Crown Business.

Séjourné, Marion. 2006. "Les politiques récentes de traitement des quartiers illégaux au Caire." PhD diss., Université François-Rabelais, Tours.

Sgard, Jérôme. 2005. "La propriété privée et les lois du capitalisme. Que nous dit Hernando De Soto ?" *L'Economie politique*, no. 26.

El-Shorbagi, Monika. 2000. "Typologies of Informal Residential Development and Informal Practices in Greater Cairo." Unpublished report for the Institute for Liberty and Democracy, Cairo.

Sims, David. 2002. "What is Secure Tenure in Egypt?" In Geoffrey Payne, ed. *Land, Rights and Innovation: Improving Tenure Security for the Urban Poor.* London: ITDG Publishing.

Sims, David, and Marion Séjourné. 2006. "Informality and the Internal Logic of a Metropolis Out of Control." Paper presented at "Weekly Lecture Programme" lecture series held at the Netherlands-Flemish Institute in Cairo (NVIC), 23 November.

Sims, David, Kamel Hazem, and David Solomon. 2008. "Housing Study for Urban Egypt." Unpublished report, Technical Assistance for Policy Reform/USAID.

Sobel, Richard, ed. 2007. *Penser la marchandisation du monde avec Karl Polanyi.* Cahiers lillois d'économie et de sociologie. Paris: Harmattan.

Soliman, Ahmed. 2004a. *A Possible Way Out: Formalizing Housing Informality in Egyptian Cities.* Lanham, MD: University Press of America.

———. 2004b. "Titling at Sphinxes: Locating Urban Informality in Egyptian Cities." In Ananda Roy and Nezar AlSayyad, eds., *Urban Informality: Transnational Perspectives from the Middle East, Latin America, and South Asia,* 171–207. Lanham, MD: Lexington Books.

Steinberg, Florian. 1984. "Cairo: Informal Land Development and the Challenge for the Future." In Paul Baross and Jan van Der Linden, eds., *The Transformation of Land Supply Systems in Third World Cities.* Aldershot, Hants: Avebury.

Struyk, Raymond. 2007. "Egyptian Consumer Knowledge and Attitudes on Mortgage Finance and Property Registration." *Egypt Financial Services Project,* Technical report no. 90, USAID.

———. 2006. "Update on Egyptian Mortgage Lending." *Housing Finance International,* December, 33–36.

Struyk, Raymond, and Roman Ireny. 2007. "Incidence and Determinants of Housing Upgrading in Cairo." *Review of Urban and Regional Development Studies* 19 (2): 123–37.

Uzzi, Brian. 1996. "The Sources and Consequences of Embeddedness for the Economic Performance of Organizations: The Network Effect." *American Sociological Review* 61 (4): 674–98.

Walras, Léon. (1848) 1997. "La vérité par un travailleur." Chapter in *La vérité sociale,* Vol. 2 of *Œuvres économiques complètes* by Auguste Walras and Léon Walras, 7 vols. Paris: Économica.

Williamson, John. 2002. *Did the Washington Consensus Fail?.* Washington, D.C.: Peterson Institute, Center for Strategic and International Studies.

———. 1990. "What Washington Means by Policy Reform." Chapter 2 in *Latin American Adjustment: How Much Has Happened?* Washington, D.C.: Peterson Institute, Center for Strategic and International Studies (new updated edition, 2002).

Woodruff, Christopher. 2001. "Review of de Soto's The Mystery of Capital." *Journal of Economic Literature*, no. 39, 1215–23.

World Bank. 2007. *Egypt—Alexandria Development Project*. Washington D.C.: The World Bank. http://documents.worldbank.org/curated/en/2007/08/8194274/egypt-alexandria-development-project.

10

Public Policies Toward Informal Settlements in Jordan (1965–2010)

Myriam Ababsa

W hile the issue of the management of Palestinian camps in Jordan and their integration into the urban fabric of the agglomerations of Amman-Russeifa-Zarqa[1] and Irbid has been extensively studied (Destremeau 1994; Jaber 1997; Al Husseini 2011), few studies have focused on the management of informal areas developed on the periphery of the camps and in Jordanian cities more generally. Only the anthropologist Omar Razzaz and the urban planner Jamal Al Daly have addressed the issue of informal settlements; one to study the conflicts that pitted the members of the Beni Hassan tribe against the state in 1986, when the latter undertook to destroy illegal buildings on land registered in the public domain (Razzaz 1991, 1994, 1996); and the other to describe the various urban renewal projects undertaken by the Jordanian government since 1980 (Al Daly 1999). Yet the subject is interesting for two reasons: firstly because only 18 percent of Palestinian refugees in Jordan live in the camps set up by UNRWA (United Nations Relief and Works Agency),[2] and many of them built their own houses by renting plots of land from individuals or squatting on public land near the official camps; and secondly because Jordan is the leading country for policies designed to upgrade informal settlements in the Middle East, through the Housing and Urban Development Corporation (HUDC). In 1992, six of the HUDC's urban planners were awarded the prestigious Aga Khan Award for Architecture for their work in the informal settlement of East Wahdat (Amman).

From 1980 to 1997, Jordan became the first Arab country to implement the new developmentalist ideology promoted by the World Bank in Latin America and Asia, which aimed to involve the inhabitants of informal areas in every stage of the renovation of their homes and to allow them access to homeownership through long-term loans guaranteed by the state. Following the Oslo Accords of September 1993 and the Wadi Araba Treaty of January 1994, however, the Jordanian government, through the Housing and Urban Development Corporation (HUDC), changed its methods of intervention in the country's camps and informal areas, to focus solely on the provision of services, giving clear priority to security issues. Once again, Jordan found itself ahead of the other main host countries (Lebanon and Syria), as it was the first country to incorporate all of the UNRWA camps in its new urban renewal policies. While they do not constitute informal areas legally or administratively, the camps are informal areas from a structural or morphological point of view, because of their similarity to informal areas surrounding them: they are characterized by self-built stories, very high construction density, infrastructural weaknesses, and so on.

The purpose of this chapter is to analyze the evolution of management policies related to (structurally) informal housing in Jordan since 1980, focusing on the methods used to involve refugee populations living in informal areas in programs to help them secure their property. This chapter is based on a series of interviews conducted with officials of the HUDC (May 2006, autumn 2007 and 2008) and on fieldwork conducted in the informal settlement of Nahariya at the beginning and the end of the upgrading project (May 2006 and March 2007). It shows that in Jordan informal housing is treated differently depending on whether it is the result of rural depopulation or of the forced Palestinian migrations of 1948 and 1967. I assume there is a relationship between levels of citizenship of the inhabitants of informal settlements in Amman and policies of urban renewal; I also show the adjustment of targeted populations to renewal projects: their willingness to 'participate' in order to be employed as laborers, and the conversion of compensation received into property.[3]

Land Tenure and Informal Settlements in Jordan
It should be noted that in Jordan, public policies related to the management of informal settlements involve the areas populated by Palestinian refugees who arrived during the Arab–Israeli wars of 1948 (arrival of

100,000 people) and 1967 (arrival of 300,000 people). The other type of informal areas, which arose from rural depopulation in the context of demographic transition, developed on agricultural land and state land on the outskirts of Jordan's major cities (Amman–Zarqa–Russeifa, Irbid, and Aqaba). These settlements receive special treatment from the Land Registry Department and the municipalities concerned. Somewhat similar in structure, these two types of informal settlement differ in terms of the the origin of their population, which is Transjordanian in the first case and Jordanian of Palestinian origin or only Palestinian (displaced from the Gaza Strip) in the second. This key distinction is never made because so much emphasis has been placed by the authorities on the upgrading of areas populated by Palestinian refugees. These areas certainly have a larger population and surface area than the informal areas inhabited by Transjordanian rural migrants. We must note that the 200,000 to 400,000 Iraqi refugees who have arrived in Jordan since the invasion of Iraq by the forces of the US–UK coalition in March 2003 have settled throughout the capital, mostly within the existing housing stock, and sometimes even within informal settlements, as is the case in Nahariya, without creating pockets of refugees.[4] They will not be discussed in this chapter.

A specific urban informality

The predominance of informal settlements inhabited by Palestinian refugees is such that it has made the definition of informality specific to Jordan. The term *sakan 'ashwa'i* refers almost exclusively to areas inhabited by Palestinian refugees, and is not used for informal settlements with rural or Bedouin populations, for which the term 'poor areas' *(ahya' al-fuqara)* is preferred.[5] Yet the definition of 'informal' remains unclear. The Housing and Urban Development Corporation has three defining criteria of informality: two morphological criteria related to the road network (accessibility of the area) and the style of building (the view from windows and proximity of buildings), and a legal criterion related to types of ownership of property.[6] Note that the legal status of housing alone can define informality, if one considers that the absence of exclusive and inalienable rights of transfer renders property informal.[7]

The specific situation of 'poor areas'

The remaining informal settlements developed within Jordanian towns are the result of rural depopulation and changing lifestyles in a Jordanian population with considerable population growth (3 percent per year).

Thus, large areas of land have been illegally appropriated and built on by Beni Hassan and Beni Sakhr tribe members in the north and east of Amman, in Zarqa and Russeifa, leading to conflicts with the state (Razzaz 1991). It reached the point where, in 1986, a special law was enacted to regulate the appropriation of public land by Bedouins.[8] In October 2008, squatters were allowed , for the nominal fee of JD2 per donum, to purchase state land that they inhabited in Otal-Russeifa in the governorate of Zarqa. However, these areas, which are inhabited by Transjordanian tribes, pose different types of problems from those of the neighborhoods inhabited by Palestinian refugees; these are mainly problems related to real-estate and tax issues that do not involve questions of nationality and identity. The types of informality associated with rural depopulation and self-built constructions are treated differently by municipal services and the Land Registry Department. Often, mayors directly provide basic services for their residents, without requiring the intervention of the HUDC. The mayor of Russeifa, who comes from the large Beni Hassan tribe, is able to provide water supply and electricity services in informal settlements populated by underprivileged members of his tribe and located within his sphere of competence.[9]

The geographical distribution of Palestinian refugees in Jordan

Since its independence in 1946, Jordan's population has increased eleven-fold. This is due to both high rates of natural population growth (more than 3 percent), and the country's absorption of four major waves of refugees and migrants: in 1948 (100,000 Palestinian refugees), 1967 (300,000 Palestinian refugees and displaced persons),[10] 1991 (350,000 Palestinian and Jordanian migrants expelled from the Gulf), and 2003–2005 (between 200,000 and 400,000 Iraqis). These waves created high demand on residential land and urban services, as 79 percent of Jordan's 6 million inhabitants are urban, with half of them living in the Amman-Russeifa-Zarqa conurbation.

After the 1948 *Nakba* ('Catastrophe') and the arrival of 100,000 Palestinian refugees in Amman, four camps were created: in Zarqa (1949), Irbid (1951), Jabal Hussein (1952), and Wahdat (1955). These camps have been administered by UNRWA since 1950. The 1967 war brought a second wave of Palestinian refugees, generating more informal settlements and leading to the establishment of several non-recognized camps (areas not recognized as camps but which have access to a basic package of UNRWA services). Huge slums appeared. The aftermath of the war also led to the establishment of six emergency camps for refugees/displaced persons: Husn, Baqaa, Talbieh, Marka, Souf, and Jerash were all formally recognized in 1968. Four other official camps are operated under the direct supervision of the Jordanian Department of Palestinian Affairs: al-Nadhif, Madaba, Hanikin, and Sukhne.

The informal settlements presented particular challenges. They were characterized by high natural population growth (more than 6 percent per year), and were typically located on treacherous terrain, including floodable *wadi* basins and steep hillsides. They also frequently encroached on agricultural land. Because of zoning regulations introduced by the British in the 1930s, residential land in Amman is zoned into four categories: A (> 1,000 m²), B (> 750 m²), C (> 500 m²), and D (> 250 m²); the plot sizes are too large to be affordable to low-income groups. This is one reason why a variety of informal zones and non-recognized camps appeared near the official UNRWA camps in East Amman.

What constitutes an informal area has been very narrowly defined in Amman. In 2006, the HUDC evaluated the number of 'squatter areas' throughout Jordan at forty, inhabited by only 100,000 people. This figure is questionable if we compare it with Syria, where nearly 60 percent of the city of Damascus is made of structures built without permits (*ghayr nizami* or *mukhalafat*).

Informal settlement characteristics

Most of the settlements that appeared in the 1950s and late 1960s were built on the edge of hills and in the floodable areas of valleys. The average lot size was 150m², that is, only about half the size allotted by the formal building code, leaving space for only narrow footpaths. By the 1980s, three quarters of the houses had permanent wall constructions and 70 percent had concrete roofs. The remaining homes had zinc or wood roofs. The average number of inhabitants per room was 4.2. However, 15 percent of the households reached 7 inhabitants per room. Most of the houses were characterized by overcrowding, with all the associated domestic risks that entails. The infant mortality rate was high: 86 percent (Al Daly 1999). In 1980, one quarter of the city of Amman was occupied by informal settlements populated by Palestinian refugees.[11]

There are four kinds of land tenure patterns in Jordan's informal areas: squats, the *hujja* contract, property ownership (*mulk*), and the *tawsiya*. In the case of squats, refugees built their shacks on government or private land, with no transaction taking place at all. There is the specific case of tribal pastoral land, which is not registered, and is considered by the government as state land. Omar Razzaz has written extensively on the conflict that pitted the Beni Hassan tribe against the government, in Yajouz in the 1990s (Razzaz 1991). In the case of a *hujja* contract, widely used in the Middle East, a former owner sells his land and makes an oral agreement, the *hujja* ('proof'), which is not legally binding and not recognized by the Land and Survey Department, but provides a basis for the assertion of ownership in court. Property ownership, *mulk*, can be private or, in most cases, collective. Collective property ownership is of two kinds: *musha'a*, where land is co-owned with other households through shares, but with only one legal title deed for all; or *musharak*, where several associated persons buy a 250 m² plot of land (the most common size of plot usually on sale) to be divided among them. The fourth case applies when the Land and Survey Department delivers a recognition document to the occupants called a *tawsiya* (Al Daly 1999).

Prior to 1980, the Jordanian government did not have a policy on informal settlements. In 1965, the Housing Corporation was created to build affordable apartments in Amman. But their cost was too high, and they did not solve the problem of informal areas. The 1970s saw growing pressure worldwide to address the phenomenon of informal areas and refugee camps, which was linked to demographic transition and rural depopulation. In this context of international concern regarding informal settlements, an ideological shift took place worldwide.

The Successful Upgrading Phase (1980–97): The Work of the Urban Development Corporation and the Housing and Urban Development Corporation

During the 1970s, international institutions, particularly the World Bank, began to finance urban renewal programs that were strongly inspired by the theories developed by the urban planner John F.C. Turner in Peru in the 1960s (Turner 1976). The basic idea behind this new developmentalist ideology was to renovate informal areas while involving their occupants in all stages of the process: from design to construction, including funding. The idea was to make them pay a nominal fee to access homeownership through long-term loans, while training them in construction trades to help bring them out of unemployment and make them independent. The use of long-term and therefore affordable loans was a condition for the replicability of urban upgrading programs, because the reimbursement of the loans could be used to fund other, similar projects.

The impact of John Turner's upgrading theory

The ideology of John Turner inspired the work of early theorists of urban informality. During the 1970s, theorists abandoned the concepts of the Chicago School of urban sociology developed in the 1930s in order to adapt to the new realities of Latin American urban transition. They thus revolutionized the concepts of urban marginality and poverty, showing that poor new urban inhabitants of southern cities were fully integrated into society, but in a way that made them economically exploited, politically oppressed, socially stigmatized, and culturally excluded (Perlman 1976; Castells 1977). The pioneering work of the Latin American school was adapted during the 1980s to the situation in India, for the mega-cities of Calcutta and Karachi (AlSayyad and Roy 2004; Fernandes and Varley 1998; Hasan 2000). The issue of urban home ownership and the regularization of land titling then became a priority for the development programs of the UNDP (United Nations Development Programme), echoing the work of Hernando de Soto (de Soto 1989; Payne 2002). The legalistic approach conceptualized by Hernando de Soto has been a great influence on the design of policies for the upgrading of informal settlements, and on the World Bank since the 1990s. It encourages home ownership by the poor via the registration of their property as collateral for future loans. However, it is strongly criticized due to the fact that home ownership implies integration into the market economy, and therefore often leads to the eviction of squatters who are unable to compete.

The Urban Development Department and the World Bank

In this context, a new agency was created in the 1980s inside the Municipality of Greater Amman: the Urban Development Department (UDD). It aimed to solve the informal settlement issue. The UDD's mandate was to develop infrastructure services and community facilities in informal areas, and to provide low-income housing. It adopted the new World Bank concepts of upgrading by involving the population. Three development projects were launched. The first Urban Development Project (UDP 1) was directed from 1981 to 1986 by Dr. Khaled Jayyoussi. It consisted in the upgrading of four sites: East Wahdat, Jabal Jofeh, Rimam, and Nozeh, and the creation of three sites with services: Marka, Quweisma, and Russeifa 1. The sites and services projects aimed at preparing the land for purchase at affordable prices, based on the division of property into small plots of 150 m^2 (thus creating the E-zoning type), with core units and all services provided. Most of the upgrading process of informal areas has taken place in downtown Amman since 1980. However, 'future' projects planned by the HUDC in 2006, but still awaiting funding in 2010, relate to the east of the city (Fig. 10.1).

The main components of the upgrading policy were: land tenure consolidation (the UDD bought the land and sold it to the squatters); cost recovery (in order to ensure the principle of replicability of the projects); self-help (in order for the squatters to acquire building skills); job opportunities (at least half of the workers had to come from the local population); community involvement (in order to facilitate the process and cope with the population's needs); incremental housing (starting with a core unit equipped with a sanitary section).[12] The upgrading program was based on full cost-recovery. Beneficiaries had to pay the full cost of onsite infrastructure services as well as the cost of the land, through a long-term mortgage loan from the Jordan Housing Bank. Meanwhile the government was responsible for the cost of the community facilities and off-site infrastructure. The Jordan Housing Bank usually asked the beneficiaries to provide a guarantor; in many cases, beneficiaries failed to satisfy the bank's requirements, while others rejected the idea of taking out a bank loan for religious reasons. Therefore, the government took the initiative to allow this category to pay directly to the UDD with reasonable arrangements, which do not require any guarantee, although the beneficiaries are still charged an interest rate equivalent to that charged by the bank (Al Daly 1999).

The UDD built a community center on each of the project sites. The objectives of the community center were to mobilize and organize local community initiatives, promote income-generating activities and literacy campaigns, raise public awareness, and encourage women's involvement in the community development process. Furthermore, women's vocational training centers were built to provide vocational training for women and promote their economic activities through an access to credit program (Al Daly 1999).

The model of East Wahdat upgrading (Aga Khan Prize 1992)

East Wahdat was chosen for upgrading due to its particularly bad conditions. It suffered from high rates of infant mortality (68 percent), very poor hygiene, a total lack of services, and poor squatter housing. East Wahdat was an informal extension of the UNRWA Wahdat camp. It was set up by Palestinian refugees, most of them holders of an UNRWA card, near Wahdat in order to have access to camp services. However, the contrast between the UNRWA concrete-built camp and the shacks with zinc roofs of East Wahdat was huge.

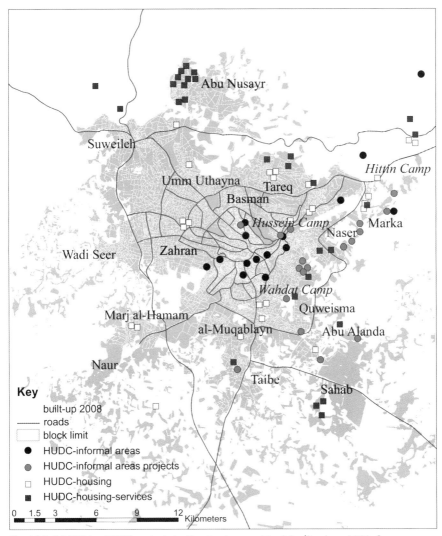

Fig. 10.1: HUDC (ex-UDD) projects in Greater Amman Municipality since 1966. Sources: GAM and HUDC (Ababsa and Daher 2011).

The program had two main underlying principles: minimum destruction, and the participation of the entire population. Walls were created around the lots, and the shanty houses were kept during the construction of the house, on the same lot. This is called 'incremental housing.' The inhabitants were not expelled, but on the contrary kept on their lot. They were asked to build a wall around their house, following an urban plan.

Each lot received a sanitary core (tap water and sewerage). This core can still be found at the entrance of each house in most of the camps and upgraded areas in Amman. During the upgrading process, the squatters first constructed a 12 to 20–square meter room into which they moved while their old shacks were being destroyed and a second room being built (Fig. 10.2).

The UDD social team was active in contacting the residents. According to Khaled Jayyousi, the success of the East Wahdat upgrading program was based on the level of trust between the UDD and the local population. The project was seen as a complete success when it received the award of the Agha Khan Architecture Prize in 1992. The most important aspect of this project was that Palestinian refugees with Jordanian citizenship gained access to legal property titles.

The aim of the program was to improve the living conditions of residents of informal settlements by enabling them to secure land tenure and by providing them with basic infrastructure, shelter, and community facilities. Funds were brought together from the World Bank (31 percent), the

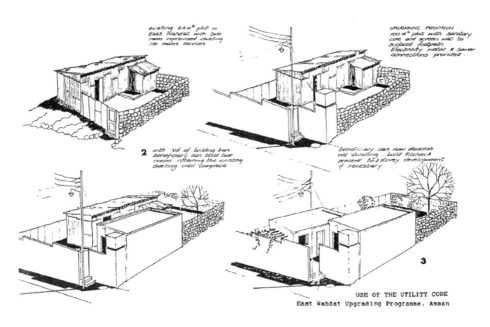

Fig. 10.2: Incremental building in East Wahdat Upgrading Program (Urban Development Department, 1980).

government of Jordan (25 percent), and the Housing Bank (44 percent). The land was bought from the original owners and mortgaged to the householders with monthly installments based on 33 percent of the income of each beneficiary.

Site selection

During my interviews, I wanted to know how the UDD proceeded with regard to site selection. Importantly, the formal camps were off limits until 1997. Thus, efforts focused on squatters inhabiting government or private land, but not did lend attention to ownership at all. Priority was given to slums that had no services. After this first success, a total of 13 squatter sites were upgraded by the UDD between 1981 and 1991: the project upgraded 11,665 units sheltering 114,000 inhabitants. The UDD bought the land from the government and reallocated it to households. In most cases, each household was allocated the plot it was already using. To secure a land title deed, each household had to pay back to the UDD the cost of the land through long-term mortgage loans. Therefore, most of the households managed to extend their houses or build new dwellings (Tables 10.1 and 10.2).

During the 1980s, some residents of informal settlements (like the area of Jabal Ali, northeast of Amman) refused the upgrading programs, because as Palestinian refugees, they still hoped to return to their homes in Palestine. They believed that the upgrading policies were unnecessary

Table 10.1: Basic information on squatter settlements included in the upgrading program.

Program	Squatter Settlement	Area (hectares)	Population	Completion date	Location
UDP 1	Wahdat	9.1	5,000	1984	Amman
UDP 1	Jofeh	2.9	2,500	1982	Amman
UDP 1	Rimam	3.7	3,500	1984	Amman
UDP 1	Nuzha	2.4	3,000	1988	Amman
UDP 2	Hayy Amir Hassan	3	2,000	1985	Amman
UDP 3	Salah al-Din	7.3	2,000	1985	Aqaba
UDP 3	Shallaleh North	11.7	5,000	1991	Aqaba

(Source: HUDC quarterly reports. Al Daly 1999).

Table 10.2: UDP upgrading projects.

	New Core Units	Upgrading Units	Beneficiaries	Cost (in JD million)
UDP 1	3,018	1,265	29,000	22
UDP 2	3,883	138	39,000	32
UDP 3	4,764	1,953	45,670	30
Total	11,665	3,356	113,670	84

(Source: Community Infrastructure Program A, 2004)

and their situation was 'temporary.' Moreover, they refused to accept Jordan or any other country as an alternative homeland (*al-watan al-badil*). They feared that the improvement of their informal areas meant converting them into permanent living areas.[13] The same had occurred in the 1970s in the UNRWA camps. Another reason upgrading in informal areas like Jabal Ali was refused is that people had already lived there for a long time without paying taxes or extra costs. If the government intervened they would start paying taxes they could not afford.[14]

In 1991 the Housing and Urban Development Corporation (HUDC) was created, merging together the Housing Corporation and the Urban Development Department. For the first time, projects were conducted at the level of the entire country, and not only in Amman. But at the same time, HUDC policy totally changed. Another shift occurred with the new peace process: official UNRWA camps started to be included in the upgrading process, but the negative consequence was that the land tenure issue was no longer addressed.

The Second Phase (1997–2007): Community Infrastructure Programs

Since the peace accords of 1993 and 1994, special attention has been given to the upgrading of housing for refugees within and without camps. Jalal Al Husseini notes that Article 8 of the Wadi Araba treaty signed by Jordan and Israel in January 1994 recognized the "massive human problems caused to both parties by the conflict in the Middle East" (paragraph 1) and recommended their alleviation, notably "through the implementation of agreed United Nations Programs and other agreed international economic programs concerning refugees and displaced persons, including assistance to their settlement" (para 2.c) (Al Husseini 2011). It is within this context that in 1997 a new policy to reduce poverty and unemployment—the National Strategic Plan—was implemented by the Jordanian government as part of structural adjustment policies imposed by the International Monetary Fund (IMF). It was a huge urban infrastructure program for the community (CIP—Community Infrastructure Program), both in camps and informal areas. For the first time in the history of the Jordanian government, all ten UNRWA camps and the three Palestinian Affairs Department camps were integrated into the work of the HUDC.

There are three types of Community Infrastructure Programs: CIP A, B, and C. CIP-A aims to renovate infrastructure in informal settlements and camps. CIP-B aims to improve infrastructure in rural areas and small towns, in coordination with the Ministry of Municipal Affairs. And CIP-C concerns the internal development of the HUDC through training and technical and computer equipment. The first infrastructure program (CIP-A) was implemented between March 1998 and February 2002, mainly in Amman, but also in Zarqa for informal areas and throughout the country for camps. The essential services included water supply and sanitation (environmentally sound wastewater and solid waste disposal); drainage systems to minimize property damage and reduce the risk of loss of human life due to floods; safety measures through accessible roads and lighting; and the provision of schools, health facilities, and community centers. Major roads were widened and lit within informal settlements, but only in areas surrounding UNRWA camps, in order to protect their physical integrity. Finally, in informal areas, eight schools, five clinics, and eight community centers (where literacy activities and association meetings are held) were built. Four hundred and fifty thousand people were affected by the CIP-A in informal areas and 220,000 in camps. Half of the cost of these projects (JD46 million) was covered by the Jordanian government (JD20 million); a quarter of the cost was funded by the World Bank (JD10 million), and the remainder was paid for by the German development bank Kreditanstalt für Wiederaufbau (KFW) (JD8.5 million), Islamic banks (JD6 million), and the Arab fund (JD1.5 million).

Strategies since 1990 only deal with the elements of housing. To satisfy needs at minimal cost, the HUDC began to organize land into small plots with special regulations, with areas of 250 m² instead of 300 m². The HUDC also started to build residential units with a surface area of

Table 10.3: Basic information on squatter settlements included in CIP-A Project.

Squatter settlements	Area (hectares)	No. of Households	Location
Wadi Abdoun	3.8	208	Amman
Al Hashemi	2.2	282	Amman
Masdar	0.7	56	Amman
Wadi Haddada	1.9	189	Amman
Lawziya	2.2	340	Amman
Zawahra	4.7	102	Amman
Qaisya	14.7	584	Amman
Nadhif	8.7	1,191	Amman
Nuzha	1.8	377	Amman
Wadi Qattar	18.0	130	Amman
Musherfa	20.5	1,306	Amman
Abu Sayah	12.5	86	Amman
Jena'a	24.0	1,673	Zarqa
Hayy Tafayla	3.9	914	Amman

(Source: Community Infrastructure Program A, 2004)

80 m²–120 m² (the average surface area of a residential unit in Jordan is 115 m²). However, construction costs on these HUDC projects are high (JD200/ m²) as compared to JD120/ m² when built by the private sector (Tables 10.3 and 10.4).

The Community Infrastructure Programs had offered opportunities. They provided a set of services while demanding nothing in return, and did not aim for cost recovery at all. They gave very good indemnities and compensations to all families affected by house demolition or displacement. Yet the fundamental aspect of land tenure was abandoned, the official reason for this being that land had become so expensive that even the government could not afford to buy and sell it. Moreover, the families concerned had become too poor to be able to take out twenty-year loans with the Housing Bank, the Islamic Bank, or the government.

Table 10.4: Basic informatioin on refugee camps included in CIP-A Project.

Refugee camps	Area (hectares)	No. of Households	Location
Madaba camp	11.2	750	Madaba
Zarqa camp	18.9	1,124	Zarqa
Souf camp	59.6	1,453	Jerash
Talbiya camp	13.3	615	Amman
Jerash camp	50.7	1,977	Jerash
al-Hussein camp	33.8	3,871	Amman
Baqaa camp	130.7	8,080	Balqa
Sukhna	6.9	565	Zarqa
Wahdat camp	47.7	4,523	Amman
Irbid camp	21.9	2,170	Irbid
Husn camp	75.4	3,400	Irbid
Marka camp	89.4	5,067	Amman
Hanikeen camp	9.6	1,161	Amman

(Source: Community Infrastructure Program A, 2004)

A Case Ctudy: Nahariya, Wahdat Camp Informal Extension

In May 2006, I started fieldwork on the ongoing Community Infrastructure Program C that was launched in February 2006, and which concerned Hayy al-Nahariya, an informal extension of Wahdat Camp inhabited mainly by refugees from Gaza, but also from Hebron and Beersheba. It is located southeast of Amman, east of Yarmouk Street. The concerned area covers 85 *dunums* (8.5 hectares) and is inhabited by eight thousand people. Most of the land is *mushtarak*-owned, that is, by groups of people. It was bought by the refugees from the Al Hadid family tribe in 1967, *lira al-mitir* (one dinar for a square meter). However, the poorest people were allowed to rent the land (JD40 to 50 per month for a two-room apartment of 40 to 50 m²) from the Al Hadid family. Houses were built without permits and are not shown on any urban plan. The plots are officially in a C zone (more than 500 m²), but the HUDC would like to convert them to the D type (> 250 m²). The area did not have a school, health center, or community center. Two main problems were underlined by the HUDC: the absence of 'service roads' from Yarmouk Street to the neighborhood and the proximity of car repair garages. Officially, the opening of roads was needed in order to provide access to fire engines and ambulances.

Thirty-three lots were targeted by the upgrading process. Eight houses were totally destroyed, and nine partly destroyed. Nine walls were removed. Most of the beneficiaries agreed with the project, since the HUDC paid well. The compensation for house destruction is paid by the square meter, according to the quality of construction (from JD55 JD/ m² for a zinc roof to JD130/m² for ceramic floors). Plus each family received compensation for eviction (JD2,250 for each family in the case of total destruction, and JD750 in the case of partial destruction). A total of JD48,450 was paid in compensation for evictions, JD112,000 was paid for land expropriation, and JD198,692 was paid in compensation for house demolitions.

It is interesting to note that the HUDC also took into consideration *hujja* type contracts to calculate levels of compensation, thus adapting to the reality of different types of land tenure in informal areas, and attempting to include the entire population. However, according to Mahmud al-Abbadi, director of CIP implementation, the HUDC took the type of contract into consideration to define compensations. People who had proof of property ownership (*tapu*, the Ottoman word for a title deed or *gushan*, the name of the document used in Ottoman-era Palestine) received 100 percent compensation.[15] People able to produce *hujja* contracts received only 90 percent of the compensation (the *hujja* has been declared illegal and non-binding by the Land and Survey Department (see Razzaz 1991, 13)). Al Abbaddi underlined the fact that this process for the calculation of compensation has a human dimension; the government cannot evict people from their houses unless it pays reasonable compensation that ensures acceptable living conditions, or at least the same conditions as those the occupants already live in.

An extreme example is given by Family 1 (lot 3): this family (nine children, made up of eight girls and one boy) received a total of JD74,047 in compensation: JD10,400 for the land, JD48,347 for the house (three floors, six apartments), and JD15,300 for eviction *(badal al-ikhla')*. With that money, in 2007 they bought a small two-story building (four apartments) built in an informal settlement in Quweisma, which is located ten minutes' walking distance east of Nahariya, for JD19,000. The transactions cost them JD1,800 in taxes.[16] They are a family of Gaza refugees who arrived in Jordan after 1967. They only have a two-year travel permit, which does not provide them with Jordanian citizenship. As Oroub El-Abed underlined, the statelessness of the Gazans in Jordan means they lack rights to individual freedoms, political participation, and a full share in the social heritage of the nation of Jordan. Although Gazan refugees in Jordan are provided with relief, health, and education services by UNRWA, they have difficulty finding jobs and entering public higher education. They are not allowed to register with professional associations and unions, or to create their own offices, firms, or clinics. Even work in the private sector is contingent upon security approval. Gaza refugees in Jordan are accordingly forced to work in the informal sector, with the resulting risk of exploitation (El-Abed 2005). For instance, the copper worker of Family 1 earned JD3 per workday instead of JD5.

The widening of the main street of Nahariya, perpendicular to Yarmouk Street, also affected the area around the Wahdat camp. On 30 May 2006, I met Latifa, a refugee from Beit Dajan who arrived in Nablus in 1948, and was driven out to Jordan in 1967. In 1973 her husband bought their 150 m² apartment for JD452 via a *hujja* contract from a refugee in the camp. In 1987, she registered the property in her name. She values her apartment at JD20,000. She has six boys and two girls and her living conditions are difficult. Her husband works as a carpenter: "*am bijib al-irsh min al-dam*" ("he is earning his living with his blood"). That same day I met her neighbor Intisar, who is forty-two, single, and works as a seamstress in the Wahdat camp. Her parents were from al-Dawalma (an area of Hebron). They arrived in Wahdat in 1950. Their house, which is part of Wahdat camp, overlooks Yarmouk Street. She greets me in the living room, which was the first room of the house built in 1950, where her parents lived with her five brothers and sisters. They had a small courtyard with a fig tree, an almond tree, and vines, where they raised a few chickens. Over time, as the family grew, the entire courtyard was built on. What remains is a central room leading on to two bedrooms, the living room, and an entrance to the kitchen and bathroom. The upgrading processes of the HUDC, and of the housing renovation program of the Department of Social Affairs, are sometimes discretely implemented within camps run by UNRWA, with the agency's agreement.

In March 2007, I carried out another series of interviews in Nahariya after the destruction of houses, the road widening, and the installation of sewers and waterworks. A family (a Palestinian widow from Lebanon whose late husband was a Palestinian Jordanian refugee and who was mother to eight girls and one boy) whose house had been destroyed had received a total sum of JD19,200 in compensation. Afaf, the mother, had thought to save the doors, which she had sold before the destruction. She bought two three-room apartments on the other side of the street, in the Wahdat camp, for JD19,000. Their owner used the money to purchase a house in Quweisma. He asked for an extra JD1,000 to vacate his apartments. Afaf leases the ground-floor apartment to Iraqis for JD60 per month.[17] One of her unmarried daughters works as a teacher, earning JD200, and gives her JD50 per month. But she complains that for the past eight months (September 2006 to March 2007) she no longer receives the JD130 of monthly assistance that the Ministry of Social Affairs paid her before the demolition of her house. She claims this is because the compensation she received was perceived as an accumulation of wealth. Yet she is confident of her fate, and certain that she will recover her rights.

On 22 March 2007 a neighboring family received a cheque for JD100 in compensation for a square meter of land lost. They were refugees from 1967, and first rented a room in the Wahdat camp before buying a 100-m² plot in Abu Han al-Hadid through *mushtaraka*, "with other poor people like us," in the name of the grandmother, Fatma. One son has migrated to Germany, another sells foam mattresses. On the other side of the street, a family has lost 50 m² from their house, which now measures only 85 m². They are refugees from Gaza who arrived in 1967 and are the owners *(mulk)* of their apartment, their ownership of the property being recorded on the same register for the entire neighborhood (with six family names on the *sanad*).

The debate about the shift of policy

The main objective of the CIP is to show the population that the state has not forgotten about them, and is not just satisfied with paying them allowances through the Ministry of Social Affairs. The goal is to unify the country and to rid the large cities of unhealthy slums as we move toward the permanent resettlement of refugees. On 13 March 2007, during a meeting involving engineers from UN-Habitat and the HUDC, it was stated clearly that the CIP obviously have a social dimension (building schools, clinics, and social centers), but above all have a security dimension; on the pretext of creating access for fire engines and ambulances they also open poor informal areas to the police force, "just as the prefect Haussmann did in Paris," stated one Jordanian engineer.

At the meeting, it was stressed that the UNRWA camps "remain as they are," with minimal intervention on the periphery for road networks. Their cheap rental to large landowners was presented as a "downside" *(noqta salbiya)* in urban management in Amman. As Jamal Al Daly wrote in 1999: "As far as the land tenure in the camps is concerned, the government has no intention to deal with this issue, since the camps are still being regarded as a temporary shelter for refugees until their political question is addressed" (Al Daly 1999). According to the director of HUDC operations in the camps, the renovation of infrastructure by the government is part of the broader political project the aim of which is to "integrate refugees in the urban fabric so that they can turn over a new leaf, forget their past, and become part of the population of Amman, with the same social characteristics and the same projects."[18]

Since 1997, the HUDC has changed its policy for two reasons: firstly, the considerable rise in the cost of land, and secondly the increased poverty of target populations that can no longer get loans from banks. The rising cost of land, which has more than tripled since 1997, is such that the government can no longer advance the funds needed to purchase property. The impoverishment of families is a genuine problem, worsened by inflation, which reached 11 percent in 2007 and 14 percent in 2008, and Amman has been ranked the most expensive city in the Middle East with respect to average Jordanian income (JD357 per month in 2004).

During my first interviews in the offices of the HUDC in Dahiyet al-Hussein in March 2006, a debate arose between the employees and a private developer involved in the paving of roads. He said the Jordanian government had no desire to solve the problem of land ownership by Palestinian refugees. This was confirmed to me in November 2007, by an employee of the HUDC who told me that the main reason for the turnaround in methods of the HUDC was more political than financial, and that the subject of registration of land ownership in informal areas was sensitive precisely because their inhabitants were Palestinian refugees. This means that their allegiance to the regime is not established,[19] but also, as I was told bluntly in October 2008 by an employee of the Department of Social Studies, "the government does not want to permanently settle Palestinian refugees."[20] The verb he used was *tawattin*, meaning permanent settlement in Jordan as a substitute homeland *(watan badil)* for Palestine. This is controversial since the great majority of these refugees have acquired Jordanian nationality. In addition, registration of property raises legal issues because the status of real estate is not always well defined. Several employees of the HUDC regret that CIP do not allow the recipients to improve their economic status, not only because housing is not guaranteed for them, but because they do not acquire any professional skills during the project, since they are merely recipients of the aid bestowed on them.[21] As a result, beneficiaries who do not become homeowners have no desire to renovate their homes at their own expense.

2008: Year of housing and year of evictions (Wadi Abdoun, Shalaleh)

After a quarter of a century of policies which focused on people, taking care not to evict them but rather to make them active in improving their housing and living conditions, 2008 marked a break. Indeed, in the context of building the new business center in Amman (Abdali) and gated communities in Aqaba, two informal settlements were displaced: the district of Qaysiya in Wadi Abdoun and the informal camp of Shalaleh. It is remarkable that these two areas had been the subject of upgrading programs by the HUDC twice during the 1990s and 2000s. In 2008, the procedure changed completely: residents were compensated for leaving their homes that were partly destroyed in September 2009. There was great controversy in Wadi Abdoun concerning the rate of compensation for the displaced inhabitants: JD80 per m², considered well below the cost of land estimated at JD200–450. In North Shalaleh, populations originating from Gaza, without Jordanian nationality, were forced to move to collective housing provided for them in al-Karama, five kilometres northeast of the town center, to where Egyptian port workers had already been displaced after the authorities destroyed their neighborhood in March 2010. These events occurred after 2008 was declared the "year of housing," by the Jordanian government, and when the HUDC ceased all its operations for the upgrading of informal areas in order to implement the royal initiative "Decent Housing for a Decent Life," which aims to build 100,000 homes in five years, to be sold for JD17,000 each. After one year, the prices of these apartments had risen to JD35,000, causing a tremendous scandal, because the minister of public works had allowed one of his private companies to control the construction of these homes. In May 2010, the entire Camp and Informal Areas Department of the HUDC was closed: employees must come to the office but do not have the right to work, because all budgets and resources are focused on the royal initiative, thus ending three decades of exemplary upgrading of informal areas in Jordan.

Conclusion

During the 1980s, Jordan was a leading country in urban upgrading projects for informal areas in the Middle East. These projects were mostly focused on neighborhoods built on the outskirts of UNRWA camps, populated by Palestinian refugees. From 1980 to 1997, the government tried to grant access to land ownership for these Jordanian citizens of Palestinian origin, and to train them in trades, especially the building trade. However, since the Wadi Araba peace accords in January 1994, the philosophy has changed completely. Now, the infrastructure is repaired to show that the improvement of living conditions is desirable for camps and informal settlements, but especially to allow improved access to these zones by state officers. However, access to property is no longer made easier. Indeed, land costs have become prohibitive and the government no longer wants these poor refugees to settle permanently *(tawtin)*. Forty or so informal areas remain in Jordan, inhabited by 100,000 people, which is a very low number compared to other Middle Eastern countries (Syria and Lebanon) where half the buildings have been built illegally (without a title deed or building permit). However, since 2008, policies have changed: in Wadi Abdoun, in the heart of the city of Amman, but also in Aqaba, in the informal Shalaleh camp near the coast, two informal settlements populated by refugees are being destroyed to make way for private investments. Thus, three types of policies have been implemented in Jordan and at the same time in other Arab countries: upgrading in the 1980s with the participation of residents; provision of services alone from the mid-1990s because of rising costs of land; and from the neoliberal wave of the mid-2000s, eviction and selective rehousing.

Notes

1   These three cities form a continuous agglomeration comprising half the population of Jordan (with three million inhabitants in 2004).

2   UNRWA is the UN agency which was created in 1949 to bring relief and assistance to Palestinian refugees.

3   This article was written as part of a research program on public policy and legal practice on the management of informal settlements directed by Baudouin Dupret within the ANR 'Citadain' program: "City and Law in the Arab world and India" (2006–2009) directed by Philippe Cadène (Paris VII).

4   The question of the number of Iraqi refugees is highly controversial. While the Jordanian government announced 700,000 people in 2005 to justify its requests for international aid, the figure has been revised

significantly downward. Thus the site of the Jordanian Department of Statistics now claims the figure of 400,000 people, after consulting the Norwegian research center Fafo, while specialists tend to speak of 200,000 people, noting that the UNHCR has only registered 50,000 *Iraqi refugees.*

5   The informal housing areas developed on the outskirts of Palestinian refugee camps are often referred to using the term camp *(mukhayyam)* by engineers of the HUDC, underlining the homogeneity of the population of Palestinian origin.

6   Interview with Bayan Jaradat, HUDC, October 22, 2008. During a joint UN Habitat-HUDC seminar, 13 March 2007, the criteria of informality adopted by the UN agency were discussed by the engineers of the HUDC with a view to adopting them in Jordan (an idea which has since been abandoned). According to UN Habitat, a parcel is informal if at least two of the following criteria are missing: access to drinking water, sewerage, sustainability of housing, sufficient surface area (fewer than two people per room), and security of tenure.

7   Definition adopted by the aforementioned ANR program.

8   Interview with engineer Hussam Madanat, advisor to the director of the Department of Land Registry, 13 October 2008.

9   Interview with Jamal Al Daly, UNRWA, November 2008.

10 'Displaced persons' refers to those Palestinians who took refuge in the West Bank in 1948 and who were subsequently expelled to the East Bank of the Jordan River in 1967.

11 Client's Record of East Wahdat Upgrading Program. Aga Khan Award for Architecture, 1992. http://www.archnet.org/library/files/one-file.jsp?file_id=925.

12 Interview with Dr. Khaled Jayyoussi, Director of the UDP 1, Amman, 2 June 2006.

13 An interview with the director of the HUDC, Dahiyet al-Hussein, 17 November 2007.

14 An interview with the director of the Refugee Camps Improvement Department, HUDC, in Dahiyet al-Hussein, 17 November 2007.

15 An interview with the director of CIP, HUDC, in Dahiyet al-Hussein, 17 November 2007.

16 Interview, 30 May 2006.

17 The camps and informal areas of Amman are home to marginalized people who are unable to pay the high rents in the rest of the city. It has been estimated that in the early 2000s there were eight thousand people, representing 16 percent of the population, who were foreign tenants, Egyptians, and Iraqis, in the Wahdat camp (al-Hamarneh 2002, 181, in al-Husseini 2010).

18 Interview, 17 November 2007.
19 Jordanians of Palestinian origin have become so numerous within the Muslim Brotherhood that a split is said to have occurred within the movement since the Second Intifada in September 2000.
20 Interview with the director of the Department of Social Studies, HUDC, 29 October 2008.
21 Interview with the director of the Department of Informal Settlements, HUDC, 17 November 2007.

References

Ababsa, Myriam. 2007. *Amman de pierre et de paix*. Paris: Autrement.
Ababsa, Myriam, and Rami Daher, eds. 2011. *Cities, Urban Practices and Nation Building in Jordan/Villes, pratiques urbaines et construction nationale en Jordanie*. Cahiers de l'IFPO (Institut français du Proche-Orient) no. 6. http://ifpo.revues.org/1675. Beirut: IFPO.
El-Abed, Oroub. 2005. "Immobile Palestinians The Impact of Policies and Practices on Palestinians from Gaza in Jordan," In Hana Jaber and France Métral, eds., *Mondes en mouvement. Migrants et migrations au Moyen-Orient au tournant du xxi*e *siècle*, 81–93. Beirut: IFPO.
AlSayyad, Nezar, and Ananda Roy, eds. 2004. *Urban Informality: Transnational Perspectives from the Middle East, Latin America, and South Asia*. Lanham, MD: Lexington Books.
Castells, M., 1977, *The urban question: a Marxist approach*, Londres: Arnold.
Cavaliere, Alfredo. 1994. "Caractères et gestion politique de l'habitat informel à Amman." Master's thesis, Tours University.
"Client's Record of East Wahdat Upgrading Program." 1992. Aga Khan Award for Architecture. http://www.archnet.org/library/ûles/one-ûle.jsp?ûle_id=925.
Al Daly, Jamal. 1999. "Informal Settlements in Jordan: Upgrading Approaches Adopted and Lessons Learned." http://www.hdm.lth.se/fileadmin/hdm/alumni/papers/ad1999/ad1999-09.pdf.
de Soto, Hernando. 1989. *The Other Path: The Invisible Revolution in the Third World*. London: I.B. Tauris.
Destremeau, Blandine. 1994. "L'espace du camp et la reproduction du provisoire: les camps de réfugiés palestiniens de Wihdat et de Jabal Hussein à Amman." In Bocco Riccardo and Mohamed-Reza Djalili, eds. *Moyen-Orient: migrations, démocratisation, médiations*. Paris: Presses Universitaires de France.
Fernandes, Edesi, and Ann Varley. 1998. *Illegal Cities: Law and Urban Change in Developing Countries*. London: Zed Books.
al-Hamarneh, Ala. 2002. "The Social and Political Effects of Transformation Processes in Palestinian Refugee Camps in the Amman Metropolitan Area (1989–99)." In Georges Joffe, ed., *Jordan in Transition*, 172–90. London: Hurst and Company.

Hannoyer, Jean, and Seteney Shami. 1996. *Amman, ville et société. The City and its society*, Beirut: CERMOC (Centre d'Etudes et de Recherches sur le Moyen-Orient Contemporain).

Hassan. A. 2000. *Housing for the Poor: Failure of Formal Sector Strategies*. Karachi: City Press.

Housing and Urban Development Corporation. 2004. "CIP-A Completion Report." Unpublished report.

Housing and Urban Development Corporation, Social Studies Direction. 2002. "Taqrir al-ittisal al-sakani al-awwal li-maqar hayy al-Nahariya." Unpublished report.

Al Husseini, Jalal. 2011. "The Palestinian Refugee Camps and Jordan's Nation Building Process." In Myriam Ababsa and Rami Daher, eds. *Cities, Urban Practices and Nation Building in Jordan/Villes, pratiques urbaines et construction nationale en Jordanie*. Cahier de l'IFPO (Institut français du Proche-Orient) no. 6. Beirut: IFPO.

————. 2004. "Community Development and Refugees: Infrastructure, Environment, Housing and Social Development." Paper presented at UNRWA Geneva Conference, "Meeting the Humanitarian Needs of the Palestine Refugees in the Near East: Building Partnerships in Support of UNRWA" (Working Group II, chaired by the Hashemite Kingdom of Jordan), 7–8 June.

Jaber, Hana. 1997. "Le camp de Wihdat à la croisée des territoires." In Bocco Riccardo, Destremeau Blandine, and Jean Hannoyer, eds. *Palestine, Palestiniens. Territoire national, espaces communautaires*, 237–58. Les Cahiers du Cermoc 17. Beirut: Centre d'Etudes et de Recherches sur le Moyen-Orient Contemporain.

Near East Report, 2007, on UNRWA intranet.

Payne, Geoffrey. 2002. *Land, Rights and Innovation: Improving Tenure Security for the Urban Poor*. London: ITDG Publishing.

Perlman, Janice. 1976. *The Myth of Marginality: Urban Poverty and Politics in Rio de Janeiro*. Berkeley: University of California Press.

Razzaz, Omar. 1996. "Land Conflicts, Property Rights and Urbanization East of Amman." In Jean Hannoyer and Seteney Shami, eds., *Amman, ville et société. The City and Its Society*, 499–526. Amman: CERMOC.

————. 1994. "Contestation and Mutual Adjustment: The Process of Controlling Land in Yajouz, Jordan." *Law and Society Review* 28 (1): 7–39.

————. 1991. "Law, Urban Land Tenure and Property Disputes in Contested Settlements: The Case of Jordan." PhD diss., Harvard University.

"Presentation Panels of East Wahdat Upgrading Program. 1992. ArchNet Digital Library. Aga Khan Award for Architecture. http://www.archnet.org/library/files/one-file.jsp?file_id=926.

Turner, John, F.C. 1976. *Housing by People. Towards Autonomy in Building Environments*. New York: Pantheon Books.

11

Mülk Allah'ındır ('This House is God's Property'): Legitimizing Land Ownership in the Suburbs of Istanbul

Jean-François Pérouse

llegal construction contained for the first time": this was the striking headline on 30 June 2007 in *Today's Zaman*, a new Turkish daily close to the current government. Published just ahead of the latest general elections, this paper leads one to believe that a new era has arrived in the public management of self-produced settlements; it argues that "for the first time" a promise of an illegal construction amnesty has been made by politicians, ahead of the general elections of July 2007.

"Istanbul: a huge illegal metropolis," should be considered as a persistent cliché to be avoided. It is used by politicians, journalists and academics; a use which prevents the improvement of a relational and dynamic analysis of the production of legality/illegality. In literature, the misuse of the term *gecekondu* as being equivalent to illegal building has contributed to the overall confusion surrounding the issue. We must abandon the term *gecekondu*, an exotic, nostalgic, but now very blurry and misleading notion, which applies mainly to the past. Moreover, as new research related to this topic tends to reveal,[1] most of the negatively stigmatized *gecekondu* were in fact built on purchased plots of land. Thus, the issue to be explored seems to be more the validity of issued property deeds and the functioning of the local system (involving politicians, [fake] plot sellers, local community leaders and so on), which allowed this land transfer to be carried out.

In this context, we must take heed of the multifold and changing types of illegality: illegalities related to land ownership and illegalities related to the building itself (violation of land use documents, lack of building permits, lack of official control during the construction process, lack of 'authorization to inhabit' permits). The different relationships between all of these types of illegality must also be taken into consideration. Consequently, in the words of Mona Fawaz, we must avoid falling "into the trap of a dualistic understanding of our cities that separates the 'legal' from the 'illegal' city and describes two different and distinct processes of city making." Legality and illegality are always subjective and relative (Fawaz 2004; Fawaz 2009).

In this context, our aim here is to address the issue of the definition of land illegality (and its socio-political construction), taking into account the relativity of this notion depending on the time and the political/economic context in which it arises. In order to cope with this relativity, special attention will be paid to the discourses and narratives deployed to affirm or to contest land legality, both by the different public actors who construct the norms and by opponents threatened with evictions and obliged to leave the land where they may have lived for decades.

Focusing on the growing suburbs of metropolitan areas, and on recent years, which have been characterized by a strong will, as expressed by public bodies, to recover the occupied lands with a view to developing them, we will try to emphasize the changes in the way both contested (Gülöksüz 2002) land legality and the issue of land illegality have been addressed.

Understanding Land Illegality and the Phenomenon of Land Occupation

Often described as a massive and homogeneous phenomenon, land illegality—which initially means the lack of a recognized property deed—in fact takes on many aspects, which are further complicated by the very complex property structure in Turkey and current transformations there:

The crucial importance of public land extension: a determining factor

To date, more than 60 percent of the land in Istanbul province could be considered as public land, under different kinds of tutelage, that is, various central or local administrations, various ministries, military departments, and so on. Most of this public land is forest. Furthermore, military sites still occupy more than 15 percent of the total land area in Istanbul province. This characteristic is more pronounced on the outskirts, as is

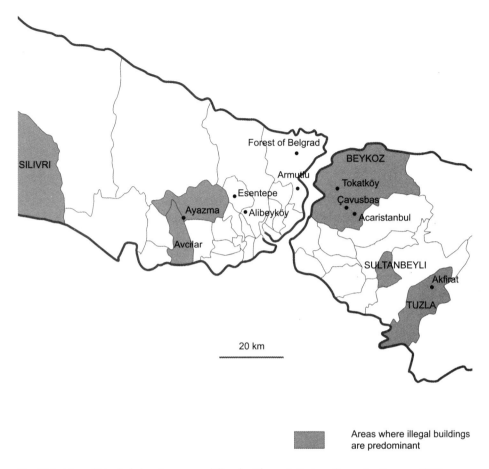

Fig. 11.1: Map of Istanbul showing areas of illegal settlement. By Jean-Françoise Perouse, 2011.

the case in the district of Beykoz, where 85 percent of the land is registered as 'public.' In these conditions, the control, sharing, and redistribution of this wonderful resource have become one of the main issues at stake in local politics. It would be very tempting to transform this huge resource into an abundant source of rent revenues. In 2008, for instance, the mayor of Akfirat, an outlying municipality located on the Asian side of the city, was forced to resign for abuse of public land. Akfirat was only instituted as an autonomous municipality in 1998 (from 1987 until then it was a village jammed between two different districts that were both trying to absorb it). With about 1,800 hectares of 'available' scrub and forest out of a total of 5,900 hectares, Akfırat rapidly became the site of intensive urban development related to the nearby motorway (called the TEM) and the opening of a Formula One racetrack. Meanwhile, the population of the small municipality had swiftly increased from fewer than 1,000 inhabitants in 1998 to more than 12,000 in 2008. In addition, the fact that its urban development is taking place exclusively in the form of luxurious villas helps us to understand the 'great expectations' generated by public land hoarding.

The long path to cadastre: breaches and loopholes;
The cadastre process isn't complete in Turkey. In 2007 the World Bank financed a project to improve the situation. Even in Istanbul, there are still many breaches and vaguely defined areas which generate litigation and abusive intervention. For instance, at the end of 2004 in Ayazma—one of my peripheral observation fields and one of the most obvious 'urban regeneration' project targets—46 percent of the land (with a population of more than 7,000) was not correctly registered in the cadastre. In spite of this vagueness regarding ownership, since the beginning of February 2007 the local municipality has undertaken to destroy houses, starting with those easy targets without title deeds. The main argument advanced by the agents of this tough 'cleansing' operation is the illegality of the whole settlement, whereas, at least regarding land status, fewer than 50 percent of all the houses concerned could be considered illegal.

Especially on the outskirts, the issue of outmoded shared title deeds (*hisseli tapu*), in which co-owners have no idea even how many other shareholders exist, constitutes a huge obstacle to clear land registration. In Sultanbeyli (in the far east of the metropolis), before the current attempts launched by local administrations to put an end to this confused situation, 70 percent of the overcrowded district was registered through shared title deeds. The continuing difficulties of clarifying matters, and sometimes identifying and locating the numerous legal owners, opens the way to inappropriate and unfair practices.

Furthermore, and especially in remote outskirts, land mafias are extremely influential. Although this phenomenon was more acute from the 1950s to the 1980s, bogus owners still sell what they do not own. The current mode of operation seems to be the exertion of pressure on owners to make them renounce their rights. These irregular practices are carried out via useful connections in the cadastre administration and registration departments, which have recently been affected by corruption cases all over the country (Ankara, Istanbul, and Antalya). Moreover, most real-estate agents operating in the market are bogus too.

In short, the conditions and secure registration of property ownership remain a problem. Subsequently, as Gülöksüz convincingly pointed out (2002), the contestation of land registration by different public agencies (such as the state treasury) is always a possibility.

Numerous and rapid changes in (urban) land status and land use
The progressive transformations and sale of forestland

Large portions of forested land have been excluded from forestry jurisdiction by the Ministry of Forests during recent decades and have become subject to regulations governing urban areas. Others might also soon be excluded, according to a new law (called "2B"), which came close to being voted on by the Turkish National Assembly at the end of January 2012. Sales of land that was previously forested are back on the government's agenda, to the delight of constructors, who have difficulty finding land for their new projects, and who ensure useful 'cash' revenues for the state treasury and municipality coffers, especially during times of financial crisis.[2] As a result, land speculators always hope for land-status transformation that would mean new capital gains opportunities. Regarding this process, the district of Beykoz is one of the most striking areas of land in the province of Istanbul: in the last thirty years, more than 35 km² of forestland have been transformed (the total district area comprises 472 km²). In this context, the illegal development project of Acaristanbul—a gated community surrounded by forest—stubbornly continues to grow, despite all the convictions declared since 2007 by different administrative courts. In short, between 1982 and 2002 about 17,000 hectares of forestland were sold in the province of Istanbul (for a total surface area now estimated to be around 250,000 hectares). The "2B" law is still under discussion; if it is adopted, more than 13,000 additional hectares will lose their original forest status.

The intense sale of public land

In practice since 2001, in order to fill treasury coffers, the systematic sale of abundant public land has clearly become one of the main aims of the AKP (Adalet ve Kalkınma Partisi, or Justice and Development Party) government since November 2002. This has been another means by which the 'public' sphere is deprived of a precious asset for urban planning. Since 2002, a set of new laws (including Law No. 4919 adopted in July 2003), bill amendments, and new regulations have established the legal framework through which to facilitate these sales. Thus, the tensions on the urban land market are intensified by the substantial income to be obtained from urban land transactions. In this context, the Mass Housing Administration (TOK), founded in 1984, has become, after the absorption of the Public Land Office (Arsa Ofisi) in 2004, the major agent of land transfer from the public to the private sector. Moreover, local municipalities were able to sell public land during the years of high migration levels to Istanbul and resulting growing pressures on urban land, without reference to the central public body, which is in fact the genuine landowner.

The long term leasing of public lands
This represents another way to transfer public lands to the private land market, through leases valid for periods of between twenty-nine to forty-nine years. This is the case in the Belgrade forest, for example, where 206 hectares of so-called protected public forest have been leased to a development company, in order to develop a very exclusive country club (which now has massive timber private housing units which were not initially planned). The development of sports and cultural activities, tourism, and educational opportunities are the pretext invoked to justify this method of transfer. Through the same proceedings, since 1991, many private universities (that is, belonging to foundations) have received large areas of public forestland. Yet in most cases, the beneficiaries of these leases do not act in the interests of the public and tend to hoard the long-term leased land, preferring lucrative ways of developing the 'leased' plot of land. Therefore, this system usually amounts in practice to a de facto sale. Let us cite the case of the major football clubs that are enjoying these special advantages: after a short period of time the allocated plot of land is developed for revenue rather than for 'popular' sports. Meanwhile, the 'BOT: Buy-Operate-Transfer' system has become a widespread method for public agents to develop plots of public land through the private sector.

The continuous changes in land-use and land-planning documents
Generally implemented by district municipalities (ilçe belediyeleri) or by the metropolitan municipality (BB), these changes cause many disappointments among citizens and demonstrate the arbitrary nature of public land-planning. For instance, some areas that are reserved for social use according to local land-planning documents, have been transformed into commercial centers or petrol stations. For example, in 2008, one of the vice-presidents

of the AKP in Turkey was forced to resign his position for his involvement in an affair of obscure land status change and land sale. This scandal took place in the district of Silivri, located at the far western periphery of Istanbul, where land transactions and development projects are extensive. Consequently, the lack of continuity in urban politics arising from short-term electoral politics reflects land-use procedures that are in turn a reflection of the relationships between citizens and land ownership.

Massive land transfers between public bodies

Following the decentralization laws passed in Turkey between 2001 and 2005, there has been a general transfer of public lands between public entities, sometimes by exchange or barter. For example, at the end of 2007 there was an exchange between the Department of Foundations and the state treasury *(Hazine)*. This exchange, which had been in the pipeline for thirty years, concerned three million square meters which were inhabited by about 350,000 people in Alibeyköy, an 'illegal' suburb on the European side of Istanbul. Thanks to the exchange, this public land became marketable, through the local municipalities in charge of organizing the sale (40 percent of the profits were to be returned to the state treasury). Once again, one of the most discussed profit-makers of this redistribution of public land was the Mass Housing Administration (TOK), which is directly associated with the office of the prime minister and was created in the early 1980s in order to supply low-income populations with accessible housing.[3]

Through all of the above-mentioned processes, the relationship of the citizen to land ownership has become quite blurred. The most striking outcome of these changes is that (public) land ownership has become very relative and unstable, always subject to redefinition. This generates a climate of flexibility and lack of determination surrounding land ownership, which can encourage all types of abusive practices.

Today's public land occupation in Istanbul: a brief overview

Although private plots of land can also be affected, in Istanbul the occupation, or squatting, phenomenon affects mostly public lands. To provide some insight into this issue, we take the case of Çavuşbaşı, a newly developed neighborhood located on the forested periphery of the Beykoz district. Although Çavuşbaşı had a population of 35,000 at the beginning of 2007, the great majority of its buildings remain without any property title deeds, due to the fact that this area is not officially suitable for urban development.

Four main public bodies are first and foremost concerned with land occupation: the government department in charge of public finance, or the state treasury *(Hazine)*, linked to the Ministry of Finance, the municipalities *(belediyeler)*, the Department of Foundations (Vakıflar Genel Müdürlüğü), and the Province Special Administration (İl Özel İdaresi). According to a report issued by the national audit office in 1999, at that time about half the plots of land registered as "*Hazine* Lands" in Istanbul were occupied by different actors (poor inhabitants and new migrants, but likewise speculators). Since the beginning of the 2000s, the efforts to recover these plots of land have slightly reduced this proportion. According to the municipalities, the proportion of occupied plots of land is comparatively lower, but remains significant. The squatted plots of land belonging to the Foundations Department are still numerous. Yet, since 2006, this administration (inherited from Ottoman times) has been trying to build a Geographic Information System (GIS) in order to clarify its properties, especially its occupied properties. For instance, in the overcrowded neighborhood of Okmeydanı (north of Taksim), more than one million square meters (officially belonging to the former Fatih Foundation) are densely occupied by about 50,000 inhabitants.[4] The Foundations Department tends to 'outsource' problematic cases of this kind by exchanging pieces of land with other public administrations more used to dealing with issues of occupation.

Although land occupations no longer take place everywhere in Istanbul as was the case during the 1950s to 1980s, the situation that has been inherited as a result continues to challenge public bodies that make any attempts to recover their 'lost' lands.

As a consequence of all the above, the qualification of land property ownership is not clear. This vagueness, which creates opportunities for both small and big actors, seems not only due to occupation, but also to state changes in land statutes and increasing numbers of land transfers.

The Sudden End of a Massive Legalization Process?
The previous system of regularization: a universal set of multi-layered measures and practices
With the previous dominant method of negotiating land ownership,[5] there was a set of 'tools' and practices which led to the transformation—with a very unpredictable time-scale and many stages—of occupied plots of land into 'legally possessed and built' plots. To sum up this method: houses were built, and the rest depended on negotiation and local opportunities.

The right to occupation title *(Tapu Tahsis Belgesi)*

In the mid-1980s the *Tapu Tahsis Belgesi* (TTB) became a very attractive and promising 'official' tool. Established by Law No. 2981, and adopted in February 1984, it is only a 'right to occupy' which grants temporary official recognition of a *fait accompli*; a first step to a 'normal' land title. Although it was interpreted by common people as a promise by the public owner to sell plots, this title does not settle the issue of legalization. However, based on 'self-denunciation,' this title has been perceived as a way to make an informal situation more official and stable. Distributed by local municipalities seeking to build a loyal and stable electorate, the TTB was issued in return for sums of money. After being granted this title, the recognized land squatter is required to pay all the taxes paid by a 'normal' urban landowner. Hundreds of thousands of TTBs have been issued, engendering a massive category of in-between urban dwellers who strongly desire official legality. However, in 1989, the Turkish Court of Annulments declared that the TTB does not represent an official document awarding stable rights to holders.

Direct and indirect land amnesties and the allocation of title deeds

Direct, indirect, national, and local (at the district level) land amnesties were the common way to regularize plots, firstly by registering individual building plots, by disbursing the *tapu* (the official land title), and granting construction rights. The amnesty represented a negotiated settlement; ending the conflict between 'illegal settlers' and the state had significant repercussions on property ownership, transferring a sizeable amount of public land to *gecekondu* dwellers. Since 1950, eleven construction amnesties *(imar affi)* have been pronounced across Turkey, mostly during the days preceding elections. Through amnesties, land plots are put up for sale by public authorities. Until the mid-1990s, the conditions of sale were relatively favorable for low-income buyers. But since then, the sums required and payment and credit conditions have become harder. For example, among the 420 households affected by a local amnesty proposed by the district municipality of Küçükçekmece (in the western outskirts of Istanbul) only ten of them could pay according to the proposed terms. Later, in the same district, occupied land was prevented from being put up for sale to its inhabitants by the price required by the Public Land Office, the special body in charge of selling lands owned by the Treasury. On a local scale, political power-relations are absolutely decisive in the amnesty process. In Tokatköy (in the district of Beykoz), after long-term negotiations and mobilizations, the local municipality progressively sold occupied Treasury land to its dwellers (first in 2003, then in 2005). In the former case, the TTB finally became an effective *hisseli tapu*; but in Armutlu (in the district of Sarıyer), considered a more 'anti-authority neighborhood,' the TTB holding land occupants are still waiting to get their *tapu*, a symbol of security.

The damaged social and political image of land squatters and new public strategies of public land use
Why this sudden change?

Among the convergent factors which can explain the changing trends in managing squatted public lands since about 2000, the evident scarcity of urban land, and the consequent increase in land values should be noted. Thus, the shrinking number of available urban land plots for local and foreign developers has created new pressures on stigmatized squatter communities. In addition to the fact that the building sector has in 2011 contributed to approximately a quarter of national growth, the current realization of local capital seems to focus on land and added values from real estate (through housing units, shopping centers, or office building programs). As proof of this trend, one can look to the recent shift from the textile or press sectors of many capital holders (such as the company Ero lu, originating from the textile sector) to the land development and construction sector. Furthermore, the efforts to promote Istanbul as a first level 'international arena of services and tourism' has led to a remaking of the city which involves setting up certain new norms and standards for dealing with urban land (particularly by referring to the EU). The Metropolitan Municipality, together with TOK , is playing a key role in this transformation of the official attitude toward 'occupied land.'

We must not forget the economic emergence of those classes that support the ruling party (AKP), since now that they have access to the system of redistribution of public resources, they tend to defend the 'legal' pattern of land ownership.

Moreover, in February 2007, Law no. 5582, a mortgage law of sorts, in preparation since 2004, was finally passed, stimulating construction firms all over the country by helping the targeted middle-class to access newly built housing units.

"No more tolerance!"[6] has become the predominant 'public' approach, ending the old system of compromises. Therefore, the flexible management of illegal settlements is denounced as an unforgivable weakness. The recent penalization of land squatting and related criminalization of land squatters and *gecekondu* owners have been embodied in the 2005 modifications to article 184 of the Turkish penal code. These modifications introduce prison sentences for those who violate city planning codes. Therefore, governments and local authorities no longer regard 'illegal settlements' as a means of solving housing problems, or as a means of ensuring voter loyalty. In this context, the legalization practices seem to be the privilege of influential private companies and relatively restricted party political members.

Since the end of the 1990s, governments and local authorities ceased to regard 'illegal settlements' as a means of solving the housing problems of the urban poor. They no longer tend to tolerate them. In this sense, the pattern of interaction between the state, local authorities, and other actors involved in deciding on urban legality has drastically changed. Most Turkish scholars now seem to agree that the motivation of appropriating land revenues was added to the motivation of acquiring shelter in the city, so that the illegal land market was rapidly commercialized (Gülöksüz 2002). With a few rare exceptions, local authorities are no longer sensitive to the demands of the populations of such 'illegal' settlements.

Creating land ownership illegality: a new urban policy?

As already suggested above, the changing attitude of public-sector actors toward the TTB, although massively settled in the 1980s, could be seen as a striking sign of the growing divide between local authorities' aims and popular occupation practices. This leads to the refusal to recognize 'occupation titles' (TTBs) on a massive scale, as well as 'official' documents concerning the payment of annual real-estate taxes for land for which recognized squatters have no official titles deeds, and the payment for various types of urban services.

Subsequently, stigmatizing local dwellers as 'squatters' has become a common means for 'public agents' to justify newly launched urban regeneration project policies. Likewise, it frequently leads to the demonization and criminalization of Kurds and Gypsies,[7] and of all the most vulnerable sectors of the urban population. For instance, in the previously cited case of Ayazma (in the district of Küçükçekmece) there is an obvious falsification of the local land ownership structure, carried out by the public agencies themselves. Besides this form of stigmatization, Ayazma has been described by the local mayor as a "dangerous den of terrorists that must be crushed as soon as possible."[8] Thus, the destruction of these modest houses, erected with the clear complicity of local authorities, was presented by the municipality as a security measure, even though the security of land titles was not totally respected.

Moreover, creating land ownership illegality by canceling title deeds seems to have become another systematic policy to enable certain regeneration projects. Hence the stepping-up of omnipresent compulsory purchase processes using newly enacted laws or laws related to exceptional situations. In such cases, the definition of 'public interest' used to justify compulsory purchases seems unclear. And the pretexts generally found are unconvincing: such as the risk of floods, the need to open new roads, the risk of earthquakes, and so on.

At this stage, vulnerable people are losing confidence in 'official documents' related to land ownership, and in the authorities supposed to guarantee land ownership. That means that even those in possession of an official title-deed, who think themselves safe, could be in for a terrible shock.

Consequently, 'legal land ownership' is definitely a fragile notion, regarded either as a sacred value or as a relative and contested quality.

Alternative Legitimacies versus Current Legality: The Divergent Grounds of Legality in the Context of Increasing Contestation

Inspired by Azuela (1987), we can support our approach here with the concept of 'forms of legitimization,' which refers to the series of social representations related to the control of land in various situations. To a certain extent, these representations establish alternative and sometimes very performative norms. Our analysis here is grounded in resistance discourses developed and displayed by 'threatened communities' over recent months. Directly threatened by the so-called urban regeneration projects, these communities are trying to find alternative ways of justifying their presence against predominant norms of legality and paradigms which would lead to immediate eviction. Thus, a new plan of action seems to have been produced.

Supra-state legitimacy: invoking God or universal human rights
Invoking God: a less successful technique
The traditional way of making self-built constructions untouchable (with the famous "This house is God's property" marked on the façades of 'illegal' buildings) seems to have progressively lost its relevance. Although such markings are still very frequent, they should now be considered as

Fig 11.2: Building in Arnavutköy with mention at front of Mülk Allah'ındır. Photograph by Jean-Françoise Perouse.

reminders of progressively outdated regulations. The sort of immunity given in the past by this type of reference no longer exists in the new governance of popular illegality.

In this respect, the conflicts between the AKP and the 'Party of Felicity' (Saadet Partisi) before the July 2007 general elections were significant. These two parties share certain traditions, including common values regarding the centrality of family in the social order, the role of women, and religion as a system of reference in national culture, but were divided in 2001 owing to differences over the issue of 'occupied' land. While the Party of Felicity, claiming divine justice, firmly supported popular land occupation, its opponent strongly denounced land occupation, based on contemporary state legality.

In addition, reference to universal human rights has become a common way to contest local urban policies, through systematic reference to the international declarations that the Turkish state has signed. "What about human rights?" has become a frequent slogan used by communities in their efforts to challenge journalists or foreign scholars. Supranational lawfulness has taken its place alongside divine lawfulness. Current mobilizations against the numerous urban transformation projects—from Avcılar to Tuzla—systematically refer to (universal) human rights, regarded as more reliable and stable than national patterns of legality, which can change according to variable and often contradictory national interests.

Playing central state legitimization against local authorities and changing governments

Protest movements sometimes refer to an idealized figure of the state purified from all forms of local interests.

In order to understand, we must keep in mind that the fundamental relationship between the state institution itself and property is underlined in all Turkish justice courts by this phrase written on the wall behind the judges: *mülk'ün temeli devlettir* ('the ground [or guarantee] of property is the state'). In this respect, belief in the central bodies of the (permanent) state is shown relative to the unstable sequence of local policies.

Hence, the Turkish flag is frequently used to protect houses that are classified as illegal against bulldozers; the flag has become a symbolic form of resistance, playing nationalism off against local allegiances. Similarly, custom prevents the public authorities from destroying the house of a family whose son is currently in military service.

Since November 2002, the ruling AKP has been denounced by opponents as an instrument of international capital aiming to seize national resources. That is why 'deep state' central institutions are seen as being better able to defend national interests.

In this context, we notice a sort of idealization of central state and of central justice institutions (such as the Constitutional Court and the Supreme Court), which are thought to be more independent of local and individual interests. More and more direct appeals to these courts are made to defend occupants' rights. Reference to the supposedly impartial state is used to stand in the way of local policies that differ from the "Tragedy of the Commons" (Hardin 1968). As one inhabitant threatened by a destruction project stated:[9]

In order to favour certain construction firms, they trample on the law. It is unfair to evict from their plot of land TTB owners who have openly asked to be regularized and who have even paid all the necessary dues for their regularization. . . . They want to destroy our houses in order to erect huge office buildings.

From this perspective, the residents of threatened neighborhoods are trying to bring to light the contradictions within the existing 'legal' outlook as the primary source of legality in setting out and promoting the inviolable state's point of view. This opposition differentiates two regimes of legality: on the one hand, rights *(hukuk ya da hak)*, and on the other hand, laws *(yasalar)*.[10] The latter are multidinous and open to changes with the passage of time, whereas the former are perceived as unique and near-permanent.

The invention of alternative legitimacies: "This was where we put down roots. This was where we finally made our city our own."[11]
The argument of anteriority

In examining the counter-discourse displayed by the opponents of urban transformation, the place now given to the past and the narratives of local, collective memory should be underlined. Disputed dwellers are often the pioneers in the contested area. In Armutlu, the first 'occupants' settled in the 1930s and 1940s, long before municipality land-contestations (which began at the end of the 1980s). Despite their lack of means and the obstacles they had to face, in seeking to improve their living conditions, they have contributed to building an appropriate environment. Just before the beginning of the demolitions in Ayazma (February 2007), a dweller based there for over twenty-five years insisted on showing me, in detail, the numerous trees he had planted and tended, demanding the recognition of his efforts by "official agents" aiming to seize the place. These relatively new claims are related to the changing pattern in the concept of citizenship, with its shift from an abstract conception—which prevailed until the end of the 1990s—toward a more concrete and territorialized one.

In order to become an owner one day, we have paid local authorities all the required fees and taxes for ten years. When we came here, there was no road, and we built a road; there was no water and we laid on water; no electricity . . . . And now, they announce to us that our land plots are resistant to earthquakes, and they want to seize this place from our hands.[12]

Using local history to reinforce the right to stay

Similarly, the forging together and use of local history narratives has become a means of resistance, by putting forth the argument that the contested areas could not be considered as areas 'without any history.' Discovering suppressed local narratives thus helps with the acknowledgement of long years of struggle, especially by the agents of urban transformation, specifically the administrators of mass housing schemes and their partners on the ground, such as district municipalities and privileged construction companies. Regarding Ayazma for example, TOK and the local municipality tend to present the 'intervention area' both as an empty area (that is, as a site of opportunities to be seized) and as an occupied one. In other terms, local and alternative urban narratives are used to defend communities whose future is threatened, in spite of their long existence (which is invisible to officialdom). The unearthing of local history that was previously not officially registered or declared gives residents of illegal settlements pride in their way of life.

Taking human inheritances into account

Consequently, raising contestation claims puts the emphasis on 'human inheritances,' which could be neither denied nor eradicated without damage. A shift could thereby be made from local dimensions to universal ones, since the protection of immaterial inheritances is now part of the agenda of agencies such as the United Nations Educational, Scientific, and Cultural Organization (UNESCO). As one inhabitant stated: "When a house is destroyed, in fact, much more than the house is destroyed. At the same time, a sense of belonging, links with the past and hopes for the future are destroyed." Therefore, intangible inheritances comprise collective ways of life and specific social relations. When demanding respect for their rights, local communities now tend to appropriate this hidden dimension, which defies any abstract definition of what is legal.

Statement of Ayazma people due to be evicted (31 May 2006)

We, the inhabitants of Ayazma for about twenty-five years, have just heard that the place where we are living will soon be destroyed in the name of so-called 'Urban Regeneration.' We have built this neighborhood with our own hands and resources, without receiving any public service and without benefit of any infrastructure. . . . We have buried our dead here. We have put in Ayazma all that we have saved and scrimped for.

Conclusion

The outskirts of Istanbul provide a striking case of a violent rupture in public regularization policies. This raises questions about the flexibility of the patterns of legal land ownership and the role assumed by public bodies in the *production of illegality*. The role of the state and of different state agencies in the production of illegality should be increasingly analyzed. Definitions of legality and the position of public agencies with respect to illegal settlements are subject to variation, due to tremendous changes in the urban land-market and new claims in city managing (in the pressing context of the launching of new ways to 'sell the city' on international markets).

While there is still an obvious "fluid nature of property rights" (Gülöksüz 2002), with time, in physical space and in the political and social spheres, this fluidity is no longer principally the outcome of negotiation processes, but of new public policies toward public urban land.

Thus, the manipulation of the legal framework by different actors (even public actors who do not necessarily represent abstract 'public interests'), the plurality of patterns of legality, and the plurality of legitimization discourses lead to the continuous reshaping of the definition of 'the common interest' in accordance with changing relationships. In this respect, we must repeat that urban land occupation is in no way the monopoly of the stigmatized poor.

Finally, as Neuwirth (2007) stressed, the key determinant of the fate of squatter communities is whether or not they have a "powerful avenue" into the political system. And as David Harvey suggests (2008), the path to the invention of other modes of legality exists around the pursuit of the right to housing, the right to life, the right to exist, that is, "the right to the city."

Notes

1 See for instance, Şükrü Aslan, *Birgün*, 27 June 2008.
2 The financial crisis which occurred at the end of 2008 seems in this respect to have offered a good excuse for relaunching the debates on "2B" forestlands amnesty. See *Milliyet-Emlak*, 25 October 2008, 3.
3 See "Mass Housing Law," no. 2985, 1984.
4 The sale of this neighborhood's land, announced in 1995, was not carried out. See *Cumhuriyet*, 30 September 1995.
5 For details, in addition to Gülöksüz (2002), see Öncü (1988): " The politics of the urban land market in Turkey: 1950–1980," IJURR.

6 See again, *Today's Zaman*, 30 June 2007, on the first page.
7 On 27 October 2008, a settlement of gypsies in Esentepe (in the district of Gaziosmanpaşa) was destroyed by local security teams, without consideration for the difficulties of the coming winterfaced by these populous households; see *Evrensel*, 28 October 2008, 5.
8 *Milliyet*, 18 November 2007, p. 8.
9 See *Cumhuriyet*, 3 November 2011, 3.
10 For instance, that is the core of the argumentation developped by associations fighting in Armutlu against municipality urban transformation/destructions: "*Tam bu noktada yasal olanla hukuki olan arasındaki ince ayrımı da dikkatlerinize sunmak isterim. . . . Halkın yoksullu undan nemalanan istismarcı politika esnafının hiç sorumluluğu yok mudur?*" ("Here, I would like to draw your attention to the subtle difference between what is legal and what is right. Do profiteering politicans who make their living off the poor have any sense of responsibility?")
11 For the declaration, "Yıkımlara Karşı Ortak Bildirisi" (Common Declaration Against Demolitions), see *Birgün*, 10 June 2007, 10.
12 See *Cumhuriyet*, 4 October 2001, 21.

References

Ameur, Mohamed. 1993. *Fès ou l'obsession du foncier*. Research booklet, no. 25. Tours: URBAMA.
"Araziler, Arsa Ofisi'ne teslim." *Cumhuriyet*, 23 December 1994.
Aveline, Natacha. 1997. "Compte rendu de la mission sur le foncier et l'immobilier à Beyrouth." Unpublished interim report.
Azuela, A. 1987. "Low Income Settlements and the Law in Mexico City." *International Journal of Urban and Regional Research* 11 (4): 522–44.
Baken, Robert J., and Jan van der Linden. 1992. *Land Delivery for Low Income Groups in Third World Cities*. Aldershot, Hants: Avebury.
Belotti, Sylvie, and Nicole Bonnet. 1982. "L'offre foncière à la périphérie de Toulouse." *Revue Géographique des Pyrénées et du Sud-Ouest* 53 (1): 64–74.
Bertaud, Marie-Agnès, and Douglas Lucious. 1989. "Land Use, Building Codes, and Infrastructure Standards as Barriers to Affordable Housing in Developing Countries." Working Paper, World Bank, Urban Development Department, Washington D.C.
Çağdaş, Volkan, Demir Hulya, and Gur Mehmet. 2002. "Concept of Ownership in Land Arrangement Studies in Turkey." Paper presented at the FIG XXII International Congress, Washington D.C., 19–26 April.
Courtney, John M. 1983. "Intervention Through Land Use Regulation." In Harold Dunkerly, ed. *Urban Land Policy Issues and Opportunities*. New York: Oxford University Press
de Soto, Hernando. 1990. *The Other Path*. New York: Harper and Row.

Durand-Lasserve, Alain, and Valérie Clerc. 1996. *Regularization and Integration of Irregular Settlements: Lessons from Experience.* UMP Working paper series no. 6, UNDP/UNCHS, World Bank.

Ekinci, Oktay. 1998. "Kaçak yapıla ma ve arazi spekülasyonu." In *75 yıl de i en kent ve mimarlık,* 191–98. stanbul: Tarih Vakfı.

Farvaque, Catherine, and Patrick McAuslan. 1991. *Reforming Urban Land Policies and Institutions in Developing Countries.* Urban Management Programme Discussion Paper, no. 5. Washington D.C.: World Bank.

Fawaz, Mona. 2009. "The State and the Production of Illegal Housing: Public Practices in Hayy el Selloum, Beirut-Lebanon." In K. Ali and M. Riker, eds., *Comparing Cities: The Middle East and South Asia.* New York: Oxford University Press.

———. 2004. "Strategizing for Housing: An Investigation of the Production and Regulation of Low-income Housing in the Suburbs of Beirut." PhD diss., Department of Urban Studies and Planning, Massachussetts Institute of Technology.

Granelle, Jean-Jacques, and Thierry Vilmin, eds. 1993. *L'articulation du foncier et de l'immobiler.* Paris: Éd. Adef.

Gülöksüz, Elvan. 2004. "Negotiation of Property Rights in Urban Land in Istanbul." In Huricihan İslamoğlu, ed. *Constituting Modernity: Private Property in the East and West,* 248–68. London/New York: I.B. Tauris.

———. 2002. Negotiation of Property Rights in Urban Land in stanbul. *International Journal of Urban and Regional Research* 26 (2): 462–76.

Güven-Erten, Mustafa. 2004. "Property Problems in the Post-earthquake Urban Redevelopment Process: A Case Study in the City of Adapazarı." Master's thesis, Department of City and Regional Planning, Natural and Applied Sciences, Middle East Technical University, Ankara.

Hardin, Garrett. 1968. "Tragedy of the Commons." *Science,* no. 162, 1243–48.

Harvey, David. 2008. "The Right to the City." *New Left Review* 53 (September–October): 23–40.

Kayser, Bernard. 1981. "Vendeurs de terre à la périphérie des villes." *Annales de la Recherche Urbaine,* nos. 10/11.

Kurtuluş, Hatice. 2007. "Türkiye'de Siyasi Otorite, Sınıflar ve Kentleşme Arasındaki İlişkiye Kentsel Arazi Bağlantıları Çerçevesinde Bir Bakış." *Mimar ist,* no. 3, 70–76.

Lipietz, Alain. 1974. *Le tribut foncier urbain.* Paris: Maspéro.

Neuwirth, Robert. 2007. "Security of Tenure in Istanbul: The Triumph of the 'Self Service City." Case study prepared for Enhancing Urban Safety and Security: Global Report on Human Settlements 2007. http://www.unhabitat.org/grhs/2007.

OCDE (Organisation for Economic Co-operation and Development). 1992. *Les marchés fonciers urbains. Quelles politiques pour les années 1990?* Paris: OCDE.

Öncü, Ayşe. 1988. "The Politics of the Urban Land Market in Turkey: 1950–1980." *International Journal of Urban and Regional Research* 12:38–64.

Özkan, Özer. 1996. "Public Lands in Urban Planning." *Planlama*, special issue, June, 8–10.

Pérouse, Jean-François. 2006. "Le marché foncier à Istanbul." *Etudes foncières*, no. 121 (May–June): 11–14.

———. 2005. "Les compétences des acteurs dans les micro-mobilisations habitantes à Istanbul." In Gilles Dorronsoro, ed., *La Turquie conteste: Mobilisations sociales et régime sécuritaire*, 127–46. Paris: Ed du CNRS.

———. 1998. "Les marchés fonciers et immobiliers à Istanbul: premiers repères méthodologiques et problématiques." *Lettre d'information de l'Observatoire Urbain d'Istanbul*, no. 14 (June), 8–18.

———. 1997. "Aux marges de la métropole stambouliote: les quartiers Nord de Gaziosmanpacha, entre varo et batıkent." In "Métropoles et métropolisation," *Cahiers d'Études de la Méditerranée Orientale et du Monde Turco-Iranien*, no. 24, 122–62.

"Régularisations de propriétés." 1995. *Les Annales de la Recherche Urbaine*, no. 66.

Tekeli, İlhan. 1992. "Kentsel Topraklarda Mülkiyet Kurumunun Varlığının Toplumsal Sonuçları ve Yeniden Düzenleme Olanakları Üzerine." *Planlama*, nos. 1–4, 48–57.

12

Law, Rights, and Justice in Informal Settlements: The Crossed Frames of Reference of Town Planning in a Large Urban Development Project in Beirut

Valérie Clerc

When faced with informal settlements, town planners usually devise urban projects that bear in mind the fact that the transformation of space has a social impact. For some of them, this social change is one of the main goals of planning: improving living conditions, encouraging social diversity, normalizing certain practices, protecting the social identity of places, defending residents' and owners' rights, encouraging access to the city, and so on. How do these planners think the transformation of space might influence social practices? The designers explain numerous causal links between existing or planned spatial shapes and the social shapes they identify or desire, based on different methods of reasoning. The selection of planning projects depends largely on these complex representations. Questions of rights, laws, and standards play a leading role therein, especially since the residents of these areas are in breach of the law. What is the impact of the issue of law and lawfulness? What is the role of the law and of rights in the creation of a project? How are decisions made, and based on which representations, for projects concerning informal settlements?

This analysis is carried out as part of research on the principles of action of town planning (Clerc-Huybrechts 2002). Research on the design and implementation of urban development projects traditionally follows two main lines. One aspect studies the design: the rhetoric and theories of urban development (Choay 1980; Nasr and Volait 2003), the skills, expertise, and methods of planners and architects (Verdeil 2002; Souami 2003), and the political and social objectives of the professionals involved (Verpraet 1989). The other aspect of research involves decision-making, public policy, understanding the mechanisms of action systems (Crozier and Friedberg 1977), and the power relations and strategies at work in the context of an urban planning project (Harb 2005; Lacaze 1997; Friedberg 1993). The first aspect mainly examines the technical stakeholders, the professionals of the city, while the second is more focused on political parties, project management, and decision-makers. This research project is positioned at the meeting point of these two approaches; it attempts to enter the 'black box' of the project's design, to identify all the factors that guide decisions, to bring to light the reasoning of the actors who have an influence on those choices, to establish when the stakeholders—the political decision-makers as well as the people working in planning—are motivated by ideal representations of the city or by the mechanisms of the system of actors in which they work (Signoles 1999).

To highlight these representations and their role in the design of urban planning projects, this paper will analyze the implementation of the Elyssar project, the biggest urban planning project of the Lebanese reconstruction period, implemented in 1995 in the southern suburbs of Beirut. Politically, this ambitious project fits into a scheme of reconciliation among the Lebanese people and reunification of a city that was fragmented into numerous communities and districts by the civil war (1975–90). It sought to open up and reinstate 560 hectares of the southwestern suburbs in the city (see Fig. 12.1). The complete restructuring of two thirds of the project's area is in response to the presence of informal settlements in the area, which are built on the land of others, and which in 1995 housed 80,000 people in a city with a population of 1.5 million.

This paper aims to analyze the Elyssar project in order to highlight the factors that influence the choice of projects, and to understand the way in which the decision-making process led to the solutions advocated by the project. Between 1998 and 2001, a survey was carried out of a hundred or so of the project's observers and parties—members of the various negotiating parties or those who were or might have been influential in defining problems, proposing solutions, or conducting negotiations for Elyssar. Interviews were conducted with representatives of the government, Amal,

Fig. 12.1: Main irregular settlements in Berut. Map by Valérie Clerc, 2010.

and Hezbollah who participated in the meetings during the various phases of negotiations, starting with the prime minister Rafiq Hariri, and including advisors, consultants, and research departments (including Oger International, Oger-Liban, Millennium, the Advisory and Development Studies Centre, Jihad al-Binaa, and so on); deputies, chairmen, and members of municipal councils in the region affected by the project; professionals (consultants, town planners, architects, engineers, economists, and so on) who were either independent or working for consultant firms that participated in various phases of the project such as Dar al-Handassah, Assaco, Laceco, and BTUTP; the employees and members of the board of directors of the Elyssar Public Company; government directors and senior officials (from the General Directorate of Town Planning, the Town Planning Board, the Architects Association, the Land Registry, the Council for Development and Reconstruction, the Public Corporation for Housing, the Ministry of Housing, the Ministry for Displaced Persons); judges and lawyers (whether advisors or professionals involved in real-estate lawsuits); owners and residents of the southwestern suburbs; planners, real-estate developers, and financial investors (banks) with projects in the area; and, finally, some observers (journalists, teachers, and researchers).

This chapter focuses on one of the frames of reference used by these actors, namely the role of notions of justice and law in the design of the town-planning project. In the first part, it shows the diversity of representations deployed, the use by the actors involved of three registers of reasoning to consider and design the project, and how these rationales combine to form very personal profiles of those actors. The second part of this chapter focuses on questions of law and justice, and shows the different value systems used in the project. Noting in particular the central choice to rehouse evicted people within the same area, or perimeter of the project, it sheds light on how these rationales and value systems are based on questions of law and justice in order to lead to decision-making.

Thinking About Town Planning
Representations, rationales, and profiles of actors
The implementation process of Elyssar in the southern suburbs of Beirut involved many political and technical participants, and therefore demonstrates a variety of representations and influences on the project.

Elyssar

In Lebanon, the informal settlements located on squatted land are found mainly in the southwestern suburbs of Beirut. Very localized informal settlements developed, particularly during the war, sometimes from former cores, owing to massive population displacements, mainly from south Lebanon and the eastern suburbs. The settling of inhabitants was organized by Shi'i militias, swelling the Palestinian camps and some small illegal settlements, by squatting on parcels that were either subject to ownership disputes, owned by public institutions, or which experienced difficulties in implementing town planning regulations and plans, which were applied to the southern suburbs for nearly a century (Clerc-Huybrechts 2008). These districts were a stronghold of the Shi'i parties Amal and Hezbollah, as are their neighboring older districts to the east: Burj al-Barajneh, Ghobeiry, and Haret Hreik, where major destruction took place during the 2006 war. Therefore, in Lebanon's political context, which is based largely on sectarian divisions, any project concerning this space took on a strong political dimension (Harb 2005).

As soon as the civil war ended in late 1990, the project was encouraged by Rafiq Hariri (who later became prime minister). From 1992 it was developed through political negotiations between the government (then headed by Hariri), which wanted to regain a foothold in those areas, and the Shi'i parties Amal and Hezbollah, which played an important role in developing the infrastructure and services for the predominantly Shi'i areas under their control. In 1995, three years of negotiations led to the decision (which was formalized by a plan and a ministerial decree) to carry out a restructuring project for the area. The project planned to create or improve infrastructure, and to develop real-estate and tourist resorts along the city's biggest beach, thus potentially adding 6.7 million square meters to the area. Thanks to negotiations, Amal and Hezbollah agreed to the project, in exchange for the guarantee that the residents would remain housed in the same area and that the project would be implemented by a public planning and development corporation. They established as a result of the negotiations the principle and methods of the destruction of the existing informal settlements, compensation for residents and building owners, and the rehousing of inhabitants in new units built within the project's domain. The project claimed to be in the public interest and to renew social ties, and sought a compromise between access to the southern suburbs for all the inhabitants of the city—requested by the government with the aim of rebuilding a unified and practical city—and the protection of the identity of those districts, of interest only to part of Beirut's population: its residents, who, defended by their representatives, wished to maintain their sectarian territorial roots.

The project was hardly implemented. Only the main roads and public facilities were built in the area, causing the demolition of part of the illegal settlements, but, fifteen years on, most of the informal settlements are still in place.

Independent representations of professions and positions

All the actors interviewed had a personal interpretation of the situation and of the project, justifying and/or criticizing its choices. Numerous opposing concepts of spatial and social recomposition were present simultaneously throughout the project's design. For instance, the inhabitants of the areas concerned were considered by the various actors involved as people who were war-displaced, poor, or living in bad conditions. Each actor interviewed established its own set of diagnoses for the purposes of the project. These were sometimes connected or consistent, generally heterogeneous, sometimes contradictory, and reflected the fact that each actor took a different line of reasoning, and that none of them had a unique strategy.

The study in Beirut revealed that these representations did not depend on the social group or profession of the relevant actors. Nor were they a function of their religious affiliation, their position within the system of actors, or their membership in the ruling or Shiʻi parties. In particular, we can see a discrepancy between the technical and political roles of the various participants and their rationales. On the one hand, the political decision-makers, both the policy makers who initiated and proposed the project (Rafiq Hariri and his team) and those who participated in the negotiations (Amal and Hezbollah party members), had a discourse that was strongly influenced by technical considerations due to their training (many political representatives are engineers, and several engineers participated in the political negotiations) and their notions of what constitutes an ideal representation of their city. In particular, at the highest political level, the prime minister, presented by all as the the project's main supporter, was originally a real-estate professional who had built his fortune (one of the biggest in the world) as an investor. From the 1980s he had begun to think about how to rebuild Beirut, then still at war, and when he became head of government he never ceased to think in terms of urban development. At the same time, town planners and technical stakeholders claimed to have taken a back seat and been restricted to their technical role because of the political sensitivites surrounding the project. But precisely because of this, they remained extremely aware of the political dimensions of the project, and many automatically used political arguments to make certain choices in their proposals, prior to discussion with the political actors (for instance, to avoid moving Shi'i inhabitants to a Druze region).

Lines of reasoning and 'topical' profiles of the actors

The various concepts used to conceive the project did not all derive from the same lines of reasoning. There were prominent lines of reasoning. Firstly, the parties reasoned within an ideal style (in the sense of both perfect and imaginary). They expressed the intention to transform from the present situation to a future one following conceptualized projects (urban and social patterns, political projects, technical improvements, social change, the implementation of rules, and so on). Secondly, the parties articulated strategies, describing the project as dynamic and taking into account issues, opposing forces, and strategies (to obtain political 'victories', economic benefits, and so on). These first two styles project into the future. The third style relies on value judgments. The actors expressed judgments, which are formulated in the language of justice and injustice, on the current situation, and on the desired outcome or means of achieving it. This style criticizes or justifies preconceptions, words, acts, and omissions identified in the two previous styles.

The combination of representations and judgments in the three lines of reasoning and how individuals manage any possible contradictions form their position concerning the project. There is no common frame of reference since each actor gives their own partial interpretation with only some elements in common. Thus, each party has a personal profile, which one might call a 'topical profile,' because it links the actor to the problematization of a place in the broad sense, and which is drawn from references to values that are external to the project but applied in a specific context. These views clash or merge to define the project.

In the first style, the ideal style, the ideas developed by the actors involved in the Elyssar project correlate with town planning theories with a social goal. Several points of view oppose one another depending on the way in which the actor takes into account the social group it wishes to promote. The vast majority of actors interviewed have progressive visions, seeking aesthetics, hygiene, and modernity. Their main leitmotifs are the improvement of living conditions and the attainment of order, movement toward urbanity, the promotion of social advancement, social diversity, or the modification of the 'traditional' social practices that these informal districts are said to have. However, others have a more cultural vision and wish to protect the current social fabric; they follow the same premise—that the transformation of space will have an impact on social practices—but they are opposed to the modification of lifestyles and settings, in favor of preserving the current forms of sociability and culture, therefore promoting a habitat suited to current practices.

In the second style, the strategies style, the space is mostly linked to organized social groups, and spatial intervention is considered as a means to protect or, to the contrary, to modify or even break up the existing collective organization in favor of another. The southeastern suburbs are mainly presented as Shi'i territory: a specific space, inhabited by a social group, controlled by a specific authority (the Shi'i Amal and Hezbollah parties), and thus a site of power, a space to be defended or won over, a marked space (Harb 2003). Consequently, the decision as to whether or not to relocate the population outside the area in question (providing compensation or rehousing elsewhere) is perceived as a major political, economic, and social issue. At the time when these discussions were underway, the population was still very conscious of the recent civil war and the project was still explained by many actors using the discourses of reconquering or defending territory, combined with economic interests.

Mixed arguments

The actors interviewed sometimes mix the first two styles (ideal and strategic), particularly when it comes to certain recurring key topics, such as the belt of poverty, rural depopulation, or Shi'i access to the city.

The belt of poverty

The prewar expression "belt of poverty" (Bourgey and Pharès 1973) refers to the poor outlying quarters of the city and the need to eradicate poverty from the suburbs. Risks were associated with rings of shantytowns surrounding the capital city Beirut; they were mostly populated with Palestinians, living in armed camps that became autonomous after the Cairo Accords (1969). The situation by the mid-1990s was completely different (for instance, 82 percent of the illegal settlements' inhabitants in Elyssar are Lebanese). Yet this expression, with its dual connotations, both strategic and ideal, is still frequently used by many actors in reference to Beirut's southern suburbs or the Elyssar project to explain why the downtown project—a small luxurious area surrounded by insanitary districts—cannot be considered independently from a project to develop the suburbs, and to give expression to the social threat that lies at the city's gates.

"Belt of poverty" allows for the differentiation between groups of inhabitants of these illegal developments: rural migrants who had no choice but to settle in the poor districts they could afford are differentiated from the people who were already living in the area, and who used their resources and often Mafia-style networks to create this supply of informal housing, and who are said to have deliberately brought together clients and people of their own confession into a single area in order to create a territory, in the military sense of the word. The project meets both these actors' concerns by improving living conditions while modifying the social fabric of this environment to break such an encirclement.

Rural depopulation and community balance

The parties interviewed believe strongly in the reversibility of the phenomenon of rural depopulation, which is closely associated with the issue of forced population displacements due to war. One of the main reasons leading to the decision to rehouse the inhabitants was the fact that refugees from South Lebanon were present in the Elyssar area. Most of them migrated during the war and some have now been urbanised for over thirty years. But they were the only residents who could not return to their region of origin, which was still occupied by Israel at the time of the project's development (Israel only withdrew from South Lebanon in 2000), and it was therefore necessary to come up with a suggestion for the area. Some suspect this assertion of reversibility to be a way of concealing community strategies aimed at getting rid of the Shi'is by sending them back to their regions of origin, with compensation. In Lebanon, poor rural inhabitants are traditionally Shi'is. In the eyes of many, migration from outlying rural areas of Lebanon toward the suburbs created a problem of population distribution in the country and a community imbalance around the city, to which the return to the countryside would be a solution.

Access of Shi'is to the city

The image of the informal settlements in the southwestern suburbs as being akin to that of a village—ties to the land, low-rise housing, outdoor spaces attached to dwellings (courtyards and gardens), a haphazard layout of buildings—is associated in the discourse of several actors with the persistence of rural attitudes, habits, and social ties, despite migration to the city that sometimes dates back a long way. Moreover, prewar studies show that although traditional forms of grouping persist in towns, they tend to break down with social advancement (Nasr 1979). The denigration of the village-like character of informal settlements, coupled with the assumption that their residents, especially the poorest, are incapable of creating urban space, is an argument from the ideal style widely used by actors to support the creation of new buildings. For some, it is also a strategic argument to deny access to the town for Shi'is, who are also associated with people living in rural areas. The Shi'is' access to the city has been cause for debate in Lebanon since before the war, and is part of the Shi'i parties' political struggle for integration into urban society (Nasr 1985). Amal and Hezbollah were therefore ready to accept the eviction of residents, on the condition that they would be rehoused in the same area, because the southern suburbs are their only gateway to the capital. But many others sought to compensate residents in a bid to clear the city of a community that they feared could threaten Christian and Sunni urban supremacy.

Justice and Town Planning Choices

In the third style of reasoning, the judgment style, the parties regularly resort, either explicitly or implicitly, to the concepts of justice, fairness, or legitimacy in order to analyze the current situation, the project's ambitions, and the system of actors to which they belong. In their discourses, the parties follow several value systems, both to criticize and to justify Elyssar, linking them in very personal, complex, and sometimes controversial ways by the same argument (Boltanski and Thévenot 1991). The concept of rights is particularly present in this, the third style.

Using different value systems to judge informal areas

Within this third style of reasoning, two value systems pervade the discourse of the project's actors. First, the *functionalist* values of improvement, efficiency, productivity, predictability, and organization, with the objective of meeting needs, guaranteeing normal functioning, and adequately determining the future in order to control it correctly. These values are used by almost all actors (thus echoing the organizational nature of town planning). Second, *civic* values, such as general interest, solidarity, law, and lawfulness, which refocus the project on the social entity which town planning affects (human settlements). These values are also used by all actors. The fact that these civic values are repeatedly drawn on by the actors is one of the main reasons for the extent of discourse about the project's social dimension. The fundamental objections and contradictions lie in the use of civic values on various levels and for several different social groups, which the project resolves through compromise.

The squatters are criticized in every value system. However, each system presents one or several reasons to judge them positively and to justify their actions. The most significant disputes about squatters revolve around civic values. A number of parties emphasize the illegitimacy of those who squatted (took others' land) by force, under the supervision and instructions of militias or of their allies, who controlled those lands during the war. They mention the fact that this phenomenon is unfair to landowners, who could not or did not know how to defend themselves, since they were not protected by state law. The judgment of certain people is focused entirely on the issue of illegality.

Yet civic values, which stigmatize these neighborhoods most violently, also provide the strongest arguments for an intervention in their favor. All the actors mention reasons not to blame these inhabitants, who sought refuge from Lebanon's successive wars. They acknowledge that they have a right to settle somewhere, and justify the settlements with reference to the lack of housing, the magnitude of the displaced population, and, often, the need for communities to rely on militia practices for their survival. These justifications of the residents' actions are all based on the state's failure, but they vary depending on designation of the social group affected. For some actors, the inhabitants developed a strategy in reaction to the state's inability to take care of the poor. For others, due to the lack of public intervention, the squatters were the victims of unequal treatment between the southern suburbs and the rest of the agglomeration. Considered as war-displaced persons, the inhabitants' attitude is forgiven by others, who cite the injustice suffered and their right to compensation. Some support the first waves who settled in those areas at the end of the 1950s, with the support of the municipality, seeking revenge against the scandal of a government considered to be neither democratic nor legitimate, and alleged to have allowed its connections to privatize beaches and public land in the southwestern suburbs. Finally, a few people mention the 1955 "Sands Trial" (Procès des Sables), which was considered to have been unfair because it ruled in favor of some private owners of parcels which were traditionally communal land and on which there had been an overlapping of rights during the previous century. The Sands Trial is referred to as a means of insisting on the legitimacy of wronged legal claimants and, by extension, that of inhabitants who sympathize with them, and to express the sentiment of injustice concerning access of the poor to land,

and their desire for a struggle of the people for democratic justice against the legal system.

All the actors have different ways of judging squatters, both negatively and positively. Some people do not point the finger at formal irregularity or the failure to adapt to needs, but to the lack of a sense of civic responsibility. Others, to the contrary, acknowledge rights, opportunistic practices, and even need, but they do not accept unlawfulness. All the actors establish personal hierarchies of rights and judgments, depending on their own personal stake in the project or their own personal worldview, or a combination of the two.

The project's choices: the case of rehousing in situ
Even when they are widely shared, the concepts arrived at do not shape the project directly. In spite of sometimes evident influences, it is impossible to credit the origin of a selection to one or more persons. The analysis of the negotiations, from press reports and especially from interviews with the three parties to the negotiations (the government, Amal, and Hezbollah), shows that the decisions taken were the result of interactions, within a context of strategic interdependency. Within the framework of this power struggle, each person aims for an agreement corresponding to his own interests and representations. Concepts take shape in some proposals. Some ideas suit everyone. They reflect a series of judgments following different value systems. Therefore the choices of the project represent the different significance awarded to them by each actor. No actor persuaded others to accept their point of view. No single justification can characterize each choice. These choices were made because a range of disparate judgments and representations led to them. They avoid dispute and make judgments compatible. They are only relevant and in line with the system as long as they support the justifications of each party.

The unanimous decision to rehouse in situ all inhabitants who so wished this, rather than compensating, renovating, or rehousing them elsewhere, combines several judgments. Based on several attitudes and representations, with regard to the law and rights, three arguments played a specific role in the reasoning processes: the arguments of social justice, respect for national law, and the rejection of social division.

From social justice to rehousing
The necessity of treating everyone equally according to the same principle led to rehousing, rather than compensation. Indeed, all the parties

involved in negotiations desire the improvement of housing conditions in these neighborhoods; for some, it is about encouraging greater social justice between communities; for others, it is a question of remedying the past neglect by the state. From a psychological point of view, it is important to provide housing and not compensation; to grant people a right to inhabit and not simply offer them a commercial good. This distinction only makes sense in the abstract. One cannot separate the qualitative value of being housed from the property value of a dwelling, and beneficiaries are able to resell their accommodation. However, the desire to grant housing, and not compensation, expresses the desire to compensate for housing inequalities; squats are the expression of a problem and there is no desire to compensate those who sought to commercialize accommodation. On a symbolic level, rehousing for Elyssar satisfies those who consider the justification of the project to be primarily the achievement of social justice.

The assertion of rights without questioning the law

The law also lies at the origin of the decision to rehouse rather than upgrade the neighborhoods. Upgrading was immediately rejected by all parties involved in negotiations, for practical purposes but also to satisfy a desire for justice for the Lebanese people who had never squatted, in order not to award legitimacy to what had been illegally acquired during the war. Above all, there is never any ambiguity regarding the legitimacy of owners. Although some people who were interviewed report that some inhabitants would prefer to stay in the property they occupy, regularization is never considered by their supporters. Despite claims that land might not have been allocated to its proper owners forty years previously, in 1990s Lebanon nmobilization on behalf of neither the poor nor the displaced, nor that for the inhabitants of the southern suburbs, was able to modify attitudes concerning property rights.

On the contrary, it is as if a scale of values was unanimously adopted, placing the established law above the civic movement that would call it into question demanding greater justice. Even if in the end legal property owners have to be expropriated (in order to obtain land for rehousing), everyone opposes the principle of expropriating them only in order to regularize the inhabitants' situation. The actual ownership of the land is never questioned; on the contrary, it itself stands in the way of the idea of upgrading.

This commitment of all actors to the current land law is remarkable in a country where the history of land ownership is so complex and unstable.

By placing the law and property rights at the heart of contentious issues, and by structuring negotiations around the law, paradoxically, all actors treat the country as a single whole, in spite of the Shiʿi parties' securing of benefits for the inhabitants of the southern suburbs that they support. After the civil war, the country's unity became a frame of reference with more significance than any other social space. By resolutely relying on the property right which survived the civil war, Elyssar can thus be read as a project of reconstruction and reconciliation, and not exclusively, as many readings of the strategies imply, as the continuation of territorial struggles by other means.

Staying in situ, a major conflict of interests

All actors agree on the importance of unity and the rejection of social division. Based on these principles, two opposing civic attitudes, which take into account the social groups at different levels, are at the heart of negotiations. On the one hand, actors reasoning at the country level reject the territorial division between communities. Although they accept the principles of compensation and rehousing, they hold that these must not be applied in situ, since that would affirm the division of society into sectarian groups. On the other hand, the actors reasoning at the level of the southern Shiʿi suburbs, oppose the reduction of the community into a series of individuals who want to free themselves from party guidelines and act in their own interests. This civic vision is internal to the community and encourages union, collective action, loyalty to a cause, and the defense of the group's interests. In this regard, it seeks to maintain the current social fabric and to gain rights and advantages for the area's residents. It was legitimized by the accession of Hezbollah members to parliament in 1992 and to the heads of municipalities in the southern suburbs in 1998. This civic system drastically opposes its predecessor since it advocates the preservation of a homogenous population in situ.

By taking into consideration part of each of these opposing attitudes, the solution chosen for Elyssar—the proposal of rehousing in situ *and* the possibility of choosing compensation—is a compromise which meets both demands while not justifying itself entirely in terms of either of them. The lack of official documents presenting a synthesis that would enable us to extract the essential facts shows how difficult it was to decide on a single project that combines two fundamentally opposed outlooks. The consensual texts written to define the project were kept to a minimum (the Elyssar decrees). They do not lay out the project's issues, put them into perspective, or record any specific general objectives. There is no overall consensual justification. The texts are sufficiently unclear so that each party can interpret and justify them in its own terms. The details of the rehousing process have therefore never been precisely defined and only part of the project was implemented.

Conclusion

Town planning takes into account both civic and functionalist values, hence the frequent link between town planning and social projects and the fact that town development plans are based on public interest. The definition and scale of the social group (neighborhood, suburb, city, or even country) targeted by the plan determine the selection of development projects. Plans to regularize informal settlements tend to give rise to opposition based on concerns for justice for the different social groups. Paradoxically, although the disagreements concerning legitimacy follow these same divisions between social groups, support for the selection of a project does not follow the same divisions. Several justifications on the same level can lead to different choices, while one choice may meet several requirements on different levels. This makes compromise possible.

A compromise, which is enough in itself

While the Elyssar project demonstrates many ways of transforming the area depending on the desired social impact, it particularly shows that different, sometimes conflicting, social impacts are the expected outcomes of a single choice of development of the area, especially that of rehousing in situ. The actors have social objectives on different levels: some give priority to city residents, others to those of the southern suburbs. However, this contradiction remains concealed.

In fact, the mere fact of agreement on the project's choices seems at least as important as their content. By its existence alone, the project constitutes common ground, which enables the progress of relations. In order for the agreement to last, contradictions should not be made visible.

The terms of the rehousing program have never been precisely defined. The negotiating actors agreed on the complex compromise of rehousing because it met their requirements, but the agreement also raised problems for them all as it involved an element that went against their various positions. The period of implementation saw an unspoken shift toward other options. The project was only partly implemented: apart from the beginning of the regrouping of lands and expropriation proceedings, only the main roads and highways passing through the project area have been completed. Therefore, notwithstanding their demands, Shi'i parties exceptionally agreed that the families living along the planned routes of these roads be evicted in return for substantial compensation. The apartments for rehousing were never built, the terms for their allocation have not been defined, and the informal settlements are still there today.

The agreement about the conflicting aspects of the project eased certain tensions, allowed relations to continue, and satisfied each party's primary social goals, through partial implementation and dispensation regarding the appointed rules. On the one hand, the party of government was able to modernize and open up the southern suburbs to the whole of the population, it could build highways across the area, and the project put an end to the expansion of informal settlements. On the other hand, the Shi'i parties obtained official acknowledgment of the rights of the residents of informal settlements, and an end to the threat of expulsion without compensation.

For the prime minister, the choice of rehousing in situ was primarily justified by the presence among the future beneficiaries of refugees from South Lebanon. When the area was liberated in 2000, he thought it would be possible to negotiate a new solution for Elyssar in which all the residents could be compensated and return to their home region. Furthermore, ten years after the war ended, it finally seemed possible for residents to deal with landowners directly (buying and selling land from one another), since they were no longer the original wronged landowners but had since bought the land with full knowledge of the facts. With the evolution of the topical profiles of the prime minister and the Shi'i parties, the period of implementation of the project became a time for its recomposition.

Town planning between the law and a sense of justice
The specificity of Beirut as a site for research highlights the contrast between existing rights and those that are in fact claimed. Town planning and building regulations were developed from the 1960s onward. For a century, the southern suburbs have been the site of town-planning projects; they are the ideal site for the expression of these rights. The right to property is guaranteed by the state upon its registration in the land register, which is an unusual situation in world terms. Therefore, the issue of irregularity does not lead to confusion. The law is used as a reference and there is no ambiguity regarding the legitimacy of owners. Moreover, nobody ever claims the transfer of property in favor of its occupiers.

In this context, it seems that political claims do not call the existing law into question, but claim rights in favor of a group: access to the city, compensation for the state's failures, and social justice. There is no overlapping reasoning on this point, unlike in countries where the law is less clearly constituted, or less known by the public. This is demonstrated by the always partial reference to the 1955 Sands Trial lawsuit, and the resulting decision to rehouse.

The importance of the role of the law in Lebanon in the actors' arguments leads one to question the conditions under which the projects of regularization of informal settlements are feasible, especially considering the role played by the law in a society which is undergoing a period of national reconciliation and/or of (re)construction of a legally constituted state.

References

Boltanski, Luc, and Laurent Thévenot. 1991. *De la justification, Les économies de la grandeur*. Paris: Gallimard.

Bourgey, André, and Joseph Pharès. 1973. "Les bidonvilles de l'agglomération de Beyrouth." *Revue de géographie de Lyon* 48 (2): 107–39.

Choay, Françoise. 1980. *La règle et le modèle*. Paris: Seuil.

Clerc-Huybrechts, Valérie. 2008. *Les quartiers irréguliers de Beyrouth, une histoire des enjeux fonciers et urbanistiques dans la banlieue sud*. Beirut: Institut français du Proche-Orient.

———. 2002. "Les principes d'action de l'urbanisme, le projet Élyssar face aux quartiers irréguliers de Beyrouth." PhD diss., l'Institut français d'urbanisme, Université Paris VIII.

Crozier, Michel, and Erhard Friedberg. 1977. *L'acteur et le système, les contraintes de l'action collective*. Paris: Seuil.

Fawaz, Mona, and Isabelle Peillen. 2003. *Understanding Slums: Case Studies for the Global Report on Human Settlements 2003—The Case of Beirut*. Beirut: UN-Habitat.

Friedberg, Erhard. 1993. *Le pouvoir et la règle. Dynamiques de l'action organisée*. Paris: Seuil.

Harb, Mona. 2005. "Action publique et système politique pluricommunautaire: les mouvements politiques chiites dans le Liban d'après-guerre." PhD diss., IEP d'Aix-en Provence.

———. 2003. "La *Dahiye* de Beyrouth: parcours d'une stigmatisation urbaine, consolidation d'un territoire politique." *Genèses*, no. 51 (June): 70–91.

Lacaze, Jean-Paul. 1997. *Les méthodes de l'urbanisme*. Paris: PUF.

Nasr, Joe, and Mercedes Volait. 2003. *Urbanism: Imported or Exported? Native Aspirations and Foreign Plans*. Chichester, UK: Wiley-Academy.

———. 1985. "La transition des chiites vers Beyrouth: mutations sociales et mobilisation communautaire à la veille de 1975." In Mona Zakaria, Bach-châr Chrabou, Waddah Charâra, Michel Seurat, Salim Nasr, Jean Pierre Thieck, Guy Leonard, *Mouvements communautaires et espaces urbains au Machreq*. Beirut: Centre d'études et de recherches sur le Moyen-Orient contemporain (CERMOC).

———. 1979. "Les formes de regroupement traditionnel dans la société de Beyrouth." In Dominique Chevallier, ed., *L'espace social de la ville arabe*. Paris: Maisonneuve et Larose.

Signoles, Pierre. 1999. "Acteurs publics et acteurs privés dans le développe-ment des villes du monde arabe." In Pierre Signoles, Galila El Kadi, and Rachid Sidi Boumedine, eds., *L'urbain dans le monde arabe, Politiques, ins-truments et acteurs*. Paris, CNRS éditions.

Souami, Taoufik. 2003. *Aménageurs de villes et territoires d'habitants, Un siècle dans le Sud algérien*. Paris: L'Harmattan.

Verdeil, Éric. 2002. "Une ville et ses urbanistes: Beyrouth en reconstruction." PhD diss., Université Paris 1.

Verpraet, Gilles. 1989. "Les théories américaines de l'aménagement urbain, la question des professions." *Les Annales de la recherche urbaine*, nos. 44–45.

13

The Coastal Settlements of Ouzaii and Jnah: Analysis of an Upgrading Project in Beirut

Falk Jähnigen

This research paper stems from a period of research spent at the Institut Français du Proche Orient (IFPO) in Beirut and the subsequent period when I completed my degree at the Technische Universität Berlin. It focuses on two neighboring informal settlements in the south of Beirut (Jnah and Ouzaii) that have grown rapidly since the onset of the civil war and continue to grow today. Therefore the purpose of the research project is to suggest appropriate planning procedures and possible initiatives to improve the lives and living conditions of the citizens in the two neighborhoods. The original dissertation is divided into two parts: the first part analyses the situation using material collected during fieldwork, while the second part presents scenarios and an action plan as a clear alternative to ongoing development. Due to the scientific nature of the workshop and limitations of space, this chapter only presents the first part of my work.

Historic, Demographic, and Economic Analysis of Ouzaii and Jnah
History of the southern suburbs of Beirut

After independence in the 1940s, the southern suburbs of Beirut were mainly rural and their few communities were still inhabited by farmers. The two Palestinian refugee camps of Sabra and Shatila were established in the southern suburbs in 1949. At the end of the 1950s, more and more people from Beirut spent their leisure time on the southern beaches, causing the area to develop more rapidly. The first informal settlements grew around the existing neighborhoods. They mainly housed rural refugees from the Bekaa Valley and South Lebanon. These inhabitants found work in the rural neighborhoods and in the newly built beach facilities. The Palestinian refugee camps' populations were increased by the large number of Palestinians moving into Beirut from 1949 onward (Fawaz and Peillen 2002).

The destruction of several informal settlements in East Beirut at the beginning of the civil war caused the expansion of most of the settlements in the southern suburbs (for example, Raml, Ouzaii, Jnah, Shatila, Sabra, and Horch Tabet). In 1982 a large proportion of the buildings in Sabra, Horch Tabet, and Shatila were destroyed during the Israeli invasion, leaving these areas uninhabited until 1992. The former inhabitants occupied the sports stadium area. The areas of Sabra, Horch Tabet, and Shatila were not repopulated until the eviction of people from the stadium. The strongholds of Hezbollah began to grow east of the southern suburbs, because of the concentration of the Shi'is from South Lebanon and the Bekaa Valley. Hezbollah's Beirut headquarters emerged in Haret Hreik. Most of the southern suburbs territory acquired a Shi'i majority over the years. In 1987 Hezbollah overtook Amal, the second biggest Shi'i movement. Consequently, Shi'i majority areas were dominated by Hezbollah (Beyhum 1991).

The Elyssar project's attempt to reconnect the southern suburbs to the Beirut city center failed during the post war years. Apart from some thoroughfares, the project remained a useless piece of paper. Through this project, the municipality of Beirut wanted to destroy large areas of the informal settlements in order to return property to the free market, but this attempt failed because of resistance from Hezbollah.

Since 1993, migrant workers from Syria, Egypt, the Philippines, and Sri Lanka have arrived in Beirut. They moved into the informal settlements in the southern suburbs because they could not afford the high rents on the formal housing market (Fawaz and Peillen 2002, 8).

History of Ouzaii and Jnah
Ouzaii (Fig. 13.1)—The development of the settlement was influenced by rural patterns and traditional family structures. Besides the occupation of land as a process of appropriation, people also bought shares of the larger parcels. The first buildings along the costal road emerged after 1948, when the municipality of Burj al-Barajneh leased big shares of

parcels for ninety-nine years to farm workers who built their cabins on the land.

Large areas of Ouzaii community land were converted into private land through a court ruling in 1953 under President Camille Chamoun (1952–58). It was impossible to appeal against the decision, by which all existing inhabitants became illegal (Clerc-Huybrecht 2002). Since the inhabitants were unable to appeal, they were encouraged by the mayor to squat on several parcels in Ouzaii and Raml. The mayor himself moved into an illegally squatted house in Raml. In 1958, the circumstances of the Lebanon crisis encouraged the inhabitants of Ouzaii to occupy more land. Shortly afterward, the state tried to resettle them (Ruppert 1999).

In 1983 the state planned an extension to the airport, which would have destroyed 30 to 40 percent of Ouzaii. The population protested and won its battle against the project (Charafeddine 1987; Clerc-Huybrecht 2002, 264f.).

Ouzaii was expanded and densified during the civil war. It mainly grew to the south along the coastal road leading to Sidon. More and more Shi'is from the south settled in Ouzaii with the aid of Hezbollah. At the same time the coastal road developed into an important economic axis. It also had a strategic position as a secure access to the south and a small harbor. Table 13.1 shows the dimensions and the nature of the occupied land in Ouzaii in 1987.

There was little change in the situation of the inhabitants of Jnah and Ouzaii following the end of the civil war. Since the people lived in illegal settlements, the municipality of Beirut refused to recognize them as citizens of Beirut. This also meant that their access to necessary public services was denied.

Jnah (Fig. 13.1)—The first wave of occupation in Jnah took place shortly after the Lebanon crisis of 1958. During this time, about twenty houses were built by Christians near the Notre Dame de Jnah church. Shortly afterward, the buildings were legalized by the municipality of Ghobeiry.

Table 13.1 General information on Jnah and Ouzaii informal settlements

Settlement	Occupied private parcels	Occupied municipal parcels	Occupied public land	Land which is shared	Surface area in hectares	Population (1987)	Founding year
Jnah		74%	15%		23	10,000	1976
Ouzaii	12%		51%	33%	50	35,000	1955

(Source: Charafeddine 1987)

Fig. 13.1: Satellite
picture of Ouzaii
and Jnah (Direction
des Affaires Géo-
graphiques 2005).

They consequently obtained a water supply, electricity, and telephone lines in 1962 (Clerc-Huybrecht 2002, 239; Harb el-Kak 1996).

A second wave of occupation started in 1975 at the beginning of the civil war. During this period, many refugees from the Bekaa Valley and southern Lebanon bought lots, which were sold illegally by fake estate agents who had occupied and subdivided the parcels illegally (Charafeddine 1987).

In 1976 the bungalows of the beach facilities of Jnah (St. Simon and St. Michel) were squatted with the support of the controlling militias. Approximately one thousand refugee families (that is, around seven thousand people) from East Beirut settled there. Half of the families were Kurds and the other half Palestinians and Syrians (Moussa 1983).

Also in 1976 the High Shi'i Council, supported by Amal's militia, started to build the al-Zahra hospital in the east of Jnah. The land surrounding the hospital was occupied after its construction and from that moment on was called Hayy al-Zahra (Figs. 13.2 and 13.6).

Administration of the informal settlements

Local self-administration exists in most of the informal settlements. Area committees have been founded in order to carry out certain infrastructural tasks and to organize a basic level of 'public' services. They require municipal financial support for this work. No formal procedure exists for the formation of these area committees; they are mostly founded by the area's dominant political power. In Ouzaii and Jnah they are currently formed by Hezbollah supporters.

The inhabitants of informal settlements are still administratively connected to their birthplace, where they vote and carry out official matters like obtaining birth and death certificates, although they have lived in Beirut for over thirty years (Charafeddine 1987; Harb 1996).

Table 13.2 Administrative status of Jnah and Ouzaii

Municipality	Quarter	Informal settlement	Palestinian refugee camp
Burj al-Barajneh	Burj al-Barajneh	Ouzaii	Burj al-Barajneh Camp
Ghobeiry	Roueiss	Raml	Shatila
	Ghobeiry	Jnah	Sabra
	Chiah	Hayy al-Zahra	
		Bir Hassan	
		Hursh Tabet	
		Hursh al-Shatil	

(Author's field research)

Fig. 13.2: al-Zahra Hospital, east Jnah. Photograph by Falk Jähnigen.

Fig. 13.3: al-Tanshi'a public secondary school in Jnah. Photograph by Falk Jähnigen.

Fig. 13.4: Mosque of al-Imam al-Ouzaii. Photograph by Falk Jähnigen.

Fig. 13.5: Ouzaii Medical Center. Photograph by Falk Jähnigen.

Infrastructure

Concerning public facilities, there is a lack of state and municipal facilities, whereas many facilities are religious or belong to political parties. The whole area is well equipped with six Hezbollah sites. There is a huge shortage of all kinds of schools; during my study I found only four, of which two were state schools and two were religious schools. There is no municipal administration in the area; however, there is a police station and a military barracks to maintain law and order. Two large social organizations work in the area and Dr. Mohammed Khaled's foundation runs a hospital ward. Overall, it is apparent that local stakeholders and their facilities are much more present than the state. A summary of all 'public' facilities can be found in Table 13.3 and Fig. 13.6.

Table 13.3 Facilities in Jnah and Ouzaii

Facilities	in Ouzaii	in Jnah
Mosques	• Sunni: al-Imam al-Ouzaii Mosque with an Islamic study center • two Shi'i mosques	• two mosques (al-Imam Moussa al-Sadr Mosque)
Husseiniyas and schools	• two Husseiniyas • two schools (al-Ahliya school)	• Two schools (al-Tanshi'a public secondary school) (al-Kifah school)
Medical centers	• two medical centers	
Public force	• one barracks (Mustafa Hassan Barracks) • one police station	• a former Syrian military center
Social organizations	• one orphanage • one social center run by Dr. Muhammad Khali	
Offices of political parties	• five for Hezbollah	• one for Hezbollah • one for Amal

(Author's field research, 2006)

Demographic characteristics

Living conditions differ widely within Ouzaii and Jnah. The zones developed during the civil war and the areas toward the sea are far poorer than other zones. These areas also suffer from a greater lack of public services.

How many people live in Ouzaii and Jnah?

Approximately 30,400 inhabitants lived in Ouzaii and 11,700 in Jnah according to a BTUTP population estimate in 1996. The coastal settlements had a total of 42,100 inhabitants (Table 13.4). My research showed that the two settlements combined have up to 61,000 inhabitants.[1]

How many square meters of living space per person?

One household consists on average of 5.71 persons and 29.3 m² living space (Fawaz and Peillen 2002). Therefore there is 5.1 m² living space per person. Sixty-one percent of households have two to three rooms (see Table. 13.5 for the distribution of the number of rooms per household) (Harb 1996).

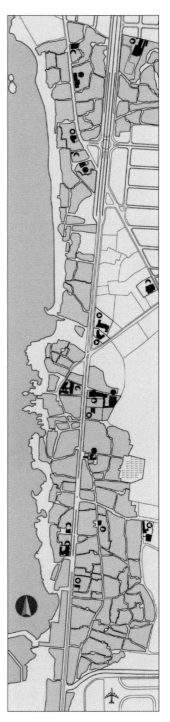

Key:
(1. mosque, Husseiniya
● 2. school
◖ 3. hospital, medical center
✪ 4. public administration (police)
◭ 5. social foundation

Fig. 13.6: Plan of public facilities in Ouzaii and Jnah (from the American University of Beirut).

Table 13.4 Population estimates 1985–96

Settlement	1984 (BTUTP)	1996 (BTUTP)
Ouzaii	3,540 buildings 19,800 inhabitants	30,400 inhabitants
Jnah	1,270 buildings 7,220 inhabitants	11,700 inhabitants
Informal settlements in the suburbs of southern Beirut	190,000 inhabitants	270,000 inhabitants

(Source: Bureau Technique d'Urbanisme et de Travaux Publics [BTUTP]).

Table 13.5 Rooms per household in Jnah and Ouzaii

16 %	of households have 1 room
33 %	of households have 2 rooms
28 %	of households have 3 rooms
16 %	of households have 4 rooms
7 %	of households have 5 or more rooms

(Source: Charafeddin 1991)

How many school-age children live in Ouzaii and Jnah?

In Lebanon, children must attend school for nine years, not counting further education. They generally attend school from the age of six until the age of fifteen. In Jnah and Ouzaii 42 percent of the population are under the age of fifteen, and 25 percent are aged between six and fifteen, and should therefore attend school (Fawaz and Peillen 2002).

If we take the number of 42,000 inhabitants in both settlements, there are 10,500 school-age children of whom only 10 percent (1,050 children) attend public schools inside the settlements and approximately 45 percent (4,700 children) attend private schools.

A 1998 study shows a high rate of illiteracy in the area: 23.5 percent of the population in Ouzaii and Jnah are illiterate, and 80 percent of women aged over forty-five are illiterate. The study also shows that 25 percent of adolescents aged eleven to fifteen work and therefore do not attend school (Feghali 1999).

Economic analysis
Businesses along the coastal road

The coastal road passes though Ouzaii and Jnah for four kilometers. A huge number of small businesses have set up along the road and serve as the economic backbone of the area. During a field study for the IFPO, 547 businesses were counted operating on both sides of the road. Another 153 were closed and 41 were under construction, making a total of 741 businesses (Tables 13.6 and 13.7).

Table 13.6 Number of businesses in Jnah and Ouzaii along the coastal road

	Number of businesses	percentage
Services	219	40.7
Of which = maintenance and repair of cars	*(189)*	
Shops	194	34.2
Of which = grocers	*(79)*	
leisure activities/tourism	33	6.1
crafts/industry	101	19
Total	**547**	**100**

(Author's field research)

Urban problems—existing and lacking integration of the settlements
To what extent are the two coastal settlements integrated into the city?

From an economic point of view it is obvious that Jnah and Ouzaii are the housing areas for many low-income earners, who work in construction, street cleaning, domestic employment, the army, and so on. Forty-eight percent of families make do with less than $300 a month (Fawaz and Peillen 2002). Since a room in most of the legal areas of Beirut costs $300, many families are forced to live in poverty. Furthermore, the settlements are home to the cheapest and most specialized car repair and maintenance garages of the city and there are many furniture and carpentry shops along the coastal road. The settlements are well connected to the transport system by the north–south route of the coastal road and by several connections with the east. A certain level of integration seems to exist in some fields. The economic sector in particular shows the dependence that characterizes the social model.

Table 13.7 Types of activities in Jnah and Ouzaii along the coastal road

SERVICES				SHOPS				INDUSTRY AND CRAFTS	
Car maintenance and repair	No.	**Other services**	No.	**Grocers**	No.	**Other shops**	No.	**Industry and Crafts**	No.
Garage	63	Bank	12	Chicken butcher	5	Shoe and bag shop	12	Furniture	
Tyres (sale and repair shop)	17	Doctor's surgery	4	Butcher	9	Pharmacy	4	Furniture production	40
Exhaust pipe garage	14	Transport company offices of building-material companies	18	Pastry shop	6	Clothes	18	Cabinet-making	11
Automobile electronics	10	Companies or refilling gas bottles	3	Bakery	15	Photo processing	3	Metal-furniture production	7
Car varnish	3	Hospital wards	1	Fishmonger	9	Magazine seller	1	Shops for processing steel, aluminum, fiberglass	26
Car interior equipment	2	**Total**	**30**	Grocery	16	Watches and jewelry	2	Plumber	2
Oil change	6			Fruit and Vegetables	8	Hairdresser	4	Production of plaster elements	3
Car glass	3	**Leisure activities** **Tourism**		Fruit juice	4	Flower shop	2	Repair and maintenance of electronic devices	7
Spare-part production	6	Restaurants	13	Grilled products	7	Home and electrical appliance	21	Production of clothing	4
Car body recycling	10	Snack bars	20	**Total**	**79**	Building materials	23	Steam-ironing	1
Sale of spare parts	29	**Total**	**33**			Fishing equipment	3	**Total**	**101**
Vehicle registration	1					Toys and gift shop	10		
Petrol stations	16					Car sale	10		
Total	**189**					**Total**	**115**		

(Author's field research)

How bad is the condition of the two settlements?

The high level of unemployment, 25 percent, shows that many of the inhabitants have only limited employment possibilities (Harb 2000). The small shabby buildings of the settlements highlight the disparity with the surrounding area, such as the growing housing developments, the airport, and the golf course. Most of the inhabitants of Ouzaii and Jnah invest little in their houses, due to the insecure tenure situation. The state of construction is therefore very poor.

There is a lack of all kinds of infrastructure and public services. Water supply is poor, the real demand for drinking water is neglected, and people use brackish and polluted ground water which they draw from their own wells. Only 30 percent of the required electricity supply is supplied; in many cases, the wires of pylons are tapped into and electricity is taken illegally. There is a shortage of state schools; 25 percent of the inhabitants are school-age children but only 10 percent of children can attend a state school inside the settlements; another 45 percent attend private schools and the rest go to school outside the area or do not go at all. Many families cannot pay for their children's education; this is proven by the high illiteracy rate of 20 percent. Medical care is very poor; for every 2,500 inhabitants there is only one hospital bed, whereas in the inner city there is one hospital bed for every 350 residents. Many diseases are caused by poor hygiene conditions (Harb 1996).

Politically, the settlements are almost self-governed by Hezbollah. There is no direct political influence from the municipal administration or Beirut city administration, since the inhabitants of the settlements do not vote in their place of residence but in their town of birth. Therefore the inhabitants depend on Hezbollah, which guarantees in return its support for the protection of the area. Socially, the inhabitants are treated as second-class citizens. The settlements themselves are very insular, so that most outsiders are quickly recognized. It is obvious that in most fields there is a lack of integration into the rest of the city; however, there are many possibilities for improvement.

Summary

My analysis highlights three essential aspects of the urban problems in Ouzaii and Jnah, which must be taken into account by all planners working in the area.
1. The growth of informal settlements and the growth of informal economic activities. This requires an independent solution for migrants' and displaced persons' living and working conditions, which are neglected by

politicians and religious leaders. This growth reinforces the breakdown of the area in terms of social standards and creates a huge supply of cheap labor, which is also an obstacle for real integration.

2. Land problems
Strategic parcels have an obscure ownership status and are occupied by informal settlements.

3. General shortages and lack of order, which concern public services and the existing infrastructure.

Analysis of the Stakeholders

Many stakeholders operate in the southern suburbs. Each has his own reasons for holding to a certain ideology, strategy, and sometimes urban planning policy. Since each stakeholder focuses on certain areas of the suburbs, they tend to overlap, exclude, compete with, and oppose one another; their conflicts structure space (Harb 1996).

There are two groups of stakeholders: public parties, that is, the government and the municipal administration; and local parties, that is, Hezbollah, the High Shi'i Council, the Amal movement, the al-Mabarrat foundation, and various NGOs.

Public stakeholders
Evolution

The southern suburbs gained little from the urban planning interventions of the state. The first major projects concerning land use regulation were implemented under President Chamoun. Facilities such as the 'Sports City' and the golf club were built during this time. Michel Ecochard's master plan was aimed at forming an area with predominantly low-density housing developments. Several public schools, hospital wards, and the Lebanese University in Hadath, south of the southern suburbs, were established under President Chebab (1958–64). President Hélou (1964–70) tried to divide the local municipalities into uniform social and denominational entities, and therefore changed the size of the municipality of Burj al-Barajneh (containing Ouzaii). No major urban regulation projects were started in the southern suburbs under presidents Frangié or Sarkis (1970–82). The state tried to reduce the density of the area by partially destroying informal settlements under President Gemayel (1982–88). From 1988 to 1990, there was a turbulent period under President Aoun, during which Hezbollah and Amal fought each other in the area while the state looked on (Harb 1996, 18).

The Taif Agreement of 1989 stipulated decentralization and increased authority for governors and mayors. The government was regaining control of the Lebanese administration, which had suffered (like all Lebanese institutions) from structural paralysis during the fifteen-year long civil war. From this time on the administration began to operate normally once again. However, it remained very corrupt and affected by favoritism. Projects for its reorganization are emerging, but the implementation of reforms concerning the renewal of the state apparatus is still suffering from inefficiency and disagreements (Fawaz and Peillen 2002).

Structures

Ministry of Public Works—Ministère des Travaux publics (MTP). The MTP was founded during the French Mandate. It is responsible for a wide range of activities, including urban planning, regional planning, transport planning, and tourism. It was exclusively responsible for the creation of master plans before the civil war. Thereafter it was in competition with the CDR.

Council for Development and Reconstruction—Conseil pour le développement et la reconstruction (CDR). The CDR was founded in 1977 to deal with land use regulations more quickly than the MTP. The CDR is directly connected to the council of ministers and has a lot of freedom concerning financial and administrative decision-making. It is responsible for major projects outside Beirut city center.

Directorate-General for Urban Development—Direction générale de l'urbanisme (DGU). The DGU is subordinate to the MTP. It has a wide scope for decision-making in the field of regional planning and during the planning and execution of projects. However, its limited financial budget restricts its activities in the southern suburbs to the issue of building permits (Harb 1996, 19f).

Municipalities. The municipality of Burj al-Barajneh manages an area of 482 hectares with 120,000 inhabitants. Burj al-Barajneh was created in 1922, and in 1974 Ouzaii was attached to it. The original municipality was founded in the historic village center. Now it includes city quarters like Roueiss, where most of the buildings are eight to eleven stories high, but it also includes informal settlements such as Ouzaii and Raml, where most of the buildings are one to four stories high.

The municipality of Ghobeiry manages an area of 450 hectares with 100,000 inhabitants. Before 1956 it was part of a larger municipality that included Chiah and Ain al-Rimmaneh. Its foundation core includes an old city quarter with a street grid plan. Today, the informal settlements of Sabra, Jnah, and Horch el-Chatil are located on its territory. The municipalities of Burj al-Barajneh and Ghobeiry are composed of legal quarters, informal settlements, and Palestinian refugee camps (Table 13.2).

Municipalities have an elected municipal council and an elected mayor (Fawaz and Peillen 2002). The urban planning services are limited to the issuing of construction permits, the asphalting of streets, minor repairs of all kinds, and the positioning of some road signs. The lion's share of the municipalities' budget is used for operating costs; therefore little is left for investments. A large proportion of expenses is taken up with labor costs, whereas fines for the violation of building laws represent the biggest revenues.

Over the years, municipal budgets have been reduced by the government and former municipal tasks have been removed; for example, the CDR instructed the private company Sukleen to organise waste collection in Burj al-Barajneh and Ghobeiry (Fawaz and Peillen 2002).

Structural problems and limited financial resources give municipalities almost no opportunity to play a major role in the urban planning process. Therefore they support reconstruction in the southern suburbs, without taking part in it. The state seems to have little interest in strengthening their position, and the municipalities themselves show no effort to gain greater influence in the urban planning process (Harb 2001).

An important aspect in the relation between municipalities and inhabitants of informal settlements concerns political representation. Lebanese citizens vote in the municipality of their birthplace, or the birthplace of their parents if they are born in an illegal settlement. Since most of the inhabitants of informal settlements are rural migrants or foreigners, none of them vote in the municipality of their place of residence. Therefore mayors have no sense of responsibility toward the inhabitants of settlements. Yet the inhabitants expect a certain level of responsibility, since they pay electricity bills (which they mistake for paying taxes) to the municipality (Fawaz and Peillen 2002, 47).

Local stakeholders

During the civil war, the southern suburbs were governed by local parties who helped inhabitants with their daily problems (water supply, electricity, establishment of hospital wards, cooperatives, pharmacies, schools, and so on). The state did not offer any help to create the necessary facilities in these quarters. Over the years the local stakeholders benefited from the lack of state presence and supplied more and more services. During the civil war, Hezbollah established itself as the main stakeholder in the southern suburbs and overtook Amal in terms of power and influence, which was once the strongest Shi'i party (Harb 1995, 39; Kramer 1988). Other local players are the High Shi'i Council, the al-Mabarrat Association, the Movement Social, and several other NGOs.

Hezbollah

The primacy of Hezbollah over other intervening parties is characterized by the three following points:
1. It has a large number of facilities, which offer a wide range of services.
2. It provides part of the potable water supply.
3. It takes an effective and firm stand on political decisions regarding projects in the southern suburbs.

Hezbollah has divided Ouzaii into three sections and Jnah into two. These sections function like community units of a larger city.

Development. Hezbollah was founded in the summer of 1982 by a group of Amal dissidents. In Baalbek and with the support of the Iranian Revolution's Guards, Sayyed Hussein al-Moussawi formed a group called 'Islamic Amal,' which announced their existence under the name Hezbollah in 1984. In that same year, Hezbollah started to establish cooperatives, schools, hospital wards, hospitals, mosques, and husseiniyas in the southern suburbs.[2] Simultaneously, many organizations were founded in order to take care of the welfare of people in need, who depended on Hezbollah. The large number of facilities created a whole range of employment, although it was not obligatory for employees to join the party. They simply had to respect the ideology, for example, dress in accordance with Islamic principles. Job proposals were especially tempting, since Hezbollah offered its employees advantages such as financial support for school children, loans to buy apartments, health insurance, and so on, and last, but not least, it paid salaries in U.S. dollars. Over the years Hezbollah facilities multiplied and further services were established, such as an Islamic bank, a research center, and a publishing house.

Hezbollah attracted attention in the public space of the southern suburbs with slogans and pictures in honor of its leaders and martyrs and the leaders of the Islamic revolution in Iran. Facilities which show their connection or their affiliation to Hezbollah are also numerous in the southern suburbs. Since 1992 Hezbollah has run for parliamentary elections; the southern suburbs always have one or two representatives in parliament. Therefore it seems that Hezbollah has the southern suburbs quite well under control (Harb 1996; Rosiny 1996).

Today, Hezbollah has deep roots in several regions of Lebanon: in the Bekaa Valley, in South Lebanon, part of North Lebanon, and in the southern suburbs of Beirut. It characterizes itself as the only powerful political party with a Shi'i ideology, although Hezbollah is a 'mission' and a 'way of life' at the same time.

Structures. Hezbollah has a clear hierarchical structure. The party leadership makes decisions and transfers duties to the lower level. Projects in the field of urban planning are drafted by the CCED and carried out by the Jihad al-Binaa, a sub-organization of Hezbollah.

Some examples of sub-organizations:
- al-Imdad cares for children in need and orphans
- al-Shahid looks after the families of war martyrs
- al-Juraha looks after the families of the war injured
- al-Hay'a al-sihhiya takes care of all matters concerning health care

Other sub-organizations deal with the electricity supply, water supply, financial aid, reconstruction, and environmental protection. Hezbollah's most important sub-organizations have partner organizations in Iran. Therefore many of its projects are financed with generous sponsorship from Iran (Rosiny 1996, 126ff).

The *Centre consultatif d'études et de documentation* (CCED)/*al-Markaz al-Istishari li-l-Durus wa-l-Tawthiqi* (The Consultancy Center for Studies and Documentation) is responsible for Hezbollah's project planning. It carries out preliminary studies based on its own research and feasibility studies. Projects are implemented by the various sub-organizations of Hezbollah. It has a library and archives that are open to the public and conducts studies for other organizations, not only Hezbollah.

According to the CCED the southern suburbs are suffering from a serious problem of overpopulation caused by population growth and several waves of migration. The resulting living condition problems and infrastructure problems can be alleviated by the CCED's projects. Two committees

have been formed to deal with the problems of illegal settlements:
1. The committee for violations of building laws in the southern suburbs.
2. The committee for the reduction of problems concerning the violation of public land and illegality.

These committees are subordinate to the CCED. They make alternative proposals, which are handed over to the party leadership for discussion with the public administration. Furthermore, the CCED has written a report about the real living conditions and the needs of the population of the southern suburbs. This report addresses the issues of living space, roads and pathways, education, health care, public administration, water supply, electricity supply, and waste disposal (Harb 1996, 31).

Jihad al-Binaa is Hezbollah's only organization involved in the preparation and implementation of construction projects. It was founded in 1988 under the order of Imam Ayatollah Khomeini, the former supreme leader of Iran. Its main objective is the construction (which is regarded as *jihad*, struggle or combat) of community facilities for the entire population. The field of activities includes architecture, development, road construction, agriculture, and research projects. Priority is given to areas that are badly damaged and poorly equipped with infrastructure.

Jihad al-Binaa has three local administrations (the southern suburbs of Beirut, Bekaa, and South Lebanon) with several subdivisions: civil engineering, mechanics, electrical equipment, water supply, agriculture, architecture, and so on. A committee of skilled employees is responsible for each section. The architecture division supervises construction projects. Its main task consists in the construction and rebuilding of schools (a boys' school in Ouzaii), (al-Hadid Mosque in Ouzaii), husseiniyas, and residential houses which have been destroyed by Israeli air raids (Harb 1996, 33; Rosiny 1996, 126).

During the civil war, Jihad al-Binaa assumed the duties of the municipal administration in many fields. For example, it took care of the installation of infrastructure, waste disposal, street cleaning, and the rebuilding of public schools. In 1988, for instance, the "committee of cleanliness" was founded to compensate for the inadequate refuse collection service by the municipalities of the southern suburbs. Jihad al-Binaa bought twelve garbage trucks and hired forty-five employees, who were put in charge of the daily collection of three hunded tons of domestic waste. This service cost $550,000 annually. The municipalities only resumed their work in 2000.

Jihad al-Binaa has supplied the southern suburbs with drinking water since 1991. It has divided the area into four regions, with ninety-six cisterns in each region to guarantee supply. This partly alleviates the chronic shortage of drinking water in the southern suburbs. The project is financed by Iran (Harb 1996, 67).

Objectives. Hezbollah's objective is for the communities it controls to be less dependent on the state. It tries to educate as many community residents as possible in order to increase their potential. Its urban planning policy also follows a strategy of greater independence from the state. Therefore Hezbollah implements its reform ideas via projects for community facilities which aim for greater autonomy in the southern suburbs. This autonomy is illusory regarding the necessary integration of the southern suburbs into the rest of the city; in terms of public services guaranteed by Hezbollah, however, it is a reality.

Hezbollah as a party not only spreads its ideology and way of life, it is also deeply rooted in society through the establishment of a wide range of facilities and urban services. This approach is no coincidence; indeed it depends on a spatial and social logic. Through this urban policy Hezbollah structures urban space via a plan to reinforce its presence in political and social matters; its presence in mosques in the southern suburbs makes Hezbollah heard by the government (Harb 1996).

Other local stakeholders
High Shiʻi Council. The High Shiʻi Council is a Shiʻi authority that is consulted on matters concerning the Shiʻi community in Lebanon. Public authorities as well as the local parties contact the Council. It is formed by the representatives of the Shiʻi community who are the Shiʻi deputies in parliament and ministers. Al-Zahra Hospital in Hayy al-Zahra east of Jnah is one example of the urban intervention implemented by the Council. However, it has only carried out a few urban interventions in the southern suburbs, and its importance as a player is mostly due to its religious status.

Amal Movement. Amal was founded in 1974 by Imam Moussa Sadr and appeared on the political stage with the name "movement of the disinherited." Amal was the main player in the southern suburbs before Hezbollah was formed. However, it was weakened by the fight against the Palestinian camps from March 1986 to December 1988. There was a serious conflict within the Shiʻi community of the southern suburbs in September 1987;

Amal and Hezbollah were in conflict, whereupon Amal withdrew into the peripheral zones, such as Jnah and Horch al-Chatil, and Hezbollah took control of the municipalities of Burj al-Barajneh and Ghobeiry. Amal is headed by Nabih Berry, who has been speaker of the parliament since 1992 (Rosiny 1996, 81; Harb 1996, 27).

In Jnah, Amal runs an office for education that supports education for war orphans. Approximately one thousand children benefit from this service. It also manages a football pitch and several youth clubs there. Amal cooperates with private schools in order to allocate scholarships and aid for children of families in need.

It has also formed a committee that works with resident-committees in order to guarantee basic infrastructure and supply: electricity, waste disposal, asphalting of roads, and so on. Amal has no direct structures that deal with urban planning tasks; its guaranteed services, such as access to electricity and the provision of fresh water tanks, are therefore limited.

Posters, placards, and murals show that the area of Jnah is claimed by Amal and Hezbollah. In contrast to Hezbollah, Amal is against the 'ghettoisation' of the southern suburbs, and lobbies for Christian–Islamic coexistence, which Amal claims to be the guarantor for the peaceful development of Lebanese society (Kiwan 1993; Harb 1996, 27).

al-Mabarrat Association. This was founded in 1978 in order to support orphans by guaranteeing them an education. The foundation has its head office in Haret Hreik and is governed by Sayyed Fadlallah. Al-Mabarrat is close to Hezbollah, but operates with a completely independent financial and administrative structure. The foundation runs a television station (al-Manara), two radio stations (al-Nour and al-Imam), a publishing house (Dar al-Malak), a hospital in Haret Hreik with two hundred and fifty beds, several mosques and cultural centers, three orphanages, and two schools for the handicapped. In Ouzaii it operates an orphanage and has built a mosque.

Its structure is hierarchical, with a directorate general and several special councils that carry out the preliminary work for the directorate general. Planning offices and execution offices are subordinate to the councils. Eight hundred employees fulfill the duties of the foundation. In 2000 it was responsible for 1,800 orphans. Al-Mabarrat is one of the biggest foundations in Lebanon, and as far as urban planning is concerned, it is one of the most dynamic parties in the southern suburbs. Its relationship to Hezbollah is characterized by mutual cooperation (Harb 1996, 29).

The Relationship between the State and Hezbollah
During the civil war

In the southern suburbs, Hezbollah took over the unaccomplished duties of the collapsing Lebanese state. Unlike other militias, it not only supplied its own clientele, but also helped people in need from other religious faiths. Its sub-organizations benefited from generous financial support from Iran, which allowed Hezbollah to do without the criminal methods frequently used by other militias (Rosiny 1996, 135).

The Lebanese state and its institutions did not care about urban and regional planning in the southern suburbs during the civil war. After the start of the civil war the state gradually withdrew from the supply of public services. Local players rose up the ranks without any resistance from the state and ensured these services. The state took up a position of laisser-faire with Hezbollah, assuming that Hezbollah would be more useful than harmful to the state. Hezbollah supplied services that were under state responsibility, such as a water supply, hospital wards, hospitals, free schools, mortgages, and support for families in need. So the state no longer had to worry about providing decent living conditions (Kramer 1988).

After the civil war

Having neglected its services during the civil war, the state gradually started to reclaim its role after the Taif Agreement, with the execution of infrastructure projects and the construction of community facilities in the *legal* settlements. However, the informal settlements continued to be neglected. Hezbollah therefore accused the state of deliberately neglecting services in order to burden the inhabitants and local parties with urban problems and to prevent any development. Extremist voices in Hezbollah even accused the state of practicing a policy of encouraging decay in order to be able to demolish buildings later. Hezbollah also blamed the state for overpopulation and shortages, citing a report by Jihad al-Binaa which proves that the fifty-year-long refusal of the state to subdivide large parcels in the southern suburbs provoked the construction of informal settlements in this area (Harb 1996, 68). It is clear that the relationship between the state and Hezbollah is asymmetric, with Hezbollah in opposition to the state and the state adopting a laissez-faire position toward Hezbollah.

The Strategies of the State and Hezbollah. The strategy of Hezbollah is to achieve greater autonomy in the southern suburbs, which should enable stronger growth with its own resources. Therefore violations of building laws and the informal economy are a justified self-help response of the population.

Why Does Hezbollah Not Intervene to Reduce Informal Settlements? The director of the CCED's answer to this question indicates that this is not a party issue, but a state issue. Hezbollah considers that certain tasks, such as infrastructure maintenance, and the enforcement of building laws do not fall within its ambit and are the responsibility of the public administration. During the civil war, Hezbollah took care of certain problems for inhabitants, such as the lack of housing, but this is no longer the case. However, if the state does not take action in the informal settlements, the inhabitants have the right to give themselves a decent life (Harb 1996, 66). The state is continuing its strategy of withholding necessary supplies and worsening the population's situation. Private institutions and the state have an economic interest in gradually regaining the territory of the settlements. Ouzaii and Jnah have outstanding sandy beaches which are very valuable for tourism, and therefore have an economic value; in Ramlet al-Baida, the area just north of Jnah, each square meter is worth $2,000 (Clerc-Huybrecht 2002).

Sixteen years after the end of the civil war, most of the administration had accepted that the inhabitants of the huge informal settlements in the southern suburbs should not be evicted and their houses demolished and that without any clear policy those areas will further densify and expand. However, if the state wishes to work together with Hezbollah, it must combat prejudices that have grown over the years. In January 2006, when I was conducting my field research, it was not ready to do so.

Examples of the Conflict: The Construction of the Motorway in Ouzaii—May 1995. In Ouzaii, Hezbollah is the main player; this is evident in the many examples of its public advertisements with slogans and pictures of its leaders and martyrs along the coast road and the number of facilities managed by the group. The inhabitants of the houses along the coastal road were due to be evicted and the houses demolished in order to make room for the motorway, and the inhabitants' claims against this course of action were rejected. The press reported on the inhabitants' protest against the evictions. The protest grew stronger and was closely followed by the press. Finally the eviction was cancelled under pressure from high-ranking Hezbollah representatives and Nabih Berry. It was later announced that the incident would be ignored (*L'Orient-Le Jour*, 24 June 1995). In 2002, when the state wanted to build a motorway bridge over the whole area, the inhabitants of Ouzaii resisted once again, with the support of Hezbollah. At that time the newspapers emphasised the illegality of the neighborhood and denied the inhabitants any right of residence (*al-Nahar*, June 2002).

The construction of the motorway in Hayy al-Zahra, north of Ouzaii, was completely different. The houses along the road in Hayy al-Zahra had to be demolished and their residents compensated for the building of the first section of the motorway from Ramlet al-Baida to Ouzaii. In this process, Amal played a decisive role in negotiating adequate compensation and in exerting pressure on the inhabitants to leave their homes. Hezbollah did not interfere at all. The inhabitants were evicted, the houses demolished, and the inhabitants compensated. However, the inhabitants of the surrounding houses were subsequently evicted without compensation. The urban context was destroyed, as was the internal unity of the inhabitants. None of the remaining inhabitants are currently assisted by any party; they are left to their own devices and are waiting to see what will happen.

From the edge of the city center to the southern suburbs, state policy states that construction should be erected wherever possible, and illegal housing should be demolished when there is no support for the inhabitants. Lost parcels are gradually regained by interventions from the north of Jnah. It is more cost-efficient to compensate inhabitants whose daily lives are destroyed by nearby construction work and who subsequently leave as a result than it is to negotiate compensation upfront based on how they might be affected. In this case, the state counts on the demoralization of residents who are no longer supported by any party. When there are no players, the area seems abandoned and the inhabitants seem to fight a losing battle (Harb 1996, 39). This state policy strengthens the position of Hezbollah in Ouzaii, since the residents know that they would rapidly lose their rights without Hezbollah.

The Relation between Jihad al-Binaa and the Municipalities. Jihad al-Binaa has taken charge of many municipal services (waste collection, maintenance of infrastructure, rebuilding of public schools).

What is the Position of Municipalities Regarding This Task Fulfillment? The municipalities try to belittle and deride Jihad al-Binaa's projects. However, there is also some cooperation between Jihad al-Binaa and the municipalities; while the municipalities collect refuse, the waste containers are provided by Jihad al-Binaa. Although the municipalities are aware that

Jihad al-Binaa is rebuilding the sewerage system, their technical team is not supporting Jihad al-Binaa. This cooperation is far more successful in municipalities which are already governed by Hezbollah, like Burj al-Bara-jneh; however, the limited municipal budget only allows for the realization of a few projects, mainly in the legal neighborhoods.

Summary. If Hezbollah had not intervened, the situation in the southern suburbs would have been far worse. However, the area would be less densely populated and therefore easier to improve. The current population density in the informal settlements prevents major urban planning projects that involve eviction and demolition, unless the state wishes to provoke serious social and political conflicts. The state, which has long been absent, is now only one player among many. This status of the state strengthens the position of Hezbollah, which is the main player defending the neglected interests of the Shi'is.

Integration of Hezbollah into state structures

In the future, the state must become a stronger player. Although it was absent during most of the civil war, it is currently working to intervene more frequently than it once did. Its initiatives are undermined by local stakeholders so that public projects are adapted to suit them. Space is being shaped through negotiations between public and private (local) stake-holders (Harb 1996, 79). Since the relationship between Hezbollah and the state is politicized, their behavior does not meet the scientific nature of urban and regional planning. On the one hand, the state has difficulty accepting that Hezbollah has a say in the improvement of settlements' facilities; on the other, Hezbollah refuses to leave urban decision-making to the state in the areas where it is dominant. The state cannot ignore the fact that Hezbollah is the main player (Harb 1996, 69).

Conclusion

The antagonism between the state and local stakeholders has left the two settlements without any urban development provided for by urban management plans. Hence the importance of exposing the consequences of the conflict between the main stakeholders. Research showed that the main obstacle to urban development in the informal settlements is the conflict between local stakeholders and the state. The local players and the settlements' residents constantly blame the state for its inability to fulfill its duties toward its citizens.

Adequate urban development and the integration of the settlements into the rest of the city can only be achieved if the main players enter into dialogue with a view to getting results and finding compromises. The settlements would have great potential if this rapprochement came about: the coastal road could become the economic backbone for services and production, while the beach could become a leisure area.

Notes

1 The surface area of all buildings (taken from satellite photographs) added together and divided by the average household area of 29.3 m² equals a number of 7,400 households in Ouzaii and 3,300 households in Jnah (based on photos from the IFPO and a map from the AUB). The number of households multiplied by the average number of persons per household equals around 42,000 inhabitants in Ouzaii and 19,000 in Jnah.

2 A husseiniya is a place used by Shi'is for political, religious, and social meetings. They were built in memory of the Imam al-Hussein. They are also used for funerals as well as for the 'ashura ceremony in memory of martyrs.

References

"'Ashar sanawat min balsamat al-jirah, 1988–1998." 1999. *al-Hay'a al-sihhiya*.

"al-'Ata': lamha mujaza 'an nashatat mu'assasat al-Jumhuriya al-Islamiya al-Iraniya fi Lubnan." 2003. Public relations department of the Islamic Republic of Iran, Beirut.

"Aydi al-'ata' fi khams sanawat." 2002. *al-Imdad.* Beydoun, R.. 1995. "Elissar: un projet ambitieux pour résoudre une série de problèmes." *L'Orient-Le Jour,* 24 June.

Beyhum, Nabil. 1991. "Espaces Eclates, Espaces Domines: Etude de la recomposition des espaces publics centraux de Beyrouth 1975 à 1990." PhD diss., l'Université de Lyon.

Bourgey, André. 1985. "La Guerre et ses Conséquences Géographiques au Liban." *Annales de Géographies 1985*, no. 521 (94th year): 1–37.

BTUTP (Bureau Technique d'Urbanisme et de Travaux Publics). 1996. "Projet de Réaménagement de la Cote Sud de Beyrouth." Unpublished report, Beirut.

Charafeddine, Wafa. 1991. "L'Habitat illégal dans la Banlieue Sud." PhD diss., Université de Paris IV.

———. 1987. "La banlieue-sud de Beyrouth: Structure urbaine et économique." PhD diss., Université de Paris IV.

Clerc-Huybrecht, Valérie. 2002. "Les principes d'action de l'urbanisme: Le projet Elyssar face aux quartiers irréguliers de Beyrouth." PhD diss., l'Institut français d'urbanisme, Université Paris VIII.

Fawaz, Mona, and Isabelle Peillen. 2002. "The Slums of Beirut: History and Development 1930–2002." Paper presented for the United Nations Center for Human Settlements.

Feghali, Kamal. 1999. "Les déplacés au Liban—Stratégie de retour et développement." In *Lettre d'information* n°11 *de l'Observatoire de recherches sur Beyrouth et la reconstruction*. Beirut: CERMOC.

Harb el-Kak, Mona. 2001. "Pratiques comparées de participation dans deux municipalités de la banlieue de Beyrouth: Ghobeiry et Burj Brajneh." In Agnès Favier, ed. *Municipalités et pouvoirs locaux au Liban*, 157–77. Beirut: CERMOC.

———. 2000. "Post-War Beirut: Resources Negotiations, and Contestations in the Elyssar Project." *The Arab World Geographer* 3 (4): 272–88.

———. 1996. *Politiques urbaines dans la banlieue sud de Beyrouth*. Collection des études urbaines. Beirut: CERMOC.

———. 1995. *Maîtrise de l'espace dans la banlieue sud de Beyrouth: Recompositions des territoires entre pouvoir public et intervenants privés*. Research report. Tours: Université François-Rabelais.

Kiwan, Fadia. 1993. "Forces politiques nouvelles, système politique ancien." In Fadia Kiwan, ed. *Le Liban d'aujourd'hui*, 64–67. Paris: CERMOC-CNRS.

Kramer, Martin. 1988. "La Morale du Hizballah et sa logique." *Maghreb-Machreq*, no. 119, 39–59.

Moussa, Wafaa. 1983. *Etude d'une population réfugiée dans des stations balnéaires au sud de Beyrouth*. Thesis for third cycle. Paris: Université Paris Diderot-Paris 7.

Mouvement Social. 2005. *Rapport Annuel 2003–2004*.

Rosiny, Stephan. 1996. *Islamismus bei den Schiiten im Libanon: Religion im Übergang von Tradition zur Moderne*. Berlin: Das Arabische Buch.

Ruppert, Helmut. 1999. "Beyrouth, une ville d'Orient marquée par l'Occident." *Les Cahiers du Cermoc*, no. 21.

United Nations Human Settlements Programme. "The Challenge of Slums." 2003. *Global Report on Human Settlement 2003*. London: United Nations Human Settlements Programme.

Yad al-'ata': sitt sanawat min al-jihad wal binaa' 1988–94. 1994. Brochure by Jihad al-Binaa, August, Beirut.